STOCK
TRADER'S
ALMANAC
2019

Jeffrey A. Hirsch & Christopher Mistal

D1611556

WILEY

www.stocktradersalmanac.com

Editor in Chief	Jeffrey A. Hirsch
Editor Emeritus	Yale Hirsch
Director of Research	Christopher Mistal
Production Editor	Kimberly Monroe-Hill

For general information about our other products and services, please contact our Customer Care Department within the United States at 800-762-2974, outside the United States at 317-572-3993, or fax at 317-572-4002.

Wiley publishes in a variety of print and electronic formats and by print-on-demand. Some material included with standard print versions of this book may not be included in e-books or in print-on-demand. If this book refers to media such as a CD or DVD that is not included in the version you purchased, you may download this material at http://booksupport.wiley.com. For more information about Wiley products, visit our website at www.wiley.com.

ISBN: 978-1-119-52931-6 (paper)
ISBN: 978-1-119-52928-6 (ePDF)
ISBN: 978-1-119-52932-3 (ePub)

Printed in the United States of America.

V092096_091118

This Fifty-Second Edition is respectfully dedicated to:

Arthur D. Cashin, Jr.

Art is a Managing Director of UBS Financial Services, Inc., and is the Director of Floor Operations for UBS at the New York Stock Exchange. When he appears on CNBC, we all turn up the volume or take the TV off mute and scoot a little closer to hear what this wise, learned, and experienced Wall Street guru has to say about the market and get our daily dose of clever Wall Street repartee. Art has been on the trading floor for 50 years, so we have grown up together, so to speak.

Art has been a great friend and colleague over the years. He always has an eye on seasonality, cycles and patterns in the mix. His calm presence, wit and wisdom are a daily tonic in the rain of market commentary. We have all stood on his shoulders and learned immeasurably from him. It is a privilege and a joy to read his daily missives; they are like manna from heaven.

THE 2019 STOCK TRADER'S ALMANAC

CONTENTS

10   2019 Strategy Calendar
12   **January Almanac**
14   January's First Five Days: An Early Warning System
16   The Incredible January Barometer (Devised 1972):
      Only Nine Significant Errors in 68 Years
18   January Barometer in Graphic Form Since 1950
20   **February Almanac**
22   Down Januarys: A Remarkable Record
24   The Ninth Year of Decades
26   Market Charts of Pre–Presidential Election Years
28   **March Almanac**
30   Pre–Presidental Election Years: Only One Loser in 80 Years
32   Why a 50% Gain in the Dow Is Possible from Its 2018 Low to Its 2019 High
34   The December Low Indicator: A Useful Prognosticating Tool
36   How to Trade Best Months Switching Strategies
38   **April Almanac**
40   Dow Jones Industrials One-Year Seasonal Pattern Charts Since 1901
42   S&P 500 One-Year Seasonal Pattern Charts Since 1930
44   NASDAQ, Russell 1000 & 2000 One-Year Seasonal Pattern Charts Since 1971
46   **May Almanac**
48   Summer Market Volume Doldrums Drive Worst Six Months
50   Top Performing Months Past 68½ Years:
      Standard & Poor's 500 and Dow Jones Industrials
52   "Best Six Months": Still an Eye-Popping Strategy
54   **June Almanac**
56   MACD-Timing Triples "Best Six Months" Results
58   Top Performing NASDAQ Months Past 47⅓ Years
60   Get More Out of NASDAQ's "Best Eight Months" with MACD Timing
62   Triple Returns, Fewer Trades: Best 6 + 4-Year Cycle
64   **July Almanac**
66   First Month of Quarters Is the Most Bullish
68   2017 Daily Dow Point Changes
70   Don't Sell Stocks on Monday or Friday
72   **August Almanac**
74   A Rally for All Seasons
76   Take Advantage of Down Friday/Down Monday Warning

78 Aura of the Triple Witch—4th Quarter Most Bullish:
Down Weeks Trigger More Weakness Week After
80 **September Almanac**
82 Market Gains More on Super-8 Days Each Month Than on All 13 Remaining
Days Combined
84 A Correction for All Seasons
86 First-Trading-Day-of-the-Month Phenomenon
88 Market Behavior Three Days Before and Three Days After Holidays
90 **October Almanac**
92 Sector Seasonality: Selected Percentage Plays
94 Sector Index Seasonality Strategy Calendar
98 **November Almanac**
100 Best Investment Book of the Year: *Big Mistakes: The Best Investors and Their
Worst Investments*
102 Fourth-Quarter Market Magic
104 Trading the Thanksgiving Market
106 **December Almanac**
108 Most of the So-Called January Effect Takes Place in the Last Half of December
110 January Effect Now Starts in Mid-December
112 Wall Street's Only "Free Lunch" Served Before Christmas
114 If Santa Claus Should Fail to Call, Bears May Come to Broad and Wall
116 Year's Top Investment Books
118 2020 Strategy Calendar

DIRECTORY OF TRADING PATTERNS AND DATABANK

121 Dow Jones Industrials Market Probability Calendar 2019
122 Recent Dow Jones Industrials Market Probability Calendar 2019
123 S&P 500 Market Probability Calendar 2019
124 Recent S&P 500 Market Probability Calendar 2019
125 NASDAQ Composite Market Probability Calendar 2019
126 Recent NASDAQ Composite Market Probability Calendar 2019
127 Russell 1000 Index Market Probability Calendar 2019
128 Russell 2000 Index Market Probability Calendar 2019
129 Decennial Cycle: A Market Phenomenon
130 Presidential Election/Stock Market Cycle: The 185-Year Saga Continues
131 Dow Jones Industrials Bull and Bear Markets Since 1900
132 Standard & Poor's 500 Bull and Bear Markets Since 1929
NASDAQ Composite Since 1971
133 Dow Jones Industrials 10-Year Daily Point Changes: January and February
134 Dow Jones Industrials 10-Year Daily Point Changes: March and April
135 Dow Jones Industrials 10-Year Daily Point Changes: May and June
136 Dow Jones Industrials 10-Year Daily Point Changes: July and August
137 Dow Jones Industrials 10-Year Daily Point Changes: September and October
138 Dow Jones Industrials 10-Year Daily Point Changes: November and December
139 A Typical Day in the Market
140 Through the Week on a Half-Hourly Basis
141 Tuesday Most Profitable Day of Week
142 NASDAQ Strongest Last 3 Days of Week
143 S&P Daily Performance Each Year Since 1952

144 NASDAQ Daily Performance Each Year Since 1971
145 Monthly Cash Inflows into S&P Stocks
146 Monthly Cash Inflows into NASDAQ Stocks
147 November, December and January: Year's Best Three-Month Span
148 November Through June: NASDAQ's Eight-Month Run
149 Dow Jones Industrials Annual Highs, Lows & Closes Since 1901
150 S&P 500 Annual Highs, Lows & Closes Since 1930
151 NASDAQ, Russell 1000 & 2000 Annual Highs, Lows & Closes Since 1971
152 Dow Jones Industrials Monthly Percent Changes Since 1950
153 Dow Jones Industrials Monthly Point Changes Since 1950
154 Dow Jones Industrials Monthly Closing Prices Since 1950
155 Standard & Poor's 500 Monthly Percent Changes Since 1950
157 Standard & Poor's 500 Monthly Closing Prices Since 1950
158 NASDAQ Composite Monthly Percent Changes Since 1971
159 NASDAQ Composite Monthly Closing Prices Since 1971
160 Russell 1000 Index Monthly Percent Changes Since 1979
161 Russell 1000 Index Monthly Closing Prices Since 1979
162 Russell 2000 Index Monthly Percent Changes Since 1979
163 Russell 2000 Index Monthly Closing Prices Since 1979
164 10 Best Days by Percent and Point
165 10 Worst Days by Percent and Point
166 10 Best Weeks by Percent and Point
167 10 Worst Weeks by Percent and Point
168 10 Best Months by Percent and Point
169 10 Worst Months by Percent and Point
170 10 Best Quarters by Percent and Point
171 10 Worst Quarters by Percent and Point
172 10 Best Years by Percent and Point
173 10 Worst Years by Percent and Point

STRATEGY PLANNING AND RECORD SECTION

175 Portfolio at Start of 2019
176 Additional Purchases
178 Short-Term Transactions
180 Long-Term Transactions
182 Interest/Dividends Received During 2019/Brokerage Account Data 2019
183 Weekly Portfolio Price Record 2019
185 Weekly Indicator Data 2019
187 Monthly Indicator Data 2019
188 Portfolio at End of 2019
189 If You Don't Profit from Your Investment Mistakes, Someone Else Will;
    Performance Record of Recommendations
190 Individual Retirement Account (IRA):
    Most Awesome Mass Investment Incentive Ever Devised
191 G. M. Loeb's "Battle Plan" for Investment Survival
192 G. M. Loeb's Investment Survival Checklist

INTRODUCTION TO THE FIFTY-SECOND EDITION

Once again we have the honor of introducing the Fifty-Second Edition of the *Stock Trader's Almanac*. The *Almanac* provides you with the necessary tools to invest successfully in the twenty-first century.

J. P. Morgan's classic retort, "Stocks will fluctuate," is often quoted with a wink-of-the-eye implication that the only prediction one can make about the stock market is that it will go up, down, or sideways. Many investors agree that no one ever really knows which way the market will move. Nothing could be further from the truth.

We discovered that while stocks do indeed fluctuate, they do so in well-defined, often predictable patterns. These patterns recur too frequently to be the result of chance or coincidence. How else do we explain that since 1950 90% of the gains in the market were made during November through April, compared to a minor gain May through October? (See page 52.)

The *Almanac* is a practical investment tool. It alerts you to those little-known market patterns and tendencies on which shrewd professionals enhance profit potential. You will be able to forecast market trends with accuracy and confidence when you use the *Almanac* to help you understand:

- How presidential elections affect the economy and the stock market—just as the moon affects the tides. Many investors have made fortunes following the political cycle. You can be sure that money managers who control billions of dollars are also political cycle watchers. Astute people do not ignore a pattern that has been working effectively throughout most of our economic history.
- How the passage of the Twentieth Amendment to the Constitution fathered the January Barometer. This barometer has an outstanding record for predicting the general course of the stock market each year, with only nine major errors since 1950, for an 86.6% accuracy ratio. (See page 16.)
- Why there is a significant market bias at certain times of the day, week, month and year.

Even if you are an investor who pays scant attention to cycles, indicators and patterns, your investment survival could hinge on your interpretation of one of the recurring patterns found within these pages. One of the most intriguing and important patterns is the symbiotic relationship between Washington and Wall Street. Aside from the potential profitability in seasonal patterns, there's the pure joy of seeing the market very often do just what you expected.

The *Stock Trader's Almanac* is also an organizer. Its wealth of information is presented on a calendar basis. The *Almanac* puts investing into a business framework and makes investing easier because it:

- Updates investment knowledge and informs you of new techniques and tools.
- Is a monthly reminder and refresher course.
- Alerts you to both seasonal opportunities and dangers.
- Furnishes a historical viewpoint by providing pertinent statistics on past market performance.
- Supplies forms necessary for portfolio planning, record keeping and tax preparation.

 The WITCH icon signifies THIRD FRIDAY OF THE MONTH on calendar pages and alerts you to extraordinary volatility due to the expiration of equity and index options and index futures contracts. Triple-witching days appear during March, June, September, and December.

The BULL icon on calendar pages signifies favorable trading day based on the S&P 500 rising 60% or more of the time on a particula trading day during the 21-year period January 1997 to December 2017 The BEAR icon on calendar pages signifies unfavorable tradin; days based on the S&P falling 60% or more of the time for the sam(21-year period.

Also, to give you even greater perspective, we have listed next to the date of ever' day that the market is open the Market Probability numbers for the same 21-yea period for the Dow (D), S&P 500 (S) and NASDAQ (N). You will see a "D," "S" anc "N" followed by a number signifying the actual Market Probability number for tha trading day, based on the recent 21-year period. On pages 121–128, you will finc complete Market Probability Calendars, both long-term and 21-year for the Dow S&P and NASDAQ, as well as for the Russell 1000 and Russell 2000 indices.

Other seasonalities near the ends, beginnings and middles of months—option expirations, around holidays, and other significant times—as well as all FOM(Meeting dates are noted for *Almanac* investors' convenience on the weekl planner pages. All other important economic releases are provided in the Strateg Calendar every month in our e-newsletter, *Almanac Investor*, available at our web site, *www.stocktradersalmanac.com.*

One-year seasonal pattern charts for the Dow, S&P 500, NASDAQ, Russel 1000 and Russell 2000 appear on pages 40, 42 and 44. There are three charts eacl for the Dow and S&P 500 spanning our entire database starting in 1901 and on(each for the younger indices. As 2019 is a pre–presidential election year, each char contains typical pre-election year performance compared to all years.

Over the past few years, our research had been restructured to flow better witl the rhythm of the year. This has also allowed us more room for added data. Again we have included historical data on the Russell 1000 and Russell 2000 indices. Th Russell 2000 is an excellent proxy for small and mid-caps, which we have used ove the years, and the Russell 1000 provides a broader view of large caps. Annual high and lows for all five indices covered in the *Almanac* appear on pages 149–151, an(we've tweaked the Best & Worst section.

In order to cram in all this material, some of our Record Keeping section wa cut. We have converted many of these paper forms into computer spreadsheets fo our own internal use. As a service to our faithful readers, we are making thes forms available at our website, *www.stocktradersalmanac.com.*

Pre-election years have been the best year of the four-year cycle, while ninth year of decades have been the third best, so on paper the prospects for 2019 are good. Th(last nine ninth years of decades appear on page 24. You can find all the market chart of pre-election years since the Depression on page 26, "Pre–Presidental Electioi Years: Only One Loser in 80 Years" on page 30 and "Why a 50% Dow Gain Is Possibl(from Its 2018 Low to Its 2019 High" on page 32.

In our 2019 Outlook on page 6 we discuss that if the market continues to rall without any major correction before year end 2018, market gains will be harder t(come by through year end 2019. We have brought back "How to Trade Best Month Switching Strategies" on page 36. And last year's new page on how "Summe Market Volume Doldrums Drives Worst Six Months" is updated on page 48.

On page 100 is our Best Investment Book of the Year, *Big Mistakes: The Bes Investors and Their Worst Investments*, by Michael Batnick, CFA (Bloomber; Press). Other top books are listed on page 116. Sector seasonalities include severa consistent shorting opportunities and appear on pages 92–96.

We are constantly searching for new insights and nuances about the stock mar ket and welcome any suggestions from our readers.

Have a healthy and prosperous 2019!

2019 OUTLOOK

Normally, the prospects for a pre–presidential election year like 2019 would be quite bullish. Despite suffering the first loss since 1939 in 2015, pre-election years are still the best year of the 4-year cycle (pages 26, 30 & 130). Since 1943, the third year of the cycle is up 15.0% on average for the Dow and 15.4% for the S&P 500. Since 1971, NASDAQ averages a whopping 28.8% in the third year of the 4-year cycle. The ninth year of the decade is also rather solid, up an average of 10.0% in the past thirteen decades with a record of 10 up and 3 down (pages 24 & 129).

The market is holding up well so far during the worst two quarters of the 4-year cycle, Q2–3 of the midterm year. At a bare minimum we expect the market to tread water through Q3. Then expect the rally to resume during the best three quarters of the 4-year cycle (midterm Q4 & pre-election Q1–2, page 102). The typical near 50% move from the midterm low to the pre-election year high (page 32) will likely be more in the 20–30% range as it has the past several times. A move from the February/March 2018 lows to a high most likely in early 2019 would put the Dow near 30,000, the S&P over 3000 and NASDAQ in the 10,000 area.

Geopolitics and technology shares have been driving market action for much of 2018. U.S. economic expansion presses on through the Fed's measured pace of tightening and the passing of the FOMC chair baton from Yellen to Powell. But a steady stream of news out of Washington and international capitals has been testing the resolve of almost every strategic and economic alliance on the planet.

After the market's return to earth in January and February from its visit to two standard deviations above the trading range, technology issues and small caps have led stock markets higher. President Trump's trade and tariff policy initiatives have taken center stage in the second half of 2018 as the market has been rising and falling on his art of the deal shots across the bow and subsequent retracements.

If the Russian collusion investigation does not find any personal transgressions on Mr. Trump's part, if he negotiates new more beneficial trade deals without a trade war and manages to avoid the usual congressional losses in the midterm elections, the market is likely to elude any major midterm-year correction. If so, that puts a damper on the prospects for 2019.

Historically low interest rates, deregulation, tax cuts and strong corporate earnings continue to drive this market higher. If the market can withstand the midterm election pressure, rising rates and geopolitics, and we avoid a Q3 selloff, we will likely be in store for the comeuppance in 2019. Unless we get a correction before the end of 2018 that takes out the Q1 lows, the major market gains in 2019 will be hard to come by.

With all the gains paid forward in 2017 and 2018, mushrooming levels of debt and deficits are likely to begin to weigh down the economy and stock market in 2019. The waning positive impact of the tax cuts and tougher quarterly earnings comparisons, not to mention the potential for a yield curve inversion, could push the economy into a recession or at least a slowdown that could awaken the long-hibernating bear in 2019.

—*Jeffrey A. Hirsch, July 14, 2018*

2019 STRATEGY CALENDAR

(Option expiration dates circled)

	MONDAY	TUESDAY	WEDNESDAY	THURSDAY	FRIDAY	SATURDAY	SUNDAY
JANUARY	31	1 JANUARY New Year's Day	2	3	4	5	6
	7	8	9	10	11	12	13
	14	15	16	17	(18)	19	20
	21 Martin Luther King Day	22	23	24	25	26	27
	28	29	30	31	1 FEBRUARY	2	3
FEBRUARY	4	5	6	7	8	9	10
	11	12	13	14 ♥	(15)	16	17
	18 Presidents' Day	19	20	21	22	23	24
	25	26	27	28	1 MARCH	2	3
MARCH	4	5	6 Ash Wednesday	7	8	9	10 Daylight Saving Time Begins
	11	12	13	14	(15)	16	17 ♣ St. Patrick's Day
	18	19	20	21	22	23	24
	25	26	27	28	29	30	31
APRIL	1 APRIL	2	3	4	5	6	7
	8	9	10	11	12	13	14
	15 Tax Deadline	16	17	(18)	19 Good Friday	20 Passover	21 Easter
	22	23	24	25	26	27	28
	29	30	1 MAY	2	3	4	5
MAY	6	7	8	9	10	11	12 Mother's Day
	13	14	15	16	(17)	18	19
	20	21	22	23	24	25	26
	27 Memorial Day	28	29	30	31	1 JUNE	2
JUNE	3	4	5	6	7	8	9
	10	11	12	13	14	15	16 Father's Day
	17	18	19	20	(21)	22	23
	24	25	26	27	28	29	30

Market closed on shaded weekdays; closes early when half-shaded.

2019 STRATEGY CALENDAR

(Option expiration dates circled)

MONDAY	TUESDAY	WEDNESDAY	THURSDAY	FRIDAY	SATURDAY	SUNDAY	
1 JULY	2	3	4 Independence Day	5	6	7	JULY
8	9	10	11	12	13	14	
15	16	17	18	(19)	20	21	
22	23	24	25	26	27	28	
29	30	31	1 AUGUST	2	3	4	AUGUST
5	6	7	8	9	10	11	
12	13	14	15	(16)	17	18	
19	20	21	22	23	24	25	
26	27	28	29	30	31	1 SEPTEMBER	SEPTEMBER
2 Labor Day	3	4	5	6	7	8	
9	10	11	12	13	14	15	
16	17	18	19	(20)	21	22	
23	24	25	26	27	28	29	
30 Rosh Hashanah	1 OCTOBER	2	3	4	5	6	OCTOBER
7	8	9 Yom Kippur	10	11	12	13	
14 Columbus Day	15	16	17	(18)	19	20	
21	22	23	24	25	26	27	
28	29	30	31	1 NOVEMBER	2	3 Daylight Saving Time Ends	NOVEMBER
4	5 Election Day	6	7	8	9	10	
11 Veterans' Day	12	13	14	(15)	16	17	
18	19	20	21	22	23	24	
25	26	27	28 Thanksgiving Day	29	30	1 DECEMBER	DECEMBER
2	3	4	5	6	7	8	
9	10	11	12	13	14	15	
16	17	18	19	(20)	21	22	
23 Chanukah	24	25 Christmas	26	27	28	29	
30	31	1 JANUARY New Year's Day	2	3	4	5	

JANUARY ALMANAC

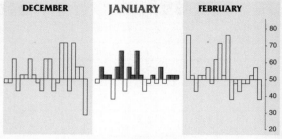

| | DECEMBER | JANUARY | FEBRUARY |

JANUARY						
S	M	T	W	T	F	S
			1	2	3	4	5
6	7	8	9	10	11	12
13	14	15	16	17	18	19
20	21	22	23	24	25	26
27	28	29	30	31		

FEBRUARY						
S	M	T	W	T	F	S
					1	2
3	4	5	6	7	8	9
10	11	12	13	14	15	16
17	18	19	20	21	22	23
24	25	26	27	28		

Market Probability Chart above is a graphic representation of the S&P 500 Recent Market Probability Calendar on page 124.

◆ January Barometer predicts year's course with .750 batting average (page 16) ◆ 15 of last 17 pre–presidential election years followed January's direction ◆ Every down January on the S&P since 1950, *without exception*, preceded a new or extended bear market, a flat market, or a 10% correction (page 22) ◆ S&P gains in January's first five days preceded full-year gains 83.7% of the time, 12 of last 17 pre–presidential election years followed first five days' direction (page 14) ◆ November, December and January constitute the year's best three-month span, a 4.1% S&P gain (pages 50 & 147) ◆ January NASDAQ powerful 2.7% since 1971 (pages 58 & 148) ◆ "January Effect" now starts in mid-December and favors small-cap stocks (pages 108 & 110) ◆ 2009 has the dubious honor of the worst S&P 500 January on record.

January Vital Statistics

	DJIA		S&P 500		NASDAQ		Russell 1K		Russell 2K	
Rank	6		5		1		5		5	
Up	44		42		31		25		22	
Down	25		27		17		15		18	
Average % Change	0.9%		1.0%		2.7%		1.0%		1.4%	
Pre-Election Year	3.7%		3.9%		6.6%		2.9%		3.2%	
Best & Worst January										
	% Change		% Change		% Change		% Change		% Change	
Best	1976	14.4	1987	13.2	1975	16.6	1987	12.7	1985	13.1
Worst	2009	−8.8	2009	−8.6	2008	−9.9	2009	−8.3	2009	−11.2
Best & Worst January Weeks										
Best	01/09/76	6.1	01/02/09	6.8	01/12/01	9.1	01/02/09	6.8	01/09/87	7.0
Worst	01/08/16	−6.2	01/08/16	−6.0	01/28/00	−8.2	01/08/16	−6.0	01/08/16	−7.9
Best & Worst January Days										
Best	01/17/91	4.6	01/03/01	5.0	01/03/01	14.2	1/3/01	5.3	01/21/09	5.3
Worst	01/08/88	−6.9	01/08/88	−6.8	01/02/01	−7.2	1/8/88	−6.1	01/20/09	−7.0
First Trading Day of Expiration Week: 1980–2018										
Record (#Up − #Down)	25–14		22–17		20–19		20–19		20–19	
Current Streak	D2		D2		D6		D6		D6	
Avg % Change	0.09		0.05		0.06		0.03		0.01	
Options Expiration Day: 1980–2018										
Record (#Up − #Down)	22–17		22–17		22–17		22–17		23–16	
Current Streak	U8		U4		U4		U4		U4	
Avg % Change	0.001		0.02		−0.02		0.001		0.04	
Options Expiration Week: 1980–2018										
Record (#Up − #Down)	21–18		17–22		22–17		17–22		21–18	
Current Streak	U1		U1		U1		U1		U1	
Avg % Change	−0.13		−0.04		0.27		−0.05		0.21	
Week After Options Expiration: 1980–2018										
Record (#Up − #Down)	22–17		25–14		23–16		25–14		27–12	
Current Streak	U4		U4		U4		U4		U4	
Avg % Change	0.11		0.29		0.23		0.27		0.25	
First Trading Day Performance										
% of Time Up	59.4		49.3		56.3		45.0		47.5	
Avg % Change	0.25		0.17		0.21		0.16		0.06	
Last Trading Day Performance										
% of Time Up	56.5		60.9		64.6		57.5		72.5	
Avg % Change	0.21		0.25		0.29		0.32		0.27	

Dow & S&P 1950–June 2018, NASDAQ 1971–June 2018, Russell 1K & 2K 1979–June 2018.

20th Amendment made "lame ducks" disappear.
Now, "As January goes, so goes the year."

DECEMBER 2018/JANUARY 2019

Last Trading Day of the Year, NASDAQ Down 15 of Last 18
NASDAQ Was Up 29 Years in a Row 1971–1999

MONDAY
D 33.3
S 28.6
N 28.6
31

Those that forget the past are condemned to repeat its mistakes, and those that mis-state the past should be condemned.
— Eugene D. Cohen (Letter to the Editor, *Financial Times*, 10/30/06)

New Year's Day *(Market Closed)*

TUESDAY
1

If we did all the things we are capable of doing, we would literally astound ourselves.
— Thomas Alva Edison (American inventor, 1,093 patents, 1847–1931)

Small Caps Punished First Trading Day of Year
Russell 2000 Down 17 of Last 28, But Up 7 of Last 10

WEDNESDAY
D 61.9
S 47.6
N 66.7
2

[A contrarian's opportunity] If everybody is thinking alike, then somebody isn't thinking.
— General George S. Patton, Jr. (U.S. Army field commander, WWII, 1885–1945)

Second Trading Day of the Year, Dow Up 19 of Last 27
Santa Claus Rally Ends (Page 114)

THURSDAY
D 66.7
S 57.1
N 52.4
3

The universal line of distinction between the strong and the weak is that one persists,
while the other hesitates, falters, trifles and at last collapses or caves in.
— Edwin Percy Whipple (American essayist, 1819–1886)

FRIDAY
D 47.6
S 52.4
N 52.4
4

Entrepreneurs who believe they're in business to vanquish the competition are less successful
than those who believe their goal is to maximize profits or increase their company's value.
— Kaihan Krippendorff (Business consultant, author, *The Art of the Advantage*, The Strategic Learning Center, b. 1971)

SATURDAY
5

January Almanac Investor Sector Seasonalities: See Pages 92, 94 and 96

SUNDAY
6

JANUARY'S FIRST FIVE DAYS: AN EARLY WARNING SYSTEM

The last 43 up First Five Days were followed by full-year gains 36 times for an 83.7% accuracy ratio and a 13.7% average gain in all 43 years. The seven exceptions include flat 1994, 2011, 2015 and four related to war. Vietnam military spending delayed the start of the 1966 bear market. Ceasefire imminence early in 1973 raised stocks temporarily. Saddam Hussein turned 1990 into a bear. The war on terrorism, instability in the Mideast and corporate malfeasance shaped 2002 into one of the worst years on record. The 25 down First Five Days were followed by 14 up years and 11 down (44.0% accurate) and an average gain of 1.0%.

In pre–presidential election years this indicator has a fair record. In the last 17 pre–presidential election years, 12 full years followed the direction of the First Five Days.

THE FIRST-FIVE-DAYS-IN-JANUARY INDICATOR

	Chronological Data					Ranked by Performance		
	Previous Year's Close	January 5th Day	5-Day Change	Year Change		Rank	5-Day Change	Year Change
1950	16.76	17.09	2.0%	21.8%		1	1987	6.2%	2.0%
1951	20.41	20.88	2.3	16.5		2	1976	4.9	19.1
1952	23.77	23.91	0.6	11.8		3	1999	3.7	19.5
1953	26.57	26.33	−0.9	−6.6		4	2003	3.4	26.4
1954	24.81	24.93	0.5	45.0		5	2006	3.4	13.6
1955	35.98	35.33	−1.8	26.4		6	1983	3.3	17.3
1956	45.48	44.51	−2.1	2.6		7	1967	3.1	20.1
1957	46.67	46.25	−0.9	−14.3		8	1979	2.8	12.3
1958	39.99	40.99	2.5	38.1		9	2018	2.8	??
1959	55.21	55.40	0.3	8.5		10	2010	2.7	12.8
1960	59.89	59.50	−0.7	−3.0		11	1963	2.6	18.9
1961	58.11	58.81	1.2	23.1		12	1958	2.5	38.1
1962	71.55	69.12	−3.4	−11.8		13	1984	2.4	1.4
1963	63.10	64.74	2.6	18.9		14	1951	2.3	16.5
1964	75.02	76.00	1.3	13.0		15	2013	2.2	29.6
1965	84.75	85.37	0.7	9.1		16	1975	2.2	31.5
1966	92.43	93.14	0.8	−13.1		17	1950	2.0	21.8
1967	80.33	82.81	3.1	20.1		18	2004	1.8	9.0
1968	96.47	96.62	0.2	7.7		19	2012	1.8	13.4
1969	103.86	100.80	−2.9	−11.4		20	1973	1.5	−17.4
1970	92.06	92.68	0.7	0.1		21	1972	1.4	15.6
1971	92.15	92.19	0.04	10.8		22	1964	1.3	13.0
1972	102.09	103.47	1.4	15.6		23	2017	1.3	19.4
1973	118.05	119.85	1.5	−17.4		24	1961	1.2	23.1
1974	97.55	96.12	−1.5	−29.7		25	1989	1.2	27.3
1975	68.56	70.04	2.2	31.5		26	2011	1.1	−0.003
1976	90.19	94.58	4.9	19.1		27	2002	1.1	−23.4
1977	107.46	105.01	−2.3	−11.5		28	1997	1.0	31.0
1978	95.10	90.64	−4.7	1.1		29	1980	0.9	25.8
1979	96.11	98.80	2.8	12.3		30	1966	0.8	−13.1
1980	107.94	108.95	0.9	25.8		31	1994	0.7	−1.5
1981	135.76	133.06	−2.0	−9.7		32	1965	0.7	9.1
1982	122.55	119.55	−2.4	14.8		33	2009	0.7	23.5
1983	140.64	145.23	3.3	17.3		34	1970	0.7	0.1
1984	164.93	168.90	2.4	1.4		35	1952	0.6	11.8
1985	167.24	163.99	−1.9	26.3		36	1954	0.5	45.0
1986	211.28	207.97	−1.6	14.6		37	1996	0.4	20.3
1987	242.17	257.28	6.2	2.0		38	1959	0.3	8.5
1988	247.08	243.40	−1.5	12.4		39	1995	0.3	34.1
1989	277.72	280.98	1.2	27.3		40	1992	0.2	4.5
1990	353.40	353.79	0.1	−6.6		41	1968	0.2	7.7
1991	330.22	314.90	−4.6	26.3		42	2015	0.2	−0.7
1992	417.09	418.10	0.2	4.5		43	1990	0.1	−6.6
1993	435.71	429.05	−1.5	7.1		44	1971	0.04	10.8
1994	466.45	469.90	0.7	−1.5		45	2007	−0.4	3.5
1995	459.27	460.83	0.3	34.1		46	2014	−0.6	11.4
1996	615.93	618.46	0.4	20.3		47	1960	−0.7	−3.0
1997	740.74	748.41	1.0	31.0		48	1957	−0.9	−14.3
1998	970.43	956.04	−1.5	26.7		49	1953	−0.9	−6.6
1999	1229.23	1275.09	3.7	19.5		50	1974	−1.5	−29.7
2000	1469.25	1441.46	−1.9	−10.1		51	1998	−1.5	26.7
2001	1320.28	1295.86	−1.8	−13.0		52	1988	−1.5	12.4
2002	1148.08	1160.71	1.1	−23.4		53	1993	−1.5	7.1
2003	879.82	909.93	3.4	26.4		54	1986	−1.6	14.6
2004	1111.92	1131.91	1.8	9.0		55	2001	−1.8	−13.0
2005	1211.92	1186.19	−2.1	3.0		56	1955	−1.8	26.4
2006	1248.29	1290.15	3.4	13.6		57	2000	−1.9	−10.1
2007	1418.30	1412.11	−0.4	3.5		58	1985	−1.9	26.3
2008	1468.36	1390.19	−5.3	−38.5		59	1981	−2.0	−9.7
2009	903.25	909.73	0.7	23.5		60	1956	−2.1	2.6
2010	1115.10	1144.98	2.7	12.8		61	2005	−2.1	3.0
2011	1257.64	1271.50	1.1	−0.003		62	1977	−2.3	−11.5
2012	1257.60	1280.70	1.8	13.4		63	1982	−2.4	14.8
2013	1426.19	1457.15	2.2	29.6		64	1969	−2.9	−11.4
2014	1848.36	1837.49	−0.6	11.4		65	1962	−3.4	−11.8
2015	2058.90	2062.14	0.2	−0.7		66	1991	−4.6	26.3
2016	2043.94	1922.03	−6.0	9.5		67	1978	−4.7	1.1
2017	2238.83	2268.90	1.3	19.4		68	2008	−5.3	−38.5
2018	2673.61	2747.71	2.8	??		69	2016	−6.0	9.5

Based on S&P 500

14

MONDAY
7

D 47.6
S 52.4
N 52.4

Big money is made in the stock market by being on the right side of major moves. I don't believe in swimming against the tide.
— Martin Zweig (Fund manager, *Winning on Wall Street*)

January's First Five Days Act as an "Early Warning" (Page 14)

TUESDAY
8

D 33.3
S 38.1
N 57.1

There are two kinds of people who lose money: those who know nothing and those who know everything.
— Henry Kaufman (German-American economist, b. 1927, to Robert Lenzner in *Forbes*, 10/19/98,
who added, "With two Nobel Prize winners in the house, Long-Term Capital clearly fits the second case.")

WEDNESDAY
9

D 47.6
S 57.1
N 61.9

---

*We are nowhere near a capitulation point because it's at that point where it's despair, not hope,
that reigns supreme, and there was scant evidence of any despair at any of the meetings I gave.*
— David Rosenberg (Economist, Merrill Lynch, *Barron's*, 4/21/08)

THURSDAY
10

D 57.1
S 66.7
N 71.4

---

*The fear of capitalism has compelled socialism to widen freedom,
and the fear of socialism has compelled capitalism to increase equality.*
— Will and Ariel Durant

FRIDAY
11

D 52.4
S 42.9
N 42.9

---

*There is a perfect inverse correlation between inflation rates and price/earnings ratios.
When inflation has been very high... P/E has been [low].*
— Liz Ann Sonders (Chief Investment Strategist, Charles Schwab, June 2006)

SATURDAY
12

SUNDAY
13

THE INCREDIBLE JANUARY BAROMETER (DEVISED 1972): ONLY NINE SIGNIFICANT ERRORS IN 68 YEARS

Devised by Yale Hirsch in 1972, our January Barometer states that as the S&P 500 goes in January, so goes the year. The indicator has registered **only nine major errors since 1950, for an 86.8% accuracy ratio.** Vietnam affected 1966 and 1968; 1982 saw the start of a major bull market in August; two January rate cuts and 9/11 affected 2001; the anticipation of military action in Iraq held down the market in January 2003; 2009 was the beginning of a new bull market; the Fed saved 2010 with QE2; QE3 likely staved off declines in 2014; and global growth fears sparked selling in January 2016. (*Almanac Investor* newsletter subscribers receive full analysis of each reading as well as its potential implications for the full year.)

Including the eight flat-year errors (less than +/– 5%) yields a 75.0% accuracy ratio. A full comparison of all monthly barometers for the Dow, S&P and NASDAQ can be seen in the January 4, 2018, Alert at *www.stocktradersalmanac.com*. Bear markets began or continued when Januarys suffered a loss (*see page 22*). Full years followed January's direction in 15 of the last 17 pre–presidential election years. *See page 18 for more.*

AS JANUARY GOES, SO GOES THE YEAR

Market Performance in January

	Previous Year's Close	January Close	January Change	Year Change	
1950	16.76	17.05	1.7%	21.8%	
1951	20.41	21.66	6.1	16.5	
1952	23.77	24.14	1.6	11.8	
1953	26.57	26.38	–0.7	–6.6	
1954	24.81	26.08	5.1	45.0	
1955	35.98	36.63	1.8	26.4	
1956	45.48	43.82	–3.6	2.6	flat
1957	46.67	44.72	–4.2	–14.3	
1958	39.99	41.70	4.3	38.1	
1959	55.21	55.42	0.4	8.5	
1960	59.89	55.61	–7.1	–3.0	flat
1961	58.11	61.78	6.3	23.1	
1962	71.55	68.84	–3.8	–11.8	
1963	63.10	66.20	4.9	18.9	
1964	75.02	77.04	2.7	13.0	
1965	84.75	87.56	3.3	9.1	
1966	92.43	92.88	0.5	–13.1	X
1967	80.33	86.61	7.8	20.1	
1968	96.47	92.24	–4.4	7.7	X
1969	103.86	103.01	–0.8	–11.4	
1970	92.06	85.02	–7.6	0.1	flat
1971	92.15	95.88	4.0	10.8	
1972	102.09	103.94	1.8	15.6	
1973	118.05	116.03	–1.7	–17.4	
1974	97.55	96.57	–1.0	–29.7	
1975	68.56	76.98	12.3	31.5	
1976	90.19	100.86	11.8	19.1	
1977	107.46	102.03	–5.1	–11.5	
1978	95.10	89.25	–6.2	1.1	flat
1979	96.11	99.93	4.0	12.3	
1980	107.94	114.16	5.8	25.8	
1981	135.76	129.55	–4.6	–9.7	
1982	122.55	120.40	–1.8	14.8	X
1983	140.64	145.30	3.3	17.3	
1984	164.93	163.41	–0.9	1.4	flat
1985	167.24	179.63	7.4	26.3	
1986	211.28	211.78	0.2	14.6	
1987	242.17	274.08	13.2	2.0	flat
1988	247.08	257.07	4.0	12.4	
1989	277.72	297.47	7.1	27.3	
1990	353.40	329.08	–6.9	–6.6	
1991	330.22	343.93	4.2	26.3	
1992	417.09	408.79	–2.0	4.5	flat
1993	435.71	438.78	0.7	7.1	
1994	466.45	481.61	3.3	–1.5	flat
1995	459.27	470.42	2.4	34.1	
1996	615.93	636.02	3.3	20.3	
1997	740.74	786.16	6.1	31.0	
1998	970.43	980.28	1.0	26.7	
1999	1229.23	1279.64	4.1	19.5	
2000	1469.25	1394.46	–5.1	–10.1	
2001	1320.28	1366.01	3.5	–13.0	X
2002	1148.08	1130.20	–1.6	–23.4	
2003	879.82	855.70	–2.7	26.4	X
2004	1111.92	1131.13	1.7	9.0	
2005	1211.92	1181.27	–2.5	3.0	flat
2006	1248.29	1280.08	2.5	13.6	
2007	1418.30	1438.24	1.4	3.5	flat
2008	1468.36	1378.55	–6.1	–38.5	
2009	903.25	825.88	–8.6	23.5	X
2010	1115.10	1073.87	–3.7	12.8	X
2011	1257.64	1286.12	2.3	–0.003	flat
2012	1257.60	1312.41	4.4	13.4	
2013	1426.19	1498.11	5.0	29.6	
2014	1848.36	1782.59	–3.6	11.4	X
2015	2058.90	1994.99	–3.1	–0.7	flat
2016	2043.94	1940.24	–5.1	9.5	X
2017	2238.83	2278.87	1.8	19.4	
2018	2673.61	2823.81	5.6	??	

January Performance by Rank

Rank		January Change	Year's Change	
1	1987	13.2%	2.0%	flat
2	1975	12.3	31.5	
3	1976	11.8	19.1	
4	1967	7.8	20.1	
5	1985	7.4	26.3	
6	1989	7.1	27.3	
7	1961	6.3	23.1	
8	1997	6.1	31.0	
9	1951	6.1	16.5	
10	1980	5.8	25.8	
11	2018	5.6	??	
12	1954	5.1	45.0	
13	2013	5.0	29.6	
14	1963	4.9	18.9	
15	2012	4.4	13.4	
16	1958	4.3	38.1	
17	1991	4.2	26.3	
18	1999	4.1	19.5	
19	1971	4.0	10.8	
20	1988	4.0	12.4	
21	1979	4.0	12.3	
22	2001	3.5	–13.0	X
23	1965	3.3	9.1	
24	1983	3.3	17.3	
25	1996	3.3	20.3	
26	1994	3.3	–1.5	flat
27	1964	2.7	13.0	
28	2006	2.5	13.6	
29	1995	2.4	34.1	
30	2011	2.3	–0.003	flat
31	1972	1.8	15.6	
32	1955	1.8	26.4	
33	2017	1.8	19.4	
34	1950	1.7	21.8	
35	2004	1.7	9.0	
36	1952	1.6	11.8	
37	2007	1.4	3.5	flat
38	1998	1.0	26.7	
39	1993	0.7	7.1	
40	1966	0.5	–13.1	X
41	1959	0.4	8.5	
42	1986	0.2	14.6	
43	1953	–0.7	–6.6	
44	1969	–0.8	–11.4	
45	1984	–0.9	1.4	flat
46	1974	–1.0	–29.7	
47	2002	–1.6	–23.4	
48	1973	–1.7	–17.4	
49	1982	–1.8	14.8	X
50	1992	–2.0	4.5	flat
51	2005	–2.5	3.0	flat
52	2003	–2.7	26.4	X
53	2015	–3.1	–0.7	flat
54	2014	–3.6	11.4	X
55	1956	–3.6	2.6	flat
56	2010	–3.7	12.8	X
57	1962	–3.8	–11.8	
58	1957	–4.2	–14.3	
59	1968	–4.4	7.7	X
60	1981	–4.6	–9.7	
61	1977	–5.1	–11.5	
62	2000	–5.1	–10.1	
63	2016	–5.1	9.5	X
64	2008	–6.1	–38.5	
65	1978	–6.2	1.1	flat
66	1990	–6.9	–6.6	
67	1960	–7.1	–3.0	flat
68	1970	–7.6	0.1	flat
69	2009	–8.6	23.5	X

X = major error   Based on S&P 500

JANUARY 2019

First Trading Day of January Expiration Week, Dow Up 17 of Last 26

MONDAY
D 52.4
S 57.1
N 52.4
14

Sometimes the best investments are the ones you don't make.
— Donald Trump (45th U.S. President, Real estate mogul and entrepreneur, *Trump: How to Get Rich*, 2004)

TUESDAY
D 52.4
S 52.4
N 38.1
15

Nothing gives one person so much advantage over another as to remain always cool and unruffled under all circumstances.
— Thomas Jefferson (3rd U.S. President, 1743–1826)

January Expiration Week, Dow Down 11 of Last 20
Average Dow Loss: −1.0%

WEDNESDAY
D 52.4
S 66.7
N 71.4
16

I don't believe in intuition. When you get sudden flashes of perception, it is just the brain working faster than usual.
— Katherine Anne Porter (American author, 1890–1980)

THURSDAY
D 42.9
S 52.4
N 57.1
17

The whole problem with the world is that fools and fanatics are always so certain of themselves,
but wiser people so full of doubts.
— Bertrand Russell (British mathematician and philosopher, 1872–1970)

January Expiration Day Improving Since 2009, Dow Up 9 of Last 10

FRIDAY
D 38.1
S 42.9
N 38.1
18

If investing is entertaining, if you're having fun, you're probably not making any money. Good investing is boring.
— George Soros (Financier, philanthropist, political activist, author and philosopher, b. 1930)

SATURDAY
19

SUNDAY
20

JANUARY BAROMETER IN GRAPHIC FORM SINCE 1950

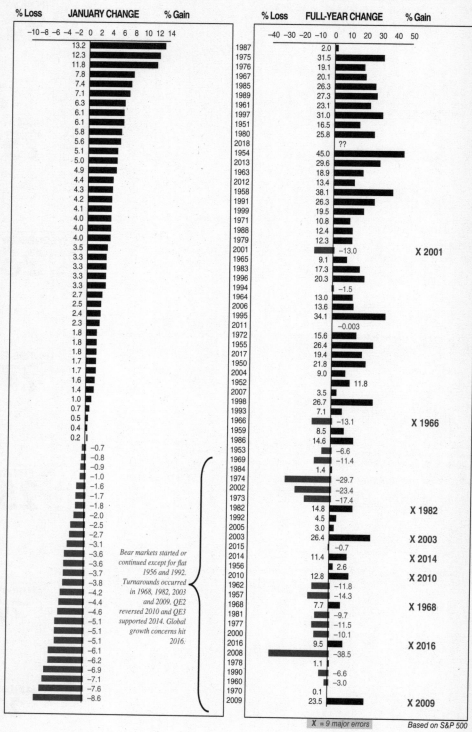

% Loss	JANUARY CHANGE	% Gain		% Loss	FULL-YEAR CHANGE	% Gain	
	−10 −8 −6 −4 −2 0 2 4 6 8 10 12 14				−40 −30 −20 −10 0 10 20 30 40 50		
	13.2		1987	2.0			
	12.3		1975	31.5			
	11.8		1976	19.1			
	7.8		1967	20.1			
	7.4		1985	26.3			
	7.1		1989	27.3			
	6.3		1961	23.1			
	6.1		1997	31.0			
	6.1		1951	16.5			
	5.8		1980	25.8			
	5.6		2018	??			
	5.1		1954	45.0			
	5.0		2013	29.6			
	4.9		1963	18.9			
	4.4		2012	13.4			
	4.3		1958	38.1			
	4.2		1991	26.3			
	4.1		1999	19.5			
	4.0		1971	10.8			
	4.0		1988	12.4			
	4.0		1979	12.3			
	3.5		2001	−13.0		X 2001	
	3.3		1965	9.1			
	3.3		1983	17.3			
	3.3		1996	20.3			
	3.3		1994	−1.5			
	2.7		1964	13.0			
	2.5		2006	13.6			
	2.4		1995	34.1			
	2.3		2011	−0.003			
	1.8		1972	15.6			
	1.8		1955	26.4			
	1.8		2017	19.4			
	1.7		1950	21.8			
	1.7		2004	9.0			
	1.6		1952	11.8			
	1.4		2007	3.5			
	1.0		1998	26.7			
	0.7		1993	7.1			
	0.5		1966	−13.1		X 1966	
	0.4		1959	8.5			
	0.2		1986	14.6			
−0.7			1953	−6.6			
−0.8			1969	−11.4			
−0.9			1984	1.4			
−1.0			1974	−29.7			
−1.6			2002	−23.4			
−1.7			1973	−17.4			
−1.8			1982	14.8		X 1982	
−2.0			1992	4.5			
−2.5			2005	3.0			
−2.7			2003	26.4		X 2003	
−3.1			2015	−0.7			
−3.6			2014	11.4		X 2014	
−3.6			1956	2.6			
−3.7			2010	12.8		X 2010	
−3.8			1962	−11.8			
−4.2			1957	−14.3			
−4.4			1968	7.7		X 1968	
−4.6			1981	−9.7			
−5.1			1977	−11.5			
−5.1			2000	−10.1			
−5.1			2016	9.5		X 2016	
−6.1			2008	−38.5			
−6.2			1978	1.1			
−6.9			1990	−6.6			
−7.1			1960	−3.0			
−7.6			1970	0.1			
−8.6			2009	23.5		X 2009	

Bear markets started or continued except for flat 1956 and 1992. Turnarounds occurred in 1968, 1982, 2003 and 2009. QE2 reversed 2010 and QE3 supported 2014. Global growth concerns hit 2016.

X = 9 major errors   Based on S&P 500

JANUARY 2019

MONDAY
21

Civility is not a sign of weakness, and sincerity is always subject to proof. Let us never negotiate out of fear. But let us never fear to negotiate.
— John F. Kennedy (35th U.S. President, Inaugural Address, 1/20/1961, 1917–1963)

TUESDAY

D 33.3
S 47.6
N 38.1
22

If I owe a million dollars I am lost. But if I owe $50 billion the bankers are lost.
— Celso Ming (Brazilian journalist)

WEDNESDAY

D 47.6
S 52.4
N 47.6
23

"Sell in May and go away." However, no one ever said it was the beginning of the month.
— John L. Person (Professional trader, author, speaker, *Commodity Trader's Almanac*, nationalfutures.com, 6/19/09, b. 1961)

January Ends "Best Three-Month Span" (Pages 50, 58, 147 and 148)

THURSDAY

D 38.1
S 47.6
N 57.1
24

A person's greatest virtue is his ability to correct his mistakes and continually make a new person of himself.
— Yang-Ming Wang (Chinese philosopher, 1472–1529)

FRIDAY

D 61.9
S 57.1
N 52.4
25

The principles of successful stock speculation are based on the supposition that people will continue in the future to make the mistakes that they have made in the past.
— Thomas F. Woodlock (*Wall Street Journal* editor & columnist, quoted in *Reminiscences of a Stock Operator*, 1866–1945)

SATURDAY
26

February Almanac Investor Sector Seasonalities: See Pages 92, 94 and 96

SUNDAY
27

FEBRUARY ALMANAC

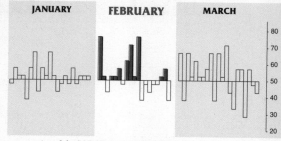

JANUARY | FEBRUARY | MARCH

Market Probability Chart above is a graphic representation of the S&P 500 Recent Market Probability Calendar on page 124.

◆ February is the weak link in "Best Six Months" (pages 50, 52 & 147)
◆ RECENT RECORD: S&P up 10, down 5, average change 0.5% last 15 years ◆ Fifth best NASDAQ month in pre–presidential election years, average gain 2.8%, up 9, down 3 (page 158), #5 Dow, up 11, down 6 and #5 S&P, up 11, down 6 (pages 152 & 155) ◆ Day before Presidents' Day weekend S&P down 17 of 27, 11 straight 1992–2002, day after up 7 of last 9 (see pages 88 & 133) ◆ Many technicians modify market predictions based on January's market.

February Vital Statistics

	DJIA		S&P 500		NASDAQ		Russell 1K		Russell 2K	
Rank	8		9		7		9		7	
Up	41		38		26		24		23	
Down	28		31		22		16		17	
Average % Change	0.2%		0.04%		0.7%		0.3%		1.1%	
Pre-Election Year	1.2%		1.1%		2.8%		1.5%		2.5%	
	Best & Worst February									
	% Change		% Change		% Change		% Change		% Change	
Best	1986	8.8	1986	7.1	2000	19.2	1986	7.2	2000	16.4
Worst	2009	−11.7	2009	−11.0	2001	−22.4	2009	−10.7	2009	−12.3
	Best & Worst February Weeks									
Best	02/01/08	4.4	02/06/09	5.2	02/04/00	9.2	02/06/09	5.3	02/01/91	6.6
Worst	02/20/09	−6.2	02/20/09	−6.9	02/09/01	−7.1	02/20/09	−6.9	02/20/09	−8.3
	Best & Worst February Days									
Best	02/24/09	3.3	02/24/09	4.0	02/11/99	4.2	02/24/09	4.1	02/24/09	4.5
Worst	02/10/09	−4.6	02/10/09	−4.9	02/16/01	−5.0	02/10/09	−4.8	02/10/09	−4.7
	First Trading Day of Expiration Week: 1980–2018									
Record (#Up – #Down)	24–15		28–11		23–16		28–11		24–15	
Current Streak	U4		U5		U5		U5		U5	
Avg % Change	0.34		0.30		0.14		0.27		0.16	
	Options Expiration Day: 1980–2018									
Record (#Up – #Down)	20–19		17–22		16–23		18–21		19–20	
Current Streak	U2		U2		D1		U2		U5	
Avg % Change	−0.04		−0.11		−0.23		−0.11		−0.06	
	Options Expiration Week: 1980–2018									
Record (#Up – #Down)	24–15		22–17		22–17		22–17		26–13	
Current Streak	U4		U4		U5		U9		U9	
Avg % Change	0.52		0.33		0.28		0.34		0.42	
	Week After Options Expiration: 1980–2018									
Record (#Up – #Down)	19–20		19–20		23–16		19–20		21–18	
Current Streak	U3		U3		U5		U3		U1	
Avg % Change	−0.21		−0.14		−0.11		−0.11		−0.04	
	First Trading Day Performance									
% of Time Up	62.3		60.9		70.8		65.0		65.0	
Avg % Change	0.14		0.15		0.32		0.18		0.32	
	Last Trading Day Performance									
% of Time Up	47.8		53.6		47.9		52.5		52.5	
Avg % Change	−0.03		−0.04		−0.10		−0.10		−0.001	

Dow & S&P 1950–June 2018, NASDAQ 1971–June 2018, Russell 1K & 2K 1979–June 2018.

*Either go short, or stay away
the day before Presidents' Day.*

JANUARY/FEBRUARY 2019

No other country can substitute for the U.S. The U.S. is still No. 1 in military, No. 1 in economy, No. 1 in promoting human rights and No. 1 in idealism. Only the U.S. can lead the world. No other country can.
— Senior Korean official (to Thomas L. Friedman, *New York Times* Foreign Affairs columnist, 2/25/09)

FOMC Meeting (2 Days)

TUESDAY
D 52.4
S 52.4
N 61.9
29

There's nothing wrong with cash. It gives you time to think.
— Robert Prechter Jr. (Elliott Wave Theorist)

WEDNESDAY
D 47.6
S 52.4
N 47.6
30

Buy when you are scared to death; sell when you are tickled to death.
— Market Maxim (*Cabot Market Letter*, April 12, 2001)

"January Barometer" 86.8% Accurate (Page 16)
Almanac Investor Subscribers Emailed Official Results (See Insert)

THURSDAY
D 47.6
S 52.4
N 52.4
31

Today's generation of young people holds more power than any generation before it to make a positive impact on the world.
— William J. Clinton (42nd U.S. President, Clinton Global Initiative, b. 1946)

First Day Trading in February, Dow Up 13 of Last 16

FRIDAY
D 71.4
S 76.2
N 81.0
1

The most valuable executive is one who is training somebody to be a better man than he is.
— Robert G. Ingersoll (American lawyer and orator, "the Great Agnostic," 1833–1899)

SATURDAY
2

SUNDAY
3

DOWN JANUARYS: A REMARKABLE RECORD

In the first third of the 20th century, there was no correlation between January markets and the year as a whole (page 24). Then, in 1972, Yale Hirsch discovered that the 1933 "Lame Duck" Amendment to the Constitution changed the political calendar, and the January Barometer was born—its record has been quite accurate (page 16).

Down Januarys are harbingers of trouble ahead in the economic, political, or military arena. Eisenhower's heart attack in 1955 cast doubt on whether he could run in 1956—a flat year. Two other election years with down Januarys were also flat (1984 & 1992). Thirteen bear markets began, and ten continued into second years with poor Januarys. 1968 started down, as we were mired in Vietnam, but Johnson's "bombing halt" changed the climate. Imminent military action in Iraq held January 2003 down before the market triple-bottomed in March. After Baghdad fell, pre-election and recovery forces fueled 2003 into a banner year. 2005 was flat, registering the narrowest Dow trading range on record. 2008 was the worst January on record and preceded the worst bear market since the Great Depression. A negative reading in 2015 and 2016 preceded an official Dow bear market declaration in February 2016.

Unfortunately, bull and bear markets do not start conveniently at the beginnings and ends of months or years. Though some years ended higher, **every down January since 1950 was followed by a new or continuing bear market, a 10% correction, or a flat year**. Down Januarys were followed by substantial declines averaging *minus* **12.9%**, providing excellent buying opportunities later in most years.

FROM DOWN JANUARY S&P CLOSES TO LOW NEXT 11 MONTHS

Year	January Close	% Change	11-Month Low	Date of Low	Jan Close to Low %	% Feb to Dec	Year % Change	
1953	26.38	−0.7%	22.71	14-Sep	−13.9%	−6.0%	−6.6%	bear
1956	43.82	−3.6	43.42	14-Feb	−0.9	6.5	2.6	FLAT/bear
1957	44.72	−4.2	38.98	22-Oct	−12.8	−10.6	−14.3	Cont. bear
1960	55.61	−7.1	52.30	25-Oct	−6.0	4.5	−3.0	bear
1962	68.84	−3.8	52.32	26-Jun	−24.0	−8.3	−11.8	bear
1968	92.24	−4.4	87.72	5-Mar	−4.9	12.6	7.7	−10%/bear
1969	103.01	−0.8	89.20	17-Dec	−13.4	−10.6	−11.4	Cont. bear
1970	85.02	−7.6	69.20	26-May	−18.6	8.4	0.1	Cont. bear
1973	116.03	−1.7	92.16	5-Dec	−20.6	−15.9	−17.4	bear
1974	96.57	−1.0	62.28	3-Oct	−35.5	−29.0	−29.7	Cont. bear
1977	102.03	−5.1	90.71	2-Nov	−11.1	−6.8	−11.5	bear
1978	89.25	−6.2	86.90	6-Mar	−2.6	7.7	1.1	Cont. bear/bear
1981	129.55	−4.6	112.77	25-Sep	−13.0	−5.4	−9.7	bear
1982	120.40	−1.8	102.42	12-Aug	−14.9	16.8	14.8	Cont. bear
1984	163.42	−0.9	147.82	24-Jul	−9.5	2.3	1.4	Cont. bear/FLAT
1990	329.07	−6.9	295.46	11-Oct	−10.2	0.4	−6.6	bear
1992	408.79	−2.0	394.50	8-Apr	−3.5	6.6	4.5	FLAT
2000	1394.46	−5.1	1264.74	20-Dec	−9.3	−5.3	−10.1	bear
2002	1130.20	−1.6	776.76	9-Oct	−31.3	−22.2	−23.4	bear
2003	855.70	−2.7	800.73	11-Mar	−6.4	29.9	26.4	Cont. bear
2005	1181.27	−2.5	1137.50	20-Apr	−3.7	5.7	3.0	FLAT
2008	1378.55	−6.1	752.44	20-Nov	−45.4	−34.5	−38.5	bear
2009	825.88	−8.6	676.53	9-Mar	−18.1	35.0	23.5	Cont. bear
2010	1073.87	−3.7	1022.58	2-Jul	−4.8	17.1	12.8	−10%/no bear
2014	1782.59	−3.6	1741.89	3-Feb	−2.3	15.5	11.4	−10% intraday
2015	1994.99	−3.1	1867.61	25-Aug	−6.4	2.5	−0.7	bear
2016	1940.24	−5.1	1829.08	11-Feb	−5.7	15.4	9.5	Cont. bear
				Totals	−348.8%	32.3%	−76.0%	
				Average	−12.9%	1.2%	−2.8%	

MONDAY

D 42.9
S 52.4
N 47.6

4

Live beyond your means; then you're forced to work hard, you have to succeed.
— Edward G. Robinson (American actor)

TUESDAY

D 47.6
S 42.9
N 38.1

5

Bear markets don't act like a medicine ball rolling down a smooth hill. Instead, they behave like a basketball bouncing down a rock-strewn mountainside; there's lots of movement up and sideways before the bottom is reached.
— Daniel Turov (*Turov on Timing, Barron's*, 5/21/01, b. 1947)

Week Before February Expiration Week, NASDAQ Down 11 of Last 18, 2010 Up 2.0%, 2011 Up 1.5%, 2014 Up 2.9%, 2015 Up 3.2%

WEDNESDAY

D 52.4
S 52.4
N 52.4

6

What counts more than luck, is determination and perseverance. If the talent is there, it will come through. Don't be too impatient.
— Fred Astaire (The report from his first screen test stated, "Can't act. Can't sing. Balding. Can dance a little.")

THURSDAY

D 52.4
S 52.4
N 57.1

7

Methodology is the last refuge of a sterile mind.
— Marianne L. Simmel (Psychologist)

FRIDAY

D 42.9
S 57.1
N 57.1

8

The usual bull market successfully weathers a number of tests until it is considered invulnerable, whereupon it is ripe for a bust.
— George Soros (Financier, philanthropist, political activist, author and philosopher, b. 1930)

SATURDAY

9

SUNDAY

10

THE NINTH YEAR OF DECADES

Excluding the Crash of 1929, the bear market of 1969 (both post-election years) and the small loss in pre–World War II 1939, all other "nine" years were up during the past twelve decades. Being a pre–presidential election year further improves the prospects for 2019.

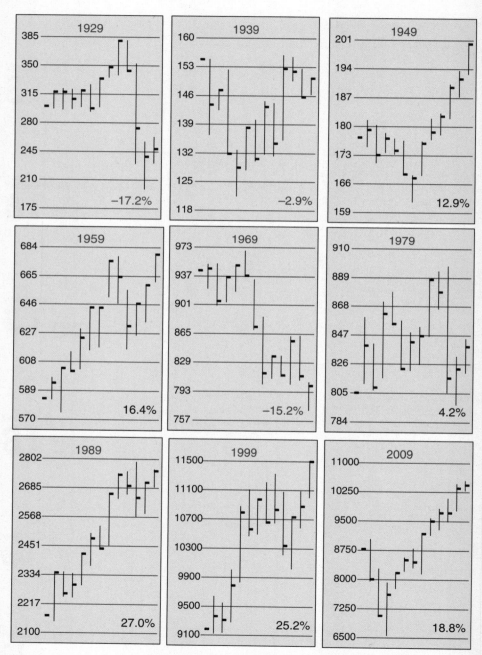

Based on Dow Jones Industrial Average monthly ranges and closing

FEBRUARY 2019

First Trading Day of February Expiration Week Dow Up 18 of Last 25,
Up Four Straight

MONDAY

D 57.1
S 47.6
N 42.9

11

The man who can master his time can master nearly anything.
— Winston Churchill (British statesman, 1874–1965)

TUESDAY

D 52.4
S 61.9
N 57.1

12

Banking establishments are more dangerous than standing armies; and that the principle of spending money to be paid by posterity, under the name of funding, is but swindling futurity on a large scale.
— Thomas Jefferson (3rd U.S. President, 1743–1826, 1816 letter to John Taylor of Carolina)

WEDNESDAY

D 61.9
S 71.4
N 71.4

13

Today's Ponzi-style acute fragility and speculative dynamics dictate that he who panics first panics best.
— Doug Noland (Prudent Bear Funds, *Credit Bubble Bulletin*, 10/26/07)

Valentine's Day ♥

THURSDAY

D 52.4
S 52.4
N 66.7

14

To change one's life: Start immediately. Do it flamboyantly. No exceptions.
— William James (Philosopher, psychologist, 1842–1910)

February Expiration Day, NASDAQ Down 13 of Last 19
Day Before Presidents' Day Weekend, S&P Down 17 of Last 27

FRIDAY

D 71.4
S 76.2
N 57.1

15

It is better to be out wishing you were in, than in wishing you were out.
— Albert W. Thomas (Trader, *Over My Shoulder*, mutualfundmagic.com, *If It Doesn't Go Up, Don't Buy It!*, b. 1927)

SATURDAY

16

SUNDAY

17

MARKET CHARTS OF PRE–PRESIDENTIAL ELECTION YEARS

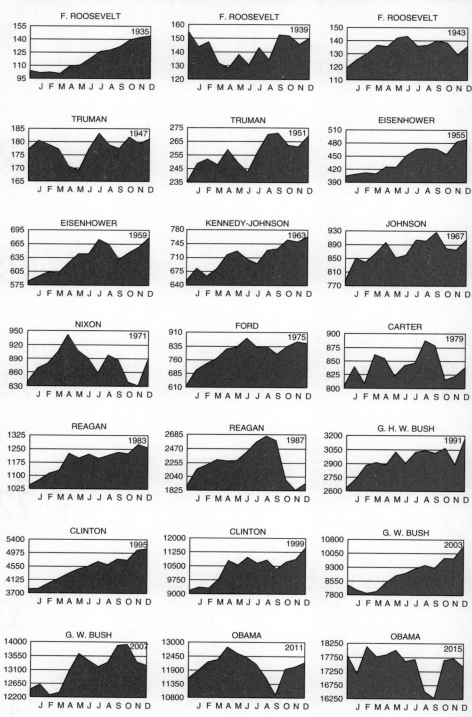

Based on Dow Jones Industial Average monthly closing prices

FEBRUARY 2019

Presidents' Day *(Market Closed)*

If I had eight hours to chop down a tree, I'd spend six sharpening my axe.
— Abraham Lincoln (16th U.S. President, 1809–1865)

Day After Presidents' Day, NASDAQ Down 15 of Last 24

TUESDAY

D 47.6
S 38.1
N 42.9

19

A government which robs Peter to pay Paul can always depend on the support of Paul.
— George Bernard Shaw (Irish dramatist, 1856–1950)

Week After February Expiration Week, Dow Down 11 of Last 20,
But Up 6 of Last 7

WEDNESDAY

D 42.9
S 47.6
N 52.4

20

There are no secrets to success. Don't waste your time looking for them. Success is the result of
perfection, hard work, learning from failure, loyalty to those for whom you work, and persistence.
— General Colin Powell (Chairman, Joint Chiefs 1989–1993, secretary of state 2001–2005, *New York Times*, 10/22/08, b. 1937)

THURSDAY

D 47.6
S 42.9
N 42.9

21

Financial markets will find and exploit hidden flaws, particularly in untested new innovations—
and do so at a time that will inflict the most damage to the most people.
— Raymond F. DeVoe Jr. (Market strategist, Jesup & Lamont, *The DeVoe Report*, 3/30/07)

End of February Miserable in Recent Years (Pages 20 and 133)

FRIDAY

D 47.6
S 47.6
N 57.1

22

The first human who hurled an insult instead of a stone was the founder of civilization.
— Sigmund Freud (Austrian neurologist, psychiatrist, "father of psychoanalysis," 1856–1939)

SATURDAY

23

March Almanac Investor Sector Seasonalities: See Pages 92, 94 and 96

SUNDAY

24

MARCH ALMANAC

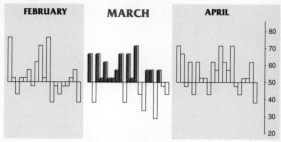

Market Probability Chart above is a graphic representation of the S&P 500 Recent Market Probability Calendar on page 124.

◆ Midmonth strength and late-month weakness are most evident above ◆ RECENT RECORD: S&P 13 up, 8 down, average gain 1.8%, second best ◆ Rather turbulent in recent years with wild fluctuations and large gains and losses ◆ March has been taking some mean end-of-quarter hits (page 134), down 1469 Dow points March 9–22, 2001 ◆ Last three or four days Dow a net loser 19 out of last 29 years ◆ NASDAQ hard hit in 2001, down 14.5% after 22.4% drop in February ◆ Fourth best NASDAQ month during pre–presidential election years, average gain 3.1%, up 10, down 2 ◆ Third Dow month to gain more than 1000 points in 2016.

March Vital Statistics

	DJIA		S&P 500		NASDAQ		Russell 1K		Russell 2K	
Rank	5		4		6		4		4	
Up	44		44		30		26		29	
Down	25		25		18		14		11	
Average % Change	1.1%		1.2%		0.9%		1.1%		1.4%	
Pre-Election Year	2.0%		1.9%		3.1%		2.0%		3.1%	
	Best & Worst March									
	% Change		% Change		% Change		% Change		% Change	
Best	2000	7.8	2000	9.7	2009	10.9	2000	8.9	1979	9.7
Worst	1980	−9.0	1980	−10.2	1980	−17.1	1980	−11.5	1980	−18.5
	Best & Worst March Weeks									
Best	03/13/09	9.0	03/13/09	10.7	03/13/09	10.6	03/13/09	10.7	03/13/09	12.0
Worst	03/16/01	−7.7	03/06/09	−7.0	03/16/01	−7.9	03/06/09	−7.1	03/06/09	−9.8
	Best & Worst March Days									
Best	03/23/09	6.8	03/23/09	7.1	03/10/09	7.1	03/23/09	7.0	03/23/09	8.4
Worst	03/02/09	−4.2	03/02/09	−4.7	03/12/01	−6.3	03/02/09	−4.8	03/27/80	−6.0
	First Trading Day of Expiration Week: 1980–2018									
Record (#Up – #Down)	25–14		25–14		20–19		23–16		21–18	
Current Streak	D2		D1		U6		D1		U2	
Avg % Change	0.17		0.07		−0.23		0.01		−0.29	
	Options Expiration Day: 1980–2018									
Record (#Up – #Down)	21–18		23–16		20–19		21–18		19–19	
Current Streak	U1		U1		U4		U1		U4	
Avg % Change	0.09		0.03		−0.03		0.03		0.001	
	Options Expiration Week: 1980–2018									
Record (#Up – #Down)	27–11		26–13		24–15		25–14		22–17	
Current Streak	D1		D1		D1		D1		D1	
Avg % Change	0.86		0.72		0.08		0.66		0.27	
	Week After Options Expiration: 1980–2018									
Record (#Up – #Down)	16–23		12–27		18–21		12–27		17–22	
Current Streak	D4		D6		D6		D7		D7	
Avg % Change	−0.43		−0.35		−0.21		−0.21		−0.28	
	First Trading Day Performance									
% of Time Up	66.7		63.8		62.5		60.0		65.0	
Avg % Change	0.17		0.18		0.26		0.16		0.26	
	Last Trading Day Performance									
% of Time Up	42.0		40.6		64.6		47.5		82.5	
Avg % Change	−0.09		0.01		0.20		0.11		0.40	

Dow & S&P 1950–June 2018, NASDAQ 1971–June 2018, Russell 1K & 2K 1979–June 2018.

March has Ides and St. Patrick's Day;
Begins bullishly, then fades away.

FEBRUARY/MARCH 2019

MONDAY
D 42.9
S 47.6
N 57.1
25

The biggest change we made was the move to a boundary-less company. We got rid of the corner offices, the bureaucracy, and the not-invented-here syndrome. Instead we got every mind in the game, got the best out of all our people.
— Jack Welch (retiring CEO of General Electric, *Business Week*, September 10, 2001)

TUESDAY
D 52.4
S 52.4
N 61.9
26

Let me end my talk by abusing slightly my status as an official representative of the Federal Reserve. I would like to say to Milton [Friedman]: regarding the Great Depression, you're right; we did it. We're very sorry. But thanks to you, we won't do it again.
— Ben Bernanke (Fed Chairman 2006–2014, 11/8/02 speech as Fed Governor)

WEDNESDAY
D 52.4
S 57.1
N 57.1
27

There is no one who can replace America. Without American leadership, there is no leadership. That puts a tremendous burden on the American people to do something positive. You can't be tempted by the usual nationalism.
— Lee Hong-koo (South Korean prime minister 1994–1995 and ambassador to U.S. 1998–2000, *N Y Times*, 2/25/09)

THURSDAY
D 38.1
S 38.1
N 23.8
28

I sold enough papers last year of high school to pay cash for a BMW.
— Michael Dell (Founder, Dell Computer, *Forbes*)

First Trading Day in March, Dow Up 15 of Last 23

FRIDAY
D 66.7
S 66.7
N 66.7
1

In investing, the return you want should depend on whether you want to eat well or sleep well.
— J. Kenfield Morley

SATURDAY
2

SUNDAY
3

PRE–PRESIDENTIAL ELECTION YEARS ONLY ONE LOSER IN 80 YEARS

Investors should feel somewhat secure going into 2019. There has only been one down year in the third year of a presidential term since war-torn 1939, Dow off 2.9%. That one loss occurred in 2015, Dow off 2.2%. The only severe loss in a pre–presidential election year going back 100 years occurred in 1931 during the Depression.

Electing a president every four years has set in motion a 4-year political stock market cycle. Most bear markets take place in the first or second years after elections (see pages 130–131). Then, the market improves. Typically, each administration usually does everything in its power to juice up the economy so that voters are in a positive mood at election time.

Quite an impressive record. Chances are the winning streak will continue and that the market in pre–presidential election year 2019 will gain ground. Prospects improve considerably if the market takes a breather in 2018 following the robust run of 2017.

THE RECORD SINCE 1915

1915	Wilson (D)	World War I in Europe, but Dow up 81.7%.
1919	Wilson (D)	Post-Armistice 45.5% gain through Nov 3 top. Dow +30.5%
1923	Harding/ Coolidge (R)	Teapot Dome scandal a depressant. Dow loses 3.3%.
1927	Coolidge (R)	Bull market rolls on, up 28.8%.
1931	Hoover (R)	Depression, stocks slashed in half. Dow −52.7%, S&P −47.1%
1935	Roosevelt (D)	Almost straight up year, S&P 500 up 41.2%, Dow 38.5%.
1939	Roosevelt (D)	War clouds, Dow −2.9% but 23.7% Apr–Dec gain. S&P −5.5%.
1943	Roosevelt (D)	U.S. at war, prospects brighter, S&P +19.4%, Dow +13.8%.
1947	Truman (D)	S&P unchanged, Dow up 2.2%.
1951	Truman (D)	Dow +14.4%, S&P +16.5%.
1955	Eisenhower (R)	Dow +20.8%, S&P +26.4%.
1959	Eisenhower (R)	Dow +16.4%, S&P +8.5%.
1963	Kennedy/ Johnson (D)	Dow +17.0%, S&P +18.9%.
1967	Johnson (D)	Dow +15.2%, S&P +20.1%.
1971	Nixon (R)	Dow +6.1%, S&P +10.8%, NASDAQ +27.4%.
1975	Ford (R)	Dow +38.3%, S&P +31.5%, NASDAQ +29.8%.
1979	Carter (D)	Dow +4.2%, S&P +12.3%, NASDAQ +28.1%.
1983	Reagan (R)	Dow +20.3%, S&P +17.3%, NASDAQ +19.9%.
1987	Reagan (R)	Dow +2.3%, S&P +2.0% despite Oct meltdown. NASDAQ −5.4%.
1991	G.H.W. Bush (R)	Dow +20.3%, S&P +26.3%, NASDAQ +56.8%.
1995	Clinton (D)	Dow +33.5%, S&P +34.1%, NASDAQ +39.9%.
1999	Clinton (D)	Millennial fever crescendo: Dow +25.2%, S&P +19.5%, NASDAQ +85.6%.
2003	G.W. Bush (R)	Straight up after fall of Saddam Hussein: Dow +25.3%, S&P +26.4%, NASDAQ +50.0%.
2007	G.W. Bush (R)	Credit bubble fuels all-time market highs before bear starts & Great Recession: Dow +6.4%, S&P +3.5%, NASDAQ 9.8%.
2011	Obama (D)	Debt Ceiling Debacle & U.S. credit rating downgrade: Dow +5.5%, S&P −0.003%, NASDAQ −1.8%.
2015	Obama (D)	Tepid growth: mild bear market ending February 2016: Dow −2.2%, S&P −0.7%, NASDAQ +5.7%.

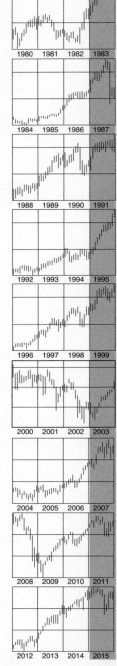

Graph shows Pre-Election years screened.
Based on Dow Jones Industial Average monthly ranges.

MARCH 2019

Ash Wednesday

MONDAY
D 42.9
S 38.1
N 38.1
4

Knowing others is intelligence; knowing yourself is true wisdom.
Mastering others is strength; mastering yourself is true power.
— Lau Tzu (Shaolin monk, founder of Taoism, circa 6th–4th century B.C.)

March Historically Strong Early in the Month (Pages 28 and 134)

TUESDAY
D 57.1
S 66.7
N 66.7
5

A generation from now, Americans may marvel at the complacency that assumed the dollar's dominance would never end.
— Floyd Norris (Chief financial correspondent, New York Times, 2/2/07)

WEDNESDAY
D 47.6
S 52.4
N 42.9
6

Nothing will improve a person's hearing more than sincere praise.
— Harvey Mackay (Pushing the Envelope, 1999)

THURSDAY
D 61.9
S 61.9
N 38.1
7

Government is like fire—useful when used legitimately, but dangerous when not.
— David Brooks (New York Times columnist, 10/5/07)

Dow Down 1469 Points March 9–22 in 2001

FRIDAY
D 47.6
S 52.4
N 52.4
8

Always grab the reader by the throat in the first paragraph, sink your thumbs into his windpipe
in the second, and hold him against the wall until the tag line.
— Paul O'Neil (Marketer, Writing Changes Everything)

SATURDAY
9

Daylight Saving Time Begins

SUNDAY
10

WHY A 50% GAIN IN THE DOW IS POSSIBLE FROM ITS 2018 LOW TO ITS 2019 HIGH

Normally, major corrections occur sometime in the first or second years following presidential elections. In the last 14 midterm election years, bear markets began or were in progress nine times—we experienced bull years in 1986, 2006, 2010 and 2014, while 1994 was flat.

The puniest midterm advance, 14.5% from the 1946 low, was during the industrial contraction after World War II. The next five smallest advances were: 2014 (tepid global growth) 19.1%, 1978 (OPEC–Iran) 21.0%, 1930 (economic collapse) 23.4%, 1966 (Vietnam) 26.7% and 2010 (European debt) 32.3%.

Since 1914 the Dow has gained 47.4% on average from its midterm election year low to its subsequent high in the following pre-election year. A swing of such magnitude is equivalent to a move from the current 2018 midterm low of 23533 to 34688.

POST–ELECTION HIGH TO MIDTERM LOW: –20.4%

Conversely, since 1913 the Dow has dropped –20.4% on average from its post–election year high to its subsequent low in the following midterm year. The Dow's 2017 post–election year high is 21206.29. A 20.4% decline would put the Dow back at 16880.20 at the 2018 midterm bottom. Historically low interest rates, deregulation, tax cuts and strong corporate earnings make a decline back to this level unlikely, save a diplomatic fiasco or fallout from the Mueller investigation. Whatever the level, the rally off the 2018 midterm low could be another great buying opportunity.

Pretty impressive seasonality! There is no reason to think the quadrennial Presidential Election/Stock Market Cycle will not continue. Page 130 shows how effectively most presidents "managed" to have much stronger economies in the third and fourth years of their terms than in their first two.

% CHANGE IN DOW JONES INDUSTRIALS BETWEEN THE MIDTERM YEAR LOW AND THE HIGH IN THE FOLLOWING YEAR

	Midterm Year Low Date of Low		Dow	Pre–Election Year High Date of High		Dow	% Gain
1	Jul 30	1914*	52.32	Dec 27	1915	99.21	89.6%
2	Jan 15	1918**	73.38	Nov 3	1919	119.62	63.0
3	Jan 10	1922**	78.59	Mar 20	1923	105.38	34.1
4	Mar 30	1926*	135.20	Dec 31	1927	202.40	49.7
5	Dec 16	1930*	157.51	Feb 24	1931	194.36	23.4
6	Jul 26	1934*	85.51	Nov 19	1935	148.44	73.6
7	Mar 31	1938*	98.95	Sep 12	1939	155.92	57.6
8	Apr 28	1942*	92.92	Jul 14	1943	145.82	56.9
9	Oct 9	1946	163.12	Jul 24	1947	186.85	14.5
10	Jan 13	1950**	196.81	Sep 13	1951	276.37	40.4
11	Jan 11	1954**	279.87	Dec 30	1955	488.40	74.5
12	Feb 25	1958**	436.89	Dec 31	1959	679.36	55.5
13	Jun 26	1962*	535.74	Dec 18	1963	767.21	43.2
14	Oct 7	1966*	744.32	Sep 25	1967	943.08	26.7
15	May 26	1970*	631.16	Apr 28	1971	950.82	50.6
16	Dec 6	1974*	577.60	Jul 16	1975	881.81	52.7
17	Feb 28	1978*	742.12	Oct 5	1979	897.61	21.0
18	Aug 12	1982*	776.92	Nov 29	1983	1287.20	65.7
19	Jan 22	1986	1502.29	Aug 25	1987	2722.42	81.2
20	Oct 11	1990*	2365.10	Dec 31	1991	3168.84	34.0
21	Apr 4	1994	3593.35	Dec 13	1995	5216.47	45.2
22	Aug 31	1998*	7539.07	Dec 31	1999	11497.12	52.5
23	Oct 9	2002*	7286.27	Dec 31	2003	10453.92	43.5
24	Jan 20	2006	10667.39	Oct 9	2007	14164.53	32.8
25	Jul 2	2010**	9686.48	Apr 29	2011	12810.54	32.3
26	Feb 3	2014	15372.80	May 19	2015	18312.39	19.1
27	Mar 23	2018	23533.20	At Press Time, July 6, 2018.			

*Bear Market ended **Bear previous year

Average   **47.4%**

PROBABILITIES FUND

PROBABILITIES
FUND MANAGEMENT, LLC

gory: Liquid Alternative - Class A: PROAX Class I: PROTX Class C: PROCX

June 2018

Cumulative Growth Chart (1/1/2008 – 6/30/2018)

- Probabilities I Share
- S&P 500
- Morningstar Diversified Alternatives Index

169.04%
132.02%
38.19%

Past Performance is no indication of future returns. Since inception, January 1, 2008 to present. The Morningstar Diversified Alternatives Index is comprised of seven alternative asset classes that broadly represent the alternative landscape, hedge funds, long/short equity, merger arbitrage, managed futures, breakeven Inflation, global Infrastructure, and listed private equity. The hypothetical scenario does not take into account federal, state or municipal takes. If taxes were taken into account, the hypothetical values shown would have been lower.

Using historical trends and patterns to obtain dynamic exposure to the US stock market.

Statistical Analysis vs S&P 500

	Probabilities I Share	MDAI	S&P 500
Cumulative Performance	169.04%	38.19%	132.02%
Annualized Alpha	6.10%	-0.20%	0.00%
Beta	0.50	0.35	1.00
Sharpe Ratio	0.65	0.44	0.58
Standard Deviation	15.83%	6.44%	14.90%
Maximum Drawdown	-22.29%	-15.25%	-48.45%
Correlation	0.47	0.81	1.00
Up Capture of S&P 500	79.94%	37.03%	100%
Down Capture of S&P 500	61.73%	37.32%	100%

Standardized Returns As of 6/30/2018 (Greater than one year, annualized)

Updated Quarterly	YTD	1 Year	3 Years	5 Years	10 Years	Since Inception
Probabilities Fund I Share (Inception 01/01/2008)	-6.51%	-0.20%	3.42%	3.00%	11.83%	9.90%
Probabilities Fund A at NAV (Inception 01/16/2014)	-6.67%	-0.58%	3.12%	N/A	N/A	2.37%
Probabilities Fund A at Maximum Load	-12.05%	-6.31%	1.10%	N/A	N/A	1.01%
Probabilities Fund C (Inception 01/16/2014)	-7.09%	-1.36%	2.36%	N/A	N/A	1.60%
S&P 500 Total Return	2.65%	14.37%	11.93%	13.42%	10.17%	8.35%

Historical Performance (PROTX)

	Jan	Feb	Mar	Apr	May	Jun	Jul	Aug	Sep	Oct	Nov	Dec	YTD	MDAI*	S&P 500	ITD
2018	4.40%	-6.50%	-4.13%	1.18%	-1.94%	0.69%							-6.51%	-0.84%	2.65%	169.04
2017	1.05%	4.26%	-0.27%	2.27%	0.18%	0.98%	0.79%	-0.61%	0.26%	1.84%	2.67%	1.65%	16.03%	2.70%	21.83%	187.76
2016	-6.02%	-1.36%	9.89%	0.19%	-0.48%	0.78%	0.10%	-1.64%	-0.39%	-2.85%	3.74%	1.95%	3.16%	2.31%	11.96%	148.01
2015	-7.56%	7.58%	-1.95%	-1.14%	0.29%	-0.95%	1.35%	-3.61%	0.39%	3.83%	1.04%	-3.93%	-5.35%	-3.66%	1.38%	140.42
2014	-4.46%	2.98%	1.35%	0.19%	0.10%	-0.47%	0.00%	1.62%	-0.66%	2.27%	1.85%	0.61%	5.30%	3.04%	13.69%	154.02
2013	5.91%	0.53%	6.57%	-0.24%	0.62%	0.28%	0.71%	-2.23%	-0.35%	0.71%	2.53%	2.61%	18.73%	8.64%	32.39%	141.29
2012	6.19%	5.83%	2.04%	2.38%	-2.80%	0.18%	4.19%	1.77%	-0.26%	0.70%	5.13%	0.07%	28.07%	6.82%	16.00%	103.17
2011	4.16%	7.75%	2.12%	6.09%	0.81%	-3.26%	-0.49%	-8.86%	-6.67%	5.79%	4.38%	2.54%	13.65%	-3.67%	2.11%	58.64
2010	-6.75%	10.41%	4.41%	2.16%	-3.56%	0.62%	-2.97%	1.22%	1.70%	0.62%	3.09%	5.45%	16.43%	11.83%	15.06%	39.48
2009	-0.94%	-15.90%	1.44%	10.98%	15.15%	0.75%	3.01%	-1.84%	-1.82%	-7.96%	8.31%	5.76%	13.88%	21.73%	26.46%	19.89
2008	1.68%	-15.28%	-8.28%	5.59%	6.07%	-0.61%	-0.07%	-2.56%	-2.33%	10.19%	11.65%	2.30%	5.27%	-12.21%	-37.00%	5.28

* Morningstar Diversified Alternatives Index.

Important Disclosures

Investors should carefully consider the investment objectives, risks, charges and expenses of the Probabilities Fun This and other importantinformation about the Fund is contained in the Prospectus, which can be obtained b contacting your financial advisor, or by calling 1.888.868.9501. The Prospectus should be read carefully befo investing. Probabilities Fund is distributed by Northern Lights Distributors, LLC member FINRA/SIPC. Probabiliti Fund Management, LLC and Northern Lights Distributors are not affiliated.

Performance shown before the inception date of the mutual fund, December 12, 2013, is for the Fund's predecessor limited partnership. T prior performance is net of management fee and other expenses, including the effect of the performance fee. The Fund's investment goa policies, guidelines and restrictions are similar to the predecessor limited partnership. From its inception date, the predecessor limite partnership was not subject to certain investment restrictions,diversification requirements and other restrictions of the Investment Compa Act of 1940 which if they had been applicable, it might have adversely affected its performance. In addition, the predecessor limite partnership was not subject to sales loads that would have adversely affected performance. Performance of the predecessor fund is not a indicator of future results.

Mutual Funds involve risk including the possible loss of principal.

ETFs are subject to investment advisory and other expenses, which will be indirectly paid by the Fund. As a result, your cost of investing the Fund will behigher than the cost of investing directly in the ETFs and may be higher than other mutual funds that invest directly in stoc and bonds. Each ETF is subject to specific risks, depending on its investments. Leveraged ETFs employ leverage, which magnifies t changes in the value of the Leveraged ETFs, which could result in significant losses to the Fund. The Fund invests in Leveraged ETFs in effort to deliver daily performance at twice the rate of the underlying index and if held over long periods of time, particularly in volat markets, the ETFs may not achieve their objective and may, in fact, perform contrary to expectations. Inverse ETFs are designed to rise price when stock prices are falling.

Inverse ETFs tend to limit the Fund's participation in overall market-wide gains. Accordingly, their performance over longer terms can perfo very differently than underlying assets and benchmarks, and volatile markets can amplify this effect.

The advisor's judgment about the attractiveness, value and potential appreciation of particular security or derivative in which the Fund inves or sells short may prove to be incorrect and may not produce the desired results. Equity prices can fall rapidly in response to developmer affecting a specific company or industry, or to changing economic, political or market conditions. A higher portfolio turnover may result higher transactional and brokerage costs. The indices shown are for informational purposes only and are not reflective of any investment. A it is not possible to invest in the indices, the data shown does not reflect or compare features of an actual investment, such as its objective costs and expenses, liquidity, safety, guarantees or insurance, fluctuation of principal or return, or tax features. Past performance does n guaranteed future results. The S&P 500 Index is an unmanaged composite of 500 large capitalization companies. This index is widely us by professional investors as a performance benchmark for large-cap stocks.

Alpha is a measure of the excess return of a fund over an index. Beta is a measure of a fund's volatility relative to market movements. Sharp Ratio is a measure of risk adjusted performance calculated by subtracting the risk-free rate from the rate of return of the portfolio a dividing the result by the standard deviation of the portfolio returns. The 3 month T-Bill rate was used in the calculation.

Standard Deviation is a statistical measurement of volatility risk based on historical returns. Maximum Drawdown represents the large peak-to-trough decline during a specific period of time. Correlation is a statistical measure of how two investments move inrelation to each oth

Up and Down Capture ratios reflect how a particular investment performed when a specific index has either risen or fallen. Long positio entail buying asecurity such as a stock, commodity or currency, with the expectation that the asset will rise in value. Short positions entail sale that is completed by thedelivery of a security borrowed by the seller. Short sellers assume they will be able to buy the stock at a low amount that the price at which they sold short.

Monday Before March Triple Witching, Dow Up 22 of Last 31

MONDAY

D 57.1
S 52.4
N 42.9

11

A statistician is someone who can draw a straight line from an unwarranted assumption to a foregone conclusion.
— Anonymous

TUESDAY

D 57.1
S 57.1
N 47.6

12

The reading of all good books is indeed like a conversation with the noblest men of past centuries, in which they reveal to us the best of their thoughts.
— René Descartes (French philosopher, mathematician and scientist, 1596–1650)

WEDNESDAY

D 57.1
S 66.7
N 66.7

13

Capitalism without bankruptcy is like Christianity without hell.
— Frank Borman (NASA Astronaut, Gemini 7, CDR Apollo 8, CEO, Eastern Airlines, April 1986)

THURSDAY

D 57.1
S 38.1
N 42.9

14

The investor who concentrated on the 50 stocks in the S&P 500 that are followed by the fewest Wall Street analysts wound up with a rousing 24.6% gain in [2006 versus] 13.6% [for] the S&P 500.
— Rich Bernstein (Chief Investment Strategist, Merrill Lynch, *Barron's*, 1/8/07)

March Triple-Witching Day Mixed Last 29 Years, but Dow Down 6 of Last 10

FRIDAY

D 76.2
S 66.7
N 47.6

15

People do not change when you tell them they should; they change when they tell themselves they must.
— Michael Mandelbaum (Johns Hopkins foreign policy specialist, *New York Times*, 6/24/09, b. 1946)

SATURDAY

16

St. Patrick's Day ♣

SUNDAY

17

THE DECEMBER LOW INDICATOR:
A USEFUL PROGNOSTICATING TOOL

When the Dow closes below its December closing low in the first quarter, it is frequently an excellent warning sign. Jeffrey Saut, Managing Director, Chief Investment Strategist at Raymond James, brought this to our attention many years ago. The December Low Indicator was originated by Lucien Hooper, a *Forbes* columnist and Wall Street analyst back in the 1970s. Hooper dismissed the importance of January and January's first week as reliable indicators. He noted that the trend could be random or even manipulated during a holiday-shortened week. Instead, said Hooper, "Pay much more attention to the December low. If that low is violated during the first quarter of the New Year, watch out!"

Twenty of the 34 occurrences were followed by gains for the rest of the year—and 18 full-year gains—after the low for the year was reached. For perspective we've included the January Barometer readings for the selected years. Hooper's "Watch Out" warning was absolutely correct, though. All but two of the instances since 1952 experienced further declines, as the Dow fell an additional 10.5% on average when December's low was breached in Q1.

Only three significant drops occurred (not shown) when December's low was not breached in Q1 (1974, 1981 and 1987). Both indicators were wrong seven times and nine years ended flat. If the December low is not crossed, turn to our January Barometer for guidance. It has been virtually perfect, right nearly 100% of these times (view the complete results at *www.stocktradersalmanac.com*).

YEARS DOW FELL BELOW DECEMBER LOW IN FIRST QUARTER

Year	Previous Dec Low	Date Crossed	Crossing Price	Subseq. Low	% Change Cross-Low	Rest of Year % Change	Full Year % Change	Jan Bar
1952	262.29	2/19/52	261.37	256.35	−1.9%	11.7%	8.4%	1.6%[2]
1953	281.63	2/11/53	281.57	255.49	−9.3	−0.2	−3.8	−0.7[3]
1956	480.72	1/9/56	479.74	462.35	−3.6	4.1	2.3	−3.6[1, 2, 3]
1957	480.61	1/18/57	477.46	419.79	−12.1	−8.7	−12.8	−4.2
1960	661.29	1/12/60	660.43	566.05	−14.3	−6.7	−9.3	−7.1
1962	720.10	1/5/62	714.84	535.76	−25.1	−8.8	−10.8	−3.8
1966	939.53	3/1/66	938.19	744.32	−20.7	−16.3	−18.9	0.5[1]
1968	879.16	1/22/68	871.71	825.13	−5.3	8.3	4.3	−4.4[1, 2, 3]
1969	943.75	1/6/69	936.66	769.93	−17.8	−14.6	−15.2	−0.8
1970	769.93	1/26/70	768.88	631.16	−17.9	9.1	4.8	−7.6[2, 3]
1973	1000.00	1/29/73	996.46	788.31	−20.9	−14.6	−16.6	−1.7
1977	946.64	2/7/77	946.31	800.85	−15.4	−12.2	−17.3	−5.1
1978	806.22	1/5/78	804.92	742.12	−7.8	0.01	−3.1	−6.2[3]
1980	819.62	3/10/80	818.94	759.13	−7.3	17.7	14.9	5.8[2]
1982	868.25	1/5/82	865.30	776.92	−10.2	20.9	19.6	−1.8[1, 2]
1984	1236.79	1/25/84	1231.89	1086.57	−11.8	−1.6	−3.7	−0.9[3]
1990	2687.93	1/15/90	2669.37	2365.10	−11.4	−1.3	−4.3	−6.9[3]
1991	2565.59	1/7/91	2522.77	2470.30	−2.1	25.6	20.3	4.2[2]
1993	3255.18	1/8/93	3251.67	3241.95	−0.3	15.5	13.7	0.7[2]
1994	3697.08	3/30/94	3626.75	3593.35	−0.9	5.7	2.1	3.3[2, 3]
1996	5059.32	1/10/96	5032.94	5032.94	NC	28.1	26.0	3.3[2]
1998	7660.13	1/9/98	7580.42	7539.07	−0.5	21.1	16.1	1.0[2]
2000	10998.39	1/4/00	10997.93	9796.03	−10.9	−1.9	−6.2	−5.1
2001	10318.93	3/12/01	10208.25	8235.81	−19.3	−1.8	−7.1	3.5[1]
2002	9763.96	1/16/02	9712.27	7286.27	−25.0	−14.1	−16.8	−1.6
2003	8303.78	1/24/03	8131.01	7524.06	−7.5	28.6	25.3	−2.7[1, 2]
2005	10440.58	1/21/05	10392.99	10012.36	−3.7	3.1	−0.6	−2.5[3]
2006	10717.50	1/20/06	10667.39	10667.39	NC	16.8	16.3	2.5
2007	12194.13	3/2/07	12114.10	12050.41	−0.5	9.5	6.4	1.4[2]
2008	13167.20	1/2/08	13043.96	7552.29	−42.1	−32.7	−33.8	−6.1
2009	8149.09	1/20/09	7949.09	6547.05	−17.6	31.2	18.8	−8.6[1, 2]
2010	10285.97	1/22/10	10172.98	9686.48	−4.8	13.8	11.0	−3.7[1, 2]
2014	15739.43	1/31/14	15698.85	15372.80	−2.1	13.5	7.5	−3.6[1, 2]
2016	17128.55	1/6/16	16906.51	15660.18	−7.4	16.9	13.4	−5.1[1, 2]
2018	24140.91	2/8/18	23860.46	23533.20	−1.4			
				Average Drop	**−10.5%**			

[1]*January Barometer wrong.* [2]*December Low Indicator wrong.* [3]*Year Flat.*

MONDAY
D 47.6
S 52.4
N 57.1
18

Show me a good phone receptionist and I'll show you a good company.
— Harvey Mackay (*Pushing the Envelope*, 1999)

FOMC Meeting (2 Days)

TUESDAY
D 66.7
S 71.4
N 71.4
19

There is always plenty of capital for those who can create practical plans for using it.
— Napoleon Hill (Author, *Think and Grow Rich*, 1883–1970)

Week After Triple Witching, Dow Down 21 of Last 31, 2000 Up 4.9%, 2007 Up 3.1%, 2009 Up 6.8%, 2011 Up 3.1%, Down 5 of Last 6

WEDNESDAY
D 57.1
S 42.9
N 66.7
20

Whatever method you use to pick stocks…, your ultimate success or failure will depend on your ability to ignore the worries of the world long enough to allow your investments to succeed. It isn't the head but the stomach that determines the fate of the stockpicker.
— Peter Lynch (Fidelity Investments, *Beating the Street*, 1994)

THURSDAY
D 38.1
S 33.3
N 52.4
21

You know a country is falling apart when even the government will not accept its own currency.
— Jim Rogers (Financier, *Adventure Capitalist*, b. 1942)

March Historically Weak Later in the Month (Pages 28 and 134)

FRIDAY
D 33.3
S 57.1
N 57.1
22

The generally accepted view is that markets are always right—that is, market prices tend to discount future developments accurately even when it is unclear what those developments are. I start with the opposite point of view. I believe that market prices are always wrong in the sense that they present a biased view of the future.
— George Soros (1987, Financier, philanthropist, political activist, author and philosopher, b. 1930)

SATURDAY
23

SUNDAY
24

HOW TO TRADE BEST MONTHS SWITCHING STRATEGIES

Our Best Months Switching Strategies found on pages 52, 56, 60 and 62 are simple and reliable, with a proven 68-year track record. Thus far we have failed to find a similar trading strategy that even comes close over the past six decades. And to top it off, the strategy has only been improving since we first discovered it in 1986.

Exogenous factors and cultural shifts must be considered. "Backward" tests that go back to 1925 or even 1896 and conclude that the pattern does not work are best ignored. They do not take into account these factors. Farming made August the best month from 1900 to 1951. Since 1987 it is the worst month of the year for the Dow and S&P. Panic caused by the financial crisis in 2007–08 caused every asset class aside from U.S. Treasuries to decline substantially. But the bulk of the major decline in equities in the worst months of 2008 was sidestepped using these strategies.

Our Best Months Switching Strategy will not make you an instant millionaire as other strategies claim they can do. What it will do is steadily build wealth over time with half the risk (or less) of a "buy and hold" approach.

A sampling of tradable funds for the Best and Worst Months appears in the table below. These are just a starting point and only skim the surface of possible trading vehicles currently available to take advantage of these strategies. Your specific situation and risk tolerance will dictate a suitable choice. If you are trading in a tax-advantaged account such as a company-sponsored 401(k) or Individual Retirement Account (IRA), your investment options may be limited to what has been selected by your employer or IRA administrator. But if you are a self-directed trader with a brokerage account, then you likely have unlimited choices (perhaps too many).

TRADABLE BEST AND WORST MONTHS SWITCHING STRATEGY FUNDS

Best Months		Worst Months	
Exchange Traded Funds (ETF)		**Exchange Traded Funds (ETF)**	
Symbol	Name	Symbol	Name
DIA	SPDR Dow Jones Industrial Average	SHY	iShares 1–3 Year Treasury Bond
SPY	SPDR S&P 500	IEI	iShares 3–7 Year Treasury Bond
QQQ	Invesco QQQ	IEF	iShares 7–10 Year Treasury Bond
IWM	iShares Russell 2000	TLT	iShares 20+ Year Treasury Bond
Mutual Funds		**Mutual Funds**	
Symbol	Name	Symbol	Name
VWNDX	Vanguard Windsor Fund	VFSTX	Vanguard Short-Term Investment-Grade Bond Fund
FMAGX	Fidelity Magellan Fund	FBNDX	Fidelity Investment Grade Bond Fund
AMCPX	American Funds AMCAP Fund	ABNDX	American Funds Bond Fund of America
FCGAX	Franklin Growth Fund	FKUSX	Franklin U.S. Government Securities Fund
SECEX	Guggenheim Large Cap Core Fund	SIUSX	Guggenheim Investment Grade Bond Fund

Generally speaking, during the Best Months you want to be invested in equities that offer similar exposure to the companies that constitute the Dow, S&P 500, and NASDAQ indices. These would typically be large-cap growth and value stocks as well as technology concerns. Reviewing the holdings of a particular ETF or mutual fund and comparing them to the index members is an excellent way to correlate.

During the Worst Months switch into Treasury bonds, money market funds or a bear/short fund. **Grizzly Short** (GRZZX) and **AdvisorShares Ranger Equity Bear** (HDGE) are two possible choices. Money market funds will be the safest, but are likely to offer the smallest return, while bear/short funds offer potentially greater returns, but more risk. If the market moves sideways or higher during the Worst Months, a bear/short fund is likely to lose money. Treasuries can offer a combination of fair returns with limited risk.

Additional Worst Month possibilities include precious metals and the companies that mine them. **SPDR Gold Shares** (GLD), **VanEck Vectors Gold Miners** (GDX) and **ETF Securities Physical Swiss Gold** (SGOL) are a few well-recognized names available from the ETF universe.

BECOME AN *ALMANAC INVESTOR*

Almanac Investor subscribers receive specific buy and sell recommendations based upon the Best Months Switching Strategies online and via email. Sector Index Seasonalities, found on page 92, are also put into action throughout the year with corresponding ETF trades. Buy limits, stop losses, and auto-sell price points for the majority of seasonal trades are delivered directly to your inbox. Visit *www.stocktradersalmanac.com* or see the insert for details and a special offer for new subscribers.

MARCH 2019

You have to keep digging, keep asking questions, because otherwise you'll be seduced or brainwashed into the idea that it's somehow a great privilege, an honor, to report the lies they've been feeding you.
— David Halberstam (American writer, war reporter, 1964 Pulitzer Prize winner, 1934–2007)

TUESDAY
D 28.6
S 28.6
N 28.6
26

Keep me away from the wisdom which does not cry, the philosophy which does not laugh and the greatness which does not bow before children.
— Kahlil Gibran (Lebanese-born American mystic, poet and artist, 1883–1931)

Start Looking for the Dow and S&P MACD SELL Signal (Pages 52 and 56)

WEDNESDAY
D 52.4
S 57.1
N 52.4
27

Cannot people realize how large an income is thrift?
— Marcus Tullius Cicero (Great Roman orator, politician, 106–43 B.C.)

THURSDAY
D 57.1
S 47.6
N 57.1
28

Those heroes of finance are like beads on a string, when one slips off, the rest follow.
— Henrik Ibsen (Norwegian playwright, 1828–1906)

Last Day of March, Dow Down 18 of Last 29, Russell 2000 Up 21 of Last 28

FRIDAY
D 38.1
S 42.9
N 52.4
29

Everything possible today was at one time impossible. Everything impossible today may at some time in the future be possible.
— Edward Lindaman (Apollo space project, president, Whitworth College, 1920–1982)

SATURDAY
30

April Almanac Investor Sector Seasonalities: See Pages 92, 94 and 96

SUNDAY
31

APRIL ALMANAC

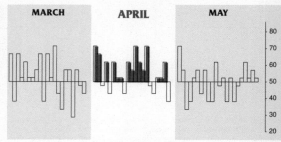

APRIL						
S	M	T	W	T	F	S
	1	2	3	4	5	6
7	8	9	10	11	12	13
14	15	16	17	18	19	20
21	22	23	24	25	26	27
28	29	30				

MAY						
S	M	T	W	T	F	S
			1	2	3	4
5	6	7	8	9	10	11
12	13	14	15	16	17	18
19	20	21	22	23	24	25
26	27	28	29	30	31	

Market Probability Chart above is a graphic representation of the S&P 500 Recent Market Probability Calendar on page 124.

◆ April is still the best Dow month (average 1.9%) since 1950 (page 50) ◆ April 1999 first month ever to gain 1000 Dow points, 856 in 2001, knocked off its high horse in 2002 down 458, 2003 up 488 ◆ Up thirteen straight, average gain 2.3% ◆ Prone to weakness after midmonth tax deadline ◆ Stocks anticipate great first-quarter earnings by rising sharply before earnings are reported, rather than after ◆ Rarely a dangerous month, recent exceptions are 2002, 2004 and 2005 ◆ "Best Six Months" of the year end with April (page 52) ◆ Pre–presidential election year Aprils stellar since 1950 (Dow 4.0%, S&P 3.5%, NASDAQ 3.5%) ◆ End of April NASDAQ strength (pages 125 & 126).

April Vital Statistics

	DJIA		S&P 500		NASDAQ		Russell 1K		Russell 2K	
Rank	1		3		4		3		3	
Up	47		49		31		28		25	
Down	22		20		17		12		15	
Average % Change	1.9%		1.4%		1.3%		1.5%		1.4%	
Pre-Election Year	4.0%		3.5%		3.5%		2.8%		2.8%	
				Best & Worst April						
	% Change		% Change		% Change		% Change		% Change	
Best	1978	10.6	2009	9.4	2001	15.0	2009	10.0	2009	15.3
Worst	1970	−6.3	1970	−9.0	2000	−15.6	2002	−5.8	2000	−6.1
				Best & Worst April Weeks						
Best	04/11/75	5.7	04/20/00	5.8	04/12/01	14.0	04/20/00	5.9	04/03/09	6.3
Worst	04/14/00	−7.3	04/14/00	−10.5	04/14/00	−25.3	04/14/00	−11.2	04/14/00	−16.4
				Best & Worst April Days						
Best	04/05/01	4.2	04/05/01	4.4	04/05/01	8.9	04/05/01	4.6	04/09/09	5.9
Worst	04/14/00	−5.7	04/14/00	−5.8	04/14/00	−9.7	04/14/00	−6.0	04/14/00	−7.3
			First Trading Day of Expiration Week: 1980–2018							
Record (#Up – #Down)	24–15		22–17		21–18		21–18		18–21	
Current Streak	U2		U2		U2		U2		U2	
Avg % Change	0.22		0.14		0.13		0.13		0.02	
			Options Expiration Day: 1980–2018							
Record (#Up – #Down)	24–15		24–15		21–18		24–15		24–15	
Current Streak	D5		D4		D4		D4		D2	
Avg % Change	0.14		0.13		−0.07		0.12		0.16	
			Options Expiration Week: 1980–2018							
Record (#Up – #Down)	31–8		28–11		26–13		26–13		29–10	
Current Streak	U3		U3		U3		U3		U3	
Avg % Change	1.04		0.86		0.92		0.84		0.85	
			Week After Options Expiration: 1980–2018							
Record (#Up – #Down)	26–13		26–13		27–12		26–13		26–13	
Current Streak	D1		D1		D1		D1		D1	
Avg % Change	0.45		0.45		0.70		0.45		0.84	
			First Trading Day Performance							
% of Time Up	58.0		60.9		45.8		57.5		47.5	
Avg % Change	0.14		0.11		−0.14		0.11		−0.13	
			Last Trading Day Performance							
% of Time Up	49.3		53.6		62.5		52.5		62.5	
Avg % Change	0.06		0.05		0.11		0.02		0.01	

Dow & S&P 1950–June 2018, NASDAQ 1971–June 2018, Russell 1K & 2K 1979–June 2018.

April "Best Month" for Dow since 1950;
Day-before-Good Friday gains are nifty.

First Trading Day in April, Dow Up 17 of Last 24

MONDAY

D 71.4
S 71.4
N 61.9

1

*Bill [Gates] isn't afraid of taking long-term chances. He also understands that you have
to try everyhting because the real secret to innovation is failing fast.*
— Gary Starkweather (Inventor of laser printer in 1969 at Xerox, *Fortune*, 7/8/02)

TUESDAY

D 66.7
S 66.7
N 61.9

2

*Corporate guidance has become something of an art. The CFO has refined and perfected his art,
gracefully leading on the bulls with the calculating grace and cunning of a great matador.*
— Joe Kalinowski (I/B/E/S)

April is the Best Month for the Dow, Average 1.9% Gain Since 1950

WEDNESDAY

D 38.1
S 47.6
N 61.9

3

*Early in March (1960), Dr. Arthur F. Burns called on me... Burns' conclusion was that unless some decisive action was taken,
and taken soon, we were heading for another economic dip which would hit its low point in October, just before the elections.*
— Richard M. Nixon (37th U.S. President, *Six Crises*, 1913–1994)

THURSDAY

D 66.7
S 61.9
N 57.1

4

*But how do we know when irrational exuberance has unduly escalated asset values, which then become
subject to unexpected and prolonged contractions as they have in Japan over the past decade?*
— Alan Greenspan (Fed Chairman 1987–2006, 12/5/96 speech to American Enterprise Institute, b. 1926)

April is 3rd Best Month for S&P, 4th Best for NASDAQ (Since 1971)

FRIDAY

D 42.9
S 42.9
N 33.3

5

*If the market does not rally, as it should during bullish seasonal periods, it is a sign that other forces are
stronger and that when the seasonal period ends those forces will really have their say.*
— Edson Gould (Stock market analyst, *Findings & Forecasts*, 1902–1987)

SATURDAY

6

SUNDAY

7

DOW JONES INDUSTRIALS ONE-YEAR SEASONAL PATTERN CHARTS SINCE 1901

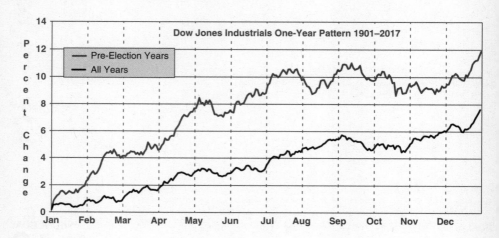

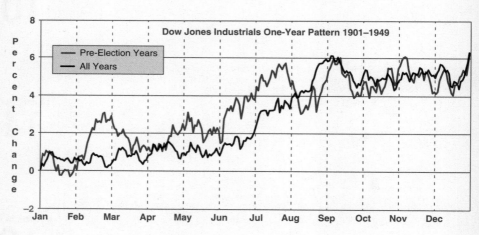

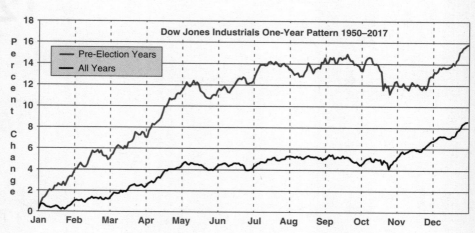

D 57.1
S 61.9
N 66.7

A day will come when all nations on our continent will form a European brotherhood... A day will come when we shall see... the United States of Europe... reaching out for each other across the seas.
— Victor Hugo (French novelist, playwright, *Hunchback of Notre Dame* and *Les Misérables*, 1802–1885)

TUESDAY
9

D 57.1
S 52.4
N 47.6

When everbody thinks alike, everyone is likely to be wrong.
— Humphrey B. Neill (Investor, analyst, author, *Art of Contrary Thinking,* 1954, 1895–1977)

April 1999 First Month Ever to Gain 1000 Dow Points

WEDNESDAY
10

D 57.1
S 52.4
N 61.9

Don't be overly concerned about your heirs. Usually, unearned funds do them more harm than good.
— Gerald M. Loeb (E. F. Hutton, *The Battle for Investment Survival*, predicted 1929 Crash, 1900–1974)

THURSDAY
11

D 47.6
S 42.9
N 38.1

The "canonical" market peak typically features rich valuations, rising interest rates, often a reasonably extended and "flattish" period... despite marginal new highs... and finally, an abrupt reversal in leadership... to a preponderance of new lows... with the reversal often occurring over a period of just a week or two.
— John P. Hussman, Ph.D. (Hussman Funds, 5/22/06)

🐻 **FRIDAY**
12

D 76.2
S 61.9
N 52.4

We're not believers that the government is bigger than the business cycle.
— David Rosenberg (Economist, Merrill Lynch, *Barron's*, 4/21/08)

SATURDAY
13

SUNDAY
14

S&P 500 ONE-YEAR SEASONAL PATTERN CHARTS SINCE 1930

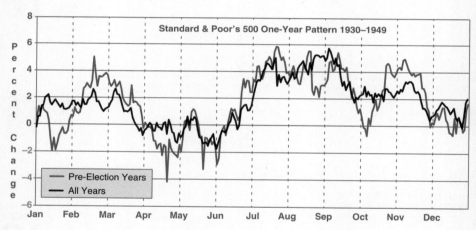

Monday Before Expiration, Dow Up 20 of Last 30, Mixed Last 14 Years
Income Tax Deadline

MONDAY

D 61.9
S 57.1
N 42.9

15

Taxes are what we pay for civilized society.
— Oliver Wendell Holmes Jr. (U.S. Supreme Court Justice, 1902–1932, "The Great Dissenter,"
inscribed above IRS HQ entrance, 1841–1935)

April Prone to Weakness After Tax Deadline (Pages 38 and 134)

TUESDAY

D 61.9
S 71.4
N 66.7

16

The government would not look fondly on Caesar's Palace if it opened a table for wagering on corporate failure.
It should not give greater encouragement for Goldman Sachs [et al.] to do so.
— Roger Lowenstein (Financial journalist and author, *End of Wall Street, New York Times* op-ed, 4/20/10, b. 1954)

WEDNESDAY

D 57.1
S 61.9
N 52.4

17

The symbol of all relationships among such men, the moral symbol of respect for human beings, is the trader.
— Ayn Rand (Russian-born American novelist and philosopher, from Galt's Speech, *Atlas Shrugged*, 1957, 1905–1982)

April Expiration Day Dow Up 14 of Last 22, But Down 5 Straight
NASDAQ Up 17 of Last 18 Days Before Good Friday

THURSDAY

D 66.7
S 57.1
N 57.1

18

When Paris sneezes, Europe catches cold.
— Prince Klemens Metternich (Austrian statesman, 1773–1859)

Good Friday *(Market Closed)*

FRIDAY

19

Life is like riding a bicycle. You don't fall off unless you stop pedaling.
— Claude D. Pepper (U.S. Senator from Florida, 1936–1951, 1900–1989)

Passover Begins

SATURDAY

20

Easter

SUNDAY

21

NASDAQ, RUSSELL 1000 & 2000 ONE-YEAR SEASONAL PATTERN CHARTS SINCE 1971

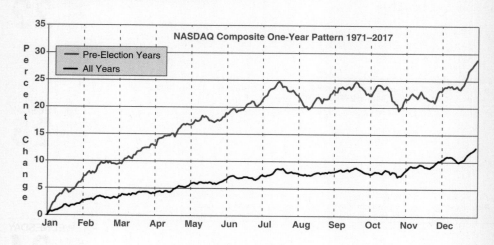

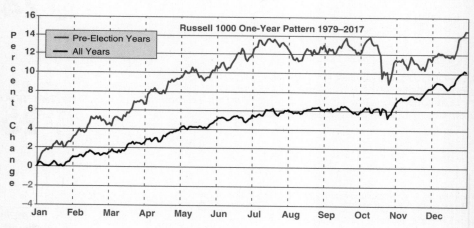

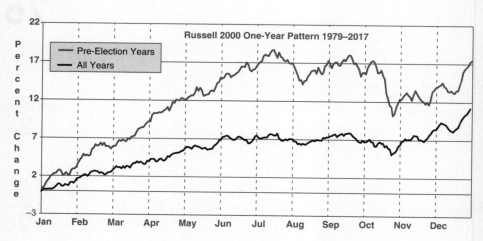

Day After Easter, Second Worst Post-Holiday (Page 88)

Politics ought to be the part-time profession of every citizen who would protect the rights and privileges of free people and who would preserve what is good and fruitful in our national heritage.
— Dwight D. Eisenhower (34th U.S. President, 1890–1969)

Knowledge born from actual experience is the answer to why one profits; lack of it is the reason one loses.
— Gerald M. Loeb (E. F. Hutton, *The Battle for Investment Survival*, predicted 1929 Crash, 1900–1974)

If you torture the data long enough, it will confess to anything.
— Darrell Huff (*How to Lie With Statistics*, 1954)

Whoso would be a man, must be a non-conformist. . . . Nothing is at last sacred but the integrity of your own mind.
— Ralph Waldo Emerson (American author, poet and philosopher, *Self-Reliance*, 1803–1882)

Capitalism works because it encourages and rewards those who successfully take risks, adapt to change, and develop profitable opportunities.
— Henry Blodget (former stock analyst, *New York Times* op-ed, 12/20/06, *The Wall Street Self-Defense Manual*)

May Almanac Investor Sector Seasonalities: See Pages 92, 94 and 96

MAY ALMANAC

	MAY					
S	M	T	W	T	F	S
			1	2	3	4
5	6	7	8	9	10	11
12	13	14	15	16	17	18
19	20	21	22	23	24	25
26	27	28	29	30	31	

	JUNE					
S	M	T	W	T	F	S
						1
2	3	4	5	6	7	8
9	10	11	12	13	14	15
16	17	18	19	20	21	22
23	24	25	26	27	28	29
30						

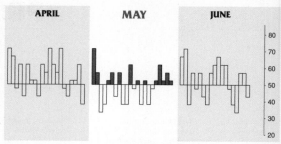

Market Probability Chart above is a graphic representation of the S&P 500 Recent Market Probability Calendar on page 124.

◆ "May/June disaster area" between 1965 and 1984 with S&P down 15 out of 20 Mays ◆ Between 1985 and 1997 May was the best month with 13 straight gains, gaining 3.3% per year on average, up 13, down 8 since ◆ Worst six months of the year begin with May (page 52) ◆ A $10,000 investment compounded to $1,008,721 for November–April in 68 years compared to a $1,031 gain for May–October ◆ Dow Memorial Day week record: up 12 years in a row (1984–1995), down 14 of the last 23 years ◆ Since 1950, pre–presidential election year Mays rank poorly: #10 Dow, #10 S&P and #7 NASDAQ.

May Vital Statistics

	DJIA		S&P 500		NASDAQ		Russell 1K		Russell 2K	
Rank	9		8		5		6		6	
Up	37		41		30		28		26	
Down	32		28		18		12		14	
Average % Change	−0.001%		0.3%		1.1%		1.0%		1.4%	
Pre-Election Year	0.1%		0.2%		1.9%		1.2%		2.7%	
	Best & Worst May									
		% Change		% Change		% Change		% Change		% Change
Best	1990	8.3	1990	9.2	1997	11.1	1990	8.9	1997	11.0
Worst	2010	−7.9	1962	−8.6	2000	−11.9	2010	−8.1	2010	−7.7
	Best & Worst May Weeks									
Best	05/29/70	5.8	05/02/97	6.2	05/17/02	8.8	05/02/97	6.4	05/14/10	6.3
Worst	05/25/62	−6.0	05/25/62	−6.8	05/07/10	−8.0	05/07/10	−6.6	05/07/10	−8.9
	Best & Worst May Days									
Best	05/27/70	5.1	05/27/70	5.0	05/30/00	7.9	05/10/10	4.4	05/10/10	5.6
Worst	05/28/62	−5.7	05/28/62	−6.7	05/23/00	−5.9	05/20/10	−3.9	05/20/10	−5.1
	First Trading Day of Expiration Week: 1980–2018									
Record (#Up – #Down)	25–14		26–13		22–17		24–15		20–19	
Current Streak	U3		U3		U3		U3		D1	
Avg % Change	0.19		0.18		0.18		0.16		0.03	
	Options Expiration Day: 1980–2018									
Record (#Up – #Down)	20–19		22–17		19–20		22–17		20–19	
Current Streak	U6		D1		D1		D1		U3	
Avg % Change	−0.07		−0.07		−0.08		−0.06		0.04	
	Options Expiration Week: 1980–2018									
Record (#Up – #Down)	19–20		19–20		20–19		18–21		21–18	
Current Streak	D3		D2		D2		D2		U1	
Avg % Change	0.04		0.01		0.16		0.02		−0.10	
	Week After Options Expiration: 1980–2018									
Record (#Up – #Down)	22–17		25–14		27–12		25–14		29–10	
Current Streak	U3		U5		U5		U5		U5	
Avg % Change	0.05		0.20		0.32		0.23		0.39	
	First Trading Day Performance									
% of Time Up	56.5		59.4		64.6		60.0		62.5	
Avg % Change	0.20		0.24		0.35		0.27		0.28	
	Last Trading Day Performance									
% of Time Up	58.0		59.4		64.6		52.5		62.5	
Avg % Change	0.16		0.24		0.18		0.18		0.28	

Dow & S&P 1950–June 2018, NASDAQ 1971–June 2018, Russell 1K & 2K 1979–June 2018.

May's new pattern, a smile or a frown,
Odd years UP and even years DOWN.

APRIL/MAY 2019

We will have to pay more and more attention to what the funds are doing. They are the ones who have been contributing to the activity, especially in the high-fliers.
— Humphrey B. Neill (Investor, analyst, author, *New York Times*, 6/11/66, 1895–1977)

End of "Best Six Months" of the Year (Pages 52, 56, 62 and 147)
FOMC Meeting (2 Days)

TUESDAY
30

D 33.3
S 38.1
N 52.4

Explosive growth of shadow banking was about the invisible hand having a party, a non-regulated drinking party, with rating agencies handing out fake IDs.
— Paul McCulley (Economist, bond investor, PIMCO, coined "shadow banking" in 2007, *NY Times*, 4/26/10, b. 1957)

First Trading Day in May, Dow Up 14 of Last 21

WEDNESDAY
1

D 66.7
S 71.4
N 76.2

The future now belongs to societies that organize themselves for learning. What we know and can do holds the key to economic progress.
— Ray Marshall (b. 1928) and Marc Tucker (b. 1939) (*Thinking for a Living: Education and the Wealth of Nations*, 1992)

THURSDAY
2

D 66.7
S 57.1
N 61.9

With respect to trading Sugar futures, if they give it away for free at restaurants you probably don't want to be trading it.
— John L. Person (Professional trader, author, speaker, *Commodity Trader's Almanac*, 2/22/11, TradersExpo, b. 1961)

FRIDAY
3

D 33.3
S 33.3
N 38.1

All there is to investing is picking good stocks at good times and staying with them as long as they remain good companies.
— Warren Buffett (CEO, Berkshire Hathaway, investor and philanthropist, b. 1930)

SATURDAY
4

SUNDAY
5

SUMMER MARKET VOLUME DOLDRUMS DRIVE WORST SIX MONTHS

In recent years, Memorial Day weekend has become the unofficial start of summer. Not long afterward trading activity typically begins to slowly decline (barring any external event triggers) toward a later summer low. We refer to this summertime slow-down in trading as the doldrums due to the anemic volume and uninspired trading on Wall Street. The individual trader, if he is looking to sell a stock, is generally met with disinterest from The Street. It becomes difficult to sell a stock at a good price. That is also why many summer rallies tend to be short lived and are quickly followed by a pullback or correction.

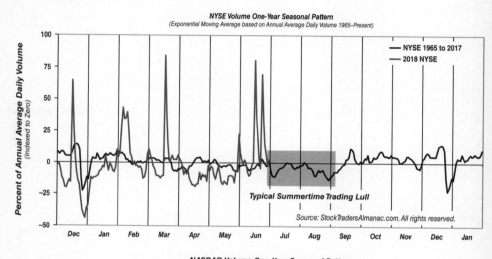

NYSE Volume One-Year Seasonal Pattern
(Exponential Moving Average based on Annual Average Daily Volume 1965–Present)

Source: StockTradersAlmanac.com. All rights reserved.

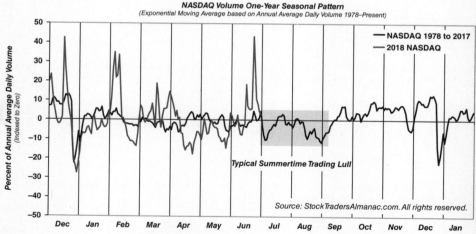

NASDAQ Volume One-Year Seasonal Pattern
(Exponential Moving Average based on Annual Average Daily Volume 1978–Present)

Source: StockTradersAlmanac.com. All rights reserved.

Above are plotted the one-year seasonal volume patterns since 1965 for the NYSE and since 1978 for NASDAQ against the annual average daily volume moving average for 2018 as of the close on June 29, 2018. The typical summer lull is highlighted in the shaded box. A prolonged surge in volume during the typically quiet summer months, especially when accompanied by gains, can be an encouraging sign that the bull market will continue. However, should traders lose their conviction and participate in the annual summer exodus from The Street, a market pullback or correction could quickly unfold.

MONDAY

D 38.1
S 38.1
N 42.9

6

The wisdom of the ages is the fruits of freedom and democracy.
— Lawrence Kudlow (Economist, 24th Annual Paulson SmallCap Conference, Waldorf Astoria NYC, 11/8/01)

TUESDAY

D 57.1
S 52.4
N 47.6

7

Today we deal with 65,000 more pieces of information each day than did our ancestors 100 years ago.
— Dr. Jean Houston (A founder of the Human Potential Movement, b. 1937)

WEDNESDAY

D 66.7
S 57.1
N 76.2

8

Anyone who believes that exponential growth can go on forever in a finite world is either a madman or an economist.
— Kenneth Ewart Boulding (Economist, activist, poet, scientist, philosopher, cofounder, General Systems Theory, 1910–1993)

THURSDAY

D 47.6
S 42.9
N 47.6

9

The worst trades are generally when people freeze and start to pray and hope rather than take some action.
— Robert Mnuchin (Partner, Goldman Sachs, b. 1933)

Friday Before Mother's Day, Dow Up 16 of Last 24

FRIDAY

D 61.9
S 57.1
N 47.6

10

The only function of economic forecasting is to make astrology look respectable.
— John Kenneth Galbraith (Canadian/American economist and diplomat, 1908–2006)

SATURDAY

11

Mother's Day

SUNDAY

12

TOP PERFORMING MONTHS PAST 68½ YEARS: STANDARD & POOR'S 500 AND DOW JONES INDUSTRIALS

Monthly performance of the S&P and the Dow is ranked over the past 68½ years. NASDAQ monthly performance is shown on page 58.

April, November and December still hold the top three positions in both the Dow and the S&P. March has reclaimed the fourth spot on the S&P. Disastrous Januarys in 2008, 2009 and 2016 knocked January into fifth. This, in part, led to our discovery in 1986 of the market's most consistent seasonal pattern. You can divide the year into two sections and have practically all the gains in one six-month section and very little in the other. September is the worst month on both lists. (See "Best Six Months" on page 52.)

MONTHLY % CHANGES (JANUARY 1950–MAY 2018)

Standard & Poor's 500					Dow Jones Industrials				
Month	Total % Change	Avg. % Change	# Up	# Down	Month	Total % Change	Avg. % Change	# Up	# Down
Jan	70.2%	1.0%	42	27	Jan	64.0%	0.9%	44	25
Feb	2.9	0.04	38	31	Feb	14.6	0.2	41	28
Mar	80.7	1.2	44	25	Mar	73.3	1.1	44	25
Apr	100.0	1.4	49	20	Apr	129.1	1.9	47	22
May	17.9	0.3	41	28	May	−0.1	−0.001	37	32
Jun	−1.6	−0.02	36	32	Jun	−19.5	−0.3	32	36
Jul	70.0	1.0	38	30	Jul	81.2	1.2	43	25
Aug	−6.0	−0.1	37	31	Aug	−11.9	−0.2	38	30
Sep*	−32.4	−0.5	30	37	Sep	−48.5	−0.7	27	41
Oct	62.6	0.9	41	27	Oct	46.7	0.7	41	27
Nov	105.2	1.5	46	22	Nov	108.3	1.6	46	22
Dec	109.5	1.6	51	17	Dec	112.9	1.7	48	20
% Rank					**% Rank**				
Dec	109.5%	1.6%	51	17	Apr	129.1%	1.9%	47	22
Nov	105.2	1.5	46	22	Dec	112.9	1.7	48	20
Apr	100.0	1.4	49	20	Nov	108.3	1.6	46	22
Mar	80.7	1.2	44	25	Jul	81.2	1.2	43	25
Jan	70.2	1.0	42	27	Mar	73.3	1.1	44	25
Jul	70.0	1.0	38	30	Jan	64.0	0.9	44	25
Oct	62.6	0.9	41	27	Oct	46.7	0.7	41	27
May	17.9	0.3	41	28	Feb	14.6	0.2	41	28
Feb	2.9	0.04	38	31	May	−0.1	−0.001	37	32
Jun	−1.6	−0.02	36	32	Aug	−11.9	−0.2	38	30
Aug	−6.0	−0.1	37	31	Jun	−19.5	−0.3	32	36
Sep*	−32.4	−0.5	30	37	Sep	−48.5	−0.7	27	41
Totals	**579.0%**	**8.3%**			**Totals**	**550.1%**	**8.1%**		
Average		**0.69%**			**Average**		**0.67%**		

*No change 1979

Anticipators, shifts in cultural behavior and faster information flow have altered seasonality in recent years. Here is how the months ranked over the past 15½ years (186 months) using total percentage gains on the S&P 500: April 32.4, March 22.9, July 22.5, December 22.3, October 18.8, November 14.7, May 10.1, September 5.6, February 5.2, August −5.1, January −10.7 and June −11.3.

During the last 15½ years front-runners of our Best Six Months may have helped push October into the number-five spot. January has declined in 10 of the last 20 years. Sizable turnarounds in "bear killing" October were a common occurrence from 1999 to 2007. Recent big Dow losses in the period were: September 2001 (9/11 attack), off 11.1%; September 2002 (Iraq war drums), off 12.4%; June 2008, off 10.2%; October 2008, off 14.1%; and February 2009 (financial crisis), off 11.7%.

MAY 2019

Monday After Mother's Day, Dow Up 16 of Last 24
Monday Before May Expiration, Dow Up 24 of Last 31, Average
Gain 0.4%

MONDAY
D 38.1
S 38.1
N 47.6
13

A "tired businessman" is one whose business is usually not a successful one.
— Joseph R. Grundy (U.S. Senator from Pennsylvania, 1929–1930, businessman, 1863–1961)

TUESDAY
D 47.6
S 38.1
N 42.9
14

A weak currency is the sign of a weak economy, and a weak economy leads to a weak nation.
— H. Ross Perot (American businessman, *The Dollar Crisis*, 2-time 3rd-party presidential candidate, 1992 & 1996, b. 1930)

WEDNESDAY
D 57.1
S 61.9
N 57.1
15

War is God's way of teaching Americans geography.
— Ambrose Bierce (Writer, satirist, Civil War hero, *The Devil's Dictionary*, 1842–1914)

THURSDAY
D 42.9
S 47.6
N 52.4
16

There is no great mystery to satisfying your customers. Build them a quality product and treat them with respect. It's that simple.
— Lee Iacocca (American industrialist, former Chrysler CEO, b. 1924)

May Expiration Day Mixed, Dow Up 12 of Last 18

FRIDAY
D 52.4
S 52.4
N 57.1
17

Age is a question of mind over matter. If you don't mind, it doesn't matter.
— Leroy Robert "Satchel" Paige (Negro League and Hall of Fame Pitcher, 1906–1982)

SATURDAY
18

SUNDAY
19

"BEST SIX MONTHS": STILL AN EYE-POPPING STRATEGY

Our Best Six Months Switching Strategy consistently delivers. Investing in the Dow Jones Industrial Average between November 1 and April 30 each year and then switching into fixed income for the other six months has produced reliable returns with reduced risk since 1950.

The chart on page 147 shows November, December, January, March and April to be the top months since 1950. Add February, and an excellent strategy is born! These six consecutive months gained 21576.80 Dow points in 68 years, while the remaining May-through-October months gained 2624.71 points. The S&P gained 2174.61 points in the same best six months versus 455.37 points in the worst six.

Percentage changes are shown along with a compounding $10,000 investment. The November–April $1,008,721 gain overshadows May–October's $1,031 gain. (S&P results are $757,335 to $9,079.) Just three November–April losses were double-digit: April 1970 (Cambodian invasion), 1973 (OPEC oil embargo) and 2008 (financial crisis). Similarly, Iraq muted the Best Six and inflated the Worst Six in 2003. When we discovered this strategy in 1986, November–April outperformed May–October by $88,163 to minus $1,522. Results improved substantially these past 31 years, $920,558 to $2,553. A simple timing indicator nearly triples results (page 56).

SIX-MONTH SWITCHING STRATEGY

	DJIA % Change May 1–Oct 31	Investing $10,000	DJIA % Change Nov 1–Apr 30	Investing $10,000
1950	5.0%	$10,500	15.2%	$11,520
1951	1.2	10,626	–1.8	11,313
1952	4.5	11,104	2.1	11,551
1953	0.4	11,148	15.8	13,376
1954	10.3	12,296	20.9	16,172
1955	6.9	13,144	13.5	18,355
1956	–7.0	12,224	3.0	18,906
1957	–10.8	10,904	3.4	19,549
1958	19.2	12,998	14.8	22,442
1959	3.7	13,479	–6.9	20,894
1960	–3.5	13,007	16.9	24,425
1961	3.7	13,488	–5.5	23,082
1962	–11.4	11,950	21.7	28,091
1963	5.2	12,571	7.4	30,170
1964	7.7	13,539	5.6	31,860
1965	4.2	14,108	–2.8	30,968
1966	–13.6	12,189	11.1	34,405
1967	–1.9	11,957	3.7	35,678
1968	4.4	12,483	–0.2	35,607
1969	–9.9	11,247	–14.0	30,622
1970	2.7	11,551	24.6	38,155
1971	–10.9	10,292	13.7	43,382
1972	0.1	10,302	–3.6	41,820
1973	3.8	10,693	–12.5	36,593
1974	–20.5	8,501	23.4	45,156
1975	1.8	8,654	19.2	53,826
1976	–3.2	8,377	–3.9	51,727
1977	–11.7	7,397	2.3	52,917
1978	–5.4	6,998	7.9	57,097
1979	–4.6	6,676	0.2	57,211
1980	13.1	7,551	7.9	61,731
1981	–14.6	6,449	–0.5	61,422
1982	16.9	7,539	23.6	75,918
1983	–0.1	7,531	–4.4	72,578
1984	3.1	7,764	4.2	75,626
1985	9.2	8,478	29.8	98,163
1986	5.3	8,927	21.8	119,563
1987	–12.8	7,784	1.9	121,835
1988	5.7	8,228	12.6	137,186
1989	9.4	9,001	0.4	137,735
1990	–8.1	8,272	18.2	162,803
1991	6.3	8,793	9.4	178,106
1992	–4.0	8,441	6.2	189,149
1993	7.4	9,066	0.03	189,206
1994	6.2	9,628	10.6	209,262
1995	10.0	10,591	17.1	245,046
1996	8.3	11,470	16.2	284,743
1997	6.2	12,181	21.8	346,817
1998	–5.2	11,548	25.6	435,602
1999	–0.5	11,490	0.04	435,776
2000	2.2	11,743	–2.2	426,189
2001	–15.5	9,923	9.6	467,103
2002	–15.6	8,375	1.0	471,774
2003	15.6	9,682	4.3	492,060
2004	–1.9	9,498	1.6	499,933
2005	2.4	9,726	8.9	544,427
2006	6.3	10,339	8.1	588,526
2007	6.6	11,021	–8.0	541,444
2008	–27.3	8,012	–12.4	474,305
2009	18.9	9,526	13.3	537,388
2010	1.0	9,621	15.2	619,071
2011	–6.7	8,976	10.5	684,073
2012	–0.9	8,895	13.3	775,055
2013	4.8	9,322	6.7	826,984
2014	4.9	9,779	2.6	848,486
2015	–1.0	9,681	0.6	853,577
2016	2.1	$9,884	15.4	$985,223
2017	11.6	$11,031	3.4	$1,018,721
Average/Gain	**0.6%**	**$1,031**	**7.5%**	**$1,008,721**
# Up/Down	**41/27**		**54/14**	

52

MONDAY

D 38.1
S 38.1
N 33.3

20

Investors operate with limited funds and limited intelligence, they don't need to know everything.
As long as they understand something better than others, they have an edge.
— George Soros (Financier, philanthropist, political activist, author and philosopher, b. 1930)

TUESDAY

D 52.4
S 52.4
N 61.9

21

Wall Street's graveyards are filled with men who were right too soon.
— William Peter Hamilton (Editor, *Wall Street Journal, The Stock Market Barometer*, 1922, 1867–1929)

WEDNESDAY

D 28.6
S 38.1
N 42.9

22

If I have seen further, it is by standing upon the shoulders of giants.
— Sir Isaac Newton (English physicist, mathematician, letter to Robert Hooke, 2/15/1676, 1643–1727)

THURSDAY

D 42.9
S 47.6
N 47.6

23

Governments last as long as the under-taxed can defend themselves against the over-taxed.
— Bernard Berenson (American art critic, 1865–1959)

Friday Before Memorial Day Tends to Be Lackluster with Light Trading,
Dow Down 11 of Last 19, Average –0.2%

FRIDAY

D 47.6
S 52.4
N 47.6

24

Being uneducated is sometimes beneficial. Then you don't know what can't be done.
— Michael Ott (Venture capitalist)

SATURDAY

25

June Almanac Investor Sector Seasonalities: See Pages 92, 94 and 96

SUNDAY

26

JUNE ALMANAC

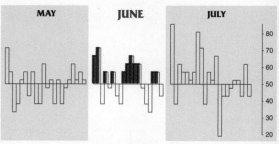

Market Probability Chart above is a graphic representation of the S&P 500 Recent Market Probability Calendar on page 124.

◆ The "summer rally" in most years is the weakest rally of all four seasons (page 74)
◆ Week after June Triple-Witching Day Dow down 25 of last 29 (page 78)
◆ RECENT RECORD: S&P up 12, down 9, average loss 0.4%, ranks tenth ◆ Stronger for NASDAQ, average gain 0.7% last 21 years ◆ Watch out for end-of-quarter "portfolio pumping" on last day of June, Dow down 17 of last 28, NASDAQ up 7 of last 8 ◆ Pre–presidential election year Junes: #5 S&P, #8 Dow, #6 NASDAQ ◆ June ends NASDAQ's Best Eight Months.

June Vital Statistics

	DJIA		S&P 500		NASDAQ		Russell 1K		Russell 2K	
Rank	11		10		9		11		8	
Up	32		37		26		24		25	
Down	37		32		22		16		15	
Average % Change	−0.3%		−0.02%		0.6%		0.2%		0.6%	
Pre-Election Year	0.8%		1.2%		1.9%		1.1%		1.4%	
Best & Worst June										
	% Change		% Change		% Change		% Change		% Change	
Best	1955	6.2	1955	8.2	2000	16.6	1999	5.1	2000	8.6
Worst	2008	−10.2	2008	−8.6	2002	−9.4	2008	−8.5	2010	−7.9
Best & Worst June Weeks										
Best	06/07/74	6.4	06/02/00	7.2	06/02/00	19.0	06/02/00	8.0	06/02/00	12.2
Worst	06/30/50	−6.8	06/30/50	−7.6	06/15/01	−8.4	06/15/01	−4.2	06/09/06	−4.9
Best & Worst June Days										
Best	06/28/62	3.8	06/28/62	3.4	06/02/00	6.4	06/10/10	3.0	06/02/00	4.2
Worst	06/26/50	−4.7	06/26/50	−5.4	06/24/16	−4.1	06/24/16	−3.6	06/04/10	−5.0
First Trading Day of Expiration Week: 1980–2018										
Record (#Up – #Down)	20–19		22–17		17–22		20–19		15–23	
Current Streak	U1		U1		U1		U1		U1	
Avg % Change	−0.04		−0.11		−0.26		−0.12		−0.33	
Options Expiration Day: 1980–2018										
Record (#Up – #Down)	23–16		24–15		20–19		24–15		21–18	
Current Streak	D1		D1		D4		D1		D4	
Avg % Change	−0.06		0.02		−0.04		−0.01		0.01	
Options Expiration Week: 1980–2018										
Record (#Up – #Down)	22–17		21–18		17–22		19–20		18–21	
Current Streak	D1		U2		U1		U2		U1	
Avg % Change	−0.08		−0.10		−0.29		−0.16		−0.26	
Week After Options Expiration: 1980–2018										
Record (#Up – #Down)	12–27		18–21		22–17		18–21		20–19	
Current Streak	D1		D1		D1		D1		U2	
Avg % Change	−0.50		−0.20		0.12		−0.17		−0.09	
First Trading Day Performance										
% of Time Up	56.5		55.1		60.4		62.5		65.0	
Avg % Change	0.16		0.13		0.15		0.10		0.19	
Last Trading Day Performance										
% of Time Up	55.1		52.2		68.8		55.0		65.0	
Avg % Change	0.06		0.11		0.32		0.06		0.40	

Dow & S&P 1950–June 2018, NASDAQ 1971–June 2018, Russell 1K & 2K 1979–June 2018.

Last Day of June not hot for the Dow;
Down 17 of 28, WOW!

Memorial Day *(Market Closed)*

Never tell people how to do things. Tell them what to do and they will surprise you with their ingenuity.
— General George S. Patton Jr. (U.S. Army field commander, WWII, 1885–1945)

Day After Memorial Day, Dow Up 21 of Last 33
Memorial Day Week Dow Down 14 of Last 23, Up 12 Straight 1984–1995

The authority of a thou and is not worth the humble reasoning of a single individual.
— Galileo Galilei (Italian physicist and astronomer, 1564–1642)

A senior European diplomat said he was convinced that the choice of starting a war this spring was made for political as well as military reasons. [The President] clearly does not want to have a war raging on the eve of his presumed reelection campaign.
— Reported by Steven R. Weisman (*New York Times*, 3/14/03)

Another factor contributing to productivity is technology, particularly the rapid introduction of new microcomputers based on single-chip circuits. . . . The results over the next decade will be a second industrial revolution.
— Yale Hirsch (Creator of *Stock Trader's Almanac, Smart Money Newsletter,* 9/22/76, b. 1923)

If you have an important point to make, don't try to be subtle or clever. Use a pile driver. Hit the point once. Then come back and hit it again. Then hit it a third time—a tremendous whack.
— Winston Churchill (British statesman, 1874–1965)

MACD-TIMING TRIPLES "BEST SIX MONTHS" RESULTS

Using the simple MACD (Moving Average Convergence Divergence) indicator developed by our friend Gerald Appel to better time entries and exits into and out of the Best Six Months (page 52) period nearly triples the results. Several years ago, Sy Harding (RIP) enhanced our Best Six Months Switching Strategy with MACD triggers, dubbing it the "best mechanical system ever." In 2006, we improved it even more, achieving similar results with just four trades every four years (page 60).

Our *Almanac Investor eNewsletter* (see ad insert) implements this system with quite a degree of success. Starting October 1, we look to catch the market's first hint of an up-trend after the summer doldrums, and beginning April 1, we prepare to exit these seasonal positions as soon as the market falters.

In up-trending markets, MACD signals get you in earlier and keep you in longer. But if the market is trending down, entries are delayed until the market turns up, and exit points can come a month earlier.

The results are astounding, applying the simple MACD signals. Instead of $10,000 gaining $1,008,721 over the 68 recent years when invested only during the Best Six Months (page 52), the gain nearly tripled to $2,836,350. The $1,031 gain during the Worst Six Months became a loss of $6,059.

Impressive results for being invested during only 6.3 months of the year on average! For the rest of the year consider money markets, bonds, puts, bear funds, covered calls, or credit call spreads.

Updated signals are emailed to our *Almanac Investor eNewsletter* subscribers as soon as they are triggered. Visit *www .stocktradersalmanac.com,* or see the ad insert for details and a special offer for new subscribers.

BEST SIX-MONTH SWITCHING STRATEGY+TIMING

	DJIA % Change May 1–Oct 31*	Investing $10,000	DJIA % Change Nov 1–Apr 30*	Investing $10,000
1950	7.3%	$10,730	13.3%	$11,330
1951	0.1	10,741	1.9	11,545
1952	1.4	10,891	2.1	11,787
1953	0.2	10,913	17.1	13,803
1954	13.5	12,386	16.3	16,053
1955	7.7	13,340	13.1	18,156
1956	−6.8	12,433	2.8	18,664
1957	−12.3	10,904	4.9	19,579
1958	17.3	12,790	16.7	22,849
1959	1.6	12,995	−3.1	22,141
1960	−4.9	12,358	16.9	25,883
1961	2.9	12,716	−1.5	25,495
1962	−15.3	10,770	22.4	31,206
1963	4.3	11,233	9.6	34,202
1964	6.7	11,986	6.2	36,323
1965	2.6	12,298	−2.5	35,415
1966	−16.4	10,281	14.3	40,479
1967	−2.1	10,065	5.5	42,705
1968	3.4	10,407	0.2	42,790
1969	−11.9	9,169	−6.7	39,923
1970	−1.4	9,041	20.8	48,227
1971	−11.0	8,046	15.4	55,654
1972	−0.6	7,998	−1.4	54,875
1973	−11.0	7,118	0.1	54,930
1974	−22.4	5,524	28.2	70,420
1975	0.1	5,530	18.5	83,448
1976	−3.4	5,342	−3.0	80,945
1977	−11.4	4,733	0.5	81,350
1978	−4.5	4,520	9.3	88,916
1979	−5.3	4,280	7.0	95,140
1980	9.3	4,678	4.7	99,612
1981	−14.6	3,995	0.4	100,010
1982	15.5	4,614	23.5	123,512
1983	2.5	4,729	−7.3	114,496
1984	3.3	4,885	3.9	118,961
1985	7.0	5,227	38.1	164,285
1986	−2.8	5,081	28.2	210,613
1987	−14.9	4,324	3.0	216,931
1988	6.1	4,588	11.8	242,529
1989	9.8	5,038	3.3	250,532
1990	−6.7	4,700	15.8	290,116
1991	4.8	4,926	11.3	322,899
1992	−6.2	4,621	6.6	344,210
1993	5.5	4,875	5.6	363,486
1994	3.7	5,055	13.1	411,103
1995	7.2	5,419	16.7	479,757
1996	9.2	5,918	21.9	584,824
1997	3.6	6,131	18.5	693,016
1998	−12.4	5,371	39.9	969,529
1999	−6.4	5,027	5.1	1,018,975
2000	−6.0	4,725	5.4	1,074,000
2001	−17.3	3,908	15.8	1,243,692
2002	−25.2	2,923	6.0	1,318,314
2003	16.4	3,402	7.8	1,421,142
2004	−0.9	3,371	1.8	1,446,723
2005	−0.5	3,354	7.7	1,558,121
2006	4.7	3,512	14.4	1,782,490
2007	5.6	3,709	−12.7	1,556,114
2008	−24.7	2,793	−14.0	1,338,258
2009	23.8	3,458	10.8	1,482,790
2010	4.6	3,617	7.3	1,591,034
2011	−9.4	3,277	18.7	1,888,557
2012	0.3	3,287	10.0	2,077,413
2013	4.1	3,422	7.1	2,224,909
2014	2.3	3,501	7.4	2,389,552
2015	−6.0	3,291	4.9	2,506,640
2016	3.5	3,406	13.1	2,835,010
2017	15.7	3,941	0.4	2,846,350
Average	−0.8%		9.1%	
# Up	37		59	
# Down	31		9	
68-Year Gain (Loss)		($6,059)		$2,836,350

*MACD generated entry and exit points (earlier or later) can lengthen or shorten six-month periods.

56

First Trading Day in June, Dow Up 24 of Last 31
Down 2008/2010 –1.1%, 2011/12 –2.2%

🐂 **MONDAY**

D 71.4
S 66.7
N 57.1

3

There's a lot of talk about self-esteem these days. It seems pretty basic to me. If you want to feel good about yourself, you've got to do things that you can be proud of.
— Osceola McCarty (American author, *Simple Wisdom for Rich Living*, 1908–1999)

Start Looking for NASDAQ MACD Sell Signal on June 1 (Page 60)
Almanac Investor Subscribers Emailed When It Triggers (See Insert)

🐂 **TUESDAY**

D 52.4
S 71.4
N 66.7

4

Whenever a well-known bearish analyst is interviewed [Cover story] in the financial press, it usually coincides with an important near-term market bottom.
— Clif Droke (Clifdroke.com, 11/15/04)

🐻 **WEDNESDAY**

D 42.9
S 38.1
N 42.9

5

We prefer to cut back exposure on what's going against us and add exposure where it's more favorable to our portfolio. This way, we're always attempting to tilt the odds in our favor. This is the exact opposite of a long investor that would average down. Averaging down is a very dangerous practice.
— John Del Vecchio and Brad Lamensdorf (Portfolio managers, Active Bear ETF, 5/10/12 *Almanac Investor* Interview)

June Ends NASDAQ's "Best Eight Months" (Pages 58, 60 and 148)

THURSDAY

D 57.1
S 57.1
N 57.1

6

We were fairly arrogant, until we realized the Japanese were selling quality products for what it cost us to make them.
— Paul A. Allaire (former chairman of Xerox)

FRIDAY

D 66.7
S 47.6
N 47.6

7

It is totally unproductive to think the world has been unfair to you. Every tough stretch is an opportunity.
— Charlie Munger (Vice-Chairman, Berkshire Hathaway, 2007 Wesco Annual Meeting, b. 1924)

SATURDAY

8

SUNDAY

9

TOP PERFORMING NASDAQ MONTHS PAST 47⅓ YEARS

NASDAQ stocks continue to run away during three consecutive months, November, December and January, with an average gain of 6.0% despite the slaughter of November 2000, −22.9%, December 2000, −4.9%, December 2002, −9.7%, November 2007, −6.9%, January 2008, −9.9%, November 2008, −10.8%, January 2009, −6.4%, January 2010, −5.4% and January 2016, −7.9%. Solid gains in November and December 2004 offset January 2005's 5.2% Iraq turmoil–fueled drop.

You can see the months graphically on page 148. January by itself is impressive, up 2.7% on average. April, May and June also shine, creating our NASDAQ Best Eight Months strategy. What appears as a Death Valley abyss occurs during NASDAQ's bleakest months: July, August and September. NASDAQ's Best Eight Months seasonal strategy using MACD timing is displayed on page 60.

MONTHLY % CHANGES (JANUARY 1971–MAY 2018)

	NASDAQ Composite*					Dow Jones Industrials			
Month	Total % Change	Avg. % Change	# Up	# Down	Month	Total % Change	Avg. % Change	# Up	# Down
Jan	127.3	2.7	31	17	Jan	54.3%	1.1%	30	18
Feb	32.5	0.7	26	22	Feb	20.2	0.4	29	19
Mar	39.8	0.8	30	18	Mar	52.1	1.1	31	17
Apr	64.2	1.3	31	17	Apr	98.1	2.0	32	16
May	51.2	1.1	30	18	May	13.3	0.3	27	21
Jun	30.2	0.6	25	22	Jun	−2.3	−0.05	24	23
Jul	19.5	0.4	25	22	Jul	37.7	0.8	27	20
Aug	6.7	0.1	26	21	Aug	−14.6	−0.3	26	21
Sep	−23.3	−0.5	26	21	Sep	−44.6	−0.9	17	30
Oct	38.0	0.8	26	21	Oct	35.3	0.8	29	18
Nov	76.7	1.6	32	15	Nov	64.3	1.4	32	15
Dec	85.2	1.8	28	19	Dec	76.6	1.6	33	14
% Rank					**% Rank**				
Jan	127.3%	2.7%	31	17	Apr	98.1%	2.0%	32	16
Dec	85.2	1.8	28	19	Dec	76.6	1.6	33	14
Nov	76.7	1.6	32	15	Nov	64.3	1.4	32	15
Apr	64.2	1.3	31	17	Jan	54.3	1.1	30	18
May	51.2	1.1	30	18	Mar	52.1	1.1	31	17
Mar	39.8	0.8	30	18	Jul	37.7	0.8	27	20
Oct	38.0	0.8	26	21	Oct	35.3	0.8	29	18
Feb	32.5	0.7	26	22	Feb	20.2	0.4	29	19
Jun	30.2	0.6	25	22	May	13.3	0.3	27	21
Jul	19.5	0.4	25	22	Jun	−2.3	−0.05	24	23
Aug	6.7	0.1	26	21	Aug	−14.6	−0.3	26	21
Sep	−23.3	−0.5	26	21	Sep	−44.6	−0.9	17	30
Totals	**548.0%**	**11.4%**			**Totals**	**390.4%**	**8.2%**		
Average		**0.95%**			**Average**		**0.69%**		

*Based on NASDAQ composite; prior to February 5, 1971, based on National Quotation Bureau indices.

For comparison, Dow figures are shown. During this period, NASDAQ averaged a 0.95% gain per month, 37.7 percent more than the Dow's 0.69% per month. Between January 1971 and January 1982, NASDAQ's composite index doubled in 12 years, while the Dow stayed flat. But while NASDAQ plummeted 77.9% from its 2000 highs to the 2002 bottom, the Dow only lost 37.8%. The Great Recession and bear market of 2007–2009 spread its carnage equally across the Dow and NASDAQ. Recent market moves are increasingly more correlated.

MONDAY
D 61.9
S 57.1
N 42.9
10

We always live in an uncertain world. What is certain is that the United States will go forward over time.
— Warren Buffett (CEO, Berkshire Hathaway, investor and philanthropist, CNBC, 9/22/10, b. 1930)

TUESDAY
D 38.1
S 42.9
N 38.1
11

A man isn't a man until he has to meet a payroll.
— Ivan Shaffer (The Stock Promotion Game)

2008 Second Worst June Ever, Dow –10.2%, S&P –8.6%,
Only 1930 Was Worse, NASDAQ –9.1%, June 2002 –9.4%

WEDNESDAY
D 42.9
S 38.1
N 33.3
12

Markets are constantly in a state of uncertainty and flux and money is made by discounting the obvious
and betting on the unexpected.
— George Soros (Financier, philanthropist, political activist, author and philosopher, b. 1930)

THURSDAY
D 57.1
S 57.1
N 52.4
13

Successful innovation is not a feat of intellect, but of will.
— Joseph A. Schumpeter (Austrian-American economist, *Theory of Economic Development*, 1883–1950)

FRIDAY
D 66.7
S 61.9
N 52.4
14

I went to a restaurant that serves "breakfast at any time." So I ordered French toast during the Renaissance.
— Steven Wright (Comedian, b. 1955)

SATURDAY
15

Father's Day

SUNDAY
16

GET MORE OUT OF NASDAQ'S "BEST EIGHT MONTHS" WITH MACD TIMING

NASDAQ's amazing eight-month run from November through June is hard to miss on pages 58 and 148. A $10,000 investment in these eight months since 1971 gained $702,412 versus a loss of $68 during the void that is the four-month period July–October (as of June 29, 2018).

Using the same MACD timing indicators on the NASDAQ as is done for the Dow (page 56) has enabled us to capture much of October's improved performance, pumping up NASDAQ's results considerably. Over the 47 years since NASDAQ began, the gain on the same $10,000 more than doubles to $1,849,187 and the loss during the four-month void increases to $6,220. Only four sizable losses occurred during the favorable period, and the bulk of NASDAQ's bear markets were avoided, including the worst of the 2000–2002 bear.

Updated signals are emailed to our monthly newsletter subscribers as soon as they are triggered. Visit *www.stocktradersalmanac.com*, or see the ad insert for details and a special offer for new subscribers.

BEST EIGHT MONTHS STRATEGY + TIMING

MACD Signal Date	Worst 4 Months July 1–Oct 31* NASDAQ	% Change	Investing $10,000	MACD Signal Date	Best 8 Months Nov 1–June 30* NASDAQ	% Change	Investing $10,000
22-Jul-71	109.54	−3.6	$9,640	4-Nov-71	105.56	24.1	$12,410
7-Jun-72	131.00	−1.8	9,466	23-Oct-72	128.66	−22.7	9,593
25-Jun-73	99.43	−7.2	8,784	7-Dec-73	92.32	−20.2	7,655
3-Jul-74	73.66	−23.2	6,746	7-Oct-74	56.57	47.8	11,314
11-Jun-75	83.60	−9.2	6,125	7-Oct-75	75.88	20.8	13,667
22-Jul-76	91.66	−2.4	5,978	19-Oct-76	89.45	13.2	15,471
27-Jul-77	101.25	−4.0	5,739	4-Nov-77	97.21	26.6	19,586
7-Jun-78	123.10	−6.5	5,366	6-Nov-78	115.08	19.1	23,327
3-Jul-79	137.03	−1.1	5,307	30-Oct-79	135.48	15.5	26,943
20-Jun-80	156.51	26.2	6,697	9-Oct-80	197.53	11.2	29,961
4-Jun-81	219.68	−17.6	5,518	1-Oct-81	181.09	−4.0	28,763
7-Jun-82	173.84	12.5	6,208	7-Oct-82	195.59	57.4	45,273
1-Jun-83	307.95	−10.7	5,544	3-Nov-83	274.86	−14.2	38,844
1-Jun-84	235.90	5.0	5,821	15-Oct-84	247.67	17.3	45,564
3-Jun-85	290.59	−3.0	5,646	1-Oct-85	281.77	39.4	63,516
10-Jun-86	392.83	−10.3	5,064	1-Oct-86	352.34	20.5	76,537
30-Jun-87	424.67	−22.7	3,914	2-Nov-87	328.33	20.1	91,921
8-Jul-88	394.33	−6.6	3,656	29-Nov-88	368.15	22.4	112,511
13-Jun-89	450.73	0.7	3,682	9-Nov-89	454.07	1.9	114,649
11-Jun-90	462.79	−23.0	2,835	2-Oct-90	356.39	39.3	159,706
11-Jun-91	496.62	6.4	3,016	1-Oct-91	528.51	7.4	171,524
11-Jun-92	567.68	1.5	3,061	14-Oct-92	576.22	20.5	206,686
7-Jun-93	694.61	9.9	3,364	1-Oct-93	763.23	−4.4	197,592
17-Jun-94	729.35	5.0	3,532	11-Oct-94	765.57	13.5	224,267
1-Jun-95	868.82	17.2	4,140	13-Oct-95	1018.38	21.6	272,709
3-Jun-96	1238.73	1.0	4,181	7-Oct-96	1250.87	10.3	300,798
4-Jun-97	1379.67	24.4	5,201	3-Oct-97	1715.87	1.8	306,212
1-Jun-98	1746.82	−7.8	4,795	15-Oct-98	1611.01	49.7	458,399
1-Jun-99	2412.03	18.5	5,682	6-Oct-99	2857.21	35.7	622,047
29-Jun-00	3877.23	−18.2	4,648	18-Oct-00	3171.56	−32.2	421,748
1-Jun-01	2149.44	−31.1	3,202	1-Oct-01	1480.46	5.5	444,944
3-Jun-02	1562.56	−24.0	2,434	2-Oct-02	1187.30	38.5	616,247
20-Jun-03	1644.72	15.1	2,802	6-Oct-03	1893.46	4.3	642,746
21-Jun-04	1974.38	−1.6	2,757	1-Oct-04	1942.20	6.1	681,954
8-Jun-05	2060.18	1.5	2,798	19-Oct-05	2091.76	6.1	723,553
1-Jun-06	2219.86	3.9	2,907	5-Oct-06	2306.34	9.5	792,291
7-Jun-07	2541.38	7.9	3,137	1-Oct-07	2740.99	−9.1	724,796
2-Jun-08	2491.53	−31.3	2,155	17-Oct-08	1711.29	6.1	769,000
15-Jun-09	1816.38	17.8	2,539	9-Oct-09	2139.28	1.6	781,313
7-Jun-10	2173.90	18.6	3,011	4-Nov-10	2577.34	7.4	839,130
1-Jun-11	2769.19	−10.5	2,695	7-Oct-11	2479.35	10.8	929,756
1-Jun-12	2747.48	9.6	2,954	6-Nov-12	3011.93	16.2	1,080,376
4-Jun-13	3445.26	10.1	3,252	15-Oct-13	3794.01	15.4	1,227,442
26-Jun-14	4379.05	0.9	3,281	21-Oct-14	4419.48	14.5	1,405,421
4-Jun-15	5059.12	−5.5	3,101	5-Oct-15	4781.26	1.4	1,425,097
13-Jun-16	4848.44	9.5	3,396	24-Oct-16	5309.83	18.8	1,693,015
9-Jun-17	6207.92	11.3	3,780	28-Nov-17	6912.36	11.6	1,859,187
21-Jun-18	7713.89						
	47-Year Loss (US$6,220)				**47-Year Gain**		**US$1,849,187**

* *MACD-generated entry and exit points (earlier or later) can lengthen or shorten eight-month periods.*

Monday of Triple-Witching Week, Dow Down 12 of Last 21

MONDAY
17

D 52.4
S 66.7
N 66.7

Anytime there is change there is opportunity. So it is paramount that an organization get energized rather than paralyzed.
— Jack Welch (General Electric CEO, *Fortune*)

FOMC Meeting (2 Days)

TUESDAY
18

D 61.9
S 61.9
N 57.1

No one ever claimed that managed care was either managed or cared.
— Anonymous

Triple-Witching Week Often Up in Bull Markets and Down in Bears (Page 78)

WEDNESDAY
19

D 57.1
S 61.9
N 66.7

In business, the competition will bite you if you keep running; if you stand still, they will swallow you.
— William Knudsen (Former president of General Motors)

THURSDAY
20

D 52.4
S 47.6
N 47.6

It isn't the incompetent who destroy an organization. It is those who have achieved something and want to rest upon their achievements who are forever clogging things up.
— Charles E. Sorenson (Danish-American engineer, officer, director of Ford Motor Co., 1907–1950, helped develop first auto assembly line, 1881–1968)

June Triple-Witching Day, Dow Up 9 of Last 15

FRIDAY
21

D 38.1
S 42.9
N 42.9

Of a stock's move, 31% can be attributed to the general stock market, 12% to the industry influence, 37% to the influence of other groupings, and the remaining 20% is peculiar to the one stock.
— Benjamin F. King (*Market and Industry Factors in Stock Price Behavior, Journal of Business*, January 1966)

SATURDAY
22

SUNDAY
23

TRIPLE RETURNS, FEWER TRADES: BEST 6 + 4-YEAR CYCLE

We first introduced this strategy to *Almanac Investor* newsletter subscribers in October 2006. Recurring seasonal stock market patterns and the four-year Presidential Election/Stock Market Cycle (page 130) have been integral to our research since the first Almanac 52 years ago. Yale Hirsch discovered the Best Six Months in 1986 (page 60), and it has been a cornerstone of our seasonal investment analysis and strategies ever since.

Most of the market's gains have occurred during the Best Six Months, and the market generally hits a low point every four years in the first (post-election) or second (midterm) year and exhibits the greatest gains in the third (pre-election) year. This strategy combines the best of these two market phenomena, the Best Six Months and the four-year cycle, timing entries and exits with MACD (pages 56 and 60).

We've gone back to 1949 to include the full four-year cycle that began with post-election year 1949. Only four trades every four years are needed to nearly triple the results of the Best Six Months. Buy and sell during the post-election and midterm years and then hold from the mid-term MACD seasonal buy signal sometime after October 1 until the post-election MACD seasonal sell signal sometime after April 1, approximately 2.5 years: solid returns, less effort, lower transaction fees and fewer taxable events.

FOUR TRADES EVERY FOUR YEARS		
	Worst Six Months	Best Six Months
Year	May–Oct	Nov–April
Post-election	Sell	Buy
Midterm	Sell	Buy
Pre-election	Hold	Hold
Election	Hold	Hold

BEST SIX MONTHS+TIMING+4-YEAR CYCLE STRATEGY

	DJIA % Change May 1–Oct 31*	Investing $10,000	DJIA % Change Nov 1–Apr 30*	Investing $10,000
1949	3.0%	$10,300	17.5%	$11,750
1950	7.3	11,052	19.7	14,065
1951		11,052		14,065
1952		11,052		14,065
1953	0.2	11,074	17.1	16,470
1954	13.5	12,569	35.7	22,350
1955		12,569		22,350
1956		12,569		22,350
1957	−12.3	11,023	4.9	23,445
1958	17.3	12,930	27.8	29,963
1959		12,930		29,963
1960		12,930		29,963
1961	2.9	13,305	−1.5	29,514
1962	−15.3	11,269	58.5	46,780
1963		11,269		46,780
1964		11,269		46,780
1965	2.6	11,562	−2.5	45,611
1966	−16.4	9,666	22.2	55,737
1967		9,666		55,737
1968		9,666		55,737
1969	−11.9	8,516	−6.7	52,003
1970	−1.4	8,397	21.5	63,184
1971		8,397		63,184
1972		8,397		63,184
1973	−11.0	7,473	0.1	63,247
1974	−22.4	5,799	42.5	90,127
1975		5,799		90,127
1976		5,799		90,127
1977	−11.4	5,138	0.5	90,578
1978	−4.5	4,907	26.8	114,853
1979		4,907		114,853
1980		4,907		114,853
1981	−14.6	4,191	0.4	115,312
1982	15.5	4,841	25.9	145,178
1983		4,841		145,178
1984		4,841		145,178
1985	7.0	5,180	38.1	200,491
1986	−2.8	5,035	33.2	267,054
1987		5,035		267,054
1988		5,035		267,054
1989	9.8	5,528	3.3	275,867
1990	−6.7	5,158	35.1	372,696
1991		5,158		372,696
1992		5,158		372,696
1993	5.5	5,442	5.6	393,455
1994	3.7	5,643	88.2	740,482
1995		5,643		740,482
1996		5,643		740,482
1997	3.6	5,846	18.5	877,471
1998	−12.4	5,121	36.3	1,195,993
1999		5,121		1,195,993
2000		5,121		1,195,993
2001	−17.3	4,235	15.8	1,384,960
2002	−25.2	3,168	34.2	1,858,616
2003		3,168		1,858,616
2004		3,168		1,858,616
2005	−0.5	3,152	7.7	2,001,729
2006	4.7	3,300	−31.7	1,367,181
2007		3,300		1,367,181
2008		3,300		1,367,181
2009	23.8	4,085	10.8	1,514,738
2010	4.6	4,273	27.4	1,929,777
2011		4,273		1,929,777
2012		4,273		1,929,777
2013	4.1	4,448	7.1	2,066,791
2014	2.3	4,550	24.0	2,562,820
2015		4,550		2,562,820
2016		4,550		2,562,820
2017	15.7	$5,265	0.4	$2,573,072
Average	**−0.6%**		**9.6%**	
# Up	**19**		**31**	
# Down	**16**		**4**	
69-Year Gain (Loss)	**($4,735)**			**$2,563,072**

* MACD and 2.5-year hold lengthen and shorten six-month periods.

MONDAY
D 33.3
S 38.1
N 33.3
24

Regardless of current economic conditions, it's always best to remember that the stock market is a barometer and not a thermometer.
— Yale Hirsch (Creator of *Stock Trader's Almanac*, b. 1923)

TUESDAY
D 38.1
S 33.3
N 42.9
25

The years teach much which the days never know.
— Ralph Waldo Emerson (American author, poet and philosopher, *Self-Reliance*, 1803–1882)

Week After June Triple Witching, Dow Down 25 of Last 29
Average Loss Since 1990, 1.1%

WEDNESDAY
D 61.9
S 57.1
N 71.4
26

You get stepped on, passed over, knocked down, but you have to come back.
— 90-year-old Walter Watson (MD, *Fortune*, 11/13/00)

THURSDAY
D 57.1
S 57.1
N 61.9
27

Laws are like sausages. It's better not to see them being made.
— Otto von Bismarck (German-Prussian politician, first Chancellor of Germany, 1815–1898)

Last Day of Q2 Bearish for Dow, Down 17 of Last 28
But Bullish for NASDAQ, Up 19 of 27

FRIDAY
D 42.9
S 42.9
N 61.9
28

New indicator: CFO Magazine gave Excellence awards to WorldCom's Scott Sullivan (1998), Enron's Andrew Fastow (1999), and to Tyco's Mark Swartz (2000). All were subsequently indicted.
— Roger Lowenstein (Financial journalist and author, *Origins of the Crash*, b. 1954)

SATURDAY
29

July Almanac Investor Sector Seasonalities: See Pages 92, 94 and 96

SUNDAY
30

JULY ALMANAC

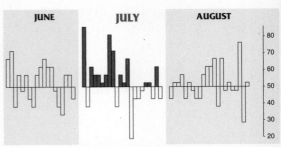

JULY								AUGUST					
S	M	T	W	T	F	S		S	M	T	W	T	F	S
	1	2	3	4	5	6							1	2	3
7	8	9	10	11	12	13		4	5	6	7	8	9	10
14	15	16	17	18	19	20		11	12	13	14	15	16	17
21	22	23	24	25	26	27		18	19	20	21	22	23	24
28	29	30	31					25	26	27	28	29	30	31

Market Probability Chart above is a graphic representation of the S&P 500 Recent Market Probability Calendar on page 124.

◆ July is the best month of the third quarter (page 66) ◆ Start of 2nd half brings an inflow of retirement funds ◆ First trading day Dow up 25 of last 30 ◆ Graph above shows strength in the first half of July ◆ Huge gain in July usually provides better buying opportunity over next 4 months ◆ Start of NASDAQ's worst four months of the year (page 60) ◆ Pre–presidential election year Julys are ranked #6 Dow (up 10, down 7) #7 S&P (up 10, down 7) and #8 NASDAQ (up 6, down 6).

July Vital Statistics

	DJIA		S&P 500		NASDAQ		Russell 1K		Russell 2K	
Rank	4		6		10		8		11	
Up	43		38		25		19		19	
Down	25		30		22		20		20	
Average % Change	1.2%		1.0%		0.4%		0.7%		−0.3%	
Pre-Election Year	1.0%		0.9%		0.9%		0.5%		0.3%	
	Best & Worst July									
	% Change		% Change		% Change		% Change		% Change	
Best	1989	9.0	1989	8.8	1997	10.5	1989	8.2	1980	11.0
Worst	1969	−6.6	2002	−7.9	2002	−9.2	2002	−7.5	2002	−15.2
	Best & Worst July Weeks									
Best	07/17/09	7.3	07/17/09	7.0	07/17/09	7.4	07/17/09	7.0	07/17/09	8.0
Worst	07/19/02	−7.7	07/19/02	−8.0	07/28/00	−10.5	07/19/02	−7.4	07/02/10	−7.2
	Best & Worst July Days									
Best	07/24/02	6.4	07/24/02	5.7	07/29/02	5.8	07/24/02	5.6	07/29/02	4.9
Worst	07/19/02	−4.6	07/19/02	−3.8	07/28/00	−4.7	07/19/02	−3.6	07/23/02	−4.1
	First Trading Day of Expiration Week: 1980–2017									
Record (#Up – #Down)	23–15		24–14		26–12		24–14		22–16	
Current Streak	D1		D1		U5		U5		U5	
Avg % Change	0.12		0.06		0.07		0.03		−0.01	
	Options Expiration Day: 1980–2017									
Record (#Up – #Down)	17–19		19–19		16–22		19–19		15–23	
Current Streak	D1		D2		D2		D2		D1	
Avg % Change	−0.24		−0.27		−0.40		−0.28		−0.44	
	Options Expiration Week: 1980–2017									
Record (#Up – #Down)	24–14		22–16		21–17		22–16		21–17	
Current Streak	D1		U6		U4		U6		U3	
Avg % Change	0.48		0.20		0.16		0.15		−0.04	
	Week After Options Expiration: 1980–2017									
Record (#Up – #Down)	20–18		18–20		17–21		19–19		14–24	
Current Streak	U2		D1		D1		D1		D1	
Avg % Change	−0.02		−0.17		−0.41		−0.18		−0.38	
	First Trading Day Performance									
% of Time Up	66.2		72.1		61.7		74.4		66.7	
Avg % Change	0.27		0.26		0.12		0.31		0.12	
	Last Trading Day Performance									
% of Time Up	50.0		60.3		48.9		56.4		64.1	
Avg % Change	0.02		0.06		−0.04		−0.03		−0.02	

Dow & S&P 1950–June 2018, NASDAQ 1971–June 2018, Russell 1K & 2K 1979–June 2018.

When Dow and S&P in July are inferior,
NASDAQ days tend to be even drearier.

Those who study market history are bound to profit from it!

ACT NOW! Visit www.STOCKTRADERSALMANAC.com
CALL 845-875-9582. TWO WAYS TO SAVE:

▸ **1-Year @ $150** – 48% Off vs. Monthly – Use promo code **1YRSTA19**

▸ **2-Years @ $250** – **BEST DEAL**, 57% Off – Use promo code **2YRSTA19**

Now you can find out which seasonal trends are on schedule and which are not, and how to take advantage of them. You will be kept abreast of upcoming market-moving events and what our indicators are saying about the next major market move. Every week you will receive timely dispatches about bullish and bearish seasonal patterns.

Our digital subscription service, *Almanac Investor*, provides all this plus unusual investing opportunities – exciting small-, mid- and large-cap stocks; seasoned, undervalued equities; timely sector ETF trades and more. Our **Data-Rich and Data-Driven Market Cycle Analysis** is the only investment tool of its kind that helps traders and investors forecast market trends with accuracy and confidence.

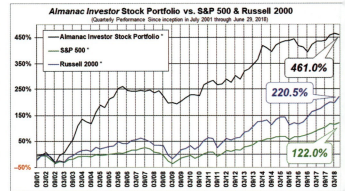

Almanac Investor Stock Portfolio vs. S&P 500 & Russell 2000
(Quarterly Performance Since inception in July 2001 through June 29, 2018)
— Almanac Investor Stock Portfolio *
— S&P 500 *
— Russell 2000 *
461.0%
220.5%
122.0%

Tactical Seasonal Switching Strategy: Best 6 Months/Worst 6 Months + MACD Timing
Annualized Performance Since 1950 + MACD Timing — 17.4% November-April, –2.9% May-October
$10K Invested in DJIA Since 1950 + MACD Timing — $2,836,350 November-April, –$6,059 May-October
Source: StockTradersAlmanac.com© Jeffrey A. Hirsch & Hirsch Holdings Inc. All rights reserved

YOU RECEIVE WEEKLY EMAIL ALERTS CONTAINING:

▸ Opportune ETF and Stock Trading Ideas with Specific Buy and Sell Price Limits

▸ Timely Data-Rich and Data-Driven Market Analysis

▸ Access to Webinars, Videos, Tools and Resources

▸ Market-Tested and Time-Proven Short- and Long-term Trading Strategies

▸ Best Six-Months Switching Strategy MACD Timing Signals.

JULY 2019

First Trading Day in July, Dow Up 25 of Last 30, Average Gain 0.5%

MONDAY
1

D 81.0
S 85.7
N 71.4

The common denominator: Something that matters! Something that counts! Something that defines! Something that is imbued with soul. And with life!
— Tom Peters (referring to projects, *Reinventing Work*, 1999, b. 1942)

TUESDAY
2

D 33.3
S 38.1
N 38.1

The critical ingredient is getting off your butt and doing something. It's as simple as that. A lot of people have ideas, but there are few who decide to do something about them now. Not tomorrow. Not next week. But today. The true entrepreneur is a doer, not a dreamer.
— Nolan Bushnell (Founder, Atari and Chuck E. Cheese's, b. 1943)

(Shortened Trading Day)

WEDNESDAY
3

D 52.4
S 61.9
N 57.1

I've never been poor, only broke. Being poor is a frame of mind. Being broke is only a temporary situation.
— Mike Todd (Movie producer, 1903–1958)

Independence Day *(Market Closed)*

THURSDAY
4

Press on. Nothing in the world can take the place of persistence. Talent will not: nothing is more common than unrewarded talent. Education alone will not: the world is full of educated failures. Persistence alone is omnipotent.
— Calvin Coolidge (30th U.S. President, 1872–1933)

Market Subject to Elevated Volatility After July 4th

FRIDAY
5

D 57.1
S 57.1
N 66.7

It wasn't raining when Noah built the ark.
— Warren Buffett (CEO, Berkshire Hathaway, investor and philanthropist, b. 1930)

SATURDAY
6

SUNDAY
7

FIRST MONTH OF QUARTERS IS THE MOST BULLISH

We have observed over the years that the investment calendar reflects the annual, semiannual and quarterly operations of institutions during January, April and July. The opening month of the first three quarters produces the greatest gains in the Dow Jones Industrials and the S&P 500. NASDAQ's record differs slightly.

The fourth quarter had behaved quite differently, since it is affected by year-end portfolio adjustments and presidential and congressional elections in even-numbered years. Since 1991, major turnarounds have helped October join the ranks of bullish first months of quarters. October transformed into a bear-killing-turnaround month, posting gains in 15 of the last 20 years; 2008 was a significant exception. (See pages 152–163.)

After experiencing the most powerful bull market of all time during the 1990s, followed by two ferocious bear markets early in the millennium, we divided the monthly average percentage changes into two groups: before 1991 and after. Comparing the month-by-month quarterly behavior of the three major U.S. averages in the table, you'll see that first months of the first three quarters perform best overall. Nasty sell-offs in April 2000, 2002, 2004 and 2005, and July 2000–2002 and 2004 hit the NASDAQ hardest. The bear market of October 2007–March 2009, which cut the markets more than in half, took a toll on every first month except April. October 2008 was the worst month in a decade. January was also a difficult month in six of the last eleven years, pulling its performance lower. (See pages 152–163.)

Between 1950 and 1990, the S&P 500 gained 1.3% (Dow, 1.4%) on average in first months of the first three quarters. Second months barely eked out any gain, while third months, thanks to March, moved up 0.23% (Dow, 0.07%) on average. NASDAQ's first month of the first three quarters averages 1.67% from 1971 to 1990, with July being a negative drag.

DOW JONES INDUSTRIALS, S&P 500 AND NASDAQ
AVERAGE MONTHLY % CHANGES BY QUARTER

	DJIA 1950–1990			S&P 500 1950–1990			NASDAQ 1971–1990		
	1st Mo	2nd Mo	3rd Mo	1st Mo	2nd Mo	3rd Mo	1st Mo	2nd Mo	3rd Mo
1Q	1.5%	−0.01%	1.0%	1.5%	−0.1%	1.1%	3.8%	1.2%	0.9%
2Q	1.6	−0.4	0.1	1.3	−0.1	0.3	1.7	0.8	1.1
3Q	1.1	0.3	−0.9	1.1	0.3	−0.7	−0.5	0.1	−1.6
Tot	4.2%	−0.1%	0.2%	3.9%	0.1%	0.7%	5.0%	2.1%	0.4%
Avg	1.40%	−0.04%	0.07%	1.30%	0.03%	0.23%	1.67%	0.70%	0.13%
4Q	−0.1%	1.4%	1.7%	0.4%	1.7%	1.6%	−1.4%	1.6%	1.4%
	DJIA 1991–May 2018			S&P 500 1991–May 2018			NASDAQ 1991–May 2018		
1Q	0.1%	0.5%	1.1%	0.3%	0.2%	1.3%	1.8%	0.3%	0.8%
2Q	2.2	0.6	−0.8	1.7	0.8	−0.5	1.1	1.2	0.3
3Q	1.3	−0.9	−0.5	0.9	−0.6	−0.2	1.1	0.2	0.3
Tot	3.6%	0.2%	−0.2%	2.9%	0.4%	0.7%	4.0%	1.7%	1.4%
Avg	1.20%	0.08%	−0.07%	0.97%	0.13%	0.22%	1.33%	0.56%	0.47%
4Q	1.9%	1.8%	1.7%	1.7%	1.4%	1.6%	2.4%	1.7%	2.1%
	DJIA 1950–May 2018			S&P 500 1950–May 2018			NASDAQ 1971–May 2018		
1Q	0.9%	0.2%	1.1%	1.0%	0.0%	1.2%	2.7%	0.7%	0.8%
2Q	1.9	−0.001	−0.3	1.4	0.3	−0.02	1.3	1.1	0.6
3Q	1.2	−0.2	−0.7	1.0	−0.09	−0.5	0.4	0.1	−0.5
Tot	4.0%	−0.001%	0.1%	3.4%	0.3%	0.7%	4.4%	1.9%	0.9%
Avg	1.33%	−0.0003%	0.03%	1.13%	0.08%	0.23%	1.47%	0.65%	0.30%
4Q	0.7%	1.6%	1.7%	0.9%	1.5%	1.6%	0.8%	1.6%	1.8%

July Begins NASDAQ's "Worst Four Months" (Pages 58, 60 and 148)

MONDAY

D 61.9
S 57.1
N 61.9

8

Beware of inside information . . . all inside information.
— Jesse Livermore (Early 20th century stock trader and speculator, *How to Trade in Stocks*, 1877–1940)

TUESDAY

D 57.1
S 52.4
N 66.7

9

Even being right 3 or 4 times out of 10 should yield a person a fortune, if he has the sense to cut his losses quickly on the ventures where he has been wrong.
— Bernard Baruch (Financier, speculator, statesman, presidential adviser, 1870–1965)

WEDNESDAY

D 57.1
S 57.1
N 61.9

10

What's going on . . . is the end of Silicon Valley as we know it. The next big thing ain't computers . . . it's biotechnology.
— Larry Ellison (Oracle CEO, quoted in the *Wall Street Journal*, 4/8/03)

July is the Best Performing Dow and S&P Month of the Third Quarter

THURSDAY

D 71.4
S 81.0
N 71.4

11

In a study of 3000 companies, researchers at the University of Pennsylvania found that spending 10% of revenue on capital improvements boosts productivity by 3.9%, but a similar investment in developing human capital increases productivity by 8.5%.
— John A. Byrne (Editor in Chief, *Fast Company Magazine*)

FRIDAY

D 71.4
S 71.4
N 76.2

12

Have not great merchants, great manufacturers, great inventors done more for the world than preachers and philanthropists. Can there be any doubt that cheapening the cost of necessities and conveniences of life is the most powerful agent of civilization and progress?
— Charles Elliott Perkins (Railroad magnate, 1888, 1840–1907)

SATURDAY

13

SUNDAY

14

2017 DAILY DOW POINT CHANGES
(DOW JONES INDUSTRIAL AVERAGE)

Week #		Monday**	Tuesday	Wednesday	Thursday	Friday** 2016 Close	Weekly Dow Close 19762.6	Net Point Change
1		Holiday	119.16	60.40	−42.87	64.51	19963.80	201.20
2	J	−76.42	−31.85	98.75	−63.28	−5.27	19885.73	−78.07
3	A	Holiday	−58.96	−22.05	−72.32	94.85	19827.25	−58.48
4	N	−27.40	112.86	155.80	32.40	−7.13	20093.78	266.53
5		−122.65	−107.04	26.85	−6.03	186.55	20071.46	−22.32
6		−19.04	37.87	−35.95	118.06	96.97	20269.37	197.91
7	F	142.79	92.25	107.45	7.91	4.28	20624.05	354.68
8	E B	Holiday	118.95	32.60	34.72	11.44	20821.76	197.71
9		15.68	−25.20	303.31	−112.58	2.74	21005.71	183.95
10		−51.37	−29.58	−69.03	2.46	44.79	20902.98	−102.73
11	M	−21.50	−44.11	112.73	−15.55	−19.93	20914.62	11.64
12	A	−8.76	−237.85	−6.71	−4.72	−59.86	20596.72	−317.90
13	R	−45.74	150.52	−42.18	69.17	−65.27	20663.22	66.50
14		−13.01	39.03	−41.09	14.80	−6.85	20656.10	−7.12
15	A	1.92	−6.72	−59.44	−138.61	Holiday	20453.25	−202.85
16	P	183.67	−113.64	−118.79	174.22	−30.95	20547.76	94.51
17	R	216.13	232.23	−21.03	6.24	−40.82	20940.51	392.75
18		−27.05	36.43	8.01	−6.43	55.47	21006.94	66.43
19	M	5.34	−36.50	−32.67	−23.69	−22.81	20896.61	−110.33
20	A	85.33	−2.19	−372.82	56.09	141.82	20804.84	−91.77
21	Y	89.99	43.08	74.51	70.53	−2.67	21080.28	275.44
22		Holiday	−50.81	−20.82	135.53	62.11	21206.29	126.01
23	J	−22.25	−47.81	37.46	8.84	89.44	21271.97	65.68
24	U	−36.30	92.80	46.09	−14.66	24.38	21384.28	112.31
25	N	144.71	−61.85	−57.11	−12.74	−2.53	21394.76	10.48
26		14.79	−98.89	143.95	−167.58	62.60	21349.63	−45.13
27		129.64*	Holiday	−1.10	−158.13	94.30	21414.34	64.71
28	J	−5.82	0.55	123.07	20.95	84.65	21637.74	223.40
29	U	−8.02	−54.99	66.02	−28.97	−31.71	21580.07	−57.67
30	L	−66.90	100.26	97.58	85.54	33.76	21830.31	250.24
31		60.81	72.80	52.32	9.86	66.71	22092.81	262.50
32		25.61	−33.08	−36.64	−204.69	14.31	21858.32	−234.49
33	A	135.39	5.28	25.88	−274.14	−76.22	21674.51	−183.81
34	U G	29.24	196.14	−87.80	−28.69	30.27	21813.67	139.16
35		−5.27	56.97	27.06	55.67	39.46	21987.56	173.89
36		Holiday	−234.25	54.33	−22.86	13.01	21797.79	−189.77
37	S	259.58	61.49	39.32	45.30	64.86	22268.34	470.55
38	E	63.01	39.45	41.79	−53.36	−9.64	22349.59	81.25
39	P	−53.50	−11.77	56.39	40.49	23.89	22405.09	55.50
40		152.51	84.07	19.97	113.75	−1.72	22773.67	368.58
41	O	−12.60	69.61	42.21	−31.88	30.71	22871.72	98.05
42	C	85.24	40.48	160.16	5.44	165.59	23328.63	456.91
43	T	−54.67	167.80	−112.30	71.40	33.33	23434.19	105.56
44		−85.45	28.50	57.77	81.25	22.93	23539.19	105.00
45	N	9.23	8.81	6.13	−101.42	−39.73	23422.21	−116.98
46	O	17.49	−30.23	−138.19	187.08	−100.12	23358.24	−63.97
47	V	72.09	160.50	−64.65	Holiday	31.81*	23557.99	199.75
48		22.79	255.93	103.97	331.67	−40.76	24231.59	673.60
49		58.46	−109.41	−39.73	70.57	117.68	24329.16	97.57
50	D	56.87	118.77	80.63	−76.77	143.08	24651.74	322.58
51	E C	140.46	−37.45	−28.10	55.64	−28.23	24754.06	102.32
52		Holiday	−7.85	28.09	63.21	−118.29	24719.22	−34.84
TOTALS		**1341.29**	**1184.32**	**882.40**	**445.43**	**1103.18**		**4956.62**

Bold Color: Down Friday, Down Monday
** Monday denotes first trading day of week, Friday denotes last trading day of week
* Shortened trading day: July 3, Nov 24

JULY 2019

Monday Before July Expiration, Dow Up 11 of Last 15

MONDAY
D 47.6
S 38.1
N 57.1
15

Get to the point! Blurt it out! Tell me plainly what's in it for me!
— Roy H. Williams (*The Wizard of Ads*, A reader's mental response to a poorly constructed advertisement.
Quoted in *Your Company*, 12/98)

TUESDAY
D 57.1
S 57.1
N 61.9
16

The first stocks to double in a bull market will usually double again.
— Michael L. Burke (*Investors Intelligence*)

WEDNESDAY
D 57.1
S 52.4
N 61.9
17

Any fool can buy. It is the wise man who knows how to sell.
— Albert W. Thomas (Trader, *Over My Shoulder*, mutualfundmagic.com, *If It Doesn't Go Up, Don't Buy It!*, b. 1927)

THURSDAY
D 66.7
S 66.7
N 71.4
18

Charts not only tell what was, they tell what is; and a trend from was to is (projected linearly into the will be)
contains better percentages than clumsy guessing.
— Robert A. Levy (Chairman, Cato Institute, founder, CDA Investment Technologies, *The Relative*
Strength Concept of Common Stock Forecasting, 1968, b. 1941)

July Expiration Day, Dow Down 11 of Last 18, –4.6% 2002, –2.5% 2010

FRIDAY
D 19.0
S 19.0
N 14.3
19

Your organization will never get better unless you are willing to admit that there is something wrong with it.
— General Norman Schwarzkopf (Ret., Commander of Allied Forces in 1990–1991 Gulf War)

SATURDAY
20

SUNDAY
21

DON'T SELL STOCKS ON MONDAY OR FRIDAY

Since 1989, Monday* and Tuesday have been the most consistently bullish days of the week for the Dow, Friday* the most bearish, as traders have become reluctant to stay long going into the weekend. Since 1989 Mondays and Tuesdays gained 15372.85 Dow points, while Fridays have gained 805.77 points. Also broken out are the last seventeen and a half years to illustrate Monday's and Friday's poor performance in bear market years 2001–2002 and 2008–2009. During uncertain market times traders often sell before the weekend and are reluctant to jump in on Monday. See pages 68, 76 and 141–144 for more.

ANNUAL DOW POINT CHANGES FOR DAYS OF THE WEEK SINCE 1953

Year	Monday*	Tuesday	Wednesday	Thursday	Friday*	Year's DJIA Closing	Year's Point Change
1953	−36.16	−7.93	19.63	5.76	7.70	280.90	−11.00
1954	15.68	3.27	24.31	33.96	46.27	404.39	123.49
1955	−48.36	26.38	46.03	−0.66	60.62	488.40	84.01
1956	−27.15	−9.36	−15.41	8.43	64.56	499.47	11.07
1957	−109.50	−7.71	64.12	3.32	−14.01	435.69	−63.78
1958	17.50	23.59	29.10	22.67	55.10	583.65	147.96
1959	−44.48	29.04	4.11	13.60	93.44	679.36	95.71
1960	−111.04	−3.75	−5.62	6.74	50.20	615.89	−63.47
1961	−23.65	10.18	87.51	−5.96	47.17	731.14	115.25
1962	−101.60	26.19	9.97	−7.70	−5.90	652.10	−79.04
1963	−8.88	47.12	16.23	22.39	33.99	762.95	110.85
1964	−0.29	−17.94	39.84	5.52	84.05	874.13	111.18
1965	−73.23	39.65	57.03	3.20	68.48	969.26	95.13
1966	−153.24	−27.73	56.13	−46.19	−12.54	785.69	−183.57
1967	−68.65	31.50	25.42	92.25	38.90	905.11	119.42
1968†	6.41	34.94	25.16	−72.06	44.19	943.75	38.64
1969	−164.17	−36.70	18.33	23.79	15.36	800.36	−143.39
1970	−100.05	−46.09	116.07	−3.48	72.11	838.92	38.56
1971	−2.99	9.56	13.66	8.04	23.01	890.20	51.28
1972	−87.40	−1.23	65.24	8.46	144.75	1020.02	129.82
1973	−174.11	10.52	−5.94	36.67	−36.30	850.86	−169.16
1974	−149.37	47.51	−20.31	−13.70	−98.75	616.24	−234.62
1975	39.46	−109.62	56.93	124.00	125.40	852.41	236.17
1976	70.72	71.76	50.88	−33.70	−7.42	1004.65	152.24
1977	−65.15	−44.89	−79.61	−5.62	21.79	831.17	−173.48
1978	−31.29	−70.84	71.33	−64.67	69.31	805.01	−26.16
1979	−32.52	9.52	−18.84	75.18	0.39	838.74	33.73
1980	−86.51	135.13	137.67	−122.00	60.96	963.99	125.25
1981	−45.68	−49.51	−13.95	−14.67	34.82	875.00	−88.99
1982	5.71	86.20	28.37	−1.47	52.73	1046.54	171.54
1983	30.51	−30.92	149.68	61.16	1.67	1258.64	212.10
1984	−73.80	78.02	−139.24	92.79	−4.84	1211.57	−47.07
1985	80.36	52.70	51.26	46.32	104.46	1546.67	335.10
1986	−39.94	97.63	178.65	29.31	83.63	1895.95	349.28
1987	−559.15	235.83	392.03	139.73	−165.56	1938.83	42.88
1988	268.12	166.44	−60.48	−230.84	86.50	2168.57	229.74
1989	−53.31	143.33	233.25	90.25	171.11	2753.20	584.63
Subtotal	**−1937.20**	**941.79**	**1708.54**	**330.82**	**1417.35**		**2461.30**
1990	219.90	−25.22	47.96	−352.55	−9.63	2633.66	−119.54
1991	191.13	47.97	174.53	254.79	−133.25	3168.83	535.17
1992	237.80	−49.67	3.12	108.74	−167.71	3301.11	132.28
1993	322.82	−37.03	243.87	4.97	−81.65	3754.09	452.98
1994	206.41	−95.33	29.98	−168.87	108.16	3834.44	80.35
1995	262.97	210.06	357.02	140.07	312.56	5117.12	1282.68
1996	626.41	155.55	−34.24	268.52	314.91	6448.27	1331.15
1997	1136.04	1989.17	−590.17	−949.80	−125.26	7908.25	1459.98
1998	649.10	679.95	591.63	−1579.43	931.93	9181.43	1273.18
1999	980.49	−1587.23	826.68	735.94	1359.81	11497.12	2315.69
2000	2265.45	306.47	−1978.34	238.21	−1542.06	10786.85	−710.27
Subtotal	**7098.52**	**1594.69**	**−327.96**	**−1299.41**	**967.81**		**8033.65**
2001	−389.33	336.86	−396.53	976.41	−1292.76	10021.50	−765.35
2002	−1404.94	−823.76	1443.69	−428.12	−466.74	8341.63	−1679.87
2003	978.87	482.11	−425.46	566.22	510.55	10453.92	2112.29
2004	201.12	523.28	358.76	−409.72	−344.35	10783.01	329.00
2005	316.23	−305.62	27.67	−128.75	24.96	10717.50	−65.51
2006	95.74	573.98	1283.87	193.34	−401.28	12463.15	1745.65
2007	278.23	−157.93	1316.74	−766.63	131.26	13264.82	801.67
2008	−1387.20	1704.51	−3073.72	−940.88	−791.14	8776.39	−4488.43
2009	−45.22	161.76	617.56	932.68	−15.12	10428.05	1651.66
2010	1236.88	−421.80	1019.66	−76.73	−608.55	11577.51	1149.46
2011	−571.02	1423.66	−776.05	246.27	317.19	12217.56	640.05
2012	254.59	−49.28	−456.37	847.34	299.30	13104.14	886.58
2013	−79.63	1091.75	170.93	653.64	1635.83	16576.66	3472.52
2014	−171.63	817.56	265.07	−337.48	672.89	17823.07	1246.41
2015	308.28	−879.14	926.70	982.16	−1736.04	17425.03	−398.04
2016	602.00	594.09	636.92	678.40	−173.84	19762.60	2337.57
2017	1341.29	1184.32	882.40	445.43	1103.18	24719.22	4956.62
2018‡	−563.01	−577.96	300.49	−394.88	972.62		
Subtotal	**1001.25**	**5678.39**	**4122.33**	**3038.70**	**−162.04**		**13932.37**
Totals	**6162.57**	**8214.87**	**5502.91**	**2070.11**	**2223.12**		**24427.32**

Monday denotes first trading day of week, Friday denotes last trading day of week
† Most Wednesdays closed last 7 months of 1968   ‡ Partial year through July 6, 2018

MONDAY

D 42.9
S 42.9
N 52.4

22

Technology will gradually strengthen democracies in every country and at every level.
— William H. Gates (Microsoft founder)

Week After July Expiration Prone to Wild Swings, Dow Up 11 of Last 16
1998 −4.3%, 2002 +3.1%, 2006 +3.2%, 2007 −4.2%, 2009 +4.0%, 2010 +3.2%

TUESDAY

D 42.9
S 42.9
N 42.9

23

The Clairvoyant Society of London will not meet Tuesday because of unforeseen circumstances.
— Advertisement in the *London Financial Times*

WEDNESDAY

D 38.1
S 47.6
N 47.6

24

Nothing is more uncertain than the favor of the crowd.
— Marcus Tullius Cicero (Great Roman orator, politician, 106–43 B.C.)

Beware the "Summer Rally" Hype
Historically the Weakest Rally of All Seasons (Page 74)

THURSDAY

D 57.1
S 52.4
N 57.1

25

A bank is a place where they lend you an umbrella in fair weather and ask for it back again when it begins to rain.
— Robert Frost (American poet, 1874–1963)

FRIDAY

D 52.4
S 52.4
N 57.1

26

When investment decisions need to consider the speed of light, something is seriously wrong.
— Frank M. Bifulco (Senior portfolio manager, Alcott Capital Management, *Barron's Letters to the Editor*, 5/24/10)

SATURDAY

27

August Almanac Investor Sector Seasonalities: See Pages 92, 94 and 96

SUNDAY

28

AUGUST ALMANAC

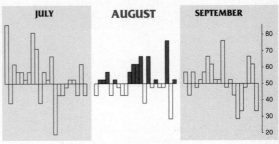

AUGUST								SEPTEMBER						
S	M	T	W	T	F	S		S	M	T	W	T	F	S
				1	2	3								1
4	5	6	7	8	9	10		2	3	4	5	6	7	
11	12	13	14	15	16	17		8	9	10	11	12	13	14
18	19	20	21	22	23	24		15	16	17	18	19	20	21
25	26	27	28	29	30	31		22	23	24	25	26	27	28
								29	30					

Market Probability Chart above is a graphic representation of the S&P 500 Recent Market Probability Calendar on page 124.

◆ Harvesting made August the best stock market month 1901–1951 ◆ Now that about 2% farm, August is the worst Dow, S&P and NASDAQ (2000 up 11.7%, 2001 down 10.9%) month since 1987 ◆ Shortest bear in history (45 days) caused by turmoil in Russia, currency crisis and hedge fund debacle ended here in 1998, 1344.22-point drop in the Dow, second worst behind October 2008, off 15.1% ◆ Saddam Hussein triggered a 10.0% slide in 1990 ◆ Best Dow gains: 1982 (11.5%) and 1984 (9.8%) as bear markets ended ◆ Next-to-last day S&P up only six times in last 22 years ◆ Pre–presidential election year Augusts' rankings: #8 S&P, #7 Dow and #10 NASDAQ.

August Vital Statistics

	DJIA		S&P 500		NASDAQ		Russell 1K		Russell 2K	
Rank	10		11		11		10		9	
Up	38		37		26		24		22	
Down	30		31		21		15		17	
Average % Change	−0.2%		−0.1%		0.1%		0.2%		0.2%	
Pre-Election Year	0.9%		0.5%		0.7%		0.3%		−0.001%	
Best & Worst August										
	% Change		% Change		% Change		% Change		% Change	
Best	1982	11.5	1982	11.6	2000	11.7	1982	11.3	1984	11.5
Worst	1998	−15.1	1998	−14.6	1998	−19.9	1998	−15.1	1998	−19.5
Best & Worst August Weeks										
Best	08/20/82	10.3	08/20/82	8.8	08/03/84	7.4	08/20/82	8.5	08/03/84	7.0
Worst	08/23/74	−6.1	08/05/11	−7.2	08/28/98	−8.8	08/05/11	−7.7	08/05/11	−10.3
Best & Worst August Days										
Best	08/17/82	4.9	08/17/82	4.8	08/09/11	5.3	08/09/11	5.0	08/09/11	6.9
Worst	08/31/98	−6.4	08/31/98	−6.8	08/31/98	−8.6	08/08/11	−6.9	08/08/11	−8.9
First Trading Day of Expiration Week: 1980–2017										
Record (#Up – #Down)	25–13		28–10		29–9		28–10		25–13	
Current Streak	U4		U4		U8		U4		U5	
Avg % Change	0.28		0.30		0.36		0.28		0.33	
Options Expiration Day: 1980–2017										
Record (#Up – #Down)	18–20		19–19		20–18		20–18		21–17	
Current Streak	D5		D5		D3		D3		D5	
Avg % Change	−0.15		−0.09		−0.15		−0.09		0.06	
Options Expiration Week: 1980–2017										
Record (#Up – #Down)	18–20		21–17		21–17		21–17		23–15	
Current Streak	D3		D3		D1		D3		D1	
Avg % Change	0.001		0.19		0.34		0.21		0.42	
Week After Options Expiration: 1980–2017										
Record (#Up – #Down)	23–15		25–13		24–14		25–13		25–13	
Current Streak	U1		U1		U1		U1		U5	
Avg % Change	0.29		0.33		0.53		0.33		0.14	
First Trading Day Performance										
% of Time Up	47.1		50.0		53.2		46.2		48.7	
Avg % Change	0.02		0.05		−0.05		0.10		−0.01	
Last Trading Day Performance										
% of Time Up	60.3		63.2		66.0		59.0		69.2	
Avg % Change	0.12		0.12		0.05		−0.04		0.06	

Dow & S&P 1950–June 2018, NASDAQ 1971–June 2018, Russell 1K & 2K 1979–June 2018.

August's a good month to go on vacation;
Trading stocks will likely lead to frustration.

MONDAY
D 42.9
S 42.9
N 42.9
29

Change is the law of life. And those who look only to the past or present are certain to miss the future.
— John F. Kennedy (35th U.S. President, 1917–1963)

FOMC Meeting (2 Days)

TUESDAY
D 42.9
S 61.9
N 66.7
30

The bigger a man's head gets, the easier it is to fill his shoes.
— Anonymous

Last Trading Day in July, NASDAQ Down 10 of Last 13

WEDNESDAY
D 33.3
S 42.9
N 38.1
31

Six words that spell business success: create concept, communicate concept, sustain momentum.
— Yale Hirsch (Creator of *Stock Trader's Almanac*, b. 1923)

First Trading Day in August, Dow Down 14 of Last 21

THURSDAY
D 33.3
S 42.9
N 47.6
1

What's money? A man is a success if he gets up in the morning and goes to bed at night and in between does what he wants to do.
— Bob Dylan (American singer-songwriter, musician and artist, b. 1941)

FRIDAY
D 57.1
S 52.4
N 38.1
2

I would rather be positioned as a petrified bull rather than a penniless bear.
— John L. Person (Trader, author, speaker, *Commodity Trader's Almanac*, nationalfutures.com, 11/3/10, b. 1961)

SATURDAY
3

SUNDAY
4

A RALLY FOR ALL SEASONS

Most years, especially when the market sells off during the first half, prospects for the perennial summer rally become the buzz on the Street. Parameters for this "rally" were defined by the late Ralph Rotnem as the lowest close in the Dow Jones Industrials in May or June to the highest close in July, August, or September. Such a big deal is made of the "summer rally" that one might get the impression the market puts on its best performance in the summertime. Nothing could be further from the truth! Not only does the market "rally" in every season of the year, but it does so with more gusto in the winter, spring and fall than in the summer.

Winters in 55 years averaged a 12.9% gain as measured from the low in November or December to the first quarter closing high. Spring rose 11.3%, followed by fall with 11.0%. Last and least was the average 8.9% "summer rally." Even 2009's impressive 19.7% "summer rally" was outmatched by spring. Nevertheless, no matter how thick the gloom or grim the outlook, don't despair! There's always a rally for all seasons, statistically.

SEASONAL GAINS IN DOW JONES INDUSTRIALS

	WINTER RALLY Nov/Dec Low to Q1 High	SPRING RALLY Feb/Mar Low to Q2 High	SUMMER RALLY May/Jun Low to Q3 High	FALL RALLY Aug/Sep Low to Q4 High
1964	15.3%	6.2%	9.4%	8.3%
1965	5.7	6.6	11.6	10.3
1966	5.9	4.8	3.5	7.0
1967	11.6	8.7	11.2	4.4
1968	7.0	11.5	5.2	13.3
1969	0.9	7.7	1.9	6.7
1970	5.4	6.2	22.5	19.0
1971	21.6	9.4	5.5	7.4
1972	19.1	7.7	5.2	11.4
1973	8.6	4.8	9.7	15.9
1974	13.1	8.2	1.4	11.0
1975	36.2	24.2	8.2	8.7
1976	23.3	6.4	5.9	4.6
1977	8.2	3.1	2.8	2.1
1978	2.1	16.8	11.8	5.2
1979	11.0	8.9	8.9	6.1
1980	13.5	16.8	21.0	8.5
1981	11.8	9.9	0.4	8.3
1982	4.6	9.3	18.5	37.8
1983	15.7	17.8	6.3	10.7
1984	5.9	4.6	14.1	9.7
1985	11.7	7.1	9.5	19.7
1986	31.1	18.8	9.2	11.4
1987	30.6	13.6	22.9	5.9
1988	18.1	13.5	11.2	9.8
1989	15.1	12.9	16.1	5.7
1990	8.8	14.5	12.4	8.6
1991	21.8	11.2	6.6	9.3
1992	14.9	6.4	3.7	3.3
1993	8.9	7.7	6.3	7.3
1994	9.7	5.2	9.1	5.0
1995	13.6	19.3	11.3	13.9
1996	19.2	7.5	8.7	17.3
1997	17.7	18.4	18.4	7.3
1998	20.3	13.6	8.2	24.3
1999	15.1	21.6	8.2	12.6
2000	10.8	15.2	9.8	3.5
2001	6.4	20.8	1.7	23.1
2002	14.8	7.9	2.8	17.6
2003	6.5	23.9	14.3	15.7
2004	11.6	5.2	4.4	10.6
2005	9.0	2.1	5.6	5.3
2006	8.8	8.3	9.5	13.0
2007	6.7	13.5	6.6	10.3
2008	2.5	11.2	3.8	4.5
2009	19.6	34.4	19.7	15.5
2010	11.6	13.1	11.1	16.0
2011	12.6	10.3	7.0	14.7
2012	18.0	4.5	12.4	5.7
2013	16.2	11.8	6.9	12.2
2014	6.0	10.2	5.5	10.3
2015	7.1	5.5	3.0	14.4
2016	3.4	15.6	8.7	10.8
2017	18.0	8.3	8.8	14.6
2018	14.4	76	2.2*	
Totals	**707.1%**	**620.3%**	**490.6%**	**595.6%**
Average	**12.9%**	**11.3%**	**8.9%**	**11.0%**

* As of 7/6/2018

74

First Nine Trading Days of August Are Historically Weak (Pages 72 and 124)

MONDAY

D 52.4
S 52.4
N 52.4

5

If banking institutions are protected by the taxpayer and they are given free rein to speculate, I may not live long enough to see the crisis, but my soul is going to come back and haunt you.
— Paul A. Volcker (Fed Chairman, 1979–1987, Chair Economic Recovery Advisory Board, 2/2/2010, b. 1927)

TUESDAY

D 52.4
S 57.1
N 52.4

6

Nothing has a stronger influence psychologically on their environment and especially on their children than the unlived life of the parent.
— Carl G. Jung (Swiss psychiatrist)

August Worst Dow and S&P Month 1988–2017
Harvesting Made August Best Dow Month 1901–1951

WEDNESDAY

D 52.4
S 42.9
N 38.1

7

Bankruptcy was designed to forgive stupidity, not reward criminality.
— William P. Barr (Verizon General Counsel, calling for gov't liquidation of MCI-WorldCom in Chapter 7, 4/14/03)

THURSDAY

D 47.6
S 52.4
N 33.3

8

An economist is someone who sees something happen, and then wonders if it would work in theory.
— Ronald Reagan (40th U.S. President, 1911–2004)

Mid-August Stronger Than Beginning and End

FRIDAY

D 47.6
S 47.6
N 42.9

9

I'm not nearly so concerned about the return on my capital as I am the return of my capital.
— Will Rogers (American humorist and showman, 1879–1935)

SATURDAY

10

SUNDAY

11

TAKE ADVANTAGE OF DOWN FRIDAY/ DOWN MONDAY WARNING

Fridays and Mondays are the most important days of the week. Friday is the day for squaring positions—trimming longs or covering shorts before taking off for the weekend. Traders want to limit their exposure (particularly to stocks that are not acting well) since there could be unfavorable developments before trading resumes two or more days later.

Monday is important because the market then has the chance to reflect any weekend news, plus what traders think after digesting the previous week's action and the many Monday morning research and strategy comments.

For over 30 years, a down Friday followed by down Monday has frequently corresponded to important market inflection points that exhibit a clearly negative bias, often coinciding with market tops and, on a few climactic occasions, such as in October 2002 and March 2009, near-major market bottoms.

One simple way to get a quick reading on which way the market may be heading is to keep track of the performance of the Dow Jones Industrial Average on Fridays and the following Mondays. Since 1995, there have been 236 occurrences of Down Friday/ Down Monday (DF/DM), with 69 falling in the bear market years of 2001, 2002, 2008, 2011 and 2015, producing an average decline of 12.1%.

To illustrate how Down Friday/Down Monday can telegraph market inflection points we created the chart below of the Dow Jones Industrials from November 2016 to July 6, 2018, with arrows pointing to occurrences of DF/DM. Use DF/DM as a warning to examine market conditions carefully.

DOWN FRIDAY/DOWN MONDAY

Year	Total Number Down Friday/ Down Monday	Subsequent Average % Dow Loss*	Average Number of Days it took
1995	8	−1.2%	18
1996	9	−3.0%	28
1997	6	−5.1%	45
1998	9	−6.4%	47
1999	9	−6.4%	39
2000	11	−6.6%	32
2001	13	−13.5%	53
2002	18	−11.9%	54
2003	9	−3.0%	17
2004	9	−3.7%	51
2005	10	−3.0%	37
2006	11	−2.0%	14
2007	8	−6.0%	33
2008	15	−17.0%	53
2009	10	−8.7%	15
2010	7	−3.1%	10
2011	11	−9.0%	53
2012	11	−4.0%	38
2013	7	−2.4%	15
2014	7	−2.5%	8
2015	12	−9.2%	44
2016	10	−2.7%	25
2017	11	−1.2%	18
2018	5	−3.0%	27
Average	**10**	**−5.6%**	**32**

* Over next 3 months, ** Ending July 6, 2018

DOW JONES INDUSTRIALS (NOVEMBER 2016–JULY 6, 2018)

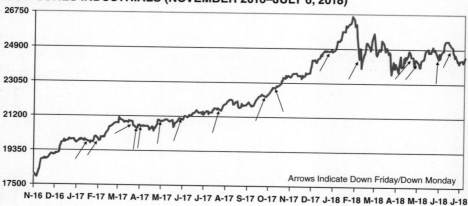

Arrows Indicate Down Friday/Down Monday

N-16 D-16 J-17 F-17 M-17 A-17 M-17 J-17 J-17 A-17 S-17 O-17 N-17 D-17 J-18 F-18 M-18 A-18 M-18 J-18 J-18

Monday Before August Expiration, Dow Up 16 of Last 23, Average Gain 0.4%

MONDAY

D 38.1
S 42.9
N 42.9

12

Don't be the last bear or last bull standing, let history guide you, be contrary to the crowd, and let the tape tell you when to act.
— Jeffrey A. Hirsch (Editor, *Stock Trader's Almanac*, b. 1966)

TUESDAY

D 47.6
S 42.9
N 52.4

13

To know values is to know the meaning of the market.
— Charles Dow (Co-founder, Dow Jones & Co, 1851–1902)

WEDNESDAY

D 61.9
S 57.1
N 61.9

14

Analysts are supposed to be critics of corporations. They often end up being public relations spokesmen for them.
— Ralph Wanger (Chief Investment Officer, Acorn Fund)

THURSDAY

D 57.1
S 61.9
N 66.7

15

A market is the combined behavior of thousands of people responding to information, misinformation and whim.
— Kenneth Chang (*New York Times* journalist)

August Expiration Day Less Bullish Lately, Dow Down 7 of Last 8 Down 531 Points (3.1%) in 2015

FRIDAY

D 57.1
S 61.9
N 66.7

16

Cooperation is essential to address 21st-century challenges; you can't fire cruise missiles at the global financial crisis.
— Nicholas D. Kristof (*New York Times* columnist, 10/23/08)

SATURDAY

17

SUNDAY

18

AURA OF THE TRIPLE WITCH—4TH QUARTER MOST BULLISH: DOWN WEEKS TRIGGER MORE WEAKNESS WEEK AFTER

Standard options expire the third Friday of every month, but in March, June, September, and December, a powerful coven gathers. Since the S&P index futures began trading on April 21, 1982, stock options, index options, and index futures all expire at the same time four times each year—known as Triple Witching. Traders have long sought to understand and master the magic of this quarterly phenomenon.

The market for single-stock and ETF futures and weekly options continues to grow. However, their impact on the market has thus far been subdued. As their availability continues to expand, trading volumes and market influence are also likely to broaden. Until such time, we do not believe the term "quadruple witching" is applicable just yet.

We have analyzed what the market does prior to, during, and following Triple-Witching expirations in search of consistent trading patterns. Here are some of our findings of how the Dow Jones Industrials perform around Triple-Witching Week (TWW).

- TWWs have become more bullish since 1990, except in the second quarter.
- Following weeks have become more bearish. Since Q1 2000, only 27 of 73 were up, and 13 occurred in December, 7 in March, 5 in September, 2 in June.
- TWWs have tended to be down in flat periods and dramatically so during bear markets.
- DOWN WEEKS TEND TO FOLLOW DOWN TWWs is a most interesting pattern. Since 1991, of 36 down TWWs, 26 following weeks were also down. This is surprising, inasmuch as the previous decade had an exactly opposite pattern: There were 13 down TWWs then, but 12 up weeks followed them.
- TWWs in the second and third quarter (Worst Six Months May through October) are much weaker, and the weeks following, horrendous. But in the first and fourth quarter (Best Six Months period November through April), only the week after Q1 expiration is negative.

Throughout the *Almanac* you will also see notations on the performance of Mondays and Fridays of TWW, as we place considerable significance on the beginnings and ends of weeks (pages 70, 76 and 141–144).

TRIPLE-WITCHING WEEK AND WEEK AFTER DOW POINT CHANGES

	Expiration Week Q1	Week After	Expiration Week Q2	Week After	Expiration Week Q3	Week After	Expiration Week Q4	Week After
1991	−6.93	−89.36	−34.98	−58.81	33.54	−13.19	20.12	167.04
1992	40.48	−44.95	−69.01	−2.94	21.35	−76.73	9.19	12.97
1993	43.76	−31.60	−10.24	−3.88	−8.38	−70.14	10.90	6.15
1994	32.95	−120.92	3.33	−139.84	58.54	−101.60	116.08	26.24
1995	38.04	65.02	86.80	75.05	96.85	−33.42	19.87	−78.76
1996	114.52	51.67	55.78	−50.60	49.94	−15.54	179.53	76.51
1997	−130.67	−64.20	14.47	−108.79	174.30	4.91	−82.01	−76.98
1998	303.91	−110.35	−122.07	231.67	100.16	133.11	81.87	314.36
1999	27.20	−81.31	365.05	−303.00	−224.80	−524.30	32.73	148.33
2000	666.41	517.49	−164.76	−44.55	−293.65	−79.63	−277.95	200.60
2001	−821.21	−318.63	−353.36	−19.05	−1369.70	611.75	224.19	101.65
2002	34.74	−179.56	−220.42	−10.53	−326.67	−284.57	77.61	−207.54
2003	662.26	−376.20	83.63	−211.70	173.27	−331.74	236.06	46.45
2004	−53.48	26.37	6.31	−44.57	−28.61	−237.22	106.70	177.20
2005	−144.69	−186.80	110.44	−325.23	−36.62	−222.35	97.01	7.68
2006	203.31	0.32	122.63	−25.46	168.66	−52.67	138.03	−102.30
2007	−165.91	370.60	215.09	−279.22	377.67	75.44	110.80	−84.78
2008	410.23	−144.92	−464.66	−496.18	−33.55	−245.31	−50.57	−63.56
2009	54.40	497.80	−259.53	−101.34	214.79	−155.01	−142.61	191.21
2010	117.29	108.38	239.57	−306.83	145.08	252.41	81.59	81.58
2011	−185.88	362.07	52.45	−69.78	516.96	−737.61	−317.87	427.61
2012	310.60	−151.89	212.97	−126.39	−13.90	−142.34	55.83	−252.73
2013	117.04	−2.08	−270.78	110.20	75.03	−192.85	465.78	257.27
2014	237.10	20.29	171.34	−95.24	292.23	−166.59	523.97	248.91
2015	378.34	−414.99	117.11	−69.27	−48.51	−69.91	−136.66	423.62
2016	388.99	−86.57	−190.18	−274.41	38.35	137.65	86.56	90.40
2017	11.64	−317.90	112.31	10.48	470.55	81.25	322.58	102.32
2018	−389.23	−1413.31	−226.05	−509.59				
Up	20	10	16	4	17	7	21	20
Down	8	18	12	24	10	20	6	7

78

MONDAY
D 66.7
S 66.7
N 61.9
19

The market can stay irrational longer than you can stay solvent.
— John Maynard Keynes (British economist, 1883–1946)

TUESDAY
D 42.9
S 38.1
N 38.1
20

There's no trick to being a humorist when you have the whole government working for you.
— Will Rogers (American humorist and showman, 1879–1935)

Week After August Expiration Mixed, Dow Down 7 of Last 13

WEDNESDAY
D 61.9
S 66.7
N 76.2
21

Stock option plans reward the executive for doing the wrong thing. Instead of asking, "Are we making the right decision?" he asks, "How did we close today?" It is encouragement to loot the corporation.
— Peter Drucker (Austrian-born pioneer management theorist, 1909–2005)

THURSDAY
D 47.6
S 47.6
N 47.6
22

If you spend more than 14 minutes a year worrying about the market, you've wasted 12 minutes.
— Peter Lynch (Fidelity Investments, *One Up on Wall Street*, b. 1944)

FRIDAY
D 52.4
S 52.4
N 47.6
23

If you are ready to give up everything else—to study the whole history and background of the market and all the principal companies . . . as carefully as a medical student studies anatomy—. . . and, in addition, you have the cool nerves of a great gambler, the sixth sense of a clairvoyant, and the courage of a lion, you have a ghost of a chance.
— Bernard Baruch (Financier, speculator, statesman, presidential adviser, 1870–1965)

SATURDAY
24

September Almanac Investor Sector Seasonalities: See Pages 92, 94 and 96

SUNDAY
25

SEPTEMBER ALMANAC

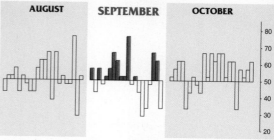

SEPTEMBER						
S	M	T	W	T	F	S
1	2	3	4	5	6	7
8	9	10	11	12	13	14
15	16	17	18	19	20	21
22	23	24	25	26	27	28
29	30					

OCTOBER						
S	M	T	W	T	F	S
		1	2	3	4	5
6	7	8	9	10	11	12
13	14	15	16	17	18	19
20	21	22	23	24	25	26
27	28	29	30	31		

Market Probability Chart above is a graphic representation of the S&P 500 Recent Market Probability Calendar on page 124.

◆ Start of business year, end of vacations and back to school made September a leading barometer month in first 60 years of 20th century; now portfolio managers back after Labor Day tend to clean house ◆ Biggest % loser on the S&P, Dow and NASDAQ since 1950 (pages 50 & 58) ◆ Streak of four great Dow Septembers averaging 4.2% gains ended in 1999 with six losers in a row averaging –5.9% (see page 152), up three straight 2005–2007, down 6% in 2008 and 2011 ◆ Day after Labor Day Dow up 16 of last 24 ◆ S&P opened strong 14 of last 23 years but tends to close weak due to end-of-quarter mutual fund portfolio restructuring, last trading day: S&P down 16 of past 25 ◆ September Triple-Witching Week can be dangerous, week after is pitiful (see page 78).

September Vital Statistics

	DJIA		S&P 500		NASDAQ		Russell 1K		Russell 2K	
Rank	12		12		12		12		12	
Up	27		30		26		19		22	
Down	41		37		21		20		17	
Average % Change	–0.7%		–0.5%		–0.5%		–0.6%		–0.4%	
Pre-Election Year	–1.0%		–0.9%		–0.9%		–1.0%		–1.6%	
Best & Worst September										
	% Change		% Change		% Change		% Change		% Change	
Best	2010	7.7	2010	8.8	1998	13.0	2010	9.0	2010	12.3
Worst	2002	–12.4	1974	–11.9	2001	–17.0	2002	–10.9	2001	–13.6
Best & Worst September Weeks										
Best	09/28/01	7.4	09/28/01	7.8	09/16/11	6.3	09/28/01	7.6	09/28/01	6.9
Worst	09/21/01	–14.3	09/21/01	–11.6	09/21/01	–16.1	09/21/01	–11.7	09/21/01	–14.0
Best & Worst September Days										
Best	09/08/98	5.0	09/30/08	5.4	09/08/98	6.0	09/30/08	5.3	09/18/08	7.0
Worst	09/17/01	–7.1	09/29/08	–8.8	09/29/08	–9.1	09/29/08	–8.7	09/29/08	–6.7
First Trading Day of Expiration Week: 1980–2017										
Record (#Up – #Down)	25–13		21–17		15–23		21–17		16–22	
Current Streak	U2		U2		U2		U2		U2	
Avg % Change	–0.01		–0.06		–0.25		–0.08		–0.17	
Options Expiration Day: 1980–2017										
Record (#Up – #Down)	19–19		20–18		24–14		21–17		24–14	
Current Streak	U1		U1		U1		U1		U1	
Avg % Change	–0.04		0.08		0.11		0.07		0.12	
Options Expiration Week: 1980–2017										
Record (#Up – #Down)	21–17		23–15		23–15		23–15		21–17	
Current Streak	U2		U2		U5		U2		U3	
Avg % Change	–0.14		0.08		0.14		0.07		0.19	
Week After Options Expiration: 1980–2017										
Record (#Up – #Down)	14–24		12–26		16–22		12–25		14–24	
Current Streak	U2		U2		D1		U2		U2	
Avg % Change	–0.67		–0.73		–0.86		–0.74		–1.24	
First Trading Day Performance										
% of Time Up	60.3		60.3		57.4		53.8		51.3	
Avg % Change	–0.001		–0.02		–0.04		–0.08		–0.01	
Last Trading Day Performance										
% of Time Up	39.7		42.6		48.9		48.7		61.5	
Avg % Change	–0.11		–0.04		0.02		0.05		0.26	

Dow & S&P 1950–June 2018, NASDAQ 1971–June 2018, Russell 1K & 2K 1979–June 2018.

September is when leaves and stocks tend to fall;
On Wall Street it's the worst month of all.

AUGUST/SEPTEMBER 2019

MONDAY

D 47.6
S 47.6
N 52.4

26

*If you bet on a horse, that's gambling. If you bet you can make three spades, that's entertainment.
If you bet cotton will go up three points, that's business. See the difference?*
— Blackie Sherrod (Sportswriter, 1919–2016)

TUESDAY

D 38.1
S 47.6
N 47.6

27

*So at last I was going to America! Really, really going, at last! The boundaries burst. The arch of heaven soared! A million
suns shone out for every star. The winds rushed in from outer space, roaring in my ears, "America! America!"*
— Mary Antin (1881–1949, Immigrant writer, The Promised Land, 1912)

WEDNESDAY

D 71.4
S 76.2
N 76.2

28

*Everyone blames the foreigners when the economy goes south. Always. It is human nature to
blame others, and it is the same all over the world.*
— Jim Rogers (Financier, Adventure Capitalist, b. 1942)

August's Next-to-Last Trading Day, S&P Down 16 of Last 22 Years

THURSDAY

D 28.6
S 28.6
N 52.4

29

*I have seen it repeatedly throughout the world: politicians get a country in trouble but swear everything is
okay in the face of overwhelming evidence to the contrary.*
— Jim Rogers (Financier, Adventure Capitalist, b. 1942)

FRIDAY

D 52.4
S 52.4
N 57.1

30

*I have noticed over the years the difficulty some people have in cutting losses, admitting an error, and moving on.
I am rather frequently—and on occasion, quite spectacularly—wrong. However, if we expect to be wrong, then there
should be no ego tied up in admitting the error, honoring the stop loss, selling the loser—and preserving your capital.*
— Barry L. Ritholtz (Founder & CIO of Ritholtz Wealth Management, Bailout Nation, The Big Picture blog, 8/12/10, b. 1961)

SATURDAY

31

SUNDAY

1

MARKET GAINS MORE ON SUPER-8 DAYS EACH MONTH THAN ON ALL 13 REMAINING DAYS COMBINED

For many years, the last day plus the first four days were the best days of the month. The market currently exhibits greater bullish bias from the last three trading days of the previous month through the first two days of the current month, and now shows significant bullishness during the middle three trading days, 9 to 11, due to 401(k) cash inflows (see pages 145 & 146). This pattern was not as pronounced during the boom years of the 1990s, with market strength all month long. Since the 2009 market bottom, the Super-8 advantage appears to be fading. In times of weakness, such as from mid-May 2015 to January 2016, strength was evident, but the Super-8 are lagging again in 2018.

SUPER-8 DAYS* DOW % CHANGES VS. REST OF MONTH

	Super-8 Days (2010)	Rest of Month	Super-8 Days (2011)	Rest of Month	Super-8 Days (2012)	Rest of Month
Jan	0.66%	−3.92%	1.70%	1.80%	1.90%	1.66%
Feb	3.31	−2.38	0.45	0.57	−0.39	2.33
Mar	1.91	3.51	−1.40	2.21	2.22	−0.55
Apr	1.13	0.18	2.30	0.95	1.00	−1.80
May	−3.08	−5.75	1.03	−2.61	−0.38	−4.52
Jun	4.33	−3.26	−1.64	−1.19	−1.30	2.08
Jul	−7.07	11.34	3.52	0.31	5.11	−2.22
Aug	0.20	−5.49	2.04	−11.39	−0.40	2.09
Sep	3.83	4.22	3.24	−3.96	−0.24	2.98
Oct	−0.18	3.47	−4.47	10.71	0.77	−3.60
Nov	−1.20	1.37	1.42	−6.66	−2.01	0.55
Dec	1.98	1.45	5.74	3.58	0.49	1.35
Totals	**5.82%**	**4.74%**	**13.93%**	**−5.68%**	**6.77%**	**0.35%**
Average	**0.49%**	**0.40%**	**1.16%**	**−0.47%**	**0.56%**	**0.03%**

	Super-8 Days (2013)	Rest of Month	Super-8 Days (2014)	Rest of Month	Super-8 Days (2015)	Rest of Month
Jan	2.28%	3.47%	0.92%	−4.26%	−3.64%	−0.07%
Feb	−0.27	−0.41	−1.99	3.66	2.65	2.00
Mar	2.93	1.82	0.77	−0.21	1.91	−4.78
Apr	0.11	1.65	2.44	−1.82	1.20	0.83
May	1.93	2.81	−0.56	2.50	1.31	−1.28
Jun	−0.27	−3.96	−0.09	1.24	−1.32	0.49
Jul	1.11	4.23	1.79	−1.10	−0.11	−1.31
Aug	−1.35	−3.75	−1.81	2.61	0.37	−8.02
Sep	2.55	0.83	0.32	−1.26	2.27	−2.04
Oct	−0.64	2.60	−3.28	3.82	1.03	6.57
Nov	1.79	1.41	2.42	2.28	0.68	0.68
Dec	−0.72	3.30	−1.66	3.14	−0.74	−0.86
Totals	**9.45%**	**14.00%**	**−0.73%**	**10.60%**	**5.61%**	**−0.86%**
Average	**0.79%**	**1.17%**	**−0.06%**	**0.88%**	**0.47%**	**−0.65%**

	Super-8 Days (2016)	Rest of Month	Super-8 Days (2017)	Rest of Month	Super-8 Days (2018)	Rest of Month
Jan	−2.95%	−4.93%	−0.44%	1.24%	2.83%	4.54%
Feb	1.69	0.30	0.62	2.90	−1.68	−3.17
Mar	4.02	2.21	1.16	−1.66	−4.26	−0.09
Apr	2.14	0.43	−0.39	1.83	0.89	−1.34
May	−1.33	0.57	−0.03	0.45	−0.79	3.59
Jun	−1.33	−2.68	1.18	−0.09	−0.67	−1.17
Jul	4.97	2.66	0.89	0.98		
Aug	−0.11	−0.30	2.12	−1.65		
Sep	0.84	−1.72	0.53	1.65		
Oct	−0.65	0.49	1.97	2.96		
Nov	−0.71	5.93	−0.15	0.93		
Dec	0.38	3.73	3.61	1.27		
Totals	**6.96%**	**6.69%**	**11.07%**	**10.81%**	**−3.68%**	**2.36%**
Average	**0.58%**	**0.56%**	**0.92%**	**0.90%**	**−0.61%**	**0.39%**

	Super-8 Days		Rest of Month (13 days)	
101 Month Totals	Net % Changes	55.20%	Net % Changes	36.08%
	Average Period	0.54%	Average Period	0.35%
	Average Day	0.07%	Average Day	0.03%

* Super-8 Days = Last 3 + First 2 + Middle 3

SEPTEMBER 2019

MONDAY

2

The way a young man spends his evenings is a part of that thin area between success and failure.
— Robert R. Young (U.S. financier and railroad tycoon, 1897–1958)

First Trading Day in September, S&P Up 14 of Last 23, But Down 7 of Last 10
Day After Labor Day, Dow Up 16 of Last 24, 1998 Up 5.0%, 2015 Up 2.4%

TUESDAY

D 57.1
S 57.1
N 66.7

3

The difference between life and the movies is that a script has to make sense, and life doesn't.
— Joseph L. Mankiewicz (Film director, writer, producer, 1909–1993)

WEDNESDAY

D 66.7
S 42.9
N 47.6

4

Why is it right-wing [conservatives] always stand shoulder to shoulder in solidarity,
while liberals always fall out among themselves?
— Yevgeny Yevtushenko (Russian poet, *Babi Yar*, quoted in London *Observer*, 12/15/91, 1933–2017)

THURSDAY

D 57.1
S 57.1
N 52.4

5

In my experience, selling a put is much safer than buying a stock.
— Kyle Rosen (Boston Capital Management, *Barron's*, 8/23/04)

FRIDAY

D 38.1
S 47.6
N 57.1

6

When teachers held high expectations of their students that alone was enough
to cause an increase of 25 points in the students' IQ scores.
— Warren Bennis (Author, *The Unconscious Conspiracy: Why Leaders Can't Lead*, 1976)

SATURDAY

7

SUNDAY

8

A CORRECTION FOR ALL SEASONS

While there's a rally for every season (page 74), almost always there's a decline or correction, too. Fortunately, corrections tend to be smaller than rallies, and that's what gives the stock market its long-term upward bias. In each season the average bounce outdoes the average setback. On average, the net gain between the rally and the correction is smallest in summer and fall.

The summer setback tends to be slightly outdone by the average correction in the fall. Tax selling and portfolio cleaning are the usual explanations—individuals sell to register a tax loss, and institutions like to get rid of their losers before preparing year-end statements. The October jinx also plays a major part. Since 1964, there have been 18 fall declines of over 10%, and in 10 of them (1966, 1974, 1978, 1979, 1987, 1990, 1997, 2000, 2002 and 2008) much damage was done in October, where so many bear markets end. Recent October lows were also seen in 1998, 1999, 2004, 2005 and 2011. Most often, it has paid to buy after fourth quarter or late third quarter "waterfall declines" for a rally that may continue into January or even beyond. Anticipation of war in Iraq put the market down in 2003 Q1. Quick success rallied stocks through Q3. Financial crisis affected the pattern in 2008–2009, producing the worst winter decline since 1932. Easy monetary policy and strong corporate earnings spared Q1 2011 and 2012 from a seasonal slump. Tax cut expectations lifted the market in Q4 2017.

SEASONAL CORRECTIONS IN DOW JONES INDUSTRIALS

	WINTER SLUMP Nov/Dec High to Q1 Low	SPRING SLUMP Feb/Mar High to Q2 Low	SUMMER SLUMP May/Jun High to Q3 Low	FALL SLUMP Aug/Sep High to Q4 Low
1964	−0.1%	−2.4%	−1.0%	−2.1%
1965	−2.5	−7.3	−8.3	−0.9
1966	−6.0	−13.2	−17.7	−12.7
1967	−4.2	−3.9	−5.5	−9.9
1968	−8.8	−0.3	−5.5	+0.4
1969	−8.7	−8.7	−172	−8.1
1970	−13.8	−20.2	−8.8	−2.5
1971	−1.4	−4.8	−10.7	−13.4
1972	−0.5	−2.6	−6.3	−5.3
1973	−11.0	−12.8	−10.9	−17.3
1974	−15.3	−10.8	−29.8	−27.6
1975	−6.3	−5.5	−9.9	−6.7
1976	−0.2	−5.1	−4.7	−8.9
1977	−8.5	−7.2	−11.5	−10.2
1978	−12.3	−4.0	−7.0	−13.5
1979	−2.5	−5.8	−3.7	−10.9
1980	−10.0	−16.0	−1.7	−6.8
1981	−6.9	−5.1	−18.6	−12.9
1982	−10.9	−7.5	−10.6	−3.3
1983	−4.1	−2.8	−6.8	−3.6
1984	−11.9	−10.5	−8.4	−6.2
1985	−4.8	−4.4	−2.8	−2.3
1986	−3.3	−4.7	−7.3	−7.6
1987	−1.4	−6.6	−1.7	−36.1
1988	−6.7	−7.0	−76	−4.5
1989	−1.7	−2.4	−3.1	−6.6
1990	−7.9	−4.0	−17.3	−18.4
1991	−6.3	−3.6	−4.5	−6.3
1992	+0.1	−3.3	−5.4	−7.6
1993	−2.7	−3.1	−3.0	−2.0
1994	−4.4	−9.6	−4.4	−7.1
1995	−0.8	−0.1	−0.2	−2.0
1996	−3.5	−4.6	−7.5	+0.2
1997	−1.8	−9.8	−2.2	−13.3
1998	−7.0	−3.1	−18.2	−13.1
1999	−2.7	−1.7	−8.0	−11.5
2000	−14.8	−7.4	−4.1	−11.8
2001	−14.5	−13.6	−27.4	−16.2
2002	−5.1	−14.2	−26.7	−19.5
2003	−15.8	−5.3	−3.1	−2.1
2004	−3.9	−7.7	−6.3	−5.7
2005	−4.5	−8.5	−3.3	−4.5
2006	−2.4	−5.4	−7.8	−0.4
2007	−3.7	−3.2	−6.1	−8.4
2008	−14.5	−11.0	−20.6	−35.9
2009	−32.0	−6.3	−7.4	−3.5
2010	−6.1	−10.4	−13.1	−1.0
2011	+0.2	−4.0	−16.3	−12.2
2012	+0.5	−8.7	−5.3	−7.8
2013	−0.2	−0.3	−4.1	−5.7
2014	−7.3	−2.6	−3.4	−6.7
2015	−4.9	−3.8	−14.4	−7.6
2016	−12.6	−3.3	−0.9	−4.0
2017	−1.2	−3.4	−1.0	+0.6
2018	−5.3	−9.7	−4.5*	
Totals	**−348.9%**	**−353.3%**	**−473.6%**	**−472.9%**
Average	**−6.3%**	**−6.4%**	**−8.6%**	**−8.8%**

* As of 7/6/2018

SEPTEMBER 2019

MONDAY
D 61.9
S 52.4
N 57.1

9

If you can buy more of your best idea, why put [the money] into your 10th-best idea or your 20th-best idea? The more positions you have, the more average you are.
— Bruce Berkowitz (Fairholme Fund, *Barron's*, 3/17/08)

TUESDAY
D 52.4
S 57.1
N 57.1

10

Don't be scared to take big steps—you can't cross a chasm in two small jumps.
— David Lloyd George (British Prime Minister, 1916–1922)

WEDNESDAY
D 66.7
S 66.7
N 61.9

11

2001 4-Day Closing,
Longest Since 9-Day Banking Moratorium in March 1933

"In Memory"

Fortune favors the brave.
— Virgil (Roman Poet, *Aeneid*, 70–19 B.C.)

THURSDAY
D 57.1
S 61.9
N 66.7

12

The four most expensive words in the English language, "This time it's different."
— Sir John Templeton (Founder, Templeton Funds, philanthropist, 1912–2008)

FRIDAY
D 47.6
S 52.4
N 76.2

13

In an uptrend, if a higher high is made but fails to carry through, and prices dip below the previous high, the trend is apt to reverse. The converse is true for downtrends.
— Victor Sperandeo (*Trader Vic—Methods of a Wall Street Master*)

SATURDAY

14

SUNDAY

15

FIRST-TRADING-DAY-OF-THE-MONTH PHENOMENON

While the Dow Jones Industrial Average has gained 17012.79 points between September 2, 1997 (7622.42) and June 1, 2018 (24635.21), it is incredible that 6763.40 points were gained on the first trading days of these 250 months. The remaining 4972 trading days combined gained 10249.39 points during the period. This averages out to gains of 27.05 points on first days, in contrast to just 2.06 points on all others.

Note September 1997 through October 2000 racked up a total gain of 2632.39 Dow points on the first trading days of these 38 months (winners except for 7 occasions). But between November 2000 and September 2002, when the 2000–2002 bear markets did the bulk of their damage, frightened investors switched from pouring money into the market on that day to pulling it out, 14 months out of 23, netting a 404.80 Dow point loss. The 2007–2009 bear market lopped off 964.14 Dow points on first days in 17 months November 2007–March 2009. First days had their worst year in 2014, declining eight times for a total loss of 820.86 Dow points.

First days of August have performed worst, declining 13 times in the last 20 years. May's first trading day is best. In rising market trends, first days tend to perform much better, as institutions are likely anticipating strong performance at each month's outset. S&P 500 first days differ slightly from Dow's pattern, with October a loser. NASDAQ first days are not as strong, with weakness in April, August and October.

DOW POINTS GAINED FIRST DAY OF MONTH
SEPTEMBER 1997–JUNE 1, 2018

	Jan	Feb	Mar	Apr	May	Jun	Jul	Aug	Sep	Oct	Nov	Dec	Totals
1997									257.36	70.24	232.31	189.98	**749.89**
1998	56.79	201.28	4.73	68.51	83.70	22.42	96.65	−96.55	288.36	−210.09	114.05	16.99	**646.84**
1999	2.84	−13.13	18.20	46.35	225.65	36.52	95.62	−9.19	108.60	−63.95	−81.35	120.58	**486.74**
2000	−139.61	100.52	9.62	300.01	77.87	129.87	112.78	84.97	23.68	49.21	−71.67	−40.95	**636.30**
2001	−140.70	96.27	−45.14	−100.85	163.37	78.47	91.32	−12.80	47.74	−10.73	188.76	−87.60	**268.11**
2002	51.90	−12.74	262.73	−41.24	113.41	−215.46	−133.47	−229.97	−355.45	346.86	120.61	−33.52	**−126.34**
2003	265.89	56.01	−53.22	77.73	−25.84	47.55	55.51	−79.83	107.45	194.14	57.34	116.59	**819.32**
2004	−44.07	11.11	94.22	15.63	88.43	14.20	−101.32	39.45	−5.46	112.38	26.92	162.20	**413.69**
2005	−53.58	62.00	63.77	−99.46	59.19	82.39	28.47	−17.76	−21.97	−33.22	−33.30	106.70	**143.23**
2006	129.91	89.09	60.12	35.62	−23.85	91.97	77.80	−59.95	83.00	−8.72	−49.71	−27.80	**397.48**
2007	11.37	51.99	−34.29	27.95	73.23	40.47	126.81	150.38	91.12	191.92	−362.14	−57.15	**311.66**
2008	−220.86	92.83	−7.49	391.47	189.87	−134.50	32.25	−51.70	−26.63	−19.59	−5.18	−679.95	**−439.48**
2009	258.30	−64.03	−299.64	152.68	44.29	221.11	57.06	114.95	−185.68	−203.00	76.71	126.74	**299.49**
2010	155.91	118.20	78.53	70.44	143.22	−112.61	−41.49	208.44	254.75	41.63	6.13	249.76	**1172.91**
2011	93.24	148.23	−168.32	56.99	−3.18	−279.65	168.43	−10.75	−119.96	−258.08	−297.05	−25.65	**−695.75**
2012	179.82	83.55	28.23	52.45	65.69	−274.88	−8.70	−37.62	−54.90	77.98	136.16	−59.98	**187.80**
2013	308.41	149.21	35.17	−5.69	−138.85	138.46	65.36	128.48	23.65	62.03	69.80	−77.64	**758.39**
2014	−135.31	−326.05	−153.68	74.95	−21.97	26.46	129.47	−69.93	−30.89	−238.19	−24.28	−51.44	**−820.86**
2015	9.92	196.09	155.93	−77.94	185.54	29.69	138.40	−91.66	−469.68	−11.99	165.22	168.43	**395.95**
2016	−276.09	−17.12	348.58	107.66	117.52	2.47	19.38	−27.73	18.42	−54.30	−105.32	68.35	**201.82**
2017	119.16	26.85	303.31	−13.01	−27.05	135.53	129.64	72.80	39.46	152.51	57.77	−40.76	**956.21**
2018	104.79	37.32	−420.22	−458.92	−64.10	219.37							**−581.76**
Totals	**738.03**	**1087.48**	**281.14**	**681.33**	**1324.14**	**299.85**	**1139.97**	**4.03**	**72.97**	**187.04**	**221.78**	**143.88**	**6181.64**

SUMMARY FIRST DAYS VS. OTHER DAYS OF MONTH

	# of Days	Total Points Gained	Average Daily Point Gain
First days	250	6763.40	27.05
Other days	4972	10249.39	2.06

SEPTEMBER 2019

Monday Before September Triple Witching, Russell 2000 Down 11 of Last 19

MONDAY
16

D 57.1
S 52.4
N 38.1

To find one man in a thousand who is your true friend from unselfish motives is to find one of the great wonders of the world.
— Leopold Mozart (Quoted by Maynard Solomon, *Mozart*)

FOMC Meeting (2 Days)

TUESDAY
17

D 76.2
S 76.2
N 76.2

Short-term volatility is greatest at turning points and diminishes as a trend becomes established.
— George Soros (Financier, philanthropist, political activist, author and philosopher, b. 1930)

Expiration Week 2001, Dow Lost 1370 Points (14.3%)
3rd Worst Weekly Point Loss Ever, 5th Worst Week Overall

WEDNESDAY
18

D 42.9
S 47.6
N 52.4

The game is lost only when we stop trying.
— Mario Cuomo (Former New York governor, *C-Span*)

THURSDAY
19

D 61.9
S 52.4
N 57.1

Bill Gates' One-Minus Staffing: For every project, figure out the bare minimum of people needed to staff it. Cut to the absolute muscle and bones, then take out one more. When you understaff, people jump on the loose ball. You find out who the real performers are. Not so when you're overstaffed. People sit around waiting for somebody else to do it.
— Quoted by Rich Karlgaard (Publisher, *Forbes*, 12/25/00)

September Triple Witching, Dow Up 11 of Last 16

FRIDAY
20

D 52.4
S 42.9
N 47.6

We go to the movies to be entertained, not see rape, ransacking, pillage and looting. We can get all that in the stock market.
— Kennedy Gammage (*The Richland Report*)

SATURDAY
21

SUNDAY
22

MARKET BEHAVIOR THREE DAYS BEFORE AND THREE DAYS AFTER HOLIDAYS

The *Stock Trader's Almanac* has tracked holiday seasonality annually since the first edition in 1968. Stocks used to rise on the day before holidays and sell off the day after, but nowadays, each holiday moves to its own rhythm. Eight holidays are separated into seven groups. Average percentage changes for the Dow, S&P 500, NASDAQ, and Russell 2000 are shown.

The Dow and S&P consist of blue chips and the largest cap stocks, whereas NASDAQ and the Russell 2000 would be more representative of smaller-cap stocks. This is evident on the last day of the year, with NASDAQ and the Russell 2000 having a field day, while their larger brethren in the Dow and S&P are showing losses on average.

Thanks to the Santa Claus Rally, the three days before and after New Year's Day and Christmas are best. NASDAQ and the Russell 2000 average gains of 1.1% to 1.6% over the six-day spans. However, trading around the first day of the year has been mixed recently. Traders have been selling more the first trading day of the year, pushing gains and losses into the New Year.

Bullishness before Labor Day and after Memorial Day is affected by strength the first day of September and June. The second worst day after a holiday is the day after Easter. Surprisingly, the following day is one of the best second days after a holiday, right up there with the second day after New Year's Day.

Presidents' Day is the least bullish of all the holidays, bearish the day before and three days after. NASDAQ has dropped 20 of the last 29 days before Presidents' Day (Dow, 16 of 29; S&P, 18 of 29; Russell 2000, 14 of 29).

HOLIDAYS: 3 DAYS BEFORE, 3 DAYS AFTER (Average % change 1980–June 2018)

	−3	−2	−1	Mixed	+1	+2	+3
S&P 500	0.03	0.19	−0.14	**New Year's**	0.21	0.29	−0.001
DJIA	0.001	0.15	−0.20	**Day**	0.30	0.28	0.10
NASDAQ	0.09	0.23	0.12	*1/1/19*	0.22	0.56	0.12
Russell 2K	0.07	0.34	0.36		0.04	0.23	0.02
S&P 500	0.36	0.05	−0.13	**Negative Before & After**	−0.15	−0.05	−0.12
DJIA	0.32	0.04	−0.07	**Presidents'**	−0.10	−0.08	−0.12
NASDAQ	0.57	0.31	−0.27	**Day**	−0.43	−0.03	−0.09
Russell 2K	0.44	0.19	−0.03	*2/18/19*	−0.30	−0.15	−0.07
S&P 500	0.12	−0.07	0.38	**Positive Before &**	−0.22	0.33	0.13
DJIA	0.10	−0.09	0.29	***Negative After***	−0.14	0.32	0.12
NASDAQ	0.30	0.16	0.49	**Good Friday**	−0.34	0.37	0.24
Russell 2K	0.16	0.02	0.49	*4/19/19*	−0.33	0.28	0.16
S&P 500	0.06	0.06	0.001	***Positive After***	0.26	0.14	0.24
DJIA	0.05	0.01	−0.06	**Memorial**	0.29	0.13	0.14
NASDAQ	0.13	0.24	0.05	**Day**	0.23	0.01	0.46
Russell 2K	−0.03	0.29	0.11	*5/27/19*	0.24	0.08	0.42
S&P 500	0.16	0.13	0.07	**Negative After**	−0.15	0.04	0.05
DJIA	0.13	0.13	0.09	**Independence**	−0.09	0.07	0.03
NASDAQ	0.29	0.14	0.06	**Day**	−0.16	−0.01	0.20
Russell 2K	0.32	0.05	0.01	*7/4/19*	−0.27	−0.05	0.04
S&P 500	0.21	−0.18	0.14	***Positive Before & After***	0.10	0.07	−0.07
DJIA	0.17	−0.24	0.14	**Labor**	0.11	0.12	−0.16
NASDAQ	0.43	0.020	0.15	**Day**	0.04	−0.05	0.08
Russell 2K	0.51	0.06	0.13	*9/2/19*	0.09	0.13	0.03
S&P 500	0.15	0.03	0.24	**Thanksgiving**	0.19	−0.43	0.32
DJIA	0.15	0.04	0.25	*11/28/19*	0.16	−0.36	0.34
NASDAQ	0.11	−0.16	0.39		0.44	−0.44	0.15
Russell 2K	0.19	−0.02	0.38		0.30	−0.52	0.30
S&P 500	0.18	0.21	0.20	**Christmas**	0.14	0.002	0.25
DJIA	0.26	0.24	0.25	*12/25/19*	0.17	0.01	0.22
NASDAQ	−0.05	0.40	0.38		0.11	0.05	0.29
Russell 2K	0.24	0.36	0.35		0.19	0.05	0.42

End of September Prone to Weakness
From End-of-Q3 Institutional Portfolio Restructuring

MONDAY

D 23.8
S 28.6
N 42.9

23

Q. What kind of grad students do you take? A. I never take a straight-A student. A real scientist
tends to be critical, and somewhere along the line, they had to rebel against their teachers.
— Lynn Margulis (University of Massachusetts science professor, *The Scientist*, 6/30/03)

Week After September Triple-Witching Dow Down 21 of Last 28
Average Loss Since 1990, 1.0%

TUESDAY

D 33.3
S 33.3
N 38.1

24

To achieve satisfactory investment results is easier than most people realize.
The typical individual investor has a great advantage over the large institutions.
— Benjamin Graham (Economist, investor, *Securities Analysis* 1934, *The Intelligent Investor*, 1949, 1894–1976)

WEDNESDAY

D 52.4
S 47.6
N 47.6

25

It was never my thinking that made the big money for me. It was always my sitting. Got that? My sitting tight!
— Jesse Livermore (Early 20th century stock trader and speculator, *How to Trade in Stocks*, 1877–1940)

Start Looking for MACD Buy Signals on October 1 (Pages 52, 56 and 60)
Almanac Investor Subscribers Emailed When It Triggers (See Insert)

THURSDAY

D 66.7
S 66.7
N 47.6

26

The single best predictor of overall excellence is a company's ability to attract, motivate, and retain talented people.
— Bruce Pfau (Vice chair, human resources, KPMG, *Fortune*, 1998)

FRIDAY

D 57.1
S 61.9
N 42.9

27

A loss never bothers me after I take it. I forget it overnight. But being wrong—not taking the loss—
that is what does damage to the pocketbook and to the soul.
— Jesse Livermore (Early 20th century stock trader and speculator, *How to Trade in Stocks*, 1877–1940)

SATURDAY

28

October Almanac Investor Sector Seasonalities: See Pages 92, 94 and 96

SUNDAY

29

OCTOBER ALMANAC

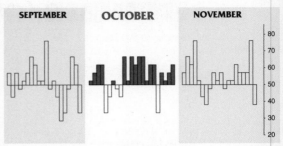

OCTOBER						
S	M	T	W	T	F	S
		1	2	3	4	5
6	7	8	9	10	11	12
13	14	15	16	17	18	19
20	21	22	23	24	25	26
27	28	29	30	31		

NOVEMBER						
S	M	T	W	T	F	S
					1	2
3	4	5	6	7	8	9
10	11	12	13	14	15	16
17	18	19	20	21	22	23
24	25	26	27	28	29	30

Market Probability Chart above is a graphic representation of the S&P 500 Recent Market Probability Calendar on page 124.

◆ Known as the jinx month because of crashes in 1929 and 1987, the 554-point drop on October 27, 1997, back-to-back massacres in 1978 and 1979, Friday the 13th in 1989, and the meltdown in 2008 ◆ Yet October is a "bear killer" and turned the tide in 12 post–WWII bear markets: 1946, 1957, 1960, 1962, 1966, 1974, 1987, 1990, 1998, 2001, 2002 and 2011 ◆ First October Dow top in 2007, 20-year 1987 Crash anniversary –2.6% ◆ Worst six months of the year ends with October (page 52) ◆ No longer worst month (pages 50 & 58) ◆ Best Dow, S&P, and NASDAQ month from 1993 to 2007 ◆ Pre–presidential election year Octobers since 1950: #11 Dow (0.5%), #12 S&P (0.9%) and #12 NASDAQ (0.9%) ◆ October is a great time to buy ◆ Big October gains five years 1999–2003 after atrocious Septembers ◆ Can get into Best Six Months earlier using MACD (page 56) ◆ October 2011, second month to gain 1000 Dow points, and again in 2015.

October Vital Statistics

	DJIA		S&P 500		NASDAQ		Russell 1K		Russell 2K	
Rank	7		7		7		7		10	
Up	41		41		26		25		22	
Down	27		27		21		14		17	
Average % Change	0.7%		0.9%		0.8%		1.0%		–0.3%	
Pre-Election Year	–0.5%		0.1%		0.1%		0.2%		–1.9%	
Best & Worst October										
	% Change		% Change		% Change		% Change		% Change	
Best	1982	10.7	1974	16.3	1974	17.2	1982	11.3	2011	15.0
Worst	1987	–23.2	1987	–21.8	1987	–27.2	1987	–21.9	1987	–30.8
Best & Worst October Weeks										
Best	10/11/74	12.6	10/11/74	14.1	10/31/08	10.9	10/31/08	10.8	10/31/08	14.1
Worst	10/10/08	–18.2	10/10/08	–18.2	10/23/08	–19.2	10/10/08	–18.2	10/23/87	–20.4
Best & Worst October Days										
Best	10/13/08	11.1	10/13/08	11.6	10/13/08	11.8	10/13/08	11.7	10/13/08	9.3
Worst	10/19/87	–22.6	10/19/87	–20.5	10/19/87	–11.4	10/19/87	–19.0	10/19/87	–12.5
First Trading Day of Expiration Week: 1980–2017										
Record (#Up – #Down)	30–8		28–10		26–12		29–9		27–11	
Current Streak	U1		U1		U1		U1		U1	
Avg % Change	0.70		0.66		0.53		0.63		0.38	
Options Expiration Day: 1980–2017										
Record (#Up – #Down)	18–20		20–18		22–16		20–18		16–22	
Current Streak	U1		U1		U5		U1		U1	
Avg % Change	–0.13		–0.19		–0.09		–0.18		–0.17	
Options Expiration Week: 1980–2017										
Record (#Up – #Down)	27–11		27–11		22–16		27–11		23–15	
Current Streak	U3		U3		U3		U3		U2	
Avg % Change	0.63		0.66		0.70		0.65		0.41	
Week After Options Expiration: 1980–2017										
Record (#Up – #Down)	19–19		17–21		20–18		17–21		17–21	
Current Streak	U5		U1		U1		U1		D2	
Avg % Change	–0.28		–0.31		–0.29		–0.33		–0.59	
First Trading Day Performance										
% of Time Up	48.5		50.0		48.9		53.8		48.7	
Avg % Change	0.06		0.05		–0.14		0.21		–0.22	
Last Trading Day Performance										
% of Time Up	52.9		54.4		63.8		64.1		71.8	
Avg % Change	0.06		0.14		0.48		0.33		0.60	

Dow & S&P 1950–June 2018, NASDAQ 1971–June 2018, Russell 1K & 2K 1979–June 2018.

October has killed many a bear,
Buy techs and small caps and soon wear a grin ear to ear.

SEPTEMBER/OCTOBER 2019

Last Day of Q3, Dow Down 14 of Last 21, Massive 4.7% Rally in 2008

Rosh Hashanah

MONDAY

D 33.3
S 33.3
N 38.1

30

Take care of your employees and they'll take care of your customers.
— John W. Marriott (Founder, Marriott International, 1900–1985)

First Trading Day in October, Dow Down 8 of Last 13, Off 2.4% in 2011

TUESDAY

D 47.6
S 52.4
N 47.6

1

The reasonable man adapts himself to the world; the unreasonable one persists in trying to adapt the world to himself.
Therefore, all progress depends on the unreasonable man.
— George Bernard Shaw (Irish dramatist, 1856–1950)

WEDNESDAY

D 52.4
S 57.1
N 61.9

2

One determined person can make a significant difference;
a small group of determined people can change the course of history.
— Sonia Johnson (author, lecturer)

October Ends Dow and S&P "Worst Six Months" (Pages 52, 56, 62 and 147)
And NASDAQ "Worst Four Months" (Pages 58, 60 and 148)

THURSDAY

D 61.9
S 61.9
N 71.4

3

It's not that I am so smart; it's just that I stay with problems longer.
— Albert Einstein (German/American physicist, 1921 Nobel Prize winner, 1879–1955)

FRIDAY

D 66.7
S 61.9
N 57.1

4

It's no coincidence that three of the top five stock option traders in a recent trading contest were all former Marines.
— Robert Prechter Jr. (Elliott Wave Theorist)

SATURDAY

5

SUNDAY

6

SECTOR SEASONALITY: SELECTED PERCENTAGE PLAYS

Sector seasonality was featured in the first *Almanac* in 1968. A Merrill Lynch study showed that buying seven sectors around September or October and selling in the first few months of 1954–1964 tripled the gains of holding them for 10 years. Over the years we have honed this strategy significantly and now devote a large portion of our time and resources to investing and trading during positive and negative seasonal periods for different sectors with Exchange Traded Funds (ETFs).

Updated seasonalities appear in the table below. Under "Ticker" we list the most commonly used symbol for each sector index. Industrials (S5INDU) have been added this year. We specify whether the seasonality starts or finishes in the beginning third (B), middle third (M), or last third (E) of the month. These selected percentage plays are geared to take advantage of the bulk of seasonal sector strength or weakness.

By design, entry points are in advance of the major seasonal moves, providing traders ample opportunity to accumulate positions at favorable prices. Conversely, exit points have been selected to capture the majority of the move.

From the major seasonalities in the table below, we created the Sector Index Seasonality Strategy Calendar on pages 94 and 96. Note the concentration of bullish sector seasonalities during the Best Six Months, November to April, and bearish sector seasonalities during the Worst Six Months, May to October.

Almanac Investor eNewsletter subscribers receive specific entry and exit points for highly correlated ETFs and detailed analysis in ETF Trades Alerts. Visit *www.stocktradersalmanac.com*, or see the ad insert for additional details and a special offer for new subscribers.

SECTOR INDEX SEASONALITY TABLE

Ticker	Sector Index	Type	Seasonality Start		Finish		Average % Return[†] 15-Year	10-Year	5-Year
XCI	Computer Tech	Short	January	B	March	B	−3.8	−1.0	1.5
XNG	Natural Gas	Long	February	E	June	B	13.8	14.1	15.6
MSH	High-Tech	Long	March	M	July	B	9.3	7.3	6.7
UTY	Utilities	Long	March	M	October	B	8.3	5.5	3.2
XCI	Computer Tech	Long	April	M	July	M	7.6	6.8	9.3
BKX	Banking	Short	May	B	July	B	−6.8	−9.6	0.3
XAU	Gold & Silver	Short	May	M	June	E	−5.5	−6.8	−8.2
S5MATR	Materials	Short	May	M	October	M	−2.6	−4.8	−2.2
XNG	Natural Gas	Short	June	M	July	E	−4.6	−5.6	−5.6
XAU	Gold & Silver	Long	July	E	December	E	7.8	−1.6	−11.1
S5INDU	Industrials	Short	July	M	October	B	−3.0	−4.9	−3.4
DJT	Transports	Short	July	M	October	M	−2.7	−3.4	−2.0
BTK	Biotech	Long	August	B	March	B	16.7	16.8	18.0
MSH	High-Tech	Long	August	M	January	M	12.5	9.3	10.8
SOX	Semiconductor	Short	August	M	October	E	−3.0	−3.4	3.0
XOI	Oil	Short	September	B	November	E	−2.6	−3.6	−0.4
BKX	Banking	Long	October	B	May	B	10.9	15.1	11.9
XBD	Broker/Dealer	Long	October	B	April	M	15.3	18.3	15.8
XCI	Computer Tech	Long	October	B	January	B	9.3	9.0	9.4
S5COND	Consumer Discretionary	Long	October	B	June	B	13.6	17.4	14.0
S5CONS	Consumer Staples	Long	October	B	June	B	8.5	8.7	7.6
S5HLTH	Healthcare	Long	October	B	May	B	9.4	11.6	9.2
S5INDU	Industrials	Long	October	E	May	M	11.0	11.9	7.8
S5MATR	Materials	Long	October	B	May	B	15.1	14.2	11.5
DRG	Pharmaceutical	Long	October	M	January	B	6.0	6.4	5.3
RMZ	Real Estate	Long	October	E	May	B	10.1	11.4	4.1
SOX	Semiconductor	Long	October	E	December	B	8.9	8.0	7.8
XTC	Telecom	Long	October	M	December	E	5.0	4.4	3.7
DJT	Transports	Long	October	B	May	B	16.0	15.9	9.8
XOI	Oil	Long	December	M	July	B	10.8	5.6	7.8

[†] *Average % Return based on full seasonality completion through May 4, 2018*

OCTOBER 2019

Executives owe it to the organization and to their fellow workers not to tolerate nonperforming individuals in important jobs.
— Peter Drucker (Austrian-born pioneer management theorist, 1909–2005)

Prosperity is a great teacher; adversity a greater.
— William Hazlitt (English essayist, 1778–1830)

Yom Kippur

Every successful enterprise requires three people—a dreamer, a businessman, and a son-of-a-bitch.
— Peter McArthur (1904)

Dow Lost 1874 Points (18.2%) on the Week Ending 10/10/08
Worst Dow Week in the History of Wall Street

Based on my own personal experience—both as an investor in recent years and an expert witness in years past—rarely do more than three or four variables really count. Everything else is noise.
— Martin J. Whitman (Founder, Third Avenue Funds, 1924–2018)

Those who cast the votes decide nothing. Those who count the votes decide everything.
— Joseph Stalin (Ruler, USSR, 1929–1953, 1879–1953)

SECTOR INDEX SEASONALITY STRATEGY CALENDAR*

* Graphic representation of the Sector Index Seasonality Percentage Plays on page 92.
L = Long Trade, S = Short Trade, ➝ = Start of Trade

(continued on page 96)

94

Columbus Day *(Bond Market Closed)*
Monday Before October Expiration, Dow Up 29 of 37

MONDAY
D 71.4
S 66.7
N 71.4
14

Doubt is the father of invention.
— Galileo Galilei (Italian physicist and astronomer, 1564–1642)

TUESDAY
D 52.4
S 52.4
N 47.6
15

*Most people have no idea of the giant capacity we can immediately command when we focus
all of our resources on mastering a single area of our lives.*
— Anthony Robbins (Motivator, advisor, consultant, author, entrepreneur, philanthropist, b. 1960)

October 2011, Second Dow Month to Gain 1000 Points

WEDNESDAY
D 57.1
S 66.7
N 57.1
16

In this age of instant information, investors can experience both fear and greed at the exact same moment.
— Sam Stovall (Chief Investment Strategist, CFRA, October 2003)

Crash of October 19, 1987, Dow Down 22.6% in One Day

THURSDAY
D 52.4
S 61.9
N 52.4
17

*The average man desires to be told specifically which particular stock to buy or sell.
He wants to get something for nothing. He does not wish to work.*
— William LeFevre (Senior analyst, Ehrenkrantz King Nussbaum, 1928–1997)

October Expiration Day, Dow Down 6 Straight 2005–2010 and 9 of Last 15

FRIDAY
D 61.9
S 66.7
N 61.9
18

I was in search of a one-armed economist so that the guy could never make a statement and then say: "on the other hand."
— Harry S. Truman (33rd U.S. President, 1884–1972)

SATURDAY
19

SUNDAY
20

(continued from page 94)

SECTOR INDEX SEASONALITY STRATEGY CALENDAR*

* Graphic representation of the Sector Index Seasonality Percentage Plays on page 92.
L = Long Trade, S = Short Trade, ——➤ = Start of Trade

96

MONDAY
D 57.1
S 66.7
N 52.4
21

Capitalism is the legitimate racket of the ruling class.
— Al Capone (American gangster, 1899–1947)

TUESDAY
D 42.9
S 52.4
N 47.6
22

I will never knowingly buy any company that has a real-time quote of their stock price in the building lobby.
— Robert Mahan (A trader commenting on Enron)

Late October Is Time to Buy Depressed Stocks
Especially Techs and Small Caps

WEDNESDAY
D 57.1
S 61.9
N 61.9
23

The greatest lie ever told: Build a better mousetrap and the world will beat a path to your door.
— Yale Hirsch (Creator of *Stock Trader's Almanac*, b. 1923)

THURSDAY
D 57.1
S 61.9
N 52.4
24

Love your enemies, for they tell you your faults.
— Benjamin Franklin (U.S. Founding Father, diplomat, inventor, 1706–1790)

FRIDAY
D 33.3
S 33.3
N 42.9
25

When new money is created on a grand scale, it must go somewhere and have some major consequences.
One of these will be greatly increased volatility and instability in the economy and financial system.
— J. Anthony Boeckh, Ph.D. (Chairman, Bank Credit Analyst, 1968–2002, *The Great Reflation, Boeckh Investment Letter*)

SATURDAY
26

November Almanac Investor Sector Seasonalities: See Pages 92, 94 and 96

SUNDAY
27

NOVEMBER ALMANAC

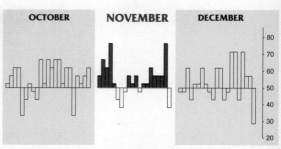

NOVEMBER								DECEMBER						
S	M	T	W	T	F	S		S	M	T	W	T	F	S
					1	2		1	2	3	4	5	6	7
3	4	5	6	7	8	9		8	9	10	11	12	13	14
10	11	12	13	14	15	16		15	16	17	18	19	20	21
17	18	19	20	21	22	23		22	23	24	25	26	27	28
24	25	26	27	28	29	30		29	30	31				

Market Probability Chart above is a graphic representation of the S&P 500 Recent Market Probability Calendar on page 124.

◆ #2 S&P and #3 Dow month since 1950, #3 on NASDAQ since 1971 (pages 50 & 58) ◆ Start of the "Best Six Months" of the year (page 52), NASDAQ's Best Eight Months and Best Three (pages 147 & 148) ◆ Simple timing indicator almost triples "Best Six Months" strategy (page 56), doubles NASDAQ's Best Eight (page 60) ◆ Day before and after Thanksgiving Day combined, only 15 losses in 66 years (page 104) ◆ Week before Thanksgiving Dow up 19 of last 25 ◆ Pre–presidential election year Novembers rank #9 Dow, S&P and NASDAQ.

November Vital Statistics

	DJIA		S&P 500		NASDAQ		Russell 1K		Russell 2K	
Rank	3		2		3		1		2	
Up	46		46		32		29		26	
Down	22		22		15		10		13	
Average % Change	1.6%		1.5%		1.6%		1.7%		2.1%	
Pre-Election Year	0.3%		0.3%		0.9%		−0.2%		1.2%	
	Best & Worst November									
	% Change		% Change		% Change		% Change		% Change	
Best	1962	10.1	1980	10.2	2001	14.2	1980	10.1	2002	8.8
Worst	1973	−14.0	1973	−11.4	2000	−22.9	2000	−9.3	2008	−12.0
	Best & Worst November Weeks									
Best	11/28/08	9.7	11/28/08	12.0	11/28/08	10.9	11/28/08	12.5	11/28/08	16.4
Worst	11/21/08	−5.3	11/21/08	−8.4	11/10/08	−12.2	11/21/08	−8.8	11/21/08	−11.0
	Best & Worst November Days									
Best	11/13/08	6.7	11/13/08	6.9	11/13/08	6.5	11/13/08	7.0	11/13/08	8.5
Worst	11/20/08	−5.6	11/20/08	−6.7	11/19/08	−6.5	11/20/08	−6.9	11/19/08	−7.9
	First Trading Day of Expiration Week: 1980–2017									
Record (#Up – #Down)	21–17		18–20		15–23		20–18		17–21	
Current Streak	U5		U1		U1		U6		D1	
Avg % Change	0.001		−0.03		−0.12		−0.04		−0.06	
	Options Expiration Day: 1980–2017									
Record (#Up – #Down)	24–14		22–16		20–18		22–16		21–16	
Current Streak	D2		D2		D2		D2		U8	
Avg % Change	0.22		0.16		0.03		0.15		0.15	
	Options Expiration Week: 1980–2017									
Record (#Up – #Down)	25–13		23–15		21–17		22–16		20–18	
Current Streak	D1		D1		U5		D1		U3	
Avg % Change	0.33		0.13		0.11		0.11		−0.12	
	Week After Options Expiration: 1980–2017									
Record (#Up – #Down)	23–15		25–13		26–12		25–13		24–14	
Current Streak	U2		U6		U6		U6		U6	
Avg % Change	0.70		0.69		0.82		0.69		0.87	
	First Trading Day Performance									
% of Time Up	63.2		63.2		63.8		71.8		59.0	
Avg % Change	0.27		0.29		0.28		0.37		0.17	
	Last Trading Day Performance									
% of Time Up	55.9		52.9		63.8		46.2		66.7	
Avg % Change	0.12		0.13		−0.08		0.02		0.14	

Dow & S&P 1950–June 2018, NASDAQ 1971–June 2018, Russell 1K & 2K 1979–June 2018.

Astute investors always smile and remember,
When stocks seasonally start soaring, and salute November.

OCTOBER/NOVEMBER 2019

MONDAY
D 66.7
S 57.1
N 47.6
28

Selling a soybean contract short is worth two years at the Harvard Business School.
— Robert Stovall (Managing director, Wood Asset Management, b. 1926)

88th Anniversary of 1929 Crash, Dow Down 23.0% in 2 Days, October 28 & 29
FOMC Meeting (2 Days)

TUESDAY
D 61.9
S 52.4
N 57.1
29

Inflation is the modern way that governments default on their debt.
— Mike Epstein (MTA, MIT/Sloan Lab for Financial Engineering)

WEDNESDAY
D 57.1
S 57.1
N 52.4
30

We are all born originals; why is it so many die copies?
— Edward Young (English poet, 1683–1765)

Halloween

THURSDAY
D 57.1
S 61.9
N 61.9
31

When Amercia sneezes, the rest of the word catches cold.
— Anonymous (circa 1929)

First Trading Day in November, Dow Down 7 of Last 13

FRIDAY
D 57.1
S 57.1
N 61.9
1

My best shorts come from research reports where there are recommendations to buy stocks
on weakness; also, where a brokerage firm changes its recommendation from a buy to a hold.
— Marc Howard (Hedge fund manager, *New York Magazine*, 1976, b. 1941)

SATURDAY
2

Daylight Saving Time Ends

SUNDAY
3

BEST INVESTMENT BOOK OF THE YEAR

Big Mistakes: The Best Investors and Their Worst Investments
By Michael Batnick, CFA

One of the first things my father, Yale Hirsch, creator of the *Almanac* (still kicking at 94!), taught me way back even before I came on board full-time to work for him in 1990 was the importance of learning from your mistakes, especially when it comes to the market and investing. In fact, page 189 in the back of the *Almanac*, titled, "If You Don't Profit from Your Investment Mistakes, Someone Else Will," has been a fixture since the beginning. Learning from our own mistakes has been vital to the continuing development and legacy of the *Stock Trader's Almanac*, our related online advisory service and our overall investment strategy.

Michael Batnick, Director of Research at Ritholtz Wealth Management, has staked another claim to Best Investment Book authorship fame for the prolific team at this top-rated RIA firm. In *Big Mistakes* Batnick boldly goes where most investment books won't get near. Instead of fawning over how brilliant these market wizards are or were, he dissects their biggest mistakes and worst trades. On top of what these big-time investors did to overcome these blunders, he layers his insights and analysis into clear and succinct lessons we can all use to improve our investment results and avoid similar mistakes.

When I am asked what's the one most important thing to know about investing, I tell people that emotion is an investor's worst enemy, sell your losers short and let your winners ride. Investing is a perpetual learning process and learning from your own investment mistakes is vital, but learning from the mistakes of others is priceless, literally, because you did not have any skin in the game. In *Big Mistakes* Batnick has done the heavy lifting for us. He examines the mental lapses of fifteen famous successful investors, the trades where they let their emotions, hubris and egos get the best of them and how the lessons they learned help hone their skills and improve their strategies.

Big Mistakes runs the gamut of failures from old-time investors like Jesse Livermore, Benjamin Graham, Mark Twain and John Maynard Keynes to more contemporary misfortunes from Bill Ackman, John Paulson and Chris Sacca. Sacca, the notorious venture capitalist, passed on Airbnb, Snapchat and Dropbox. Batnick also covers Warren Buffett's overconfident Dexter Shoe debacle; how leverage, ego and hubris destroyed Livermore and Long-Term Capital Management; and a host of other wisdom for the ages.

The bottom line, Batnick concludes, is that investing is super hard and even the best make huge mistakes. The key here and what Batnick does a superb job of focusing on and conveying simply is what lessons were learned and how to recover from these major errors. *Big Mistakes* is an extremely readable, informative and captivating book. This is not a new concept, but it is a critical one to adhere to, and Batnick does us all a service by reinforcing these investing truths.

Bloomberg Press, $34.95. **2019 Best Investment Book of the Year**.

NOVEMBER 2019

November Begins Dow and S&P "Best Six Months" (Pages 52, 56, 60, 62 and 147) and NASDAQ "Best Eight Months" (Pages 58, 60 and 148)

MONDAY

D 57.1
S 66.7
N 61.9

4

History must repeat itself because we pay such little attention to it the first time.
— Blackie Sherrod (Sportswriter, 1919–2016)

Election Day

TUESDAY

D 61.9
S 61.9
N 66.7

5

A president is elected and tries to get rid of the dirty stuff in the economy as quickly as possible, so that by the time the next election comes around, he looks like a hero. The stock market is reacting to what the politicians are doing.
— Yale Hirsch (Creator of *Stock Trader's Almanac, New York Times*, 10/10/10, b. 1923)

WEDNESDAY

D 76.2
S 76.2
N 66.7

6

Thomas Alva Edison said, "Genius is 5% inspiration and 95% perspiration!" Unfortunately, many startup "genius" entrepreneurs mistakenly switch the two percentages around, and then wonder why they can't get their projects off the ground.
— Yale Hirsch (Creator of *Stock Trader's Almanac*, b. 1923)

THURSDAY

D 61.9
S 52.4
N 57.1

7

Throughout the centuries there were men who took first steps down new roads armed with nothing but their own vision.
— Ayn Rand (Russian-born American novelist and philosopher, *The Fountainhead*, 1957, 1905–1982)

FRIDAY

D 47.6
S 42.9
N 52.4

8

As for it being different this time, it is different every time. The question is in what way, and to what extent.
— Tom McClellan (*The McClellan Market Report*)

SATURDAY

9

SUNDAY

10

FOURTH-QUARTER MARKET MAGIC

Examining market performance on a quarterly basis reveals several intriguing and helpful patterns. Fourth-quarter market gains have been magical, providing the greatest and most consistent gains over the years. First-quarter performance runs a respectable second. This should not be surprising, as cash inflows, trading volume, and buying bias are generally elevated during these two quarters.

Positive market psychology hits a fever pitch as the holiday season approaches, and does not begin to wane until spring. Professionals drive the market higher, as they make portfolio adjustments to maximize year-end numbers. Bonuses are paid and invested around the turn of the year.

The market's sweet spot of the four-year cycle begins in the fourth quarter of the midterm year. The best two-quarter span runs from the fourth quarter of the midterm year through the first quarter of the pre-election year, averaging 14.6% for the Dow, 15.4% for the S&P 500 and an amazing 22.0% for NASDAQ. Pre-election Q2 is smoking, too, the third best quarter of the cycle, creating a three-quarter sweet spot from midterm Q4 to pre-election Q2.

Quarterly strength fades in the latter half of the pre-election year, but stays impressively positive through the election year. Losses dominate the first quarter of post-election years and the second and third quarters of midterm years.

QUARTERLY % CHANGES

	Q1	Q2	Q3	Q4	Year	Q2–Q3	Q4–Q1
Dow Jones Industrials (1949–June 2018)							
Average	2.2%	1.5%	0.5%	4.1%	8.6%	2.1%	6.5%
Post-election	−0.1%	1.7%	0.5%	4.2%	6.7%	2.3%	5.5%
Midterm	1.2%	−1.4%	−0.4%	7.1%	6.7%	−1.8%	14.6%
Pre-election	7.1%	4.9%	1.0%	2.6%	15.8%	5.9%	3.5%
Election	1.8%	1.0%	0.7%	2.3%	5.3%	1.8%	2.4%
S&P 500 (1949–June 2018)							
Average	2.2%	1.7%	0.7%	4.2%	9.1%	2.4%	6.7%
Post-election	−0.2%	2.2%	0.9%	3.6%	7.0%	3.2%	4.7%
Midterm	0.9%	−2.1%	0.1%	7.8%	6.7%	−2.2%	15.4%
Pre-election	7.1%	4.9%	0.6%	3.2%	16.1%	5.5%	4.7%
Election	1.3%	1.8%	1.1%	2.0%	6.7%	2.9%	2.0%
NASDAQ Composite (1971–June 2018)							
Average	4.3%	3.1%	0.3%	4.5%	12.7%	3.6%	9.0%
Post-election	−1.2%	6.3%	2.5%	5.0%	12.6%	8.8%	6.9%
Midterm	2.0%	−1.9%	−4.5%	8.6%	2.8%	−6.7%	22.0%
Pre-election	12.9%	7.5%	0.9%	5.4%	28.8%	8.5%	9.3%
Election	3.4%	0.7%	1.8%	−0.6%	6.0%	2.8%	−1.3%

NOVEMBER 2019

Veterans' Day
Monday Before November Expiration, Dow Up 10 of Last 14

MONDAY
D 42.9
S 38.1
N 38.1
11

At a time of war, we need you to work for peace. At a time of inequality, we need you to work for opportunity.
At a time of so much cynicism and so much doubt, we need you to make us believe again.
— Barack H. Obama (44th U.S. President, Commencement Address, Wesleyan University, 5/28/08, b. 1961)

TUESDAY
D 38.1
S 47.6
N 57.1
12

Individualism, private property, the law of accumulation of wealth and the law of competition…
are the highest result of human experience, the soil in which, so far, has produced the best fruit.
— Andrew Carnegie (Scottish-born U.S. industrialist, philanthropist, *The Gospel of Wealth*, 1835–1919)

WEDNESDAY
D 66.7
S 57.1
N 66.7
13

Self-discipline is a form of freedom. Freedom from laziness and lethargy, freedom from
expectations and demands of others, freedom from weakness and fear—and doubt.
— Harvey A. Dorfman (Sports psychologist, *The Mental ABC's of Pitching*, 1935–2011)

THURSDAY
D 57.1
S 52.4
N 47.6
14

All great truths begin as blasphemies.
— George Bernard Shaw (Irish dramatist, 1856–1950)

November Expiration Day, Dow Up 12 of Last 16
Dow Surged in 2008, Up 494 Points (6.5%)

FRIDAY
D 66.7
S 57.1
N 47.6
15

I'm very big on having clarified principles. I don't believe in being reactive. You can't do that
in the markets effectively. I can't. I need perspective. I need a game plan.
— Ray Dalio (Money manager, founder, Bridgewater Associates, *Fortune*, 3/16/09, b. 1949)

SATURDAY
16

SUNDAY
17

TRADING THE THANKSGIVING MARKET

For 35 years, the "holiday spirit" gave the Wednesday before Thanksgiving and the Friday after a great track record, except for two occasions. Publishing it in the 1987 *Almanac* was the kiss of death. Since 1988, Wednesday–Friday gained 18 of 30 times, with a total Dow point gain of 781.01 versus Monday's total Dow point loss of 900.48, down 14 of 20 since 1998. The best strategy appears to be coming into the week long and exiting into strength Friday.

DOW JONES INDUSTRIALS BEFORE AND AFTER THANKSGIVING

	Tuesday Before	Wednesday Before		Friday After	Total Gain Dow Points	Dow Close	Next Monday
1952	-0.18	1.54		1.22	2.76	283.66	0.04
1953	1.71	0.65		2.45	3.10	280.23	1.14
1954	3.27	1.89		3.16	5.05	387.79	0.72
1955	4.61	0.71		0.26	0.97	482.88	-1.92
1956	-4.49	-2.16		4.65	2.49	472.56	-2.27
1957	-9.04	10.69		3.84	14.53	449.87	-2.96
1958	-4.37	8.63		8.31	16.94	557.46	2.61
1959	2.94	1.41		1.42	2.83	652.52	6.66
1960	-3.44	1.37		4.00	5.37	606.47	-1.04
1961	-0.77	1.10		2.18	3.28	732.60	-0.61
1962	6.73	4.31	T	7.62	11.93	644.87	-2.81
1963	32.03	-2.52		9.52	7.00	750.52	1.39
1964	-1.68	-5.21	H	-0.28	-5.49	882.12	-6.69
1965	2.56	N/C		-0.78	-0.78	948.16	-1.23
1966	-3.18	1.84	A	6.52	8.36	803.34	-2.18
1967	13.17	3.07		3.58	6.65	877.60	4.51
1968	8.14	-3.17	N	8.76	5.59	985.08	-1.74
1969	-5.61	3.23		1.78	5.01	812.30	-7.26
1970	5.21	1.98	K	6.64	8.62	781.35	12.74
1971	-5.18	0.66		17.96	18.62	816.59	13.14
1972	8.21	7.29	S	4.67	11.96	1025.21	-7.45
1973	-17.76	10.08		-0.98	9.10	854.00	-29.05
1974	5.32	2.03	G	-0.63	1.40	618.66	-15.64
1975	9.76	3.15		2.12	5.27	860.67	-4.33
1976	-6.57	1.66	I	5.66	7.32	956.62	-6.57
1977	6.41	0.78		1.12	1.90	844.42	-4.85
1978	-1.56	2.95	V	3.12	6.07	810.12	3.72
1979	-6.05	-1.80		4.35	2.55	811.77	16.98
1980	3.93	7.00	I	3.66	10.66	993.34	-23.89
1981	18.45	7.90		7.80	15.70	885.94	3.04
1982	-9.01	9.01	N	7.36	16.37	1007.36	-4.51
1983	7.01	-0.20		1.83	1.63	1277.44	-7.62
1984	9.83	6.40	G	18.78	25.18	1220.30	-7.95
1985	0.12	18.92		-3.56	15.36	1472.13	-14.22
1986	6.05	4.64		-2.53	2.11	1914.23	-1.55
1987	40.45	-16.58		-36.47	-53.05	1910.48	-76.93
1988	11.73	14.58		-17.60	-3.02	2074.68	6.76
1989	7.25	17.49	N	18.77	36.26	2675.55	19.42
1990	-35.15	9.16		-12.13	-2.97	2527.23	5.94
1991	14.08	-16.10	G	-5.36	-21.46	2894.68	40.70
1992	25.66	17.56		15.94	33.50	3282.20	22.96
1993	3.92	13.41		-3.63	9.78	3683.95	-6.15
1994	-91.52	-3.36		33.64	30.28	3708.27	31.29
1995	40.46	18.06		7.23*	25.29	5048.84	22.04
1996	-19.38	-29.07	D	22.36*	-6.71	6521.70	N/C
1997	41.03	-14.17		28.35*	14.18	7823.13	189.98
1998	-73.12	13.13	A	18.80*	31.93	9333.08	-216.53
1999	-93.89	12.54		-19.26*	-6.72	10988.91	-40.99
2000	31.85	-95.18	Y	70.91*	-24.27	10470.23	75.84
2001	-75.08	-66.70		125.03*	58.33	9959.71	23.04
2002	-172.98	255.26		-35.59*	219.67	8896.09	-33.52
2003	16.15	15.63		2.89*	18.52	9782.46	116.59
2004	3.18	27.71		1.92*	29.63	10522.23	-46.33
2005	51.15	44.66		15.53*	60.19	10931.62	-40.90
2006	5.05	5.36		-46.78*	-41.42	12280.17	-158.46
2007	51.70	-211.10		181.84*	-29.26	12980.88	-237.44
2008	36.08	247.14		102.43*	349.57	8829.04	-679.95
2009	-17.24	30.69		-154.48*	-123.79	10309.92	34.92
2010	-142.21	150.91		-95.28*	55.63	11092.00	-39.51
2011	-53.59	-236.17		-25.77*	-261.94	11231.78	291.23
2012	-7.45	48.38		172.79*	221.17	13009.68	-42.31
2013	0.26	24.53		-10.92*	13.61	16086.41	-77.64
2014	-2.96	-2.69		15.99*	13.30	17828.24	-51.44
2015	19.51	1.20		-14.90*	-13.70	17798.49	-78.57
2016	67.18	59.31		68.96*	128.27	19152.14	-54.24
2017	160.50	-64.65		31.81*	-32.84	23557.99	22.79

104

*Shortened trading day

MONDAY

D 47.6
S 47.6
N 57.1

18

Make sure you have a jester because people in high places are seldom told the truth.
— Radio caller to President Ronald Reagan

TUESDAY

D 47.6
S 52.4
N 47.6

19

Only those who will risk going too far can possibly find out how far one can go.
— T. S. Eliot (English poet, essayist and critic, *The Waste Land*, 1888–1965)

Week Before Thanksgiving, Dow Up 19 of Last 25,
2003 –1.4%, 2004 –0.8%, 2008 –5.3%, 2011 –2.9%, 2012 –1.8%

WEDNESDAY

D 52.4
S 52.4
N 57.1

20

Oil has fostered massive corruption in almost every country that has been "blessed" with it, and the expectation that oil wealth will transform economies has led to disastrous policy choices.
— Ted Tyson (Chief Investment Officer, Mastholm Asset Management)

Trading Thanksgiving Market: Long into Weakness Prior,
Exit into Strength After (Page 104)

THURSDAY

D 66.7
S 61.9
N 76.2

21

What investors really get paid for is holding dogs. Small stocks tend to have higher average returns than big stocks, and value stocks tend to have higher average returns than growth stocks.
— Kenneth R. French (Economist, Dartmouth, NBER, b. 1954)

FRIDAY

D 61.9
S 57.1
N 57.1

22

Unless you love EVERYBODY, you can't sell ANYBODY.
— (From *Jerry Maguire*, 1996)

SATURDAY

23

SUNDAY

24

DECEMBER ALMANAC

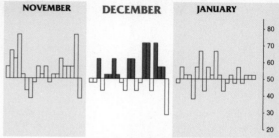

DECEMBER							JANUARY						
S	M	T	W	T	F	S	S	M	T	W	T	F	S
1	2	3	4	5	6	7			1	2	3	4	
8	9	10	11	12	13	14	5	6	7	8	9	10	11
15	16	17	18	19	20	21	12	13	14	15	16	17	18
22	23	24	25	26	27	28	19	20	21	22	23	24	25
29	30	31					26	27	28	29	30	31	

Market Probability Chart above is a graphic representation of the S&P 500 Recent Market Probability Calendar on page 124.

◆ #1 S&P (+1.6%) and #2 Dow (+1.7%) month since 1950 (page 50), #2 NASDAQ 1.8% since 1971 (page 58) ◆ 2002 worst December since 1931, down over 6% Dow and S&P, –9.7% on NASDAQ (pages 152, 155 & 158) ◆ "Free lunch" served on Wall Street before Christmas (page 112) ◆ Small caps start to outperform larger caps near middle of month (pages 108 & 110) ◆ "Santa Claus Rally" visible in graph above and on page 114 ◆ In 1998 was part of best fourth quarter since 1928 (page 170) ◆ Fourth quarter expiration week most bullish triple-witching week, Dow up 21 of last 27 (page 78) ◆ Pre–presidential election year Decembers rankings: #3 Dow and S&P, #2 NASDAQ.

December Vital Statistics

	DJIA		S&P 500		NASDAQ		Russell 1K		Russell 2K	
Rank	2		1		2		2		1	
Up	48		51		28		30		30	
Down	20		17		19		9		9	
Average % Change	1.7%		1.6%		1.8%		1.5%		2.5%	
Midterm Year	2.7%		2.9%		4.3%		2.9%		3.1%	
Best & Worst December										
	% Change		% Change		% Change		% Change		% Change	
Best	1991	9.5	1991	11.2	1999	22.0	1991	11.2	1999	11.2
Worst	2002	–6.2	2002	–6.0	2002	–9.7	2002	–5.8	2002	–5.7
Best & Worst December Weeks										
Best	12/02/11	7.0	12/02/11	7.4	12/08/00	10.3	12/02/11	7.4	12/02/11	10.3
Worst	12/04/87	–7.5	12/06/74	–7.1	12/15/00	–9.1	12/04/87	–7.0	12/12/80	–6.5
Best & Worst December Days										
Best	12/16/08	4.2	12/16/08	5.1	12/05/00	10.5	12/16/08	5.2	12/16/08	6.7
Worst	12/01/08	–7.7	12/01/08	–8.9	12/01/08	–9.0	12/01/08	–9.1	12/01/08	–11.9
First Trading Day of Expiration Week: 1980–2017										
Record (#Up – #Down)	23–15		23–15		17–21		23–15		16–22	
Current Streak	U3		U1		U1		U1		D4	
Avg % Change	0.18		0.14		–0.05		0.10		–0.19	
Options Expiration Day: 1980–2017										
Record (#Up – #Down)	24–14		27–11		26–12		27–11		24–14	
Current Streak	U1		U1		U1		U1		U1	
Avg % Change	0.26		0.33		0.32		0.32		0.42	
Options Expiration Week: 1980–2017										
Record (#Up – #Down)	29–9		27–11		22–16		26–12		20–18	
Current Streak	U2		U1		U1		U1		U1	
Avg % Change	0.75		0.76		0.30		0.70		0.61	
Week After Options Expiration: 1980–2017										
Record (#Up – #Down)	27–10		24–14		25–13		24–14		27–11	
Current Streak	U5		U5		U5		U5		U5	
Avg % Change	0.78		0.53		0.69		0.56		0.87	
First Trading Day Performance										
% of Time Up	47.1		48.5		57.4		48.7		48.7	
Avg % Change	–0.05		–0.04		0.09		–0.05		–0.16	
Last Trading Day Performance										
% of Time Up	51.5		58.8		68.1		48.7		64.1	
Avg % Change	0.05		0.08		0.27		–0.10		0.36	

Dow & S&P 1950–June 2018, NASDAQ 1971–June 2018, Russell 1K & 2K 1979–June 2018.

If Santa Claus should fail to call,
Bears may come to Broad and Wall.

NOVEMBER/DECEMBER 2019

MONDAY
D 66.7
S 57.1
N 57.1
25

Benjamin Graham was correct in suggesting that while the stock market in the short run may be a voting mechanism, in the long run it is a weighing mechanism. True value will win out in the end.
— Burton G. Malkiel (Economist, April 2003 Princeton Paper, A *Random Walk Down Wall Street*, b. 1932)

TUESDAY
D 61.9
S 57.1
N 57.1
26

Every man with a new idea is a crank until the idea succeeds.
— Mark Twain (American novelist and satirist, pen name of Samuel Langhorne Clemens, 1835–1910)

WEDNESDAY
D 61.9
S 76.2
N 66.7
27

The task of leadership is not to put greatness into humanity, but to elicit it, for the greatness is already there.
— Sir John Buchan (Scottish author, Governor General of Canada, 1935–1940, 1875–1940)

Thanksgiving *(Market Closed)*

THURSDAY
28

I'd be a bum on the street with a tin cup, if the markets were always efficient.
— Warren Buffett (CEO, Berkshire Hathaway, investor and philanthropist, b. 1930)

(Shortened Trading Day)
Last Trading Day of November, S&P Down 13 of Last 20

FRIDAY
D 52.4
S 38.1
N 42.9
29

If there is something you really want to do, make your plan and do it. Otherwise, you'll just regret it forever.
— Richard Rocco (PostNet franchisee, *Entrepreneur Magazine*, 12/06, b. 1946)

SATURDAY
30

December Almanac Investor Sector Seasonalities: See Pages 92, 94 and 96

SUNDAY
1

MOST OF THE SO-CALLED JANUARY EFFECT TAKES PLACE IN THE LAST HALF OF DECEMBER

Over the years we have reported annually on the fascinating January Effect, showing that small-cap stocks handily outperformed large-cap stocks during January 40 out of 43 years between 1953 and 1995. Readers saw that "Cats and Dogs" on average quadrupled the returns of blue chips in this period. Then the January Effect disappeared over the next four years.

Looking at the graph on page 110, comparing the Russell 1000 index of large-capitalization stocks to the Russell 2000 smaller-capitalization stocks, shows small-cap stocks beginning to outperform the blue chips in mid-December. Narrowing the comparison down to half-month segments was an inspiration and proved to be quite revealing, as you can see in the table below.

31-YEAR AVERAGE RATES OF RETURN (DEC 1987–FEB 2018)

From mid-Dec*	Russell 1000 Change	Annualized	Russell 2000 Change	Annualized
12/15–12/31	1.7%	47.1%	3.2%	105.8%
12/15–01/15	2.0	25.5	3.7	51.6
12/15–01/31	2.2	19.4	3.6	33.3
12/15–02/15	3.1	20.1	5.0	34.0
12/15–02/28	2.6	13.8	4.8	26.7
end-Dec*				
12/31–01/15	0.3	6.5	0.2	4.3
12/31–01/31	0.5	6.2	0.4	4.9
12/31–02/15	1.4	11.6	1.8	15.1
12/31–02/28	0.9	5.8	1.6	10.5

39-YEAR AVERAGE RATES OF RETURN (DEC 1979–FEB 2018)

From mid-Dec*	Russell 1000 Change	Annualized	Russell 2000 Change	Annualized
12/15–12/31	1.6%	43.9%	2.9%	92.5%
12/15–01/15	2.2	28.3	3.8	53.3
12/15–01/31	2.5	22.2	4.1	38.6
12/15–02/15	3.3	21.5	5.5	37.9
12/15–02/28	2.9	15.2	5.4	29.7
end-Dec*				
12/31–01/15	0.6	13.4	0.9	20.7
12/31–01/31	0.9	11.4	1.2	15.4
12/31–02/15	1.7	14.2	2.6	22.4
12/31–02/28	1.4	9.2	2.5	16.8

* Midmonth dates are the 11th trading day of the month; month-end dates are monthly closes.

Small-cap strength in the last half of December became even more magnified after the 1987 market crash. Note the dramatic shift in gains in the last half of December during the 31-year period starting in 1987, versus the 39 years from 1979 to 2018. With all the beaten-down small stocks being dumped for tax-loss purposes, it generally pays to get a head start on the January Effect in mid-December. You don't have to wait until December either; the small-cap sector often begins to turn around toward the beginning of November.

DECEMBER 2019

MONDAY

D 47.6
S 47.6
N 57.1

2

To succeed in the markets, it is essential to make your own decisions.
Numerous traders cited listening to others as their worst blunder.
— Jack D. Schwager (Fund manager, author, *Stock Market Wizards*, b. 1948)

TUESDAY

D 42.9
S 47.6
N 52.4

3

There are ways for the individual investor to make money in the securities markets. Buying value and
holding long term while collecting dividends has been proven over and over again.
— Robert M. Sharp (Author, *The Lore and Legends of Wall Street*)

WEDNESDAY

D 66.7
S 61.9
N 61.9

4

People who can take a risk, who believe in themselves enough to walk away [from a company]
are generally people who bring about change.
— Cynthia Danaher (Exiting GM of Hewlett-Packard's Medical Products Group, *Newsweek*)

THURSDAY

D 47.6
S 42.9
N 61.9

5

Never overpay for a stock. More money is lost than in any other way by projecting above-average growth
and paying an extra multiple for it.
— Charles Neuhauser (Bear Stearns)

FRIDAY

D 57.1
S 52.4
N 47.6

6

You have to find something that you love enough to be able to take risks, jump over the hurdles
and break through the brick walls that are always going to be placed in front of you. If you don't
have that kind of feeling for what it is you're doing, you'll stop at the first giant hurdle.
— George Lucas (director, *Star Wars*)

SATURDAY

7

SUNDAY

8

JANUARY EFFECT NOW STARTS IN MID-DECEMBER

Small-cap stocks tend to outperform big caps in January. Known as the "January Effect," the tendency is clearly revealed by the graph below. Thirty-seven years of daily data for the Russell 2000 index of smaller companies are divided by the Russell 1000 index of largest companies, and then compressed into a single year to show an idealized yearly pattern. When the graph is descending, big blue chips are outperforming smaller companies; when the graph is rising, smaller companies are moving up faster than their larger brethren.

In a typical year, the smaller fry stay on the sidelines while the big boys are on the field. Then, around early November, small stocks begin to wake up, and in mid-December they take off. Anticipated year-end dividends, payouts and bonuses could be a factor. Other major moves are quite evident just before Labor Day—possibly because individual investors are back from vacation. Small caps hold the lead through the beginning of June, though the bulk of the move is complete by early March.

RUSSELL 2000/RUSSELL 1000 ONE-YEAR SEASONAL PATTERN

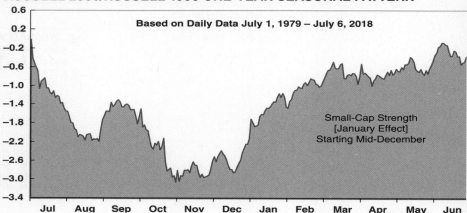

The bottom graph shows the actual ratio of the Russell 2000 divided by the Russell 1000 from 1979. Smaller companies had the upper hand for five years into 1983, as the last major bear trend wound to a close and the nascent bull market logged its first year. After falling behind for about eight years, they came back after the Persian Gulf War bottom in 1990, moving up until 1994, when big caps ruled the latter stages of the millennial bull. For six years, the picture was bleak for small fry, as the blue chips and tech stocks moved to stratospheric PE ratios. Small caps spiked in late 1999 and early 2000 and reached a peak in early 2006, as the four-year-old bull entered its final year. Note how the small-cap advantage has waned during major bull moves and intensified during weak market times.

RUSSELL 2000/RUSSELL 1000 (1979–JUNE 2018)

DECEMBER 2019

History is a collection of agreed-upon lies.
— Voltaire (French philosopher, 1694–1778)

What lies behind us and what lies before us are tiny matters, compared to what lies within us.
— Ralph Waldo Emerson (American author, poet and philosopher, *Self-Reliance*, 1803–1882)

Small Cap Strength Starts in Mid-December (Page 108)

The secret to business is to know something that nobody else knows.
— Aristotle Onassis (Greek shipping billionaire)

The first panacea for a mismanaged nation is inflation of the currency; the second is war. Both bring a temporary prosperity; both bring a permanent ruin. But both are the refuge of political and economic opportunists.
— Ernest Hemingway (American writer, 1954 Nobel Prize winner, 1899–1961)

Experience is helpful, but it is judgment that matters.
— General Colin Powell (Chairman, Joint Chiefs, 1989–93, Secretary of State, 2001–05, *N Y Times*, 10/22/08, b. 1937)

WALL STREET'S ONLY "FREE LUNCH" SERVED BEFORE CHRISTMAS

Investors tend to get rid of their losers near year-end for tax purposes, often hammering these stocks down to bargain levels. Over the years, the *Almanac* has shown that NYSE stocks selling at their lows on December 15 will usually outperform the market by February 15 in the following year. Preferred stocks, closed-end funds, splits and new issues are eliminated.

BARGAIN STOCKS VS. THE MARKET*

Short Span* Late Dec–Jan/Feb	New Lows Late Dec	% Change Jan/Feb	% Change NYSE Composite	Bargain Stocks Advantage
1974–75	112	48.9%	22.1%	26.8%
1975–76	21	34.9	14.9	20.0
1976–77	2	1.3	−3.3	4.6
1977–78	15	2.8	−4.5	7.3
1978–79	43	11.8	3.9	7.9
1979–80	5	9.3	6.1	3.2
1980–81	14	7.1	−2.0	9.1
1981–82	21	−2.6	−7.4	4.8
1982–83	4	33.0	9.7	23.3
1983–84	13	−3.2	−3.8	0.6
1984–85	32	19.0	12.1	6.9
1985–86	4	−22.5	3.9	−26.4
1986–87	22	9.3	12.5	−3.2
1987–88	23	13.2	6.8	6.4
1988–89	14	30.0	6.4	23.6
1989–90	25	−3.1	−4.8	1.7
1990–91	18	18.8	12.6	6.2
1991–92	23	51.1	7.7	43.4
1992–93	9	8.7	0.6	8.1
1993–94	10	−1.4	2.0	−3.4
1994–95	25	14.6	5.7	8.9
1995–96	5	−11.3	4.5	−15.8
1996–97	16	13.9	11.2	2.7
1997–98	29	9.9	5.7	4.2
1998–99	40	−2.8	4.3	−7.1
1999–00	26	8.9	−5.4	14.3
2000–01	51	44.4	0.1	44.3
2001–02	12	31.4	−2.3	33.7
2002–03	33	28.7	3.9	24.8
2003–04	15	16.7	2.3	14.4
2004–05	36	6.8	−2.8	9.6
2005–06	71	12.0	2.6	9.4
2006–07	43	5.1	−0.5	5.6
2007–08	71	−3.2	−9.4	6.2
2008–09	88	11.4	−2.4	13.8
2009–10	25	1.8	−3.0	4.8
2010–11	20	8.3	3.4	4.9
2011–12	65	18.1	6.1	12.0
2012–13	17	20.9	3.4	17.5
2013–14	18	25.7	1.7	24.0
2014–15	17	0.2	−0.4	0.6
2015–16	38	−9.2	5.6	−14.8
2016–17	19	2.8	0.6	2.2
2017–18	18	3.3	1.2	2.1
44-Year Totals		**524.8%**	**131.6%**	**393.2%**
Average		**11.9%**	**3.0%**	**8.9%**

* Dec 15–Feb 15 (1974–1999), Dec 1999–2018 based on actual newsletter portfolio

In response to changing market conditions, we tweaked the strategy the last 19 years, adding selections from NASDAQ and AMEX, and selling in mid-January some years. We email the list of stocks to our *Almanac Investor eNewsletter* subscribers. Visit *www.stocktradersalmanac.com*, or see the ad insert for additional details and a special offer for new subscribers.

We have come to the conclusion that the most prudent course of action is to compile our list from the stocks making new lows on Triple-Witching Friday before Christmas, capitalizing on the Santa Claus Rally (page 114). This also gives us the weekend to evaluate the issues in greater depth and weed out any glaringly problematic stocks. Subscribers will receive the list of stocks selected from the new lows made on December 21, 2018, and December 20, 2019, via email.

This "Free Lunch" strategy is an extremely short-term strategy reserved for the nimblest traders. It has performed better after market corrections and when there are more new lows to choose from. The object is to buy bargain stocks near their 52-week lows and sell after any quick, generous gains, as these issues can be real dogs.

Monday Before December Triple Witching S&P Up 12 of Last 18

MONDAY
D 61.9
S 61.9
N 57.1

16

The more feted by the media, the worse a pundit's accuracy.
— Sharon Begley (Senior editor, *Newsweek*, 2/23/09, referencing Philip E. Tetlock's 2005 *Expert Political Judgment*)

TUESDAY
D 57.1
S 61.9
N 57.1

17

Sight and Sound function differently in the mind, with sound being the surer investment.
WIN THE EARS OF THE PEOPLE, THEIR EYES WILL FOLLOW.
— Roy H. Williams (*The Wizard of Ads*)

December Triple-Witching Week, S&P Up 26 of Last 34

WEDNESDAY
D 38.1
S 42.9
N 33.3

18

That's the American way. If little kids don't aspire to make money like I did, what the hell good is this country?
— Lee Iacocca (American industrialist, Former Chrysler CEO, b. 1924)

THURSDAY
D 47.6
S 47.6
N 47.6

19

If there's anything duller than being on a board in Corporate America, I haven't found it.
— H. Ross Perot (American businessman, *NY Times*, 10/28/92, 2-time presidential candidate, 1992 and 1996, b. 1930)

December Triple Witching, S&P Up 25 of 36, Average Gain 0.3%

FRIDAY
D 71.4
S 71.4
N 61.9

20

Over the last 25 years, computer processing capacity has risen more than a millionfold,
while communication capacity has risen over a thousandfold.
— Richard Worzel (Futurist, *Facing the Future*, b. 1950)

The Only FREE LUNCH on Wall Street Is Served (Page 112)
Almanac Investors Emailed Alert Before the Open, Monday (See Insert)

SATURDAY

21

SUNDAY

22

IF SANTA CLAUS SHOULD FAIL TO CALL, BEARS MAY COME TO BROAD AND WALL

Santa Claus tends to come to Wall Street nearly every year, bringing a short, sweet, respectable rally within the last five days of the year and the first two in January. This has been good for an average 1.3% gain since 1969 (1.3% since 1950 as well). Santa's failure to show tends to precede bear markets, or times stocks could be purchased later in the year at much lower prices. We discovered this phenomenon in 1972.

DAILY % CHANGE IN S&P 500 AT YEAR END

| | Trading Days Before Year End | | | | | | First Days in January | | | Rally % |
	6	5	4	3	2	1	1	2	3	Change
1969	−0.4	1.1	0.8	−0.7	0.4	0.5	1.0	0.5	−0.7	3.6
1970	0.1	0.6	0.5	1.1	0.2	−0.1	−1.1	0.7	0.6	1.9
1971	−0.4	0.2	1.0	0.3	−0.4	0.3	−0.4	0.4	1.0	1.3
1972	−0.3	−0.7	0.6	0.4	0.5	1.0	0.9	0.4	−0.1	3.1
1973	−1.1	−0.7	3.1	2.1	−0.2	0.01	0.1	2.2	−0.9	6.7
1974	−1.4	1.4	0.8	−0.4	0.03	2.1	2.4	0.7	0.5	7.2
1975	0.7	0.8	0.9	−0.1	−0.4	0.5	0.8	1.8	1.0	4.3
1976	0.1	1.2	0.7	−0.4	0.5	0.5	−0.4	−1.2	−0.9	0.8
1977	0.8	0.9	N/C	0.1	0.2	0.2	−1.3	−0.3	−0.8	−0.3
1978	0.03	1.7	1.3	−0.9	−0.4	−0.2	0.6	1.1	0.8	3.3
1979	−0.6	0.1	0.1	0.2	−0.1	0.1	−2.0	−0.5	1.2	−2.2
1980	−0.4	0.4	0.5	−1.1	0.2	0.3	0.4	1.2	0.1	2.0
1981	−0.5	0.2	−0.2	−0.5	0.5	0.2	0.2	−2.2	−0.7	−1.8
1982	0.6	1.8	−1.0	0.3	−0.7	0.2	−1.6	2.2	0.4	1.2
1983	−0.2	−0.03	0.9	0.3	−0.2	0.05	−0.5	1.7	1.2	2.1
1984	−0.5	0.8	−0.2	−0.4	0.3	0.6	−1.1	−0.5	−0.5	−0.6
1985	−1.1	−0.7	0.2	0.9	0.5	0.3	−0.8	0.6	−0.1	1.1
1986	−1.0	0.2	0.1	−0.9	−0.5	−0.5	1.8	2.3	0.2	2.4
1987	1.3	−0.5	−2.6	−0.4	1.3	−0.3	3.6	1.1	0.1	2.2
1988	−0.2	0.3	−0.4	0.1	0.8	−0.6	−0.9	1.5	0.2	0.9
1989	0.6	0.8	−0.2	0.6	0.5	0.8	1.8	−0.3	−0.9	4.1
1990	0.5	−0.6	0.3	−0.8	0.1	0.5	−1.1	−1.4	−0.3	−3.0
1991	2.5	0.6	1.4	0.4	2.1	0.5	0.04	0.5	−0.3	5.7
1992	−0.3	0.2	−0.1	−0.3	0.2	−0.7	−0.1	−0.2	0.04	−1.1
1993	0.01	0.7	0.1	−0.1	−0.4	−0.5	−0.2	0.3	0.1	−0.1
1994	0.01	0.2	0.4	−0.3	0.1	−0.4	−0.03	0.3	−0.1	0.2
1995	0.8	0.2	0.4	0.04	−0.1	0.3	0.8	0.1	−0.6	1.8
1996	−0.3	0.5	0.6	0.1	−0.4	−1.7	−0.5	1.5	−0.1	0.1
1997	−1.5	−0.7	0.4	1.8	1.8	−0.04	0.5	0.2	−1.1	4.0
1998	2.1	−0.2	−0.1	1.3	−0.8	−0.2	−0.1	1.4	2.2	1.3
1999	1.6	−0.1	0.04	0.4	0.1	0.3	−1.0	−3.8	0.2	−4.0
2000	0.8	2.4	0.7	1.0	0.4	−1.0	−2.8	5.0	−1.1	5.7
2001	0.4	−0.02	0.4	0.7	0.3	−1.1	0.6	0.9	0.6	1.8
2002	0.2	−0.5	−0.3	−1.6	0.5	0.05	3.3	−0.05	2.2	1.2
2003	0.3	−0.2	0.2	1.2	0.01	0.2	−0.3	1.2	0.1	2.4
2004	0.1	−0.4	0.7	−0.01	0.01	−0.1	−0.8	−1.2	−0.4	−1.8
2005	0.4	0.04	−1.0	0.1	−0.3	−0.5	1.6	0.4	0.002	0.4
2006	−0.4	−0.5	0.4	0.7	−0.1	−0.5	−0.1	0.1	−0.6	0.003
2007	1.7	0.8	0.1	−1.4	0.1	−0.7	−1.4	N/C	−2.5	−2.5
2008	−1.0	0.6	0.5	−0.4	2.4	1.4	3.2	−0.5	0.8	7.4
2009	0.2	0.5	0.1	−0.1	0.02	−1.0	1.6	0.3	0.05	1.4
2010	−0.2	0.1	0.1	0.1	−0.2	−0.02	1.1	−0.1	0.5	1.1
2011	0.8	0.9	0.01	−1.3	1.1	−0.4	1.6	0.02	0.3	1.9
2012	−0.9	−0.2	−0.5	−0.1	−1.1	1.7	2.5	−0.2	0.5	2.0
2013	0.5	0.3	0.5	−0.03	−0.02	0.4	−0.9	−0.03	−0.3	0.2
2014	0.2	−0.01	0.3	0.1	−0.5	−1.0	−0.03	−1.8	−0.9	−3.0
2015	1.2	−0.2	−0.2	1.1	−0.7	−0.9	−1.5	0.2	−1.3	−2.3
2016	−0.2	0.1	0.2	−0.8	−0.03	−0.5	0.9	0.6	−0.1	0.4
2017	0.2	−0.05	−0.1	0.1	0.2	−0.5	0.8	0.6	0.4	1.1
Avg	**0.12**	**0.29**	**0.25**	**0.05**	**0.16**	**−0.01**	**0.23**	**0.36**	**−0.0004**	**1.3**

The couplet above was certainly on the mark in 1999, as the period suffered a horrendous 4.0% loss. On January 14, 2000, the Dow started its 33-month 37.8% slide to the October 2002 midterm election year bottom. NASDAQ cracked eight weeks later, falling 37.3% in 10 weeks, eventually dropping 77.9% by October 2002. Energy prices and Middle East terror woes may have grounded Santa in 2004. In 2007, the third worst reading since 1950 was recorded, as a full-blown financial crisis led to the second worst bear market in history. In 2016, the period was hit again as global growth concerns escalated and the market digested the first interest rate hike in nearly a decade.

Chanukah begins

MONDAY
D 71.4
S 71.4
N 66.7
23

[The Fed] is very smart, but [it] doesn't run the markets. In the end, the markets will run [the Fed].
The markets are bigger than any man or any group of men. The markets can even break a president.
— Richard Russell (*Dow Theory Letters*, 8/4/04)

Last Trading Day Before Christmas, Dow Up 8 of Last 11 Years
(Shortened Trading Day)

TUESDAY
D 42.9
S 42.9
N 57.1
24

We do not believe any group of men adequate enough or wise enough to operate without scrutiny
or without criticism… the only way to avoid error is to detect it, that the only way to detect it is
to be free to inquire… in secrecy error undetected will flourish and subvert.
— J. Robert Oppenheimer (American physicist, father of the A-bomb, 1904–1967)

Christmas Day *(Market Closed)*

WEDNESDAY
25

The inherent vice of capitalism is the unequal sharing of blessings;
the inherent virtue of socialism is the equal sharing of miseries.
— Winston Churchill (British statesman, 1874–1965)

THURSDAY
D 71.4
S 71.4
N 61.9
26

We can guarantee cash benefits as far out and at whatever size you like, but we cannot guarantee their purchasing power.
— Alan Greenspan (Fed Chairman, 1987–2006, on funding Social Security to Senate Banking Committee, 2/15/05)

FRIDAY
D 52.4
S 57.1
N 57.1
27

I'm not better than the next trader, just quicker at admitting my mistakes and moving on to the next opportunity.
— George Soros (Financier, philanthropist, political activist, author and philosopher, b. 1930)

SATURDAY
28

January Almanac Investor Sector Seasonalities: See Pages 92, 94 and 96

SUNDAY
29

YEAR'S TOP INVESTMENT BOOKS

Big Mistakes: The Best Investors and Their Worst Investments, Michael Batnick, Bloomberg Press, $34.95. <u>**2019 Best Investment Book of the Year**</u>. See page 100.

Dark Pool Secrets: Learn How to Profit from Wall Street's Hidden Trades That Move the Market!, Stefanie Kammerman, Stock Whisperer Trading Company, $29.95. Kammerman learned how to spot big dark pool trades on big volume in private stock exchanges under the tutelage of top prop traders. Now she teaches you how to spot them yourself and capitalize on them before they move stock prices.

Advanced Techniques in Day Trading: A Practical Guide to High Probability Strategies and Methods, Andrew Aziz, CreateSpace, $39.99. This well-reviewed engineer-turned-trader loves to teach others how to do it. In *Advanced Techniques in Day Trading* Andrew Aziz builds on his flagship book, *How to Day Trade for a Living*, with a step-by-step detailed roadmap for succeeding as a day trader.

Mastering the Market Cycle: Getting the Odds on Your Side, Howard Marks, Houghton Mifflin Harcourt, $30.00. Music to our cyclical ears from the man whom *Barron's* calls "Wall Street's Favorite Guru" and whose memos Warren Buffett says are "the first thing I open and read." Legendary manager with over $100 billion in AUM teaches us the power and opportunities hidden in the fluctuations of market cycles. Marks teaches how to learn from history.

Predicting the Markets: A Professional Autobiography, Edward Yardeni, YRI Press, $40.00. After 40 years on The Street from his early days at E. F. Hutton in 1978, Dr. Ed has learned a thing or two. Using his knack for putting economics and finance in plain language, Yardeni takes us on amazing journey through the turbulent market times of the 1970s up to the social media and technology-infused present day with lessons from the past and insights into the future.

The Socionomic Theory of Finance, Robert R. Prechter, Socionomics Institute Press, $79.00. Prechter may be preaching to the converted among us *Almanactarians* that finance and economics are inextricably linked to human social behavior. This book and original groundbreaking theory is the culmination of Prechter's 13-year-long endeavor. Supported and commended by colleagues and scholars, STF is an unconventional unified theory with real-world application.

Debts, Defaults, Depression and Other Delightful Ditties from the Dismal Science, Bryan Taylor, Global Financial Data, $12.99. We have used Taylor's unparalleled database for years as an invaluable resource. A breezy, enjoyable read on what is often a dry boring topic. Taylor dives deep, yet explains complex economic relationships in easy-to-understand lay terms. Econ class with a cool, captivating professor.

A History of the United States in Five Crashes: Stock Market Meltdowns That Defined a Nation, Scott Nations, William Morrow, $28.99. Head honcho of NationsShares, a leading developer of option-enhanced and volatility indexes, and a CNBC contributor gives us a fun, thriller-like read of how the five major crashes impacted Wall Street and the United States: the Panic of 1907, the 1929 Crash, the 1987 Crash, the 2008 Great Recession and the 2010 Flash Crash.

A First-Class Catastrophe: The Road to Black Monday, the Worst Day in Wall Street History, Diana B. Henriques, Henry Holt and Co, $32.00. Pulitzer Prize–winning investigative journalist and best-selling financial exposé author who penned the critically acclaimed *The Wizard of Lies*, the Madoff story that became an HBO TV film starring Robert De Niro, tackles the event that changed the market systemically forever. Detailed account for policy wonks.

Stock Market Crashes: Predictable and Unpredictable and What to Do About Them, William T. Ziemba, Mikhail Zhitlukhin, and Sebastien Lleo, World Scientific, $35.00. Three heavy-hitting economic and finance professors show you what makes market bubbles and their subsequent crashes tick, and how to spot them with four different models that have successfully identified bubbles over hundreds of years and predicted their subsequent crashes.

DECEMBER 2019/JANUARY 2020

MONDAY

D 47.6
S 57.1
N 42.9

30

We may face more inflation pressure than currently shows up in formal data.
— William Poole (Economist, president, Federal Reserve Bank of St. Louis, 1998–2008, June 2006 speech, b. 1937)

Last Trading Day of the Year, NASDAQ Down 15 of Last 18
NASDAQ Was Up 29 Years in a Row 1971–1999

TUESDAY

D 33.3
S 28.6
N 28.6

31

Our philosophy here is identifying change, anticipating change. Change is what drives earnings growth, and if you identify the underlying change, you recognize the growth before the market, and the deceleration of that growth.
— Peter Vermilye (Baring America Asset Management, 1987)

New Year's Day *(Market Closed)*

WEDNESDAY

1

There is a habitual nature to society and human activity. People's behavior and what they do with their money and time bears upon economics and the stock market.
— Jeffrey A. Hirsch (Editor, *Stock Trader's Almanac*, b. 1966)

Small Caps Punished First Trading Day of the Year
Russell 2000 Down 17 of Last 28, But Up 7 of Last 10

THURSDAY

D 61.9
S 47.6
N 66.7

2

When you're one step ahead of the crowd, you're a genius. When you're two steps ahead, you're a crackpot.
— Shlomo Riskin (Rabbi, author, b. 1940)

Second Trading Day of the Year, Dow Up 19 of Last 27
Santa Claus Rally Ends (Page 114)

FRIDAY

D 66.7
S 57.1
N 52.4

3

Our firm conviction is that, sooner or later, capitalism will give way to socialism. . . . We will bury you.
— Nikita Khrushchev (Soviet leader, 1953–1964, 1894–1971)

SATURDAY

4

SUNDAY

5

2020 STRATEGY CALENDAR

(Option expiration dates circled)

	MONDAY	TUESDAY	WEDNESDAY	THURSDAY	FRIDAY	SATURDAY	SUNDAY
JANUARY	30	31	1 JANUARY New Year's Day	2	3	4	5
	6	7	8	9	10	11	12
	13	14	15	16	(17)	18	19
	20 Martin Luther King Day	21	22	23	24	25	26
	27	28	29	30	31	1 FEBRUARY	2
FEBRUARY	3	4	5	6	7	8	9
	10	11	12	13	14 ♥	15	16
	17 Presidents' Day	18	19	20	(21)	22	23
	24	25	26 Ash Wednesday	27	28	29	1 MARCH
MARCH	2	3	4	5	6	7	8 Daylight Saving Time Begins
	9	10	11	12	13	14	15
	16	17 ♣ St. Patrick's Day	18	19	(20)	21	22
	23	24	25	26	27	28	29
	30	31	1 APRIL	2	3	4	5
APRIL	6	7	8	9 Passover	10 Good Friday	11	12 Easter
	13	14	15 Tax Deadline	16	(17)	18	19
	20	21	22	23	24	25	26
	27	28	29	30	1 MAY	2	3
MAY	4	5	6	7	8	9	10 Mother's Day
	11	12	13	14	(15)	16	17
	18	19	20	21	22	23	24
	25 Memorial Day	26	27	28	29	30	31
JUNE	1 JUNE	2	3	4	5	6	7
	8	9	10	11	12	13	14
	15	16	17	18	(19)	20	21 Father's Day
	22	23	24	25	26	27	28

Market closed on shaded weekdays; closes early when half-shaded.

2020 STRATEGY CALENDAR

(Option expiration dates circled)

MONDAY	TUESDAY	WEDNESDAY	THURSDAY	FRIDAY	SATURDAY	SUNDAY	
29	30	1 JULY	2	3	4 Independence Day	5	JULY
6	7	8	9	10	11	12	
13	14	15	16	(17)	18	19	
20	21	22	23	24	25	26	
27	28	29	30	31	1 AUGUST	2	
3	4	5	6	7	8	9	AUGUST
10	11	12	13	14	15	16	
17	18	19	20	(21)	22	23	
24	25	26	27	28	29	30	
31	1 SEPTEMBER	2	3	4	5	6	SEPTEMBER
7 Labor Day	8	9	10	11	12	13	
14	15	16	17	(18)	19 Rosh Hashanah	20	
21	22	23	24	25	26	27	
28 Yom Kippur	29	30	1 OCTOBER	2	3	4	OCTOBER
5	6	7	8	9	10	11	
12 Columbus Day	13	14	15	(16)	17	18	
19	20	21	22	23	24	25	
26	27	28	29	30	31	1 NOVEMBER Daylight Saving Time Ends	NOVEMBER
2	3 Election Day	4	5	6	7	8	
9	10	11 Veterans' Day	12	13	14	15	
16	17	18	19	(20)	21	22	
23	24	25	26 Thanksgiving Day	27	28	29	
30	1 DECEMBER	2	3	4	5	6	DECEMBER
7	8	9	10 Chanukah	11	12	13	
14	15	16	17	(18)	19	20	
21	22	23	24	25 Christmas	26	27	
28	29	30	31	1 JANUARY New Year's Day	2	3	

DIRECTORY OF TRADING PATTERNS AND DATABANK

CONTENTS

121   Dow Jones Industrials Market Probability Calendar 2019
122   <u>Recent</u> Dow Jones Industrials Market Probability Calendar 2019
123   S&P 500 Market Probability Calendar 2019
124   <u>Recent</u> S&P 500 Market Probability Calendar 2019
125   NASDAQ Composite Market Probability Calendar 2019
126   <u>Recent</u> NASDAQ Composite Market Probability Calendar 2019
127   Russell 1000 Index Market Probability Calendar 2019
128   Russell 2000 Index Market Probability Calendar 2019
129   Decennial Cycle: A Market Phenomenon
130   Presidential Election/Stock Market Cycle: The 185-Year Saga Continues
131   Dow Jones Industrials Bull and Bear Markets Since 1900
132   Standard & Poor's 500 Bull and Bear Markets Since 1929/NASDAQ Composite Since 1971
133   Dow Jones Industrials 10-Year Daily Point Changes: January and February
134   Dow Jones Industrials 10-Year Daily Point Changes: March and April
135   Dow Jones Industrials 10-Year Daily Point Changes: May and June
136   Dow Jones Industrials 10-Year Daily Point Changes: July and August
137   Dow Jones Industrials 10-Year Daily Point Changes: September and October
138   Dow Jones Industrials 10-Year Daily Point Changes: November and December
139   A Typical Day in the Market
140   Through the Week on a Half-Hourly Basis
141   Tuesday Most Profitable Day of Week
142   NASDAQ Strongest Last 3 Days of Week
143   S&P Daily Performance Each Year Since 1952
144   NASDAQ Daily Performance Each Year Since 1971
145   Monthly Cash Inflows into S&P Stocks
146   Monthly Cash Inflows into NASDAQ Stocks
147   November, December and January: Year's Best Three-Month Span
148   November Through June: NASDAQ's Eight-Month Run
149   Dow Jones Industrials Annual Highs, Lows & Closes Since 1901
150   S&P 500 Annual Highs, Lows & Closes Since 1930
151   NASDAQ, Russell 1000 & 2000 Annual Highs, Lows & Closes Since 1971
152   Dow Jones Industrials Monthly Percent Changes Since 1950
153   Dow Jones Industrials Monthly Point Changes Since 1950
154   Dow Jones Industrials Monthly Closing Prices Since 1950
155   Standard & Poor's 500 Monthly Percent Changes Since 1950
157   Standard & Poor's 500 Monthly Closing Prices Since 1950
158   NASDAQ Composite Monthly Percent Changes Since 1971
159   NASDAQ Composite Monthly Closing Prices Since 1971
160   Russell 1000 Index Monthly Percent Changes Since 1979
161   Russell 1000 Index Monthly Closing Prices Since 1979
162   Russell 2000 Index Monthly Percent Changes Since 1979
163   Russell 2000 Index Monthly Closing Prices Since 1979
164   10 <u>Best</u> Days by Percent and Point
165   10 <u>Worst</u> Days by Percent and Point
166   10 <u>Best</u> Weeks by Percent and Point
167   10 <u>Worst</u> Weeks by Percent and Point
168   10 <u>Best</u> Months by Percent and Point
169   10 <u>Worst</u> Months by Percent and Point
170   10 <u>Best</u> Quarters by Percent and Point
171   10 <u>Worst</u> Quarters by Percent and Point
172   10 <u>Best</u> Years by Percent and Point
173   10 <u>Worst</u> Years by Percent and Point

DOW JONES INDUSTRIALS MARKET PROBABILITY CALENDAR 2019

THE % CHANCE OF THE MARKET RISING ON ANY TRADING DAY OF THE YEAR*

(Based on the number of times the DJIA rose on a particular trading day during January 1953–December 2017)

Date	Jan	Feb	Mar	Apr	May	Jun	Jul	Aug	Sep	Oct	Nov	Dec
1	H	60.0	66.2	60.0	56.9	S	66.2	44.6	S	47.7	61.5	S
2	58.5	S	S	60.0	64.6	S	56.9	46.2	H	56.9	S	44.6
3	72.3	S	S	50.8	49.2	58.5	60.0	S	58.5	53.8	S	52.3
4	46.2	53.8	63.1	58.5	S	52.3	H	S	60.0	61.5	53.8	63.1
5	S	41.5	58.5	50.8	S	50.8	56.9	49.2	60.0	S	66.2	56.9
6	S	55.4	50.8	S	46.2	56.9	S	50.8	44.6	S	58.5	49.2
7	55.4	47.7	47.7	S	47.7	53.8	S	53.8	S	44.6	49.2	S
8	44.6	41.5	53.8	60.0	53.8	S	61.5	46.2	S	52.3	60.0	S
9	47.7	S	S	61.5	49.2	S	58.5	46.2	49.2	44.6	S	46.2
10	47.7	S	S	61.5	50.8	46.2	50.8	S	44.6	41.5	S	53.8
11	47.7	47.7	60.0	55.4	S	36.9	44.6	S	60.0	50.8	53.8	56.9
12	S	58.5	53.8	72.3	S	53.8	66.2	46.2	58.5	S	56.9	46.2
13	S	47.7	55.4	S	44.6	60.0	S	49.2	46.2	S	49.2	50.8
14	56.9	50.8	52.3	S	52.3	58.5	S	63.1	S	60.0	47.7	S
15	55.4	55.4	61.5	61.5	55.4	S	49.2	56.9	S	52.3	58.5	S
16	58.5	S	S	55.4	43.1	S	47.7	50.8	56.9	53.8	S	49.2
17	40.0	S	S	56.9	52.3	49.2	52.3	S	56.9	46.2	S	56.9
18	40.0	H	60.0	53.8	S	50.8	53.8	S	41.5	60.0	52.3	47.7
19	S	41.5	58.5	H	S	52.3	38.5	47.7	50.8	S	49.2	55.4
20	S	49.2	52.3	S	43.1	46.2	S	53.8	46.2	S	49.2	58.5
21	H	50.8	47.7	S	50.8	43.1	S	58.5	S	52.3	66.2	S
22	41.5	38.5	36.9	52.3	43.1	S	47.7	49.2	S	46.2	58.5	S
23	58.5	S	S	52.3	35.4	S	46.2	50.8	36.9	43.1	S	52.3
24	47.7	S	S	52.3	52.3	35.4	44.6	S	49.2	52.3	S	60.0
25	56.9	46.2	49.2	58.5	S	47.7	58.5	S	53.8	27.7	66.2	H
26	S	61.5	44.6	56.9	S	49.2	53.8	47.7	53.8	S	60.0	69.2
27	S	47.7	55.4	S	H	53.8	S	44.6	49.2	S	53.8	47.7
28	58.5	49.2	46.2	S	46.2	53.8	S	61.5	S	53.8	H	S
29	49.2		41.5	50.8	44.6	S	46.2	41.5	S	55.4	53.8	S
30	58.5		S	49.2	55.4	S	58.5	60.0	40.0	58.5	S	55.4
31	56.9		S		56.9		49.2	S		52.3		52.3

* See new trends developing on pages 70, 82, 141–146.

RECENT DOW JONES INDUSTRIALS MARKET PROBABILITY CALENDAR 2019

THE % CHANCE OF THE MARKET RISING ON ANY TRADING DAY OF THE YEAR*
(Based on the number of times the DJIA rose on a particular trading day during January 1997–December 2017**)

Date	Jan	Feb	Mar	Apr	May	Jun	Jul	Aug	Sep	Oct	Nov	Dec
1	H	71.4	66.7	71.4	66.7	S	81.0	33.3	S	47.6	57.1	S
2	61.9	S	S	66.7	66.7	S	33.3	57.1	H	52.4	S	47.6
3	66.7	S	S	38.1	33.3	71.4	52.4	S	57.1	61.9	S	42.9
4	47.6	42.9	42.9	66.7	S	52.4	H	S	66.7	66.7	57.1	66.7
5	S	47.6	57.1	42.9	S	42.9	57.1	52.4	57.1	S	61.9	47.6
6	S	52.4	47.6	S	38.1	57.1	S	52.4	38.1	S	76.2	57.1
7	47.6	52.4	61.9	S	57.1	66.7	S	52.4	S	33.3	61.9	S
8	33.3	42.9	47.6	57.1	66.7	S	61.9	47.6	S	42.9	47.6	S
9	47.6	S	S	57.1	47.6	S	57.1	47.6	61.9	52.4	S	52.4
10	57.1	S	S	57.1	61.9	61.9	57.1	S	52.4	47.6	S	52.4
11	52.4	57.1	57.1	47.6	S	38.1	71.4	S	66.7	38.1	42.9	52.4
12	S	52.4	57.1	76.2	S	42.9	71.4	38.1	57.1	S	38.1	52.4
13	S	61.9	57.1	S	38.1	57.1	S	47.6	47.6	S	66.7	47.6
14	52.4	52.4	57.1	S	47.6	66.7	S	61.9	S	71.4	57.1	S
15	52.4	71.4	76.2	61.9	57.1	S	47.6	57.1	S	52.4	66.7	S
16	52.4	S	S	61.9	42.9	S	57.1	57.1	57.1	57.1	S	61.9
17	42.9	S	S	57.1	52.4	52.4	57.1	S	76.2	52.4	S	57.1
18	38.1	H	47.6	66.7	S	61.9	66.7	S	42.9	61.9	47.6	38.1
19	S	47.6	66.7	H	S	57.1	19.0	66.7	61.9	S	47.6	47.6
20	S	42.9	57.1	S	38.1	52.4	S	42.9	52.4	S	52.4	71.4
21	H	47.6	38.1	S	52.4	38.1	S	61.9	S	57.1	66.7	S
22	33.3	47.6	33.3	66.7	28.6	S	42.9	47.6	S	42.9	61.9	S
23	47.6	S	S	52.4	42.9	S	42.9	52.4	23.8	57.1	S	71.4
24	38.1	S	S	47.6	47.6	33.3	38.1	S	33.3	57.1	S	42.9
25	61.9	42.9	57.1	57.1	S	38.1	57.1	S	52.4	33.3	66.7	H
26	S	52.4	28.6	66.7	S	61.9	52.4	47.6	66.7	S	61.9	71.4
27	S	52.4	52.4	S	H	57.1	S	38.1	57.1	S	61.9	52.4
28	61.9	38.1	57.1	S	57.1	42.9	S	71.4	S	66.7	H	S
29	52.4		38.1	66.7	47.6	S	42.9	28.6	S	61.9	52.4	S
30	47.6		S	33.3	57.1	S	42.9	52.4	33.3	57.1	S	47.6
31	47.6		S		42.9		33.3	S		57.1		33.3

*See new trends developing on pages 70, 82, 141–146.   ** Based on most recent 21-year period.*

S&P 500 MARKET PROBABILITY CALENDAR 2019

THE % CHANCE OF THE MARKET RISING ON ANY TRADING DAY OF THE YEAR*

(Based on the number of times the S&P 500 rose on a particular trading day during **January 1953–December 2017**)

Date	Jan	Feb	Mar	Apr	May	Jun	Jul	Aug	Sep	Oct	Nov	Dec
1	H	61.5	63.1	63.1	58.5	S	72.3	47.7	S	49.2	61.5	S
2	47.7	S	S	60.0	67.7	S	55.4	44.6	H	66.2	S	46.2
3	69.2	S	S	52.3	53.8	56.9	55.4	S	60.0	55.4	S	52.3
4	50.8	58.5	58.5	55.4	S	61.5	H	S	53.8	61.5	56.9	61.5
5	S	47.7	61.5	52.3	S	50.8	60.0	49.2	60.0	S	67.7	56.9
6	S	50.8	49.2	S	43.1	55.4	S	52.3	46.2	S	55.4	44.6
7	50.8	50.8	49.2	S	46.2	47.7	S	53.8	S	46.2	47.7	S
8	43.1	44.6	55.4	61.5	53.8	S	61.5	46.2	S	50.8	58.5	S
9	50.8	S	S	61.5	47.7	S	55.4	52.3	49.2	43.1	S	50.8
10	53.8	S	S	53.8	52.3	44.6	52.3	S	52.3	46.2	S	55.4
11	52.3	41.5	60.0	50.8	S	40.0	52.3	S	60.0	50.8	60.0	49.2
12	S	61.5	52.3	63.1	S	53.8	70.8	46.2	63.1	S	56.9	47.7
13	S	55.4	64.6	S	43.1	63.1	S	47.7	49.2	S	47.7	43.1
14	60.0	47.7	44.6	S	49.2	56.9	S	63.1	S	55.4	47.7	S
15	61.5	55.4	61.5	60.0	55.4	S	50.8	61.5	S	52.3	50.8	S
16	56.9	S	S	58.5	47.7	S	46.2	53.8	55.4	58.5	S	49.2
17	49.2	S	S	55.4	53.8	55.4	47.7	S	56.9	46.2	S	58.5
18	49.2	H	61.5	53.8	S	49.2	53.8	S	47.7	66.2	50.8	44.6
19	S	36.9	56.9	H	S	56.9	38.5	53.8	52.3	S	53.8	47.7
20	S	52.3	49.2	S	40.0	41.5	S	50.8	47.7	S	52.3	55.4
21	H	44.6	41.5	S	47.7	46.2	S	60.0	S	53.8	64.6	S
22	47.7	41.5	50.8	55.4	50.8	S	41.5	47.7	S	49.2	58.5	S
23	60.0	S	S	46.2	44.6	S	46.2	49.2	36.9	43.1	S	49.2
24	60.0	S	S	49.2	52.3	35.4	44.6	S	47.7	47.7	S	60.0
25	53.8	41.5	43.1	58.5	S	41.5	55.4	S	50.8	30.8	66.2	H
26	S	58.5	46.2	50.8	S	52.3	55.4	46.2	60.0	S	60.0	70.8
27	S	52.3	56.9	S	H	56.9	S	46.2	50.8	S	60.0	52.3
28	52.3	55.4	40.0	S	50.8	50.8	S	61.5	S	58.5	H	S
29	46.2		40.0	47.7	47.7	S	47.7	44.6	S	58.5	50.8	S
30	61.5		S	55.4	55.4	S	64.6	63.1	43.1	58.5	S	61.5
31	61.5		S		58.5		60.0	S		53.8		60.0

* See new trends developing on pages 70, 82, 141–146.

RECENT S&P 500 MARKET PROBABILITY CALENDAR 2019

THE % CHANCE OF THE MARKET RISING ON ANY TRADING DAY OF THE YEAR*
(Based on the number of times the S&P 500 rose on a particular trading day during January 1997–December 2017**)

Date	Jan	Feb	Mar	Apr	May	Jun	Jul	Aug	Sep	Oct	Nov	Dec
1	H	76.2	66.7	71.4	71.4	S	85.7	42.9	S	52.4	57.1	S
2	47.6	S	S	66.7	57.1	S	38.1	52.4	H	57.1	S	47.6
3	57.1	S	S	47.6	33.3	66.7	61.9	S	57.1	61.9	S	47.6
4	52.4	52.4	38.1	61.9	S	71.4	H	S	42.9	61.9	66.7	61.9
5	S	42.9	66.7	42.9	S	38.1	57.1	52.4	57.1	S	61.9	42.9
6	S	52.4	52.4	S	38.1	57.1	S	57.1	47.6	S	76.2	52.4
7	52.4	52.4	61.9	S	52.4	47.6	S	42.9	S	33.3	52.4	S
8	38.1	57.1	52.4	61.9	57.1	S	57.1	52.4	S	42.9	42.9	S
9	57.1	S	S	52.4	42.9	S	52.4	47.6	52.4	52.4	S	52.4
10	66.7	S	S	52.4	57.1	57.1	57.1	S	57.1	47.6	S	61.9
11	42.9	47.6	52.4	42.9	S	42.9	81.0	S	66.7	42.9	38.1	52.4
12	S	61.9	57.1	61.9	S	38.1	71.4	42.9	61.9	S	47.6	47.6
13	S	71.4	66.7	S	38.1	57.1	S	42.9	52.4	S	57.1	42.9
14	57.1	52.4	38.1	S	38.1	61.9	S	57.1	S	66.7	52.4	S
15	52.4	76.2	66.7	57.1	61.9	S	38.1	61.9	S	52.4	57.1	S
16	66.7	S	S	71.4	47.6	S	57.1	61.9	52.4	66.7	S	61.9
17	52.4	S	S	61.9	52.4	66.7	52.4	S	76.2	61.9	S	61.9
18	42.9	H	52.4	57.1	S	61.9	66.7	S	47.6	66.7	47.6	42.9
19	S	38.1	71.4	H	S	61.9	19.0	66.7	52.4	S	52.4	47.6
20	S	47.6	42.9	S	38.1	47.6	S	38.1	42.9	S	52.4	71.4
21	H	42.9	33.3	S	52.4	42.9	S	66.7	S	66.7	61.9	S
22	47.6	47.6	57.1	71.4	38.1	S	42.9	47.6	S	52.4	57.1	S
23	52.4	S	S	47.6	47.6	S	42.9	52.4	28.6	61.9	S	71.4
24	47.6	S	S	42.9	52.4	38.1	47.6	S	33.3	61.9	S	42.9
25	57.1	47.6	57.1	52.4	S	33.3	52.4	S	47.6	33.3	57.1	H
26	S	52.4	28.6	52.4	S	57.1	52.4	47.6	66.7	S	57.1	71.4
27	S	57.1	57.1	S	H	57.1	S	47.6	61.9	S	76.2	57.1
28	47.6	38.1	47.6	S	61.9	42.9	S	76.2	S	57.1	H	S
29	52.4		42.9	61.9	52.4	S	42.9	28.6	S	52.4	38.1	S
30	52.4		S	38.1	57.1	S	61.9	52.4	33.3	57.1	S	57.1
31	52.4		S		52.4		42.9	S		61.9		28.6

* See new trends developing on pages 70, 82, 141–146.   ** Based on most recent 21-year period.

NASDAQ COMPOSITE MARKET PROBABILITY CALENDAR 2019

THE % CHANCE OF THE MARKET RISING ON ANY TRADING DAY OF THE YEAR*

(Based on the number of times the NASDAQ rose on a particular trading day during **January 1971–December 2017**)

Date	Jan	Feb	Mar	Apr	May	Jun	Jul	Aug	Sep	Oct	Nov	Dec
1	H	72.3	63.8	46.8	63.8	S	61.7	53.2	S	48.9	63.8	S
2	55.3	S	S	63.8	70.2	S	46.8	40.4	H	61.7	S	57.4
3	63.8	S	S	61.7	55.3	59.6	46.8	S	57.4	59.6	S	61.7
4	57.4	66.0	55.3	55.3	S	72.3	H	S	59.6	61.7	53.2	63.8
5	S	55.3	68.1	44.7	S	55.3	55.3	51.1	59.6	S	68.1	59.6
6	S	63.8	51.1	S	51.1	59.6	S	57.4	59.6	S	57.4	44.7
7	63.8	55.3	48.9	S	55.3	51.1	S	55.3	S	57.4	48.9	S
8	55.3	53.2	57.4	63.8	63.8	S	61.7	40.4	S	59.6	55.3	S
9	59.6	S	S	61.7	55.3	S	66.0	51.1	55.3	48.9	S	55.3
10	59.6	S	S	59.6	42.6	46.8	61.7	S	48.9	51.1	S	51.1
11	57.4	48.9	57.4	51.1	S	40.4	70.2	S	55.3	68.1	57.4	42.6
12	S	63.8	48.9	59.6	S	51.1	74.5	48.9	61.7	S	61.7	44.7
13	S	61.7	72.3	S	55.3	61.7	S	57.4	59.6	S	55.3	40.4
14	61.7	66.0	51.1	S	55.3	61.7	S	61.7	S	63.8	51.1	S
15	61.7	61.7	53.2	51.1	55.3	S	61.7	59.6	S	51.1	42.6	S
16	70.2	S	S	61.7	55.3	S	51.1	51.1	40.4	53.2	S	48.9
17	57.4	S	S	55.3	51.1	55.3	55.3	S	53.2	44.7	S	57.4
18	44.7	H	63.8	55.3	S	48.9	61.7	S	55.3	66.0	51.1	48.9
19	S	48.9	59.6	H	S	53.2	36.2	57.4	61.7	S	51.1	53.2
20	S	55.3	66.0	S	42.6	46.8	S	48.9	51.1	S	53.2	59.6
21	H	40.4	55.3	S	48.9	51.1	S	68.1	S	46.8	70.2	S
22	48.9	48.9	53.2	59.6	51.1	S	44.7	53.2	S	55.3	57.4	S
23	51.1	S	S	53.2	51.1	S	46.8	51.1	44.7	48.9	S	63.8
24	59.6	S	S	53.2	53.2	40.4	53.2	S	51.1	48.9	S	68.1
25	48.9	53.2	51.1	46.8	S	46.8	55.3	S	44.7	34.0	59.6	H
26	S	63.8	42.6	63.8	S	59.6	51.1	51.1	51.1	S	68.1	70.2
27	S	59.6	55.3	S	H	66.0	S	57.4	46.8	S	66.0	51.1
28	66.0	48.9	57.4	S	55.3	68.1	S	66.0	S	42.6	H	S
29	59.6		63.8	63.8	61.7	S	44.7	59.6	S	57.4	63.8	S
30	53.2		S	63.8	57.4	S	57.4	66.0	48.9	57.4	S	61.7
31	63.8		S		66.0		48.9	S		63.8		68.1

* See new trends developing on pages 70, 82, 141–146.
Based on NASDAQ composite, prior to February 5, 1971; based on National Quotation Bureau indices.

RECENT NASDAQ COMPOSITE MARKET PROBABILITY CALENDAR 2019

THE % CHANCE OF THE MARKET RISING ON ANY TRADING DAY OF THE YEAR*
(Based on the number of times the NASDAQ rose on a particular trading day during January 1997–December 2017**)

Date	Jan	Feb	Mar	Apr	May	Jun	Jul	Aug	Sep	Oct	Nov	Dec
1	H	81.0	66.7	61.9	76.2	S	71.4	47.6	S	47.6	61.9	S
2	66.7	S	S	61.9	61.9	S	38.1	38.1	H	61.9	S	57.1
3	52.4	S	S	61.9	38.1	57.1	57.1	S	66.7	71.4	S	52.4
4	52.4	47.6	38.1	57.1	S	66.7	H	S	47.6	57.1	61.9	61.9
5	S	38.1	66.7	33.3	S	42.9	66.7	52.4	52.4	S	66.7	61.9
6	S	52.4	42.9	S	42.9	57.1	S	52.4	57.1	S	66.7	47.6
7	52.4	57.1	38.1	S	47.6	47.6	S	38.1	S	47.6	57.1	S
8	57.1	57.1	52.4	66.7	76.2	S	61.9	33.3	S	57.1	52.4	S
9	61.9	S	S	47.6	47.6	S	66.7	42.9	57.1	57.1	S	57.1
10	71.4	S	S	61.9	47.6	42.9	61.9	S	57.1	52.4	S	71.4
11	42.9	42.9	42.9	38.1	S	38.1	71.4	S	61.9	52.4	38.1	42.9
12	S	57.1	47.6	52.4	S	33.3	76.2	42.9	66.7	S	57.1	47.6
13	S	71.4	66.7	S	47.6	52.4	S	52.4	76.2	S	66.7	42.9
14	52.4	66.7	42.9	S	42.9	52.4	S	61.9	S	71.4	47.6	S
15	38.1	57.1	47.6	42.9	57.1	S	57.1	66.7	S	47.6	47.6	S
16	71.4	S	S	66.7	52.4	S	61.9	66.7	38.1	57.1	S	57.1
17	57.1	S	S	52.4	57.1	66.7	61.9	S	76.2	52.4	S	57.1
18	38.1	H	57.1	57.1	S	57.1	71.4	S	52.4	61.9	57.1	33.3
19	S	42.9	71.4	H	S	66.7	14.3	61.9	57.1	S	47.6	47.6
20	S	52.4	66.7	S	33.3	47.6	S	38.1	47.6	S	57.1	61.9
21	H	42.9	52.4	S	61.9	42.9	S	76.2	S	52.4	76.2	S
22	38.1	57.1	57.1	66.7	42.9	S	52.4	47.6	S	47.6	57.1	S
23	47.6	S	S	47.6	47.6	S	42.9	47.6	42.9	61.9	S	66.7
24	57.1	S	S	52.4	47.6	33.3	47.6	S	38.1	52.4	S	57.1
25	52.4	57.1	71.4	38.1	S	42.9	57.1	S	47.6	42.9	57.1	H
26	S	61.9	28.6	47.6	S	71.4	57.1	52.4	47.6	S	57.1	61.9
27	S	57.1	52.4	S	H	61.9	S	47.6	42.9	S	66.7	57.1
28	71.4	23.8	57.1	S	57.1	61.9	S	76.2	S	47.6	H	S
29	61.9		52.4	71.4	66.7	S	42.9	52.4	S	57.1	42.9	S
30	47.6		S	52.4	66.7	S	66.7	57.1	38.1	52.4	S	42.9
31	52.4		S		47.6		38.1	S		61.9		28.6

* See new trends developing on pages 70, 82, 141–146.   ** Based on most recent 21-year period.

RUSSELL 1000 INDEX MARKET PROBABILITY CALENDAR 2019

THE % CHANCE OF THE MARKET RISING ON ANY TRADING DAY OF THE YEAR*
(Based on the number of times the RUSSELL 1000 rose on a particular trading day during January 1979–December 2017)

Date	Jan	Feb	Mar	Apr	May	Jun	Jul	Aug	Sep	Oct	Nov	Dec
1	H	81.0	66.7	61.9	76.2	S	71.4	47.6	S	47.6	61.9	S
2	66.7	S	S	61.9	61.9	S	38.1	38.1	H	61.9	S	57.1
3	52.4	S	S	61.9	38.1	57.1	57.1	S	66.7	71.4	S	52.4
4	52.4	47.6	38.1	57.1	S	66.7	H	S	47.6	57.1	61.9	61.9
5	S	38.1	66.7	33.3	S	42.9	66.7	52.4	52.4	S	66.7	61.9
6	S	52.4	42.9	S	42.9	57.1	S	52.4	57.1	S	66.7	47.6
7	52.4	57.1	38.1	S	47.6	47.6	S	38.1	S	47.6	57.1	S
8	57.1	57.1	52.4	66.7	76.2	S	61.9	33.3	S	57.1	52.4	S
9	61.9	S	S	47.6	47.6	S	66.7	42.9	57.1	57.1	S	57.1
10	71.4	S	S	61.9	47.6	42.9	61.9	S	57.1	52.4	S	71.4
11	42.9	42.9	42.9	38.1	S	38.1	71.4	S	61.9	52.4	38.1	42.9
12	S	57.1	47.6	52.4	S	33.3	76.2	42.9	66.7	S	57.1	47.6
13	S	71.4	66.7	S	47.6	52.4	S	52.4	76.2	S	66.7	42.9
14	52.4	66.7	42.9	S	42.9	52.4	S	61.9	S	71.4	47.6	S
15	38.1	57.1	47.6	42.9	57.1	S	57.1	66.7	S	47.6	46.6	S
16	71.4	S	S	66.7	52.4	S	61.9	66.7	38.1	57.1	S	57.1
17	57.1	S	S	52.4	57.1	66.7	61.9	S	76.2	52.4	S	57.1
18	38.1	H	57.1	57.1	S	57.1	71.4	S	52.4	61.9	57.1	33.3
19	S	42.9	71.4	H	S	66.7	14.3	61.9	57.1	S	47.6	47.6
20	S	52.4	66.7	S	33.3	47.6	S	38.1	47.6	S	57.1	61.9
21	H	42.9	52.4	S	61.9	42.9	S	76.2	S	52.4	76.2	S
22	38.1	57.1	57.1	66.7	42.9	S	52.4	47.6	S	47.6	57.1	S
23	47.6	S	S	47.6	47.6	S	42.9	47.6	42.9	61.9	S	66.7
24	57.1	S	S	52.4	47.6	33.3	47.6	S	38.1	52.4	S	57.1
25	52.4	57.1	71.4	38.1	S	42.9	57.1	S	47.6	42.9	57.1	H
26	S	61.9	28.6	47.6	S	71.4	57.1	52.4	47.6	S	57.1	61.9
27	S	57.1	52.4	S	H	61.9	S	47.6	42.9	S	66.7	57.1
28	71.4	23.8	57.1	S	57.1	61.9	S	76.2	S	47.6	H	S
29	61.9		52.4	71.4	66.7	S	42.9	52.4	S	57.1	42.9	S
30	47.6		S	52.4	66.7	S	66.7	57.1	38.1	52.4	S	42.9
31	52.4		S		47.6		38.1	S		61.9		28.6

* See new trends developing on pages 70, 82, 141–146.

RUSSELL 2000 INDEX MARKET PROBABILITY CALENDAR 2019

THE % CHANCE OF THE MARKET RISING ON ANY TRADING DAY OF THE YEAR*
(Based on the number of times the RUSSELL 2000 rose on a particular trading day during January 1979–December 2017)

Date	Jan	Feb	Mar	Apr	May	Jun	Jul	Aug	Sep	Oct	Nov	Dec
1	H	64.1	66.7	48.7	61.5	S	66.7	48.7	S	48.7	59.0	S
2	46.2	S	S	59.0	64.1	S	46.2	43.6	H	51.3	S	48.7
3	64.1	S	S	46.2	56.4	64.1	43.6	S	51.3	51.3	S	61.5
4	56.4	61.5	59.0	53.8	S	69.2	H	S	59.0	66.7	69.2	64.1
5	S	53.8	64.1	43.6	S	51.3	56.4	51.3	56.4	S	61.5	61.5
6	S	66.7	53.8	S	53.8	56.4	S	51.3	64.1	S	61.5	48.7
7	59.0	59.0	59.0	S	56.4	59.0	S	48.7	S	41.0	53.8	S
8	53.8	59.0	51.3	59.0	53.8	S	51.3	46.2	S	48.7	56.4	S
9	64.1	S	S	61.5	64.1	S	61.5	56.4	56.4	46.2	S	56.4
10	56.4	S	S	61.5	48.7	41.0	53.8	S	56.4	48.7	S	48.7
11	64.1	46.2	53.8	48.7	S	46.2	61.5	S	64.1	64.1	53.8	46.2
12	S	69.2	43.6	56.4	S	51.3	66.7	46.2	66.7	S	69.2	43.6
13	S	64.1	64.1	S	51.3	59.0	S	48.7	53.8	S	48.7	41.0
14	64.1	66.7	51.3	S	46.2	61.5	S	74.4	S	59.0	48.7	S
15	64.1	59.0	51.3	61.5	48.7	S	56.4	61.5	S	59.0	48.7	S
16	69.2	S	S	59.0	56.4	S	48.7	59.0	38.5	43.6	S	43.6
17	66.7	S	S	51.3	53.8	59.0	48.7	S	51.3	51.3	S	56.4
18	35.9	H	61.5	59.0	S	48.7	53.8	S	46.2	66.7	25.6	59.0
19	S	53.8	69.2	H	S	43.6	35.9	56.4	43.6	S	61.5	61.5
20	S	43.6	56.4	S	53.8	43.6	S	48.7	46.2	S	48.7	66.7
21	H	41.0	59.0	S	53.8	51.3	S	66.7	S	53.8	64.1	S
22	51.3	51.3	48.7	66.7	51.3	S	48.7	48.7	S	51.3	64.1	S
23	48.7	S	S	53.8	53.8	S	38.5	59.0	41.0	46.2	S	66.7
24	56.4	S	S	51.3	59.0	38.5	48.7	S	46.2	48.7	S	76.9
25	48.7	53.8	53.8	61.5	S	46.2	61.5	S	33.3	30.8	61.5	H
26	S	59.0	43.6	64.1	S	59.0	61.5	59.0	56.4	S	64.1	69.2
27	S	66.7	53.8	S	H	69.2	S	59.0	56.4	S	69.2	53.8
28	66.7	53.8	56.4	S	56.4	66.7	S	66.7	S	41.0	H	S
29	56.4		82.1	56.4	64.1	S	48.7	64.1	S	56.4	66.7	S
30	53.8		S	64.1	64.1	S	56.4	69.2	61.5	53.8	S	61.5
31	74.4		S		64.1		64.1	S		71.8		64.1

* See new trends developing on pages 70, 82, 141–146.

DECENNIAL CYCLE: A MARKET PHENOMENON

By arranging each year's market gain or loss so that the first and succeeding years of each decade fall into the same column, certain interesting patterns emerge—strong fifth and eighth years; weak first, seventh, and zero years.

This fascinating phenomenon was first presented by Edgar Lawrence Smith in *Common Stocks and Business Cycles* (William-Frederick Press, 1959). Anthony Gaubis co-pioneered the decennial pattern with Smith.

When Smith first cut graphs of market prices into 10-year segments and placed them above one another, he observed that each decade tended to have three bull market cycles and that the longest and strongest bull markets seemed to favor the middle years of a decade.

Don't place too much emphasis on the decennial cycle nowadays, other than the extraordinary fifth and zero years, as the stock market is more influenced by the quadrennial presidential election cycle, shown on page 130. Also, the last half-century, which has been the most prosperous in U.S. history, has distributed the returns among most years of the decade. Interestingly, NASDAQ suffered its worst bear market ever in a zero year.

Ninth years of decades have the third best record behind fifth and eighth years. There has not been a negative ninth year since 1969, when the Dow was in the midst of a nasty bear market that lopped 35.9% off. Being a pre-election year, the outlook for 2019 is further improved.

THE 10-YEAR STOCK MARKET CYCLE
Annual % Change in Dow Jones Industrial Average
Year of Decade

DECADES	1st	2nd	3rd	4th	5th	6th	7th	8th	9th	10th
1881–1890	3.0%	−2.9%	−8.5%	−18.8%	20.1%	12.4%	−8.4%	4.8%	5.5%	−14.1%
1891–1900	17.6	−6.6	−24.6	−0.6	2.3	−1.7	21.3	22.5	9.2	7.0
1901–1910	−8.7	−0.4	−23.6	41.7	38.2	−1.9	−37.7	46.6	15.0	−17.9
1911–1920	0.4	7.6	−10.3	−5.4	81.7	−4.2	−21.7	10.5	30.5	−32.9
1921–1930	12.7	21.7	−3.3	26.2	30.0	0.3	28.8	48.2	−17.2	−33.8
1931–1940	−52.7	−23.1	66.7	4.1	38.5	24.8	−32.8	28.1	−2.9	−12.7
1941–1950	−15.4	7.6	13.8	12.1	26.6	−8.1	2.2	−2.1	12.9	17.6
1951–1960	14.4	8.4	−3.8	44.0	20.8	2.3	−12.8	34.0	16.4	−9.3
1961–1970	18.7	−10.8	17.0	14.6	10.9	−18.9	15.2	4.3	−15.2	4.8
1971–1980	6.1	14.6	−16.6	−27.6	38.3	17.9	−17.3	−3.1	4.2	14.9
1981–1990	−9.2	19.6	20.3	−3.7	27.7	22.6	2.3	11.8	27.0	−4.3
1991–2000	20.3	4.2	13.7	2.1	33.5	26.0	22.6	16.1	25.2	−6.2
2001–2010	−7.1	−16.8	25.3	3.1	−0.6	16.3	6.4	−33.8	18.8	11.0
2011–2020	5.5	7.3	26.5	7.5	−2.2	13.4	25.1			
Total % Change	**5.6%**	**30.4%**	**92.6%**	**99.3%**	**365.8%**	**101.2%**	**−6.8%**	**187.9%**	**129.4%**	**−75.9%**
Avg % Change	**0.4%**	**2.2%**	**6.6%**	**7.1%**	**26.1%**	**7.2%**	**−0.5%**	**14.5%**	**10.0%**	**−5.8%**
Up Years	9	8	7	9	12	9	8	10	10	5
Down Years	5	6	7	5	2	5	6	3	3	8

Based on annual close; Cowles indices 1881–1885; 12 Mixed Stocks, 10 Rails, 2 Inds 1886–1889;
20 Mixed Stocks, 18 Rails, 2 Inds 1890–1896; Railroad average 1897 (First industrial average published May 26, 1896).

PRESIDENTIAL ELECTION/STOCK MARKET CYCLE: THE 185-YEAR SAGA CONTINUES

It is no mere coincidence that the last two years (pre-election year and election year) of the 45 administrations since 1833 produced a total net market gain of 742.5%, dwarfing the 332.2% gain of the first two years of these administrations.

Presidential elections every four years have a profound impact on the economy and the stock market. Wars, recessions, and bear markets tend to start or occur in the first half of the term; prosperous times and bull markets, in the latter half. After nine straight annual Dow gains during the millennial bull, the four-year election cycle reasserted its overarching domination of market behavior until 2008. Recovery from the worst recession since the Great Depression produced six straight annual gains, until 2015, when the Dow suffered its first pre-election year loss since 1939.

STOCK MARKET ACTION SINCE 1833
Annual % Change in Dow Jones Industrial Average[1]

4-Year Cycle Beginning	President Elected	Post-Election Year	Midterm Year	Pre-Election Year	Election Year
1833	Jackson (D)	−0.9	13.0	3.1	−11.7
1837	Van Buren (D)	−11.5	1.6	−12.3	5.5
1841*	W. H. Harrison (W)**	−13.3	−18.1	45.0	15.5
1845*	Polk (D)	8.1	−14.5	1.2	−3.6
1849*	Taylor (W)	N/C	18.7	−3.2	19.6
1853*	Pierce (D)	−12.7	−30.2	1.5	4.4
1857	Buchanan (D)	−31.0	14.3	−10.7	14.0
1861*	Lincoln (R)	−1.8	55.4	38.0	6.4
1865	Lincoln (R)**	−8.5	3.6	1.6	10.8
1869	Grant (R)	1.7	5.6	7.3	6.8
1873	Grant (R)	−12.7	2.8	−4.1	−17.9
1877	Hayes (R)	−9.4	6.1	43.0	18.7
1881	Garfield (R)**	3.0	−2.9	−8.5	−18.8
1885*	Cleveland (D)	20.1	12.4	−8.4	4.8
1889*	B. Harrison (R)	5.5	−14.1	17.6	−6.6
1893*	Cleveland (D)	−24.6	−0.6	2.3	−1.7
1897*	McKinley (R)	21.3	22.5	9.2	7.0
1901	McKinley (R)**	−8.7	−0.4	−23.6	41.7
1905	T. Roosevelt (R)	38.2	−1.9	−37.7	46.6
1909	Taft (R)	15.0	−17.9	0.4	7.6
1913*	Wilson (D)	−10.3	−5.4	81.7	−4.2
1917	Wilson (D)	−21.7	10.5	30.5	−32.9
1921*	Harding (R)**	12.7	21.7	−3.3	26.2
1925	Coolidge (R)	30.0	0.3	28.8	48.2
1929	Hoover (R)	−17.2	−33.8	−52.7	−23.1
1933*	F. Roosevelt (D)	66.7	4.1	38.5	24.8
1937	F. Roosevelt (D)	−32.8	28.1	−2.9	−12.7
1941	F. Roosevelt (D)	−15.4	7.6	13.8	12.1
1945	F. Roosevelt (D)**	26.6	−8.1	2.2	−2.1
1949	Truman (D)	12.9	17.6	14.4	8.4
1953*	Eisenhower (R)	−3.8	44.0	20.8	2.3
1957	Eisenhower (R)	−12.8	34.0	16.4	−9.3
1961*	Kennedy (D)**	18.7	−10.8	17.0	14.6
1965	Johnson (D)	10.9	−18.9	15.2	4.3
1969*	Nixon (R)	−15.2	4.8	6.1	14.6
1973	Nixon (R)***	−16.6	−27.6	38.3	17.9
1977*	Carter (D)	−17.3	−3.1	4.2	14.9
1981*	Reagan (R)	−9.2	19.6	20.3	−3.7
1985	Reagan (R)	27.7	22.6	2.3	11.8
1989	G. H. W. Bush (R)	27.0	−4.3	20.3	4.2
1993*	Clinton (D)	13.7	2.1	33.5	26.0
1997	Clinton (D)	22.6	16.1	25.2	−6.2
2001*	G. W. Bush (R)	−7.1	−16.8	25.3	3.1
2005	G. W. Bush (R)	−0.6	16.3	6.4	−33.8
2009*	Obama (D)	18.8	11.0	5.5	7.3
2013	Obama (D)	26.5	7.5	−2.2	13.4
2017	Trump (R)	25.1			
Total % Gain		**137.7%**	**194.5%**	**467.3%**	**275.2%**
Average % Gain		**3.0%**	**4.2%**	**10.2%**	**6.0%**
# Up		22	28	34	31
# Down		24	18	12	15

*Party in power ousted   **Died in office   ***Resigned   **D**–Democrat, **W**–Whig, **R**–Republican
[1] Based on annual close; prior to 1886 based on Cowles and other indices; 12 Mixed Stocks, 10 Rails, 2 Inds 1886–1889; 20 Mixed Stocks, 18 Rails, 2 Inds 1890–1896; Railroad average 1897 (First industrial average published May 26, 1896).

DOW JONES INDUSTRIALS BULL AND BEAR MARKETS SINCE 1900

Bear markets begin at the end of one bull market and end at the start of the next bull market (10/9/07 to 3/9/09 as an example). The longest bull market on record ended on 7/17/98, and the shortest bear market on record ended on 8/31/98, when the new bull market began. The greatest bull super cycle in history that began 8/12/82 ended in 2000 after the Dow gained 1409% and NASDAQ climbed 3072%. The Dow gained only 497% in the eight-year super bull from 1921 to the top in 1929. NASDAQ suffered its worst loss ever from the 2000 top to the 2002 bottom, down 77.9%, nearly as much as the 89.2% drop in the Dow from the 1929 top to the 1932 bottom. The third-longest Dow bull since 1900 that began 10/9/02 ended on its fifth anniversary. The ensuing bear market was the second worst bear market since 1900, slashing the Dow 53.8%. At press time, the Dow has left the mild bear market ending 2/11/2016 in its dust and is currently trading above 25,000. (See page 132 for S&P 500 and NASDAQ bulls and bears.)

DOW JONES INDUSTRIALS BULL AND BEAR MARKETS SINCE 1900

— Beginning —		— Ending —		Bull		Bear	
Date	DJIA	Date	DJIA	% Gain	Days	% Change	Days
9/24/00	38.80	6/17/01	57.33	47.8%	266	−46.1%	875
11/9/03	30.88	1/19/06	75.45	144.3	802	−48.5	665
11/15/07	38.83	11/19/09	73.64	89.6	735	−27.4	675
9/25/11	53.43	9/30/12	68.97	29.1	371	−24.1	668
7/30/14	52.32	11/21/16	110.15	110.5	845	−40.1	393
12/19/17	65.95	11/3/19	119.62	81.4	684	−46.6	660
8/24/21	63.90	3/20/23	105.38	64.9	573	−18.6	221
10/27/23	85.76	9/3/29	381.17	344.5	2138	−47.9	71
11/13/29	198.69	4/17/30	294.07	48.0	155	−86.0	813
7/8/32	41.22	9/7/32	79.93	93.9	61	−37.2	173
2/27/33	50.16	2/5/34	110.74	120.8	343	−22.8	171
7/26/34	85.51	3/10/37	194.40	127.3	958	−49.1	386
3/31/38	98.95	11/12/38	158.41	60.1	226	−23.3	147
4/8/39	121.44	9/12/39	155.92	28.4	157	−40.4	959
4/28/42	92.92	5/29/46	212.50	128.7	1492	−23.2	353
5/17/47	163.21	6/15/48	193.16	18.4	395	−16.3	363
6/13/49	161.60	1/5/53	293.79	81.8	1302	−13.0	252
9/14/53	255.49	4/6/56	521.05	103.9	935	−19.4	564
10/22/57	419.79	1/5/60	685.47	63.3	805	−17.4	294
10/25/60	566.05	12/13/61	734.91	29.8	414	−27.1	195
6/26/62	535.76	2/9/66	995.15	85.7	1324	−25.2	240
10/7/66	744.32	12/3/68	985.21	32.4	788	−35.9	539
5/26/70	631.16	4/28/71	950.82	50.6	337	−16.1	209
11/23/71	797.97	1/11/73	1051.70	31.8	415	−45.1	694
12/6/74	577.60	9/21/76	1014.79	75.7	655	−26.9	525
2/28/78	742.12	9/8/78	907.74	22.3	192	−16.4	591
4/21/80	759.13	4/27/81	1024.05	34.9	371	−24.1	472
8/12/82	776.92	11/29/83	1287.20	65.7	474	−15.6	238
7/24/84	1086.57	8/25/87	2722.42	150.6	1127	−36.1	55
10/19/87	1738.74	7/17/90	2999.75	72.5	1002	−21.2	86
10/11/90	2365.10	7/17/98	9337.97	294.8	2836	−19.3	45
8/31/98	7539.07	1/14/00	11722.98	55.5	501	−29.7	616
9/21/01	8235.81	3/19/02	10635.25	29.1	179	−31.5	204
10/9/02	7286.27	10/9/07	14164.53	94.4	1826	−53.8	517
3/9/09	6547.05	4/29/11	12810.54	95.7	781	−16.8	157
10/3/11	10655.30	5/19/15	18312.39	71.9	1324	−14.5	268
2/11/16	15660.18	1/26/18	26616.71	70.0*	852*		
				*As of June 12, 2018 — not in averages			
		Average		**85.6%**	**772**	**−30.6%**	**422**

Based on Dow Jones Industrial Average.
1900–2000 Data: Ned Davis Research
The NYSE was closed from 7/31/1914 to 12/11/1914 due to World War I.
DJIA figures were then adjusted back to reflect the composition change from 12 to 20 stocks in September 1916.

STANDARD & POOR'S 500 BULL AND BEAR MARKETS SINCE 1929 NASDAQ COMPOSITE SINCE 1971

A constant debate of the definition and timing of bull and bear markets permeates Wall Street like the bell that signals the open and close of every trading day. We have relied on the Ned Davis Research parameters for years to track bulls and bears on the Dow (see page 131). Standard & Poor's 500 index has been a stalwart indicator for decades and at times marched to a slightly different beat than the Dow. The moves of the S&P 500 and NASDAQ have been correlated to the bull and bear dates on page 131. Many dates line up for the three indices, but you will notice quite a lag or lead on several occasions, including NASDAQ's independent cadence from 1975 to 1980.

STANDARD & POOR'S 500 BULL AND BEAR MARKETS

— Beginning —		— Ending —		Bull		Bear	
Date	S&P 500	Date	S&P 500	% Gain	Days	% Change	Days
11/13/29	17.66	4/10/30	25.92	46.8%	148	−83.0%	783
6/1/32	4.40	9/7/32	9.31	111.6	98	−40.6	173
2/27/33	5.53	2/6/34	11.82	113.7	344	−31.8	401
3/14/35	8.06	3/6/37	18.68	131.8	723	−49.0	390
3/31/38	8.50	11/9/38	13.79	62.2	223	−26.2	150
4/8/39	10.18	10/25/39	13.21	29.8	200	−43.5	916
4/28/42	7.47	5/29/46	19.25	157.7	1492	−28.8	353
5/17/47	13.71	6/15/48	17.06	24.4	395	−20.6	363
6/13/49	13.55	1/5/53	26.66	96.8	1302	−14.8	252
9/14/53	22.71	8/2/56	49.74	119.0	1053	−21.6	446
10/22/57	38.98	8/3/59	60.71	55.7	650	−13.9	449
10/25/60	52.30	12/12/61	72.64	38.9	413	−28.0	196
6/26/62	52.32	2/9/66	94.06	79.8	1324	−22.2	240
10/7/66	73.20	11/29/68	108.37	48.0	784	−36.1	543
5/26/70	69.29	4/28/71	104.77	51.2	337	−13.9	209
11/23/71	90.16	1/11/73	120.24	33.4	415	−48.2	630
10/3/74	62.28	9/21/76	107.83	73.1	719	−19.4	531
3/6/78	86.90	9/12/78	106.99	23.1	190	−8.2	562
3/27/80	98.22	11/28/80	140.52	43.1	246	−27.1	622
8/12/82	102.42	10/10/83	172.65	68.6	424	−14.4	288
7/24/84	147.82	8/25/87	336.77	127.8	1127	−33.5	101
12/4/87	223.92	7/16/90	368.95	64.8	955	−19.9	87
10/11/90	295.46	7/17/98	1186.75	301.7	2836	−19.3	45
8/31/98	957.28	3/24/00	1527.46	59.6	571	−36.8	546
9/21/01	965.80	1/4/02	1172.51	21.4	105	−33.8	278
10/9/02	776.76	10/9/07	1565.15	101.5	1826	−56.8	517
3/9/09	676.53	4/29/11	1363.61	101.6	781	−19.4	157
10/3/11	1099.23	5/21/15	2130.82	93.8	1326	−14.2	266
2/11/16	1829.08	1/26/18	2872.87	57.1*	852* *As of June 12, 2018 — not in averages			
			Average	81.5%	750	−29.7%	375

NASDAQ COMPOSITE BULL AND BEAR MARKETS

— Beginning —		— Ending —		Bull		Bear	
Date	NASDAQ	Date	NASDAQ	% Gain	Days	% Change	Days
11/23/71	100.31	1/11/73	136.84	36.4%	415	−59.9%	630
10/3/74	54.87	7/15/75	88.00	60.4	285	−16.2	63
9/16/75	73.78	9/13/78	139.25	88.7	1093	−20.4	62
11/14/78	110.88	2/8/80	165.25	49.0	451	−24.9	48
3/27/80	124.09	5/29/81	223.47	80.1	428	−28.8	441
8/13/82	159.14	6/24/83	328.91	106.7	315	−31.5	397
7/25/84	225.30	8/26/87	455.26	102.1	1127	−35.9	63
10/28/87	291.88	10/9/89	485.73	66.4	712	−33.0	372
10/16/90	325.44	7/20/98	2014.25	518.9	2834	−29.5	80
10/8/98	1419.12	3/10/00	5048.62	255.8	519	−71.8	560
9/21/01	1423.19	1/4/02	2059.38	44.7	105	−45.9	278
10/9/02	1114.11	10/31/07	2859.12	156.6	1848	−55.6	495
3/9/09	1268.64	4/29/11	2873.54	126.5	781	−18.7	157
10/3/11	2335.83	7/20/15	5218.86	123.4	1386	−18.2	206
2/11/16	4266.84	6/12/18	7703.79	80.6*	852* *As of June 12, 2018 — not in averages			
			Average	129.7%	879	−35.0%	275

JANUARY DAILY POINT CHANGES DOW JONES INDUSTRIALS

	2009	2010	2011	2012	2013	2014	2015	2016	2017	2018
Previous Month Close	8776.39	10428.05	11577.51	12217.56	13104.14	16576.66	17823.07	17425.03	19762.60	24719.22
1	H	H	S	S	H	H	H	H	S	H
2	258.30	S	S	H	308.41	−135.31	9.92	S	H	104.79
3	S	S	93.24	179.82	−21.19	28.64	S	S	119.16	98.67
4	S	155.91	20.43	21.04	43.85	S	S	−276.09	60.40	152.45
5	−81.80	−11.94	31.71	−2.72	S	S	−331.34	9.72	−42.87	220.74
6	62.21	1.66	−25.58	−55.78	S	−44.89	−130.01	−252.15	64.51	S
7	−245.40	33.18	−22.55	S	−50.92	105.84	212.88	−392.41	S	S
8	−27.24	11.33	S	S	−55.44	−68.20	323.35	−167.65	S	−12.87
9	−143.28	S	S	32.77	61.66	−17.98	−170.50	S	−76.42	102.80
10	S	S	−37.31	69.78	80.71	−7.71	S	S	−31.85	−16.67
11	S	45.80	34.43	−13.02	17.21	S	S	52.12	98.75	205.60
12	−125.21	−36.73	83.56	21.57	S	S	−96.53	117.65	−63.28	228.46
13	−25.41	53.51	−23.54	−48.96	S	−179.11	−27.16	−364.81	−5.27	S
14	−248.42	29.78	55.48	S	18.89	115.92	−186.59	227.64	S	S
15	12.35	−100.90	S	S	27.57	108.08	−106.38	−390.97	S	H
16	68.73	S	S	H	−23.66	−64.93	190.86	S	H	−10.33
17	S	S	H	60.01	84.79	41.55	S	S	−58.96	322.79
18	S	H	50.55	96.88	53.68	S	S	H	−22.05	−97.84
19	H	115.78	−12.64	45.03	S	S	H	27.94	−72.32	53.91
20	−332.13	−122.28	−2.49	96.50	S	H	3.66	−249.28	94.85	S
21	279.01	−213.27	49.04	S	S	−44.12	39.05	115.94	S	S
22	−105.30	−216.90	S	S	62.51	−41.10	259.70	210.83	S	142.88
23	−45.24	S	S	−11.66	67.12	−175.99	−141.38	S	−27.40	−3.79
24	S	S	108.68	−33.07	46.00	−318.24	S	S	112.86	41.31
25	S	23.88	−3.33	81.21	70.65	S	S	−208.29	155.80	140.67
26	38.47	−2.57	8.25	−22.33	S	S	6.10	282.01	32.40	223.92
27	58.70	41.87	4.39	−74.17	S	−41.23	−291.49	−222.77	−7.13	S
28	200.72	−115.70	−166.13	S	−14.05	90.68	−195.84	125.18	S	S
29	−226.44	−53.13	S	S	72.49	−189.77	225.48	396.66	S	−177.23
30	−148.15	S	S	−6.74	−44.00	109.82	−251.90	S	−122.65	−362.59
31	S	S	68.23	−20.81	−49.84	−149.76	S	S	−107.04	72.50
Close	8000.86	10067.33	11891.93	12632.91	13860.58	15698.85	17164.95	16466.30	19864.09	26149.39
Change	−775.53	−360.72	314.42	415.35	756.44	−877.81	−658.12	−958.73	101.49	1430.17

FEBRUARY DAILY POINT CHANGES DOW JONES INDUSTRIALS

	2009	2010	2011	2012	2013	2014	2015	2016	2017	2018
Previous Month Close	8000.86	10067.33	11891.93	12632.91	13860.58	15698.85	17164.95	16466.30	19864.09	26149.39
1	S	118.20	148.23	83.55	149.21	S	S	−17.12	26.85	37.32
2	−64.03	111.32	1.81	−11.05	S	S	196.09	−295.64	−6.03	−665.75
3	141.53	−26.30	20.29	156.82	S	−326.05	305.36	183.12	186.55	S
4	−121.70	−268.37	29.89	S	−129.71	72.44	6.62	79.92	S	S
5	106.41	10.05	S	S	99.22	−5.01	211.86	−211.61	S	−1175.21
6	217.52	S	S	−17.10	7.22	188.30	−60.59	S	−19.04	567.02
7	S	S	69.48	33.07	−42.47	165.55	S	S	37.87	−19.42
8	S	−103.84	71.52	5.75	48.92	S	S	−177.92	−35.95	−1032.89
9	−9.72	150.25	6.74	6.51	S	S	−95.08	−12.67	118.06	330.44
10	−381.99	−20.26	−10.60	−89.23	S	7.71	139.55	−99.64	96.97	S
11	50.65	105.81	43.97	S	−21.73	192.98	−6.62	−254.56	S	S
12	−6.77	−45.05	S	S	47.46	−30.83	110.24	313.66	S	410.37
13	−82.35	S	S	72.81	−35.79	63.65	46.97	S	142.79	39.18
14	S	S	−5.07	4.24	−9.52	126.80	S	S	92.25	253.04
15	S	H	−41.55	−97.33	8.37	S	S	H	107.45	306.88
16	H	169.67	61.53	123.13	S	S	H	222.57	7.91	19.01
17	−297.81	40.43	29.97	45.79	S	H	28.23	257.42	4.28	S
18	3.03	83.66	73.11	S	H	−23.99	−17.73	−40.40	S	S
19	−89.68	9.45	S	S	53.91	−89.84	−44.08	−21.44	S	H
20	−100.28	S	S	H	−108.13	92.67	154.67	S	H	−254.63
21	S	S	H	15.82	−46.92	−29.93	S	S	118.95	−166.97
22	S	−18.97	−178.46	−27.02	119.95	S	S	228.67	32.60	164.70
23	−250.89	−100.97	−107.01	46.02	S	S	−23.60	−188.88	34.72	347.51
24	236.16	91.75	−37.28	−1.74	S	103.84	92.35	53.21	11.44	S
25	−80.05	−53.13	61.95	S	−216.40	−27.48	15.38	212.30	S	S
26	−88.81	4.23	S	S	115.96	18.75	−10.15	−57.32	S	399.28
27	−119.15	S	S	−1.44	175.24	74.24	−81.72	S	15.68	−299.24
28	S	S	95.89	23.61	−20.88	49.06	S	S	−25.20	−380.83
29	—	—	—	−53.05				−123.47		
Close	7062.93	10325.26	12226.34	12952.07	14054.49	16321.71	18132.70	16516.50	20812.24	25029.20
Change	−937.93	257.93	334.41	319.16	193.91	622.86	967.75	50.20	948.15	−1120.19

MARCH DAILY POINT CHANGES DOW JONES INDUSTRIALS

Previous Month Close	2009	2010	2011	2012	2013	2014	2015	2016	2017	2018
	7062.93	10325.26	12226.34	12952.07	14054.49	16321.71	18132.70	16516.50	20812.24	25029.20
1	S	78.53	−168.32	28.23	35.17	S	S	348.58	303.31	−420.22
2	−299.64	2.19	8.78	−2.73	S	S	155.93	34.24	−112.58	−70.92
3	−37.27	−9.22	191.40	S	S	−153.68	−85.26	44.58	2.74	S
4	149.82	47.38	−88.32	S	38.16	227.85	−106.47	62.87	S	S
5	−281.40	122.06	S	−14.76	125.95	−35.70	38.82	S	S	336.70
6	32.50	S	S	−203.66	42.47	61.71	−278.94	S	−51.37	9.36
7	S	S	−79.85	78.18	33.25	30.83	S	67.18	−29.58	−82.76
8	S	−13.68	124.35	70.61	67.58	S	S	−109.85	−69.03	93.85
9	−79.89	11.86	−1.29	14.08	S	S	138.94	36.26	2.46	440.53
10	379.44	2.95	−228.48	S	S	−34.04	−332.78	−5.23	44.79	S
11	3.91	44.51	59.79	S	50.22	−67.43	−27.55	218.18	S	S
12	239.66	12.85	S	37.69	2.77	−11.17	259.83	S	S	−157.13
13	53.92	S	S	217.97	5.22	−231.19	−145.91	S	−21.50	−171.58
14	S	S	−51.24	16.42	83.86	−43.22	S	15.82	−44.11	−248.91
15	S	17.46	−137.74	58.66	−25.03	S	S	22.40	112.73	115.54
16	−7.01	43.83	−242.12	−20.14	S	S	228.11	74.23	−15.55	72.85
17	178.73	47.69	161.29	S	S	181.55	−128.34	155.73	−19.93	S
18	90.88	45.50	83.93	S	−62.05	88.97	227.11	120.81	S	S
19	−85.78	−37.19	S	6.51	3.76	−114.02	−117.16	S	S	−335.60
20	−122.42	S	S	−68.94	55.91	108.88	168.62	S	−8.76	116.36
21	S	S	178.01	−45.57	−90.24	−28.28	S	21.57	−237.85	−44.96
22	S	43.91	−17.90	−78.48	90.54	S	S	−41.30	−6.71	−724.42
23	497.48	102.94	67.39	34.59	S	S	−11.61	−79.98	−4.72	−424.69
24	−115.89	−52.68	84.54	S	S	−26.08	−104.90	13.14	−59.86	S
25	89.84	5.06	50.03	S	−64.28	91.19	−292.60	H	S	S
26	174.75	9.15	S	160.90	111.90	−98.89	−40.31	S	S	669.40
27	−148.38	S	S	−43.90	−33.49	−4.76	34.43	S	−45.74	−344.89
28	S	S	−22.71	−71.52	52.38	58.83	S	19.66	150.52	−9.29
29	S	45.50	81.13	19.61	H	S	S	97.72	−42.18	254.69
30	−254.16	11.56	71.60	66.22	S	S	263.65	83.55	69.17	H
31	86.90	−50.79	−30.88	S	S	134.60	−200.19	−31.57	−65.27	S
Close	7608.92	10856.63	12319.73	13212.04	14578.54	16457.66	17776.12	17685.09	20663.22	24103.11
Change	545.99	531.37	93.39	259.97	524.05	135.95	−356.58	1168.59	−149.02	−926.09

APRIL DAILY POINT CHANGES DOW JONES INDUSTRIALS

Previous Month Close	2009	2010	2011	2012	2013	2014	2015	2016	2017	2018
	7608.92	10856.63	12319.73	13212.04	14578.54	16457.66	17776.12	17685.09	20663.22	24103.11
1	152.68	70.44	56.99	S	−5.69	74.95	−77.94	107.66	S	S
2	216.48	H	S	52.45	89.16	40.39	65.06	S	S	−458.92
3	39.51	S	S	−64.94	−111.66	−0.45	H	S	−13.01	389.17
4	S	S	23.31	−124.80	55.76	−159.84	S	−55.75	39.03	230.94
5	S	46.48	−6.13	−14.61	−40.86	S	S	−133.68	−41.09	240.92
6	−41.74	−3.56	32.85	H	S	S	117.61	112.73	14.80	−572.46
7	−186.29	−72.47	−17.26	S	S	−166.84	−5.43	−174.09	−6.85	S
8	47.55	29.55	−29.44	S	48.23	10.27	27.09	35.00	S	S
9	246.27	70.28	S	−130.55	59.98	181.04	56.22	S	S	46.34
10	H	S	S	−213.66	128.78	−266.96	98.92	S	1.92	428.90
11	S	S	1.06	89.46	62.90	−143.47	S	−20.55	−6.72	−218.55
12	S	8.62	−117.53	181.19	−0.08	S	S	164.84	−59.44	293.60
13	−25.57	13.45	7.41	−136.99	S	S	−80.61	187.03	−138.61	−122.91
14	−137.63	103.69	14.16	S	S	146.49	59.66	18.15	H	S
15	109.44	21.46	56.68	S	−265.86	89.32	75.91	−28.97	S	S
16	95.81	−125.91	S	71.82	157.58	162.29	−6.84	S	S	212.90
17	5.90	S	S	194.13	−138.19	−16.31	−279.47	S	183.67	213.59
18	S	S	−140.24	−82.79	−81.45	H	S	106.70	−113.64	−38.56
19	S	73.39	65.16	−68.65	10.37	S	S	49.44	−118.79	−83.18
20	−289.60	25.01	186.79	65.16	S	S	208.63	42.67	174.22	−201.95
21	127.83	7.86	52.45	S	S	40.71	−85.34	−113.75	−30.95	S
22	−82.99	9.37	H	S	19.66	65.12	88.68	21.23	S	S
23	70.49	69.99	S	−102.09	152.29	−12.72	20.42	S	S	−14.25
24	119.23	S	S	74.39	−43.16	0.00	21.45	S	216.13	−424.56
25	S	S	−26.11	89.16	24.50	−140.19	S	−26.51	232.23	59.70
26	S	0.75	115.49	113.90	11.75	S	S	13.08	−21.03	238.51
27	−51.29	−213.04	95.59	23.69	S	S	−42.17	51.23	6.24	−11.15
28	−8.05	53.28	72.35	S	S	87.28	72.17	−210.79	−40.82	S
29	168.78	122.05	47.23	S	106.20	86.63	−74.61	−57.12	S	S
30	−17.61	−158.71	S	−14.68	21.05	45.47	−195.01	S	S	−148.04
Close	8168.12	11008.61	12810.54	13213.63	14839.80	16580.84	17840.52	17773.64	20940.51	24163.15
Change	559.20	151.98	490.81	1.59	261.26	123.18	64.40	88.55	277.29	60.04

MAY DAILY POINT CHANGES DOW JONES INDUSTRIALS

	2009	2010	2011	2012	2013	2014	2015	2016	2017	2018
Previous Month Close	8168.12	11008.61	12810.54	13213.63	14839.80	16580.84	17840.52	17773.64	20940.51	24163.15
1	44.29	S	S	65.69	-138.85	-21.97	183.54	S	-27.05	-64.10
2	S	S	-3.18	-10.75	130.63	-45.98	S	117.52	36.43	-174.07
3	S	143.22	0.15	-61.98	142.38	S	S	-140.25	8.01	5.17
4	214.33	-225.06	-83.93	-168.32	S	S	46.34	-99.65	-6.43	332.36
5	-16.09	-58.65	-139.41	S	S	17.66	-142.20	9.45	55.47	S
6	101.63	-347.80	54.57	S	-5.07	-129.53	-86.22	79.92	S	S
7	-102.43	-139.89	S	-29.74	87.31	117.52	82.08	S	S	94.81
8	164.80	S	S	-76.44	48.92	32.43	267.05	S	5.34	2.89
9	S	S	45.94	-97.03	-22.50	32.37	S	-34.72	-36.50	182.33
10	S	404.71	75.68	19.98	35.87	S	S	222.44	-32.67	196.99
11	-155.88	-36.88	-130.33	-34.44	S	S	-85.94	-217.23	-23.69	91.64
12	50.34	148.65	65.89	S	S	112.13	-36.94	9.38	-22.81	S
13	-184.22	-113.96	-100.17	S	-26.81	19.97	-7.74	-185.18	S	S
14	46.43	-162.79	S	-125.25	123.57	-101.47	191.75	S	S	68.24
15	-62.68	S	S	-63.35	60.44	-167.16	20.32	S	85.33	-193.00
16	S	S	-47.38	-33.45	-42.47	44.50	S	175.39	-2.19	62.52
17	S	5.67	-68.79	-156.06	121.18	S	S	-180.73	-372.82	-54.95
18	235.44	-114.88	80.60	-73.11	S	S	26.32	-3.36	56.09	1.11
19	-29.23	-66.58	45.14	S	S	20.55	13.51	-91.22	141.82	S
20	-52.81	-376.36	-93.28	S	-19.12	-137.55	-26.99	65.54	S	S
21	-129.91	125.38	S	135.10	52.30	158.75	0.34	S	S	298.20
22	-14.81	S	S	-1.67	-80.41	10.02	-53.72	S	89.99	-178.88
23	S	S	-130.78	-6.66	-12.67	63.19	S	-8.01	43.08	52.40
24	S	-126.82	-25.05	33.60	8.60	S	S	213.12	74.51	-75.05
25	H	-22.82	38.45	-74.92	S	S	H	145.46	70.53	-58.67
26	196.17	-69.30	8.10	S	S	H	-190.48	-23.22	-2.67	S
27	-173.47	284.54	38.82	S	H	69.23	121.45	44.93	S	S
28	103.78	-122.36	S	H	106.29	-42.32	-36.87	S	S	H
29	96.53	S	S	125.86	-106.59	65.56	-115.44	S	H	-391.64
30	S	S	H	-160.83	21.73	18.43	S	H	-50.81	306.33
31	S	H	128.21	-26.41	-208.96	S	S	-86.02	-20.82	-251.94
Close	8500.33	10136.63	12569.79	12393.45	15115.57	16717.17	18010.68	17787.20	21008.65	24415.84
Change	332.21	-871.98	-240.75	-820.18	275.77	136.33	170.16	13.56	68.14	252.69

JUNE DAILY POINT CHANGES DOW JONES INDUSTRIALS

	2008	2009	2010	2011	2012	2013	2014	2015	2016	2017
Previous Month Close	12638.32	8500.33	10136.63	12569.79	12393.45	15115.57	16717.17	18010.68	17787.20	21008.65
1	S	221.11	-112.61	-279.65	-274.88	S	S	29.69	2.47	135.53
2	-134.50	19.43	225.52	-41.59	S	S	26.46	-28.43	48.89	62.11
3	-100.97	-65.59	5.74	-97.29	S	138.46	-21.29	64.33	-31.50	S
4	-12.37	74.96	-323.31	S	-17.11	-76.49	15.19	-170.69	S	S
5	213.97	12.89	S	S	26.49	-216.95	98.58	-56.12	S	-22.25
6	-394.64	S	S	-61.30	286.84	80.03	88.17	S	113.27	-47.81
7	S	S	-115.48	-19.15	46.17	207.50	S	S	17.95	37.46
8	S	1.36	123.49	-21.87	93.24	S	S	-82.91	66.77	8.84
9	70.51	-1.43	-40.73	75.42	S	S	18.82	-2.51	-19.86	89.44
10	9.44	-24.04	273.28	-172.45	S	-9.53	2.82	236.36	-119.85	S
11	-205.99	31.90	38.54	S	-142.97	-116.57	-102.04	38.97	S	S
12	57.81	28.34	S	S	162.57	-126.79	-109.69	-140.53	S	-36.30
13	165.77	S	S	1.06	-77.42	180.85	41.55	S	-132.86	92.80
14	S	S	-20.18	123.14	155.53	-105.90	S	S	-57.66	46.09
15	S	-187.13	213.88	-178.84	115.26	S	S	-107.67	-34.65	-14.66
16	-38.27	-107.46	4.69	64.25	S	S	5.27	113.31	92.93	24.38
17	-108.78	-7.49	24.71	42.84	S	109.67	27.48	31.26	-57.94	S
18	-131.24	58.42	16.47	S	-25.35	138.38	98.13	180.10	S	S
19	34.03	-15.87	S	S	95.51	-206.04	14.84	-99.89	S	144.71
20	-220.40	S	S	76.02	-12.94	-353.87	25.62	S	129.71	-61.85
21	S	S	-8.23	109.63	-250.82	41.08	S	S	24.86	-57.11
22	S	-200.72	-148.89	-80.34	67.21	S	S	103.83	-48.90	-12.74
23	-0.33	-16.10	4.92	-59.67	S	S	-9.82	24.29	230.24	-2.53
24	-34.93	-23.05	-145.64	-115.42	S	-139.84	-119.13	-178.00	-610.32	S
25	4.40	172.54	-8.99	S	-138.12	100.75	49.38	-75.71	S	S
26	-358.41	-34.01	S	S	32.01	149.83	-21.38	56.32	S	14.79
27	-106.91	S	S	108.98	92.34	114.35	5.71	S	-260.51	-98.89
28	S	S	-5.29	145.13	-24.75	-114.89	S	S	269.48	143.95
29	S	90.99	-268.22	72.73	277.83	S	S	-350.33	284.96	-167.58
30	3.50	-82.38	-96.28	152.92	S	S	-25.24	23.16	235.31	62.60
Close	11350.01	8447.00	9774.02	12414.34	12880.09	14909.60	16826.60	17619.51	17929.99	21349.63
Change	-1288.31	-53.33	-362.61	-155.45	486.64	-205.97	109.43	-391.17	142.79	340.98

JULY DAILY POINT CHANGES DOW JONES INDUSTRIALS

	2008	2009	2010	2011	2012	2013	2014	2015	2016	2017
Previous Month Close	11350.01	8447.00	9774.02	12414.34	12880.09	14909.60	16826.60	17619.51	17929.99	21349.63
1	32.25	57.06	−41.49	168.43	S	65.36	129.47	138.40	19.38	S
2	−166.75	−223.32	−46.05	S	−8.70	−42.55	20.17	−27.80	S	S
3	73.03*	H	S	S	72.43*	56.14*	92.02	H	S	129.64*
4	H	S	S	H	H	H	H	H	H	H
5	S	S	H	−12.90	−47.15	147.29	S	S	−108.75	−1.10
6	S	44.13	57.14	56.15	−124.20	S	S	−46.53	78.00	−158.13
7	−56.58	−161.27	274.66	93.47	S	S	−44.05	93.33	−22.74	94.30
8	152.25	14.81	120.71	−62.29	S	88.85	−117.59	−261.49	250.86	S
9	−236.77	4.76	59.04	S	−36.18	75.65	78.99	33.20	S	S
10	81.58	−36.65	S	S	−83.17	−8.68	−70.54	211.79	S	−5.82
11	−128.48	S	S	−151.44	−48.59	169.26	28.74	S	80.19	0.55
12	S	S	18.24	−58.88	−31.26	3.38	S	S	120.74	123.07
13	S	185.16	146.75	44.73	203.82	S	S	217.27	24.45	20.95
14	−45.35	27.81	3.70	−54.49	S	S	111.61	75.90	134.29	84.65
15	−92.65	256.72	−7.41	42.61	S	19.96	5.26	−3.41	10.14	S
16	276.74	95.61	−261.41	S	−49.88	−32.41	77.52	70.08	S	S
17	207.38	32.12	S	S	78.33	18.67	−161.39	−33.80	S	−8.02
18	49.91	S	S	−94.57	103.16	78.02	123.37	S	16.50	−54.99
19	S	S	56.53	202.26	34.66	−4.80	S	S	25.96	66.02
20	S	104.21	75.53	−15.51	−120.79	S	S	13.96	36.02	−28.97
21	−29.23	67.79	−109.43	152.50	S	S	−48.45	−181.12	−77.80	−31.71
22	135.16	−34.68	201.77	−43.25	S	1.81	61.81	−68.25	53.62	S
23	29.88	188.03	102.32	S	−101.11	22.19	−26.91	−119.12	S	S
24	−283.10	23.95	S	S	−104.14	−25.50	−2.83	−163.39	S	−66.90
25	21.41	S	S	−88.36	58.73	13.37	−123.23	S	−77.79	100.26
26	S	S	100.81	−91.50	211.88	3.22	S	S	−19.31	97.58
27	S	15.27	12.26	−198.75	187.73	S	S	−127.94	−1.58	85.54
28	−239.61	−11.79	−39.81	−62.44	S	S	22.02	189.68	−15.82	33.76
29	266.48	−26.00	−30.72	−96.87	S	−36.86	−70.48	121.12	−24.11	S
30	186.13	83.74	−1.22	S	−2.65	−1.38	−31.75	−5.41	S	S
31	−205.67	17.15	S	S	−64.33	−21.05	−317.06	−56.12	S	60.81
Close	11378.02	9171.61	10465.94	12143.24	13008.68	15499.54	16563.30	17689.86	18432.24	21891.12
Change	28.01	724.61	691.92	−271.10	128.59	589.94	−263.30	70.35	502.25	541.49

*Shortened trading day

AUGUST DAILY POINT CHANGES DOW JONES INDUSTRIALS

	2008	2009	2010	2011	2012	2013	2014	2015	2016	2017
Previous Month Close	11378.02	9171.61	10465.94	12143.24	13008.68	15499.54	16563.30	17689.86	18432.24	21891.12
1	−51.70	S	S	−10.75	−37.62	128.48	−69.93	S	−27.73	72.80
2	S	S	208.44	−265.87	−92.18	30.34	S	S	−90.74	52.32
3	S	114.95	−38.00	29.82	217.29	S	S	−91.66	41.23	9.86
4	−42.17	33.63	44.05	−512.76	S	S	75.91	−47.51	−2.95	66.71
5	331.62	−39.22	−5.45	60.93	S	−46.23	−139.81	−10.22	191.48	S
6	40.30	−24.71	−21.42	S	21.34	−93.39	13.87	−120.72	S	S
7	−224.64	113.81	S	S	51.09	−48.07	−75.07	−46.37	S	25.61
8	302.89	S	S	−634.76	7.04	27.65	185.66	S	−14.24	−33.08
9	S	S	45.19	429.92	−10.45	−72.81	S	S	3.76	−36.64
10	S	−32.12	−54.50	−519.83	42.76	S	S	241.79	−37.39	−204.69
11	48.03	−96.50	−265.42	423.37	S	S	16.05	−212.33	117.86	14.31
12	−139.88	120.16	−58.88	125.71	S	−5.83	−9.44	−0.33	−37.05	S
13	−109.51	36.58	−16.80	S	−38.52	31.33	91.26	5.74	S	S
14	82.97	−76.79	S	S	2.71	−113.35	61.78	69.15	S	135.39
15	43.97	S	S	213.88	−7.36	−225.47	−50.67	S	59.58	5.28
16	S	S	−1.14	−76.97	85.33	−30.72	S	S	−84.03	25.88
17	S	−186.06	103.84	4.28	25.09	S	S	67.78	21.92	−274.14
18	−180.51	82.60	9.69	−419.63	S	S	175.83	−33.84	23.76	−76.22
19	−130.84	61.22	−144.33	−172.93	S	−70.73	80.85	−162.61	−45.13	S
20	68.88	70.89	−57.59	S	−3.56	−7.75	59.54	−358.04	S	S
21	12.78	155.91	S	S	−68.06	−105.44	60.36	−530.94	S	29.24
22	197.85	S	S	37.00	−30.82	66.19	−38.27	S	−23.15	196.14
23	S	S	−39.21	322.11	−115.30	46.77	S	S	17.88	−87.80
24	S	3.32	−133.96	143.95	100.51	S	S	−588.40	−65.82	−28.69
25	−241.81	30.01	19.61	−170.89	S	S	75.65	−204.91	−33.07	30.27
26	26.62	4.23	−74.25	134.72	S	−64.05	29.83	619.07	−53.01	S
27	89.64	37.11	164.84	S	−33.30	−170.33	15.31	369.26	S	S
28	212.67	−36.43	S	S	−21.68	48.38	−42.44	−11.76	S	−5.27
29	−171.63	S	S	254.71	4.49	16.44	18.88	S	107.59	56.97
30	S	S	−140.92	20.70	−106.77	−30.64	S	S	−48.69	27.06
31	S	−47.92	4.99	53.58	90.13	S	S	−114.98	−53.42	55.67
Close	11543.55	9496.28	10014.72	11613.53	13090.84	14810.31	17098.45	16528.03	18400.88	21948.10
Change	165.53	324.67	−451.22	−529.71	82.16	−689.23	535.15	−1161.83	−31.36	56.98

SEPTEMBER DAILY POINT CHANGES DOW JONES INDUSTRIALS

	2008	2009	2010	2011	2012	2013	2014	2015	2016	2017
Previous Month Close	11543.55	9496.28	10014.72	11613.53	13090.84	14810.31	17098.45	16528.03	18400.88	21948.10
1	H	−185.68	254.75	−119.96	S	S	H	−469.68	18.42	39.46
2	−26.63	−29.93	50.63	−253.31	S	H	−30.89	293.03	72.66	S
3	15.96	63.94	157.83	S	H	23.65	10.72	23.38	S	S
4	−344.65	96.66	S	S	−54.90	96.91	−8.70	−272.38	S	H
5	32.73	S	S	H	11.54	6.61	67.78	S	H	−234.25
6	S	S	H	−100.96	244.52	−14.98	S	S	46.16	54.33
7	S	H	−137.24	275.56	14.64	S	S	H	−11.98	−22.86
8	289.78	56.07	46.32	−119.05	S	S	−25.94	390.30	−46.23	13.01
9	−280.01	49.88	28.23	−303.68	S	140.62	−97.55	−239.11	−394.46	S
10	38.19	80.26	47.53	S	−52.35	127.94	54.84	76.83	S	S
11	164.79	−22.07	S	S	69.07	135.54	−19.71	102.69	S	259.58
12	−11.72	S	S	68.99	9.99	−25.96	−61.49	S	239.62	61.49
13	S	S	81.36	44.73	206.51	75.42	S	S	−258.32	39.32
14	S	21.39	−17.64	140.88	53.51	S	S	−62.13	−31.98	45.30
15	−504.48	56.61	46.24	186.45	S	S	43.63	228.89	177.71	64.86
16	141.51	108.30	22.10	75.91	S	118.72	100.83	140.10	−88.68	S
17	−449.36	−7.79	13.02	S	−40.27	34.95	24.88	−65.21	S	S
18	410.03	36.28	S	S	11.54	147.21	109.14	−290.16	S	63.01
19	368.75	S	S	−108.08	13.32	−40.39	13.75	S	−3.63	39.45
20	S	S	145.77	7.65	18.97	−185.46	S	S	9.79	41.79
21	S	−41.34	7.41	−283.82	−17.46	S	S	125.61	163.74	−53.36
22	−372.75	51.01	−21.72	−391.01	S	S	−107.06	−179.72	98.76	−9.64
23	−161.52	−81.32	−76.89	37.65	S	−49.71	−116.81	−50.58	−131.01	S
24	−29.00	−41.11	197.84	S	−20.55	−66.79	154.19	−78.57	S	S
25	196.89	−42.25	S	S	−101.37	−61.33	−264.26	113.35	S	−53.50
26	121.07	S	S	272.38	−44.04	55.04	167.35	S	−166.62	−11.77
27	S	S	−48.22	146.83	72.46	−70.06	S	S	133.47	56.39
28	S	124.17	46.10	−179.79	−48.84	S	S	−312.78	110.94	40.49
29	−777.68	−47.16	−22.86	143.08	S	S	−41.93	47.24	−195.79	23.89
30	485.21	−29.92	−47.23	−240.60	S	−128.57	−28.32	234.87	164.70	S
Close	10850.66	9712.28	10788.05	10913.38	13437.13	15129.67	17042.90	16284.00	18308.15	22405.09
Change	−692.89	216.00	773.33	−700.15	346.29	319.36	−55.55	−244.03	−92.73	456.99

OCTOBER DAILY POINT CHANGES DOW JONES INDUSTRIALS

	2008	2009	2010	2011	2012	2013	2014	2015	2016	2017
Previous Month Close	10850.66	9712.28	10788.05	10913.38	13437.13	15129.67	17042.90	16284.00	18308.15	22405.09
1	−19.59	−203.00	41.63	S	77.98	62.03	−238.19	−11.99	S	S
2	−348.22	−21.61	S	S	−32.75	−58.56	−3.66	200.36	S	152.51
3	−157.47	S	S	−258.08	12.25	−136.66	208.64	S	−54.30	84.07
4	S	S	−78.41	153.41	80.75	76.10	S	S	−85.40	19.97
5	S	112.08	193.45	131.24	34.79	S	S	304.06	112.58	113.75
6	−369.88	131.50	22.93	183.38	S	S	−17.78	13.76	−12.53	−1.72
7	−508.39	−5.67	−19.07	−20.21	S	−136.34	−272.52	122.10	−28.01	S
8	−189.01	61.29	57.90	S	−26.50	−159.71	274.83	138.46	S	S
9	−678.91	78.07	S	S	−110.12	26.45	−334.97	33.74	S	−12.60
10	−128.00	S	S	330.06	−128.56	323.09	−115.15	S	88.55	69.61
11	S	S	3.86	−16.88	−18.58	111.04	S	S	−200.38	42.21
12	S	20.86	10.06	102.55	2.46	S	S	47.37	15.54	−31.88
13	936.42	−14.74	75.68	−40.72	S	S	−223.03	−49.97	−45.26	30.71
14	−76.62	144.80	−1.51	166.36	S	64.15	−5.88	−157.14	39.44	S
15	−733.08	47.08	−31.79	S	95.38	−133.25	−173.45	217.00	S	S
16	401.35	−67.03	S	S	127.55	205.82	−24.50	74.22	S	85.24
17	−127.04	S	S	−247.49	5.22	−2.18	263.17	S	−51.98	40.48
18	S	S	80.91	180.05	−8.06	28.00	S	S	75.54	160.16
19	S	96.28	−165.07	−72.43	−205.43	S	S	14.57	40.68	5.44
20	413.21	−50.71	129.35	37.16	S	S	19.26	−13.43	−40.27	165.59
21	−231.77	−92.12	38.60	267.01	S	−7.45	215.14	−48.50	−16.64	S
22	−514.45	131.95	−14.01	S*	2.38	75.46	−153.49	320.55	S	S
23	172.04	−109.13	S	S	−243.36	−54.33	216.58	157.54	S	−54.67
24	−312.30	S	S	104.83	−25.19	95.88	127.51	S	77.32	167.80
25	S	S	5.41	−207.00	26.34	61.07	S	S	−53.76	−112.30
26	S	−104.22	−43.18	162.42	3.53	S	S	−23.65	30.06	71.40
27	−203.18	14.21	−12.33	339.51	S	S	12.53	−41.62	−29.65	33.33
28	889.35	−119.48	31.49	22.56	S	S	187.81	198.09	−8.49	S
29	−74.16	199.89	4.54	S	H*	111.42	−31.44	−23.72	S	S
30	189.73	−249.85	S	S	H*	−61.59	221.11	−92.26	S	−85.45
31	144.32	S	S	−276.10	−10.75	−73.01	195.10	S	−18.77	28.50
Close	9325.01	9712.73	11118.49	11955.01	13096.46	15545.75	17390.52	17663.54	18142.42	23377.24
Change	−1525.65	0.45	330.44	1041.63	−340.67	416.08	347.62	1379.54	−165.73	972.15

*Hurricane Sandy

Previous Month Close	2008	2009	2010	2011	2012	2013	2014	2015	2016	2017
	9325.01	9712.73	11118.49	11955.01	13096.46	15545.75	17390.52	17663.54	18142.42	23377.24
1	S	S	6.13	−297.05	136.16	69.80	S	S	−105.32	57.77
2	S	76.71	64.10	178.08	−139.46	S	S	165.22	−77.46	81.25
3	−5.18	−17.53	26.41	208.43	S	S	−24.28	89.39	−28.97	22.93
4	305.45	30.23	219.71	−61.23	S	23.57	17.60	−50.57	−42.39	S
5	−486.01	203.82	9.24	S	19.28	−20.90	100.69	−4.15	S	S
6	−443.48	17.46	S	S	133.24	128.66	69.94	46.90	S	9.23
7	248.02	S	S	85.15	−312.95	−152.90	19.46	S	371.32	8.81
8	S	S	−37.24	101.79	−121.41	167.80	S	S	73.14	6.13
9	S	203.52	−60.09	−389.24	4.07	S	S	−179.85	256.95	−101.42
10	−73.27	20.03	10.29	112.85	S	S	39.81	27.73	218.19	−39.73
11	−176.58	44.29	−73.94	259.89	S	21.32	1.16	−55.99	39.78	S
12	−411.30	−93.79	−90.52	S	−0.31	−32.43	−2.70	−254.15	S	S
13	552.59	73.00	S	S	−58.90	70.96	40.59	−202.83	S	17.49
14	−337.94	S	S	−74.70	−185.23	54.59	−18.05	S	21.03	−30.23
15	S	S	9.39	17.18	−28.57	85.48	S	S	54.37	−138.19
16	S	136.49	−178.47	−190.57	45.93	S	S	237.77	−54.92	187.08
17	−223.73	30.46	−15.62	−134.86	S	S	13.01	6.49	35.68	−100.12
18	151.17	−11.11	173.35	25.43	S	14.32	40.07	247.66	−35.89	S
19	−427.47	−93.87	22.32	S	207.65	−8.99	−2.09	−4.41	S	S
20	−444.99	−14.28	S	S	−7.45	−66.21	33.27	91.06	S	72.09
21	494.13	S	S	−248.85	48.38	109.17	91.06	S	88.76	160.50
22	S	S	−24.97	−53.59	H	54.78	S	S	67.18	−64.65
23	S	132.79	−142.21	−236.17	172.79*	S	S	−31.13	59.31	H
24	396.97	−17.24	150.91	H	S	S	7.84	19.51	H	31.81*
25	36.08	30.69	H	−25.77*	S	7.77	−2.96	1.20	68.96*	S
26	247.14	H	−95.28*	S	−42.31	0.26	−2.69	H	S	S
27	H	−154.48*	S	S	−89.24	24.53	H	−14.9*	S	22.79
28	102.43*	S	S	291.23	106.98	H	15.99*	S	−54.24	255.93
29	S	S	−39.51	32.62	36.71	−10.92*	S	S	23.70	103.97
30	S	34.92	−46.47	490.05	3.76	S	S	−78.57	1.98	331.67
Close	8829.04	10344.84	11006.02	12045.68	13025.58	16086.41	17828.24	17719.92	19123.58	24272.35
Change	−495.97	632.11	−112.47	90.67	−70.88	540.66	437.72	56.38	981.16	895.11

*Shortened trading day

Previous Month Close	2008	2009	2010	2011	2012	2013	2014	2015	2016	2017
	8829.04	10344.84	11006.02	12045.68	13025.58	16086.41	17828.24	17719.92	19123.58	24272.35
1	−679.95	126.74	249.76	−25.65	S	S	−51.44	168.43	68.35	−40.76
2	270.00	−18.90	106.63	−0.61	S	−77.64	102.75	−158.67	−21.51	S
3	172.60	−86.53	19.68	S	−59.98	−94.15	33.07	−252.01	S	S
4	−215.45	22.75	S	S	−13.82	−24.85	−12.52	369.96	S	58.46
5	259.18	S	S	78.41	82.71	−68.26	58.69	S	45.82	−109.41
6	S	S	−19.90	52.30	39.55	198.69	S	S	35.54	−39.73
7	S	1.21	−3.03	46.24	81.09	S	S	−117.12	297.84	70.57
8	298.76	−104.14	13.32	−198.67	S	S	−106.31	−162.51	65.19	117.68
9	−242.85	51.08	−2.42	186.56	S	5.33	−51.28	−75.70	142.04	S
10	70.09	68.78	40.26	S	14.75	−52.40	−268.05	82.45	S	S
11	−196.33	65.67	S	S	78.56	−129.60	63.19	−309.54	S	56.87
12	64.59	S	S	−162.87	−2.99	−104.10	−315.51	S	39.58	118.77
13	S	S	18.24	−66.45	−74.73	15.93	S	S	114.78	80.63
14	S	29.55	47.98	−131.46	−35.71	S	S	103.29	−118.68	−76.77
15	−65.15	−49.05	−19.07	45.33	S	S	−99.99	156.41	59.71	143.08
16	359.61	−10.88	41.78	−2.42	S	129.21	−111.97	224.18	−8.83	S
17	−99.80	−132.86	−7.34	S	100.38	−9.31	288.00	−253.25	S	S
18	−219.35	20.63	S	S	115.57	292.71	421.28	−367.29	S	140.46
19	−25.88	S	S	−100.13	−98.99	11.11	26.65	S	39.65	−37.45
20	S	S	−13.78	337.32	59.75	42.06	S	S	91.56	−28.10
21	S	85.25	55.03	4.16	−120.88	S	S	123.07	−32.66	55.64
22	−59.34	50.79	26.33	61.91	S	S	154.64	165.65	−23.08	−28.23
23	−100.28	1.51	14.00	124.35	S	73.47	64.73	185.34	14.93	S
24	48.99*	53.66*	H	S	−51.76*	62.94*	6.04*	−50.44*	S	S
25	H	H	S	S	H	H	H	H	S	H
26	47.07	S	S	H	−24.49	122.33	23.50	S	H	−7.85
27	S	S	−18.46	−2.65	−18.28	−1.47	S	S	11.23	28.09
28	S	26.98	20.51	−139.94	−158.20	S	S	−23.90	−111.36	63.21
29	−31.62	−1.67	9.84	135.63	S	S	−15.48	192.71	−13.90	−118.29
30	184.46	3.10	−15.67	−69.48	S	25.88	−55.16	−117.11	−57.18	S
31	108.00	−120.46	7.80	S	166.03	72.37	−160.00	−178.84	S	S
Close	8776.39	10428.05	11577.51	12217.56	13104.14	16576.66	17823.07	17425.03	19762.60	24719.22
Change	−52.65	83.21	571.49	171.88	78.56	490.25	−5.17	−294.89	639.02	446.87

*Shortened trading day

A TYPICAL DAY IN THE MARKET

Half-hourly data became available for the Dow Jones Industrial Average starting in January 1987. The NYSE switched 10:00 a.m. openings to 9:30 a.m. in October 1985. Below is the comparison between half-hourly performance from January 1987 to May 25, 2018, and hourly performance from November 1963 to June 1985. Stronger closings in a more bullish climate are evident. Morning and afternoon weaknesses appear an hour earlier.

MARKET % PERFORMANCE EACH HALF-HOUR OF THE DAY
(January 1987–May 25, 2018)

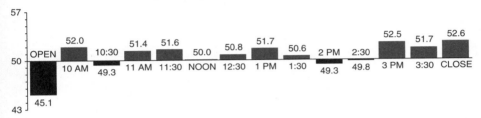

Based on the number of times the Dow Jones Industrial Average increased over the previous half-hour.

MARKET % PERFORMANCE EACH HOUR OF THE DAY
(November 1963–June 1985)

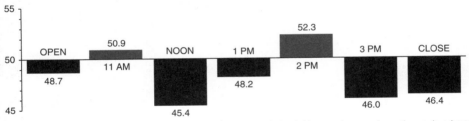

Based on the number of times the Dow Jones Industrial Average increased over the previous hour.

On the next page, half-hourly movements since January 1987 are separated by day of the week. From 1953 to 1989, Monday was the worst day of the week, especially during long bear markets, but times changed. Monday reversed positions and became the best day of the week and on the plus side eleven years in a row from 1990 to 2000.

During the last 17 years (2001–May 25, 2018) Friday is a net loser. Tuesday through Thursday are solid gainers, Tuesday the best (page 68). On all days, stocks do tend to firm up near the close with weakness in the early morning and from 1:30 to 2:30 frequently.

THROUGH THE WEEK ON A HALF-HOURLY BASIS

From the chart showing the percentage of times the Dow Jones Industrial Average rose over the preceding half-hour (January 1987 to May 15, 2018*), the typical week unfolds.

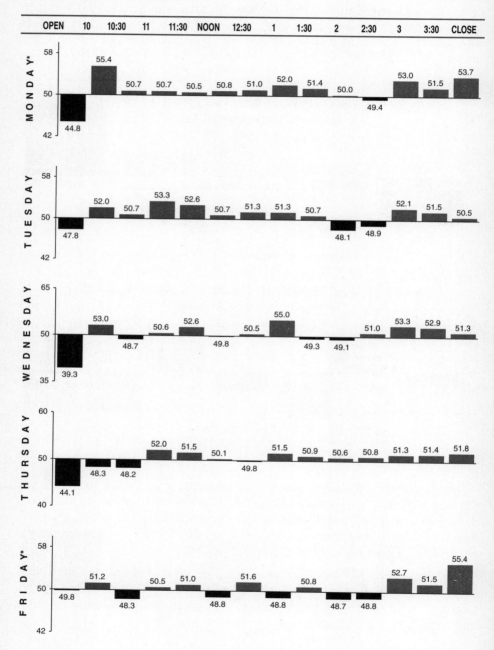

*Monday denotes first trading day of the week, Friday denotes last trading day of the week.

TUESDAY MOST PROFITABLE DAY OF WEEK

Between 1952 and 1989, Monday was the worst trading day of the week. The first trading day of the week (including Tuesday when Monday is a holiday) rose only 44.3% of the time, while the other trading days closed higher 54.8% of the time. (NYSE Saturday trading was discontinued in June 1952.)

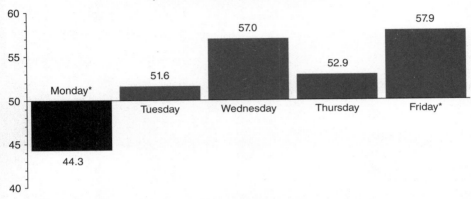

MARKET % PERFORMANCE EACH DAY OF THE WEEK
(June 1952–December 1989)

A dramatic reversal occurred in 1990—Monday became the most powerful day of the week. However, during the last 17⅓ years, Tuesday has produced the most gains. Since the top in 2000, traders have not been inclined to stay long over the weekend nor buy up equities at the outset of the week. This is not uncommon during uncertain market times. Monday was the worst day during the 2007–2009 bear, and only Tuesday was a net gainer. Since the March 2009 bottom, Tuesday and Thursday are best. See pages 68 and 143.

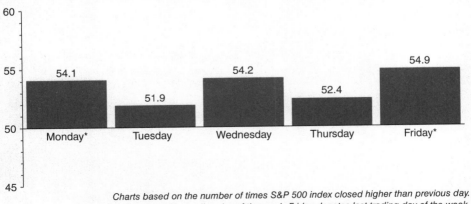

MARKET % PERFORMANCE EACH DAY OF THE WEEK
(January 1990–June 8, 2018)

Charts based on the number of times S&P 500 index closed higher than previous day.
*Monday denotes first trading day of the week, Friday denotes last trading day of the week.

NASDAQ STRONGEST LAST 3 DAYS OF WEEK

Despite 20 years less data, daily trading patterns on NASDAQ through 1989 appear to be fairly similar to the S&P on page 141, except for more bullishness on Thursdays. During the mostly flat markets of the 1970s and early 1980s, it would appear that apprehensive investors decided to throw in the towel over weekends and sell on Mondays and Tuesdays.

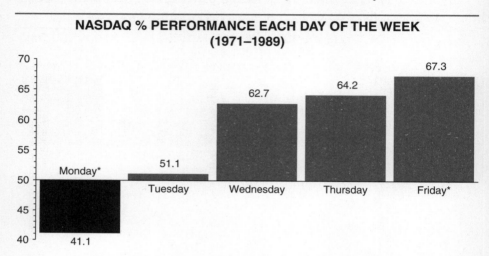

NASDAQ % PERFORMANCE EACH DAY OF THE WEEK
(1971–1989)

Notice the vast difference in the daily trading pattern between NASDAQ and S&P from January 1, 1990, to recent times. The reason for so much more bullishness is that NASDAQ moved up 1010%, over three times as much during the 1990 to 2000 period. The gain for the S&P was 332% and for the Dow Jones industrials, 326%. NASDAQ's weekly patterns are beginning to move in step with the rest of the market. Notice the similarities to the S&P since 2001 on pages 143 and 144—Monday and Friday weakness, midweek strength.

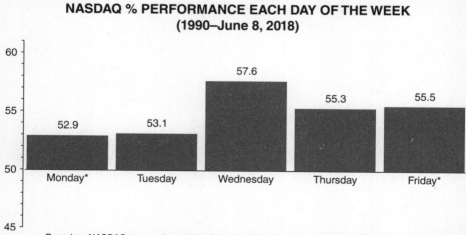

NASDAQ % PERFORMANCE EACH DAY OF THE WEEK
(1990–June 8, 2018)

Based on NASDAQ composite, prior to February 5, 1971, based on National Quotation Bureau indices.
*Monday denotes first trading day of the week, Friday denotes last trading day of the week.

S&P DAILY PERFORMANCE EACH YEAR SINCE 1952

To determine if market trend alters performance of different days of the week, we separated 23 bear years—1953, '56, '57, '60, '62, '66, '69, '70, '73, '74, '77, '78, '81, '84, '87, '90, '94, 2000, 2001, 2002, 2008, 2011, and 2015—from 43 bull market years. While Tuesdays and Thursdays did not vary much between bull and bear years, Mondays and Fridays were sharply affected. There was a swing of 10.2 percentage points in Monday's performance and 9.5 in Friday's. Tuesday is the best day of the week based on total points gained. See page 70.

PERCENTAGE OF TIMES MARKET CLOSED HIGHER THAN PREVIOUS DAY
(JUNE 1952–JUNE 8, 2018)

	Monday*	Tuesday	Wednesday	Thursday	Friday*
1952	48.4%	55.6%	58.1%	51.9%	66.7%
1953	32.7	50.0	54.9	57.5	56.6
1954	50.0	57.5	63.5	59.2	73.1
1955	50.0	45.7	63.5	60.0	78.9
1956	36.5	39.6	46.9	50.0	59.6
1957	25.0	54.0	66.7	48.9	44.2
1958	59.6	52.0	59.6	68.1	72.6
1959	42.3	53.1	55.8	48.9	69.8
1960	34.6	50.0	44.2	54.0	59.6
1961	52.9	54.4	64.7	56.0	67.3
1962	28.3	52.1	54.0	51.0	50.0
1963	46.2	63.3	51.0	57.5	69.2
1964	40.4	48.0	61.5	58.7	77.4
1965	44.2	57.5	55.8	51.0	71.2
1966	36.5	47.8	53.9	42.0	57.7
1967	38.5	50.0	60.8	64.0	69.2
1968†	49.1	57.5	64.3	42.6	54.9
1969	30.8	45.8	50.0	67.4	50.0
1970	38.5	46.0	63.5	48.9	52.8
1971	44.2	64.6	57.7	55.1	51.9
1972	38.5	60.9	57.7	51.0	67.3
1973	32.1	51.1	52.9	44.9	44.2
1974	32.7	57.1	51.0	36.7	30.8
1975	53.9	38.8	61.5	56.3	55.8
1976	55.8	55.3	55.8	40.8	58.5
1977	40.4	40.4	46.2	53.1	53.9
1978	51.9	43.5	59.6	54.0	48.1
1979	54.7	53.2	58.8	66.0	44.2
1980	55.8	54.2	71.7	35.4	59.6
1981	44.2	38.8	55.8	53.2	47.2
1982	46.2	39.6	44.2	44.9	50.0
1983	55.8	46.8	61.5	52.0	55.8
1984	39.6	63.8	31.4	46.0	44.2
1985	44.2	61.2	54.9	56.3	53.9
1986	51.9	44.9	67.3	58.3	55.8
1987	51.9	57.1	63.5	61.7	49.1
1988	51.9	61.7	51.9	48.0	59.6
1989	51.9	47.8	69.2	58.0	69.2
1990	67.9	53.2	52.9	40.0	51.9
1991	44.2	46.9	52.9	49.0	51.9
1992	51.9	49.0	53.9	56.3	45.3
1993	65.4	41.7	55.8	44.9	48.1
1994	55.8	46.8	52.9	48.0	59.6
1995	63.5	56.5	63.5	62.0	63.5
1996	54.7	44.9	51.0	57.1	63.5
1997	67.3	67.4	42.3	41.7	57.7
1998	57.7	62.5	57.7	38.3	60.4
1999	46.2	29.8	67.3	53.1	57.7
2000	51.9	43.5	40.4	56.0	46.2
2001	45.3	51.1	44.0	59.2	43.1
2002	40.4	37.5	56.9	38.8	48.1
2003	59.6	62.5	42.3	58.3	50.0
2004	51.9	61.7	59.6	52.1	52.8
2005	59.6	47.8	59.6	56.0	55.8
2006	55.8	55.6	67.3	52.0	48.1
2007	47.2	50.0	64.0	50.0	61.5
2008	42.3	50.0	41.5	60.4	55.8
2009	53.9	50.0	57.7	63.8	52.8
2010	61.5	57.5	55.8	53.1	57.7
2011	48.1	56.5	55.8	56.0	57.7
2012	52.8	48.9	50.0	58.0	53.9
2013	51.9	60.4	54.9	59.2	65.4
2014	53.9	56.3	57.7	56.3	61.5
2015	51.9	43.8	44.2	53.2	43.4
2016	50.0	58.7	55.8	50.0	46.2
2017	55.8	55.6	61.5	50.0	61.5
2018‡	60.9	57.9	52.2	45.5	69.6
Average	**48.3%**	**51.6%**	**55.8%**	**52.8%**	**56.4%**
43 Bull Years	**51.9%**	**53.2%**	**58.2%**	**53.5%**	**59.7%**
23 Bear Years	**41.7%**	**48.7%**	**51.4%**	**51.3%**	**50.2%**

Based on S&P 500

† Most Wednesdays closed last 7 months of 1968. ‡ Through 6/8/2018 only, not included in averages.
*Monday denotes first trading day of the week, Friday denotes last trading day of the week.

NASDAQ DAILY PERFORMANCE EACH YEAR SINCE 1971

After dropping a hefty 77.9% from its 2000 high (versus −37.8% on the Dow and −49.1% on the S&P 500), NASDAQ tech stocks still outpace the blue chips and big caps—but not nearly by as much as they did. From January 1, 1971, through June 8, 2018, NASDAQ moved up an impressive 8432%. The Dow (up 2918%) and the S&P (up 2916%) gained less than half as much.

Monday's performance on NASDAQ was lackluster during the three-year bear market of 2000–2002. As NASDAQ rebounded (up 50% in 2003), strength returned to Monday during 2003–2006. During the bear market from late 2007 to early 2009, weakness was most consistent on Monday and Friday. At press time, Thursdays have been challenging.

PERCENTAGE OF TIMES NASDAQ CLOSED HIGHER THAN PREVIOUS DAY (1971–JUNE 8, 2018)

	Monday*	Tuesday	Wednesday	Thursday	Friday*
1971	51.9%	52.1%	59.6%	65.3%	71.2%
1972	30.8	60.9	63.5	57.1	78.9
1973	34.0	48.9	52.9	53.1	48.1
1974	30.8	44.9	52.9	51.0	42.3
1975	44.2	42.9	63.5	64.6	63.5
1976	50.0	63.8	67.3	59.2	58.5
1977	51.9	40.4	53.9	63.3	73.1
1978	48.1	47.8	73.1	72.0	84.6
1979	45.3	53.2	64.7	86.0	82.7
1980	46.2	64.6	84.9	52.1	73.1
1981	42.3	32.7	67.3	76.6	69.8
1982	34.6	47.9	59.6	51.0	63.5
1983	42.3	44.7	67.3	68.0	73.1
1984	22.6	53.2	35.3	52.0	51.9
1985	36.5	59.2	62.8	68.8	66.0
1986	38.5	55.1	65.4	72.9	75.0
1987	42.3	49.0	65.4	68.1	66.0
1988	50.0	55.3	61.5	66.0	63.5
1989	38.5	54.4	71.2	72.0	75.0
1990	54.7	42.6	60.8	46.0	55.8
1991	51.9	59.2	66.7	65.3	51.9
1992	44.2	53.1	59.6	60.4	45.3
1993	55.8	56.3	69.2	57.1	67.3
1994	51.9	46.8	54.9	52.0	55.8
1995	50.0	52.2	63.5	64.0	63.5
1996	50.9	57.1	64.7	61.2	63.5
1997	65.4	59.2	53.9	52.1	55.8
1998	59.6	58.3	65.4	44.7	58.5
1999	61.5	40.4	63.5	57.1	65.4
2000	40.4	41.3	42.3	60.0	57.7
2001	41.5	57.8	52.0	55.1	47.1
2002	44.2	37.5	56.9	46.9	46.2
2003	57.7	60.4	40.4	60.4	46.2
2004	57.7	59.6	53.9	50.0	50.9
2005	61.5	47.8	51.9	48.0	59.6
2006	55.8	51.1	65.4	50.0	44.2
2007	47.2	63.0	66.0	56.0	57.7
2008	34.6	52.1	49.1	54.2	42.3
2009	51.9	54.2	63.5	63.8	50.9
2010	61.5	53.2	61.5	55.1	61.5
2011	50.0	56.5	50.0	64.0	53.9
2012	49.1	53.3	50.0	54.0	51.9
2013	57.7	60.4	52.9	59.2	67.3
2014	57.7	58.3	57.7	52.1	59.6
2015	55.8	39.6	53.9	59.6	49.1
2016	51.9	52.2	55.8	50.0	57.7
2017	59.6	62.2	67.3	50.0	67.3
2018†	60.9	63.2	52.2	36.4	65.2
Average	**48.1%**	**52.3%**	**59.7%**	**58.9%**	**60.3%**
34 Bull Years	**50.5%**	**54.5%**	**62.1%**	**59.7%**	**63.2%**
13 Bear Years	**41.9%**	**46.4%**	**53.4%**	**56.8%**	**52.8%**

Based on NASDAQ composite; prior to February 5, 1971, based on National Quotation Bureau indices.
† Through 6/8/2018 only, not included in averages.
*Monday denotes first trading day of the week, Friday denotes last trading day of the week.

MONTHLY CASH INFLOWS INTO S&P STOCKS

For many years, the last trading day of the month, plus the first four of the following month, were the best market days of the month. This pattern is quite clear in the first chart, showing these five consecutive trading days towering above the other 16 trading days of the average month in the 1953–1981 period. The rationale was that individuals and institutions tended to operate similarly, causing a massive flow of cash into stocks near beginnings of months.

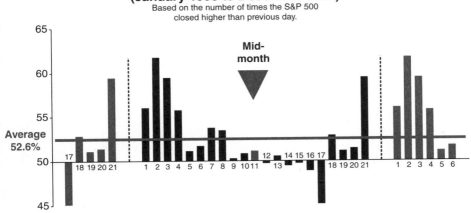

MARKET % PERFORMANCE EACH DAY OF THE MONTH
(January 1953 to December 1981)
Based on the number of times the S&P 500
closed higher than previous day.

Clearly, "front-running" traders took advantage of this phenomenon, drastically altering the previous pattern. The second chart from 1982 onward shows the trading shift caused by these "anticipators" to the last three trading days of the month, plus the first two. Another astonishing development shows the ninth, tenth, and eleventh trading days rising strongly as well. Growth of 401(k) retirement plans, IRAs, and similar plans (participants' salaries are usually paid twice monthly) is responsible for this midmonth bulge. First trading days of the month have produced the greatest gains in recent years (see page 86).

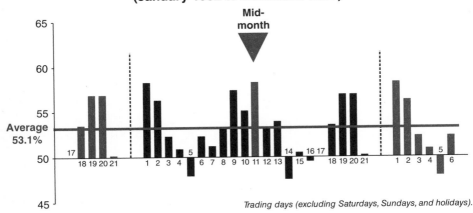

MARKET % PERFORMANCE EACH DAY OF THE MONTH
(January 1982 to December 2017)

Trading days (excluding Saturdays, Sundays, and holidays).

MONTHLY CASH INFLOWS INTO NASDAQ STOCKS

NASDAQ stocks moved up 58.1% of the time through 1981 compared to 52.6% for the S&P on page 145. Ends and beginnings of the month are fairly similar, specifically the last plus the first four trading days. But notice how investors piled into NASDAQ stocks until midmonth. NASDAQ rose 118.6% from January 1, 1971, to December 31, 1981, compared to 33.0% for the S&P.

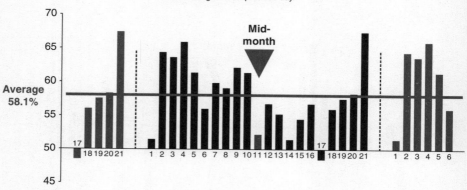

NASDAQ % PERFORMANCE EACH DAY OF THE MONTH
(January 1971 to December 1981)
Based on the number of times the NASDAQ composite
closed higher than previous day.

After the air was let out of the tech market in 2000–2002, S&P's 2,082% gain over the last 36 years is more evenly matched with NASDAQ's 3,425% gain. Last three, first four, and middle eighth and tenth days rose the most. Where the S&P has three days of the month that go down more often than up, NASDAQ has none. NASDAQ exhibits the most strength on the first trading day of the month. Over the past 19 years, last days have weakened considerably, down more often than not.

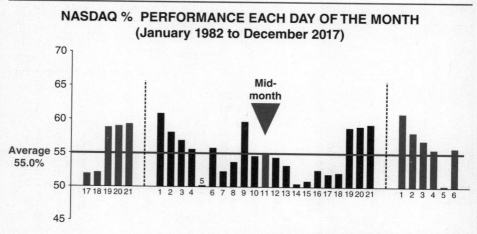

NASDAQ % PERFORMANCE EACH DAY OF THE MONTH
(January 1982 to December 2017)

Trading days (excluding Saturdays, Sundays, and holidays).
Based on NASDAQ composite, prior to February 5, 1971, based on National Quotation Bureau indices.

146

NOVEMBER, DECEMBER AND JANUARY: YEAR'S BEST THREE-MONTH SPAN

The most important observation to be made from a chart showing the average monthly percent change in market prices since 1950 is that institutions (mutual funds, pension funds, banks, etc.) determine the trading patterns in today's market.

The "investment calendar" reflects the annual, semiannual, and quarterly operations of institutions during January, April, and July. October, besides being the last campaign month before elections, is also the time when most bear markets seem to end, as in 1946, 1957, 1960, 1966, 1974, 1987, 1990, 1998, and 2002. (August and September tend to combine to make the worst consecutive two-month period.)

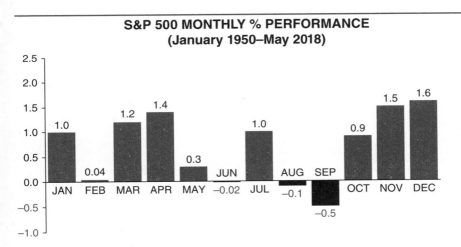

**S&P 500 MONTHLY % PERFORMANCE
(January 1950–May 2018)**

*Average month-to-month % change in S&P 500.
(Based on monthly closing prices.)*

Unusual year-end strength comes from corporate and private pension funds, producing a 4.1% gain on average between November 1 and January 31. In 2007–2008, these three months were all down for the fourth time since 1930; previously in 1931–1932, 1940–1941, and 1969–1970, also bear markets. September's dismal performance makes it the worst month of the year. However, in the last 14 years, it has been up 9 times after being down five in a row 1999–2003.

In pre-election years since 1950, January is the best month, +3.9% (15–2). April is second best with a 3.5% average gain. February, March, May, June, July, August, October, November and December are also positive. September is the sole losing month in pre-election years, averaging −0.9%, down 12 of the last 17.

See page 50 for monthly performance tables for the S&P 500 and the Dow Jones industrials. See pages 52, 56, 60 and 62 for unique switching strategies.

On page 64, you can see how the first month of the first three quarters far outperforms the second and third months since 1950, and note the improvement in May's and October's performance since 1991.

NOVEMBER THROUGH JUNE: NASDAQ'S EIGHT-MONTH RUN

The two-and-a-half-year plunge of 77.9% in NASDAQ stocks, between March 10, 2000, and October 9, 2002, brought several horrendous monthly losses (the two greatest were November 2000, −22.9%, and February 2001, −22.4%), which trimmed average monthly performance over the $47^1/_3$-year period. Ample Octobers in 14 of the last 20 years, including three huge turnarounds in 2001 (+12.8%), 2002 (+13.5%), and 2011 (+11.1%) have put bear-killing October in the number two spot since 1998. January's 2.7% average gain is still awesome, and more than twice S&P's 1.2% January average since 1971.

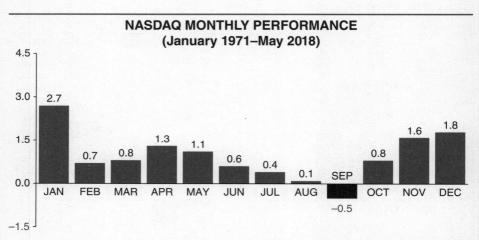

NASDAQ MONTHLY PERFORMANCE
(January 1971–May 2018)

Average month-to-month % change in NASDAQ composite, prior to February 5, 1971, based on National Quotation Bureau indices. (Based on monthly closing prices.)

Bear in mind, when comparing NASDAQ to the S&P on page 147, that there are 22 fewer years of data here. During this $47^1/_3$-year (1971–May 2018) period, NASDAQ gained 8205%, while the S&P and the Dow rose only 2836% and 2810%, respectively. On page 56, you can see a statistical monthly comparison between NASDAQ and the Dow.

Year-end strength is even more pronounced in NASDAQ, producing a 6.1% gain on average between November 1 and January 31—nearly 1.5 times greater than that of the S&P 500 on page 147. September is the worst month of the year for the over-the-counter index as well, posting an average loss of −0.5%. These extremes underscore NASDAQ's higher volatility—and moves of greater magnitude.

In pre-election years since 1971, January is best with an average gain of 6.6% (10–2). February, March, April, May, June, July, August, October, November and December are also all positive. September is the only losing month, down 0.9% on average, with six gains and six losses.

DOW JONES INDUSTRIALS ANNUAL HIGHS, LOWS & CLOSES SINCE 1901

YEAR	HIGH DATE	HIGH CLOSE	LOW DATE	LOW CLOSE	YEAR CLOSE	YEAR	HIGH DATE	HIGH CLOSE	LOW DATE	LOW CLOSE	YEAR CLOSE
1901	6/17	57.33	12/24	45.07	47.29	1960	1/5	685.47	10/25	566.05	615.89
1902	4/24	50.14	12/15	43.64	47.10	1961	12/13	734.91	1/3	610.25	731.14
1903	2/16	49.59	11/9	30.88	35.98	1962	1/3	726.01	6/26	535.76	652.10
1904	12/5	53.65	3/12	34.00	50.99	1963	12/18	767.21	1/2	646.79	762.95
1905	12/29	70.74	1/25	50.37	70.47	1964	11/18	891.71	1/2	766.08	874.13
1906	1/19	75.45	7/13	62.40	69.12	1965	12/31	969.26	6/28	840.59	969.26
1907	1/7	70.60	11/15	38.83	43.04	1966	2/9	995.15	10/7	744.32	785.69
1908	11/13	64.74	2/13	42.94	63.11	1967	9/25	943.08	1/3	786.41	905.11
1909	11/19	73.64	2/23	58.54	72.56	1968	12/3	985.21	3/21	825.13	943.75
1910	1/3	72.04	7/26	53.93	59.60	1969	5/14	968.85	12/17	769.93	800.36
1911	6/19	63.78	9/25	53.43	59.84	1970	12/29	842.00	5/26	631.16	838.92
1912	9/30	68.97	2/10	58.72	64.37	1971	4/28	950.82	11/23	797.97	890.20
1913	1/9	64.88	6/11	52.83	57.71	1972	12/11	1036.27	1/26	889.15	1020.02
1914	3/20	61.12	7/30	52.32	54.58	1973	1/11	1051.70	12/5	788.31	850.86
1915	12/27	99.21	2/24	54.22	99.15	1974	3/13	891.66	12/6	577.60	616.24
1916	11/21	110.15	4/22	84.96	95.00	1975	7/15	881.81	1/2	632.04	852.41
1917	1/3	99.18	12/19	65.95	74.38	1976	9/21	1014.79	1/2	858.71	1004.65
1918	10/18	89.07	1/15	73.38	82.20	1977	1/3	999.75	11/2	800.85	831.17
1919	11/3	119.62	2/8	79.15	107.23	1978	9/8	907.74	2/28	742.12	805.01
1920	1/3	109.88	12/21	66.75	71.95	1979	10/5	897.61	11/7	796.67	838.74
1921	12/15	81.50	8/24	63.90	81.10	1980	11/20	1000.17	4/21	759.13	963.99
1922	10/14	103.43	1/10	78.59	98.73	1981	4/27	1024.05	9/25	824.01	875.00
1923	3/20	105.38	10/27	85.76	95.52	1982	12/27	1070.55	8/12	776.92	1046.54
1924	12/31	120.51	5/20	88.33	120.51	1983	11/29	1287.20	1/3	1027.04	1258.64
1925	11/6	159.39	3/30	115.00	156.66	1984	1/6	1286.64	7/24	1086.57	1211.57
1926	8/14	166.64	3/30	135.20	157.20	1985	12/16	1553.10	1/4	1184.96	1546.67
1927	12/31	202.40	1/25	152.73	202.40	1986	12/2	1955.57	1/22	1502.29	1895.95
1928	12/31	300.00	2/20	191.33	300.00	1987	8/25	2722.42	10/19	1738.74	1938.83
1929	9/3	381.17	11/13	198.69	248.48	1988	10/21	2183.50	1/20	1879.14	2168.57
1930	4/17	294.07	12/16	157.51	164.58	1989	10/9	2791.41	1/3	2144.64	2753.20
1931	2/24	194.36	12/17	73.79	77.90	1990	7/17	2999.75	10/11	2365.10	2633.66
1932	3/8	88.78	7/8	41.22	59.93	1991	12/31	3168.83	1/9	2470.30	3168.83
1933	7/18	108.67	2/27	50.16	99.90	1992	6/1	3413.21	10/9	3136.58	3301.11
1934	2/5	110.74	7/26	85.51	104.04	1993	12/29	3794.33	1/20	3241.95	3754.09
1935	11/19	148.44	3/14	96.71	144.13	1994	1/31	3978.36	4/4	3593.35	3834.44
1936	11/17	184.90	1/6	143.11	179.90	1995	12/13	5216.47	1/30	3832.08	5117.12
1937	3/10	194.40	11/24	113.64	120.85	1996	12/27	6560.91	1/10	5032.94	6448.27
1938	11/12	158.41	3/31	98.95	154.76	1997	8/6	8259.31	4/11	6391.69	7908.25
1939	9/12	155.92	4/8	121.44	150.24	1998	11/23	9374.27	8/31	7539.07	9181.43
1940	1/3	152.80	6/10	111.84	131.13	1999	12/31	11497.12	1/22	9120.67	11497.12
1941	1/10	133.59	12/23	106.34	110.96	2000	1/14	11722.98	3/7	9796.03	10786.85
1942	12/26	119.71	4/28	92.92	119.40	2001	5/21	11337.92	9/21	8235.81	10021.50
1943	7/14	145.82	1/8	119.26	135.89	2002	3/19	10635.25	10/9	7286.27	8341.63
1944	12/16	152.53	2/7	134.22	152.32	2003	12/31	10453.92	3/11	7524.06	10453.92
1945	12/11	195.82	1/24	151.35	192.91	2004	12/28	10854.54	10/25	9749.99	10783.01
1946	5/29	212.50	10/9	163.12	177.20	2005	3/4	10940.55	4/20	10012.36	10717.50
1947	7/24	186.85	5/17	163.21	181.16	2006	12/27	12510.57	1/20	10667.39	12463.15
1948	6/15	193.16	3/16	165.39	177.30	2007	10/9	14164.53	3/5	12050.41	13264.82
1949	12/30	200.52	6/13	161.60	200.13	2008	5/2	13058.20	11/20	7552.29	8776.39
1950	11/24	235.47	1/13	196.81	235.41	2009	12/30	10548.51	3/9	6547.05	10428.05
1951	9/13	276.37	1/3	238.99	269.23	2010	12/29	11585.38	7/2	9686.48	11577.51
1952	12/30	292.00	5/1	256.35	291.90	2011	4/29	12810.54	10/3	10655.30	12217.56
1953	1/5	293.79	9/14	255.49	280.90	2012	10/5	13610.15	6/4	12101.46	13104.14
1954	12/31	404.39	1/11	279.87	404.39	2013	12/31	16576.66	1/8	13328.85	16576.66
1955	12/30	488.40	1/17	388.20	488.40	2014	12/26	18053.71	2/3	15372.80	17823.07
1956	4/6	521.05	1/23	462.35	499.47	2015	5/19	18312.39	8/25	15666.44	17425.03

YEAR	HIGH DATE	HIGH CLOSE	LOW DATE	LOW CLOSE	YEAR CLOSE	YEAR	HIGH DATE	HIGH CLOSE	LOW DATE	LOW CLOSE	YEAR CLOSE
1957	7/12	520.77	10/22	419.79	435.69	2016	12/20	19974.62	2/11	15660.18	19762.60
1958	12/31	583.65	2/25	436.89	583.65	2017	12/28	24837.51	1/19	19732.40	24719.22
1959	12/31	679.36	2/9	574.46	679.36	2018*	1/26	26616.71	3/23	23533.20	At press time

*Through June 8, 2018

S&P 500 ANNUAL HIGHS, LOWS & CLOSES SINCE 1930

YEAR	HIGH DATE	HIGH CLOSE	LOW DATE	LOW CLOSE	YEAR CLOSE	YEAR	HIGH DATE	HIGH CLOSE	LOW DATE	LOW CLOSE	YEAR CLOSE
1930	4/10	25.92	12/16	14.44	15.34	1975	7/15	95.61	1/8	70.04	90.19
1931	2/24	18.17	12/17	7.72	8.12	1976	9/21	107.83	1/2	90.90	107.46
1932	9/7	9.31	6/1	4.40	6.89	1977	1/3	107.00	11/2	90.71	95.10
1933	7/18	12.20	2/27	5.53	10.10	1978	9/12	106.99	3/6	86.90	96.11
1934	2/6	11.82	7/26	8.36	9.50	1979	10/5	111.27	2/27	96.13	107.94
1935	11/19	13.46	3/14	8.06	13.43	1980	11/28	140.52	3/27	98.22	135.76
1936	11/9	17.69	1/2	13.40	17.18	1981	1/6	138.12	9/25	112.77	122.55
1937	3/6	18.68	11/24	10.17	10.55	1982	11/9	143.02	8/12	102.42	140.64
1938	11/9	13.79	3/31	8.50	13.21	1983	10/10	172.65	1/3	138.34	164.93
1939	1/4	13.23	4/8	10.18	12.49	1984	11/6	170.41	7/24	147.82	167.24
1940	1/3	12.77	6/10	8.99	10.58	1985	12/16	212.02	1/4	163.68	211.28
1941	1/10	10.86	12/29	8.37	8.69	1986	12/2	254.00	1/22	203.49	242.17
1942	12/31	9.77	4/28	7.47	9.77	1987	8/25	336.77	12/4	223.92	247.08
1943	7/14	12.64	1/2	9.84	11.67	1988	10/21	283.66	1/20	242.63	277.72
1944	12/16	13.29	2/7	11.56	13.28	1989	10/9	359.80	1/3	275.31	353.40
1945	12/10	17.68	1/23	13.21	17.36	1990	7/16	368.95	10/11	295.46	330.22
1946	5/29	19.25	10/9	14.12	15.30	1991	12/31	417.09	1/9	311.49	417.09
1947	2/8	16.20	5/17	13.71	15.30	1992	12/18	441.28	4/8	394.50	435.71
1948	6/15	17.06	2/14	13.84	15.20	1993	12/28	470.94	1/8	429.05	466.45
1949	12/30	16.79	6/13	13.55	16.76	1994	2/2	482.00	4/4	438.92	459.27
1950	12/29	20.43	1/14	16.65	20.41	1995	12/13	621.69	1/3	459.11	615.93
1951	10/15	23.85	1/3	20.69	23.77	1996	11/25	757.03	1/10	598.48	740.74
1952	12/30	26.59	2/20	23.09	26.57	1997	12/5	983.79	1/2	737.01	970.43
1953	1/5	26.66	9/14	22.71	24.81	1998	12/29	1241.81	1/9	927.69	1229.23
1954	12/31	35.98	1/11	24.80	35.98	1999	12/31	1469.25	1/14	1212.19	1469.25
1955	11/14	46.41	1/17	34.58	45.48	2000	3/24	1527.46	12/20	1264.74	1320.28
1956	8/2	49.74	1/23	43.11	46.67	2001	2/1	1373.47	9/21	965.80	1148.08
1957	7/15	49.13	10/22	38.98	39.99	2002	1/4	1172.51	10/9	776.76	879.82
1958	12/31	55.21	1/2	40.33	55.21	2003	12/31	1111.92	3/11	800.73	1111.92
1959	8/3	60.71	2/9	53.58	59.89	2004	12/30	1213.55	8/12	1063.23	1211.92
1960	1/5	60.39	10/25	52.30	58.11	2005	12/14	1272.74	4/20	1137.50	1248.29
1961	12/12	72.64	1/3	57.57	71.55	2006	12/15	1427.09	6/13	1223.69	1418.30
1962	1/3	71.13	6/26	52.32	63.10	2007	10/9	1565.15	3/5	1374.12	1468.36
1963	12/31	75.02	1/2	62.69	75.02	2008	1/2	1447.16	11/20	752.44	903.25
1964	11/20	86.28	1/2	75.43	84.75	2009	12/28	1127.78	3/9	676.53	1115.10
1965	11/15	92.63	6/28	81.60	92.43	2010	12/29	1259.78	7/2	1022.58	1257.64
1966	2/9	94.06	10/7	73.20	80.33	2011	4/29	1363.61	10/3	1099.23	1257.60
1967	9/25	97.59	1/3	80.38	96.47	2012	9/14	1465.77	1/3	1277.06	1426.19
1968	11/29	108.37	3/5	87.72	103.86	2013	12/31	1848.36	1/8	1457.15	1848.36
1969	5/14	106.16	12/17	89.20	92.06	2014	12/29	2090.57	2/3	1741.89	2058.90
1970	1/5	93.46	5/26	69.29	92.15	2015	5/21	2130.82	8/25	1867.61	2043.94
1971	4/28	104.77	11/23	90.16	102.09	2016	12/13	2271.72	2/11	1829.08	2238.83
1972	12/11	119.12	1/3	101.67	118.05	2017	12/18	2690.16	1/3	2257.83	2673.61
1973	1/11	120.24	12/5	92.16	97.55	2018*	1/26	2872.87	2/8	2581.00	At press time
1974	1/3	99.80	10/3	62.68	68.56						

*Through June 8, 2018

NASDAQ ANNUAL HIGHS, LOWS & CLOSES SINCE 1971

YEAR	HIGH DATE	HIGH CLOSE	LOW DATE	LOW CLOSE	YEAR CLOSE
1971	12/31	114.12	1/5	89.06	114.12
1972	12/8	135.15	1/3	113.65	133.73
1973	1/11	136.84	12/24	88.67	92.19
1974	3/15	96.53	10/3	54.87	59.82
1975	7/15	88.00	1/2	60.70	77.62
1976	12/31	97.88	1/2	78.06	97.88
1977	12/30	105.05	4/5	93.66	105.05
1978	9/13	139.25	1/11	99.09	117.98
1979	10/5	152.29	1/2	117.84	151.14
1980	11/28	208.15	3/27	124.09	202.34
1981	5/29	223.47	9/28	175.03	195.84
1982	12/8	240.70	8/13	159.14	232.41
1983	6/24	328.91	1/3	230.59	278.60
1984	1/6	287.90	7/25	225.30	247.35
1985	12/16	325.16	1/2	245.91	324.93
1986	7/3	411.16	1/9	323.01	349.33
1987	8/26	455.26	10/28	291.88	330.47
1988	7/5	396.11	1/12	331.97	381.38
1989	10/9	485.73	1/3	378.56	454.82
1990	7/16	469.60	10/16	325.44	373.84
1991	12/31	586.34	1/14	355.75	586.34
1992	12/31	676.95	6/26	547.84	676.95
1993	10/15	787.42	4/26	645.87	776.80
1994	3/18	803.93	6/24	693.79	751.96
1995	12/4	1069.79	1/3	743.58	1052.13
1996	12/9	1316.27	1/15	988.57	1291.03
1997	10/9	1745.85	4/2	1201.00	1570.35
1998	12/31	2192.69	10/8	1419.12	2192.69
1999	12/31	4069.31	1/4	2208.05	4069.31
2000	3/10	5048.62	12/20	2332.78	2470.52
2001	1/24	2859.15	9/21	1423.19	1950.40
2002	1/4	2059.38	10/9	1114.11	1335.51
2003	12/30	2009.88	3/11	1271.47	2003.37
2004	12/30	2178.34	8/12	1752.49	2175.44
2005	12/2	2273.37	4/28	1904.18	2205.32
2006	11/22	2465.98	7/21	2020.39	2415.29
2007	10/31	2859.12	3/5	2340.68	2652.28
2008	1/2	2609.63	11/20	1316.12	1577.03
2009	12/30	2291.28	3/9	1268.64	2269.15
2010	12/22	2671.48	7/2	2091.79	2652.87
2011	4/29	2873.54	10/3	2335.83	2605.15
2012	9/14	3183.95	1/4	2648.36	3019.51
2013	12/31	4176.59	1/8	3091.81	4176.59
2014	12/29	4806.91	2/3	3996.96	4736.05
2015	7/20	5218.86	8/25	4506.49	5007.41
2016	12/27	5487.44	2/11	4266.84	5383.12
2017	12/18	6994.76.	1/3	5429.08	6903.39
2018*	6/6	7689.24	2/8	6777.16	At press time

RUSSELL 1000 ANNUAL HIGHS, LOWS & CLOSES SINCE 1979

YEAR	HIGH DATE	HIGH CLOSE	LOW DATE	LOW CLOSE	YEAR CLOSE
1979	10/5	61.18	2/27	51.83	59.87
1980	11/28	78.26	3/27	53.68	75.20
1981	1/6	76.34	9/25	62.03	67.93
1982	11/9	78.47	8/12	55.98	77.24
1983	10/10	95.07	1/3	76.04	90.38
1984	1/6	92.80	7/24	79.49	90.31
1985	12/16	114.97	1/4	88.61	114.39
1986	7/2	137.87	1/22	111.14	130.00
1987	8/25	176.22	12/4	117.65	130.02
1988	10/21	149.94	1/20	128.35	146.99
1989	10/9	189.93	1/3	145.78	185.11
1990	7/16	191.56	10/11	152.36	171.22
1991	12/31	220.61	1/9	161.94	220.61
1992	12/18	235.06	4/8	208.87	233.59
1993	10/15	252.77	1/8	229.91	250.71
1994	2/1	258.31	4/4	235.38	244.65
1995	12/13	331.18	1/3	244.41	328.89
1996	12/2	401.21	1/10	318.24	393.75
1997	12/5	519.72	4/11	389.03	513.79
1998	12/29	645.36	1/9	490.26	642.87
1999	12/31	767.97	2/9	632.53	767.97
2000	9/1	813.71	12/20	668.75	700.09
2001	1/30	727.35	9/21	507.98	604.94
2002	3/19	618.74	10/9	410.52	466.18
2003	12/31	594.56	3/11	425.31	594.56
2004	12/30	651.76	8/13	566.06	650.99
2005	12/14	692.09	4/20	613.37	679.42
2006	12/15	775.08	6/13	665.81	770.08
2007	10/9	852.32	3/5	749.85	799.82
2008	1/2	788.62	11/20	402.91	487.77
2009	12/28	619.22	3/9	367.55	612.01
2010	12/29	698.11	7/2	562.58	696.90
2011	4/29	758.45	10/3	604.42	693.36
2012	9/14	809.01	1/4	703.72	789.90
2013	12/31	1030.36	1/8	807.95	1030.36
2014	12/29	1161.45	2/3	972.95	1144.37
2015	5/21	1189.55	8/25	1042.77	1131.88
2016	12/13	1260.06	2/11	1005.89	1241.66
2017	12/18	1490.06	1/3	1252.11	1481.81
2018*	1/26	1588.98	2/8	1429.23	At press time

RUSSELL 2000 ANNUAL HIGHS, LOWS & CLOSES SINCE 1979

YEAR	HIGH DATE	HIGH CLOSE	LOW DATE	LOW CLOSE	YEAR CLOSE
1979	12/31	55.91	1/2	40.81	55.91
1980	11/28	77.70	3/27	45.36	74.80
1981	6/15	85.16	9/25	65.37	73.67
1982	12/8	91.01	8/12	60.33	88.90
1983	6/24	126.99	1/3	88.29	112.27
1984	1/12	116.69	7/25	93.95	101.49
1985	12/31	129.87	1/2	101.21	129.87
1986	7/3	155.30	1/9	128.23	135.00
1987	8/25	174.44	10/28	106.08	120.42
1988	7/15	151.42	1/12	121.23	147.37
1989	10/9	180.78	1/3	146.79	168.30
1990	6/15	170.90	10/30	118.82	132.16
1991	12/31	189.94	1/15	125.25	189.94
1992	12/31	221.01	7/8	185.81	221.01
1993	11/2	260.17	2/23	217.55	258.59
1994	3/18	271.08	12/9	235.16	250.36
1995	9/14	316.12	1/30	246.56	315.97
1996	5/22	364.61	1/16	301.75	362.61
1997	10/13	465.21	4/25	335.85	437.02
1998	4/21	491.41	10/8	310.28	421.96
1999	12/31	504.75	3/23	383.37	504.75
2000	3/9	606.05	12/20	443.80	483.53
2001	5/22	517.23	9/21	378.89	488.50
2002	4/16	522.95	10/9	327.04	383.09
2003	12/30	565.47	3/12	345.94	556.91
2004	12/28	654.57	8/12	517.10	651.57
2005	12/2	690.57	4/28	575.02	673.22
2006	12/27	797.73	7/21	671.94	787.66
2007	7/13	855.77	11/26	735.07	766.03
2008	6/5	763.27	11/20	385.31	499.45
2009	12/24	634.07	3/9	343.26	625.39
2010	12/27	792.35	2/8	586.49	783.65
2011	4/29	865.29	10/3	609.49	740.92
2012	9/14	864.70	6/4	737.24	849.35
2013	12/31	1163.64	1/3	872.60	1163.64
2014	12/29	1219.11	10/13	1049.30	1204.70
2015	6/23	1295.80	9/29	1083.91	1135.89
2016	12/9	1388.07	2/11	953.72	1357.13
2017	12/28	1548.93	4/13	1345.24	1535.51
2018*	6/6	1675.95	2/8	1463.79	At press time

*Through June 8, 2018

DOW JONES INDUSTRIALS MONTHLY PERCENT CHANGES SINCE 1950

	Jan	Feb	Mar	Apr	May	Jun	Jul	Aug	Sep	Oct	Nov	Dec	Year's Change
1950	0.8	0.8	1.3	4.0	4.2	−6.4	0.1	3.6	4.4	−0.6	1.2	3.4	17.6
1951	5.7	1.3	−1.6	4.5	−3.7	−2.8	6.3	4.8	0.3	−3.2	−0.4	3.0	14.4
1952	0.5	−3.9	3.6	−4.4	2.1	4.3	1.9	−1.6	−1.6	−0.5	5.4	2.9	8.4
1953	−0.7	−1.9	−1.5	−1.8	−0.9	−1.5	2.7	−5.1	1.1	4.5	2.0	−0.2	−3.8
1954	4.1	0.7	3.0	5.2	2.6	1.8	4.3	−3.5	7.3	−2.3	9.8	4.6	44.0
1955	1.1	0.7	−0.5	3.9	−0.2	6.2	3.2	0.5	−0.3	−2.5	6.2	1.1	20.8
1956	−3.6	2.7	5.8	0.8	−7.4	3.1	5.1	−3.0	−5.3	1.0	−1.5	5.6	2.3
1957	−4.1	−3.0	2.2	4.1	2.1	−0.3	1.0	−4.8	−5.8	−3.3	2.0	−3.2	−12.8
1958	3.3	−2.2	1.6	2.0	1.5	3.3	5.2	1.1	4.6	2.1	2.6	4.7	34.0
1959	1.8	1.6	−0.3	3.7	3.2	−0.03	4.9	−1.6	−4.9	2.4	1.9	3.1	16.4
1960	−8.4	1.2	−2.1	−2.4	4.0	2.4	−3.7	1.5	−7.3	0.04	2.9	3.1	−9.3
1961	5.2	2.1	2.2	0.3	2.7	−1.8	3.1	2.1	−2.6	0.4	2.5	1.3	18.7
1962	−4.3	1.1	−0.2	−5.9	−7.8	−8.5	6.5	1.9	−5.0	1.9	10.1	0.4	−10.8
1963	4.7	−2.9	3.0	5.2	1.3	−2.8	−1.6	4.9	0.5	3.1	−0.6	1.7	17.0
1964	2.9	1.9	1.6	−0.3	1.2	1.3	1.2	−0.3	4.4	−0.3	0.3	−0.1	14.6
1965	3.3	0.1	−1.6	3.7	−0.5	−5.4	1.6	1.3	4.2	3.2	−1.5	2.4	10.9
1966	1.5	−3.2	−2.8	1.0	−5.3	−1.6	−2.6	−7.0	−1.8	4.2	−1.9	−0.7	−18.9
1967	8.2	−1.2	3.2	3.6	−5.0	0.9	5.1	−0.3	2.8	−5.1	−0.4	3.3	15.2
1968	−5.5	−1.7	0.02	8.5	−1.4	−0.1	−1.6	1.5	4.4	1.8	3.4	−4.2	4.3
1969	0.2	−4.3	3.3	1.6	−1.3	−6.9	−6.6	2.6	−2.8	5.3	−5.1	−1.5	−15.2
1970	−7.0	4.5	1.0	−6.3	−4.8	−2.4	7.4	4.1	−0.5	−0.7	5.1	5.6	4.8
1971	3.5	1.2	2.9	4.1	−3.6	−1.8	−3.7	4.6	−1.2	−5.4	−0.9	7.1	6.1
1972	1.3	2.9	1.4	1.4	0.7	−3.3	−0.5	4.2	−1.1	0.2	6.6	0.2	14.6
1973	−2.1	−4.4	−0.4	−3.1	−2.2	−1.1	3.9	−4.2	6.7	1.0	−14.0	3.5	−16.6
1974	0.6	0.6	−1.6	−1.2	−4.1	0.03	−5.6	−10.4	−10.4	9.5	−7.0	−0.4	−27.6
1975	14.2	5.0	3.9	6.9	1.3	5.6	−5.4	0.5	−5.0	5.3	2.9	−1.0	38.3
1976	14.4	−0.3	2.8	−0.3	−2.2	2.8	−1.8	−1.1	1.7	−2.6	−1.8	6.1	17.9
1977	−5.0	−1.9	−1.8	0.8	−3.0	2.0	−2.9	−3.2	−1.7	−3.4	1.4	0.2	−17.3
1978	−7.4	−3.6	2.1	10.6	0.4	−2.6	5.3	1.7	−1.3	−8.5	0.8	0.7	−3.1
1979	4.2	−3.6	6.6	−0.8	−3.8	2.4	0.5	4.9	−1.0	−7.2	0.8	2.0	4.2
1980	4.4	−1.5	−9.0	4.0	4.1	2.0	7.8	−0.3	−0.02	−0.9	7.4	−3.0	14.9
1981	−1.7	2.9	3.0	−0.6	−0.6	−1.5	−2.5	−7.4	−3.6	0.3	4.3	−1.6	−9.2
1982	−0.4	−5.4	−0.2	3.1	−3.4	−0.9	−0.4	11.5	−0.6	10.7	4.8	0.7	19.6
1983	2.8	3.4	1.6	8.5	−2.1	1.8	−1.9	1.4	1.4	−0.6	4.1	−1.4	20.3
1984	−3.0	−5.4	0.9	0.5	−5.6	2.5	−1.5	9.8	−1.4	0.1	−1.5	1.9	−3.7
1985	6.2	−0.2	−1.3	−0.7	4.6	1.5	0.9	−1.0	−0.4	3.4	7.1	5.1	27.7
1986	1.6	8.8	6.4	−1.9	5.2	0.9	−6.2	6.9	−6.9	6.2	1.9	−1.0	22.6
1987	13.8	3.1	3.6	−0.8	0.2	5.5	6.3	3.5	−2.5	−23.2	−8.0	5.7	2.3
1988	1.0	5.8	−4.0	2.2	−0.1	5.4	−0.6	−4.6	4.0	1.7	−1.6	2.6	11.8
1989	8.0	−3.6	1.6	5.5	2.5	−1.6	9.0	2.9	−1.6	−1.8	2.3	1.7	27.0
1990	−5.9	1.4	3.0	−1.9	8.3	0.1	0.9	−10.0	−6.2	−0.4	4.8	2.9	−4.3
1991	3.9	5.3	1.1	−0.9	4.8	−4.0	4.1	0.6	−0.9	1.7	−5.7	9.5	20.3
1992	1.7	1.4	−1.0	3.8	1.1	−2.3	2.3	−4.0	0.4	−1.4	2.4	−0.1	4.2
1993	0.3	1.8	1.9	−0.2	2.9	−0.3	0.7	3.2	−2.6	3.5	0.1	1.9	13.7
1994	6.0	−3.7	−5.1	1.3	2.1	−3.5	3.8	4.0	−1.8	1.7	−4.3	2.5	2.1
1995	0.2	4.3	3.7	3.9	3.3	2.0	3.3	−2.1	3.9	−0.7	6.7	0.8	33.5
1996	5.4	1.7	1.9	−0.3	1.3	0.2	−2.2	1.6	4.7	2.5	8.2	−1.1	26.0
1997	5.7	0.9	−4.3	6.5	4.6	4.7	7.2	−7.3	4.2	−6.3	5.1	1.1	22.6
1998	−0.02	8.1	3.0	3.0	−1.8	0.6	−0.8	−15.1	4.0	9.6	6.1	0.7	16.1
1999	1.9	−0.6	5.2	10.2	−2.1	3.9	−2.9	1.6	−4.5	3.8	1.4	5.7	25.2
2000	−4.8	−7.4	7.8	−1.7	−2.0	−0.7	0.7	6.6	−5.0	3.0	−5.1	3.6	−6.2
2001	0.9	−3.6	−5.9	8.7	1.6	−3.8	0.2	−5.4	−11.1	2.6	8.6	1.7	−7.1
2002	−1.0	1.9	2.9	−4.4	−0.2	−6.9	−5.5	−0.8	−12.4	10.6	5.9	−6.2	−16.8
2003	−3.5	−2.0	1.3	6.1	4.4	1.5	2.8	2.0	−1.5	5.7	−0.2	6.9	25.3
2004	0.3	0.9	−2.1	−1.3	−0.4	2.4	−2.8	0.3	−0.9	−0.5	4.0	3.4	3.1
2005	−2.7	2.6	−2.4	−3.0	2.7	−1.8	3.6	−1.5	0.8	−1.2	3.5	−0.8	−0.6
2006	1.4	1.2	1.1	2.3	−1.7	−0.2	0.3	1.7	2.6	3.4	1.2	2.0	16.3
2007	1.3	−2.8	0.7	5.7	4.3	−1.6	−1.5	1.1	4.0	0.2	−4.0	−0.8	6.4
2008	−4.6	−3.0	−0.03	4.5	−1.4	−10.2	0.2	1.5	−6.0	−14.1	−5.3	−0.6	−33.8
2009	−8.8	−11.7	7.7	7.3	4.1	−0.6	8.6	3.5	2.3	0.005	6.5	0.8	18.8
2010	−3.5	2.6	5.1	1.4	−7.9	−3.6	7.1	−4.3	7.7	3.1	−1.0	5.2	11.0
2011	2.7	2.8	0.8	4.0	−1.9	−1.2	−2.2	−4.4	−6.0	9.5	0.8	1.4	5.5
2012	3.4	2.5	2.0	0.01	−6.2	3.9	1.0	0.6	2.6	−2.5	−0.5	0.6	7.3

continued

	Jan	Feb	Mar	Apr	May	Jun	Jul	Aug	Sep	Oct	Nov	Dec	Year's Change
2013	5.8	1.4	3.7	1.8	1.9	−1.4	4.0	−4.4	2.2	2.8	3.5	3.0	26.5
2014	−5.3	4.0	0.8	0.7	0.8	0.7	−1.6	3.2	−0.3	2.0	2.5	−0.03	7.5
2015	−3.7	5.6	−2.0	0.4	1.0	−2.2	0.4	−6.6	−1.5	8.5	0.3	−1.7	−2.2
2016	−5.5	0.3	7.1	0.5	0.1	0.8	2.8	−0.2	−0.5	−0.9	5.4	3.3	13.4
2017	0.5	4.8	−0.7	1.3	0.3	1.6	2.5	0.3	2.1	4.3	3.8	1.8	25.1
2018	5.8	−4.3	−3.7	0.2	1.0								
TOTALS	64.0	14.6	73.3	129.1	−0.1	−19.5	81.2	−11.9	−48.5	46.7	108.3	112.9	
AVG.	0.9	0.2	1.1	1.9	−0.001	−0.3	1.2	−0.2	−0.7	0.7	1.6	1.7	
# Up	44	41	44	47	37	32	43	38	27	41	46	48	
# Down	25	28	25	22	32	36	25	30	41	27	22	20	

DOW JONES INDUSTRIALS MONTHLY POINT CHANGES SINCE 1950

	Jan	Feb	Mar	Apr	May	Jun	Jul	Aug	Sep	Oct	Nov	Dec	Year's Close
1950	1.66	1.65	2.61	8.28	9.09	−14.31	0.29	7.47	9.49	−1.35	2.59	7.81	235.41
1951	13.42	3.22	−4.11	11.19	−9.48	−7.01	15.22	12.39	0.91	−8.81	−1.08	7.96	269.23
1952	1.46	−10.61	9.38	−11.83	5.31	11.32	5.30	−4.52	−4.43	−1.38	14.43	8.24	291.90
1953	−2.13	−5.50	−4.40	−5.12	−2.47	−4.02	7.12	−14.16	2.82	11.77	5.56	−0.47	280.90
1954	11.49	2.15	8.97	15.82	8.16	6.04	14.39	−12.12	24.66	−8.32	34.63	17.62	404.39
1955	4.44	3.04	−2.17	15.95	−0.79	26.52	14.47	2.33	−1.56	−11.75	28.39	5.14	488.40
1956	−17.66	12.91	28.14	4.33	−38.07	14.73	25.03	−15.77	−26.79	4.60	−7.07	26.69	499.47
1957	−20.31	−14.54	10.19	19.55	10.57	−1.64	5.23	−24.17	−28.05	−15.26	8.83	−14.18	435.69
1958	14.33	−10.10	6.84	9.10	6.84	15.48	24.81	5.64	23.46	11.13	14.24	26.19	583.65
1959	10.31	9.54	−1.79	22.04	20.04	−0.19	31.28	−10.47	−32.73	14.92	12.58	20.18	679.36
1960	−56.74	7.50	−13.53	−14.89	23.80	15.12	−23.89	9.26	−45.85	0.22	16.86	18.67	615.89
1961	32.31	13.88	14.55	2.08	18.01	−12.76	21.41	14.57	−18.73	2.71	17.68	9.54	731.14
1962	−31.14	8.05	−1.10	−41.62	−51.97	−52.08	36.65	11.25	−30.20	10.79	59.53	2.80	652.10
1963	30.75	−19.91	19.58	35.18	9.26	−20.08	−11.45	33.89	3.47	22.44	−4.71	12.43	762.95
1964	22.39	14.80	13.15	−2.52	9.79	10.94	9.60	−2.62	36.89	−2.29	2.35	−1.30	874.13
1965	28.73	0.62	−14.43	33.26	−4.27	−50.01	13.71	11.36	37.48	30.24	−14.11	22.55	969.26
1966	14.25	−31.62	−27.12	8.91	−49.61	−13.97	−22.72	−58.97	−14.19	32.85	−15.48	−5.90	785.69
1967	64.20	−10.52	26.61	31.07	−44.49	7.70	43.98	−2.95	25.37	−46.92	−3.93	29.30	905.11
1968	−49.64	−14.97	0.17	71.55	−13.22	−1.20	−14.80	13.01	39.78	16.60	32.69	−41.33	943.75
1969	2.30	−40.84	30.27	14.70	−12.62	−64.37	−57.72	21.25	−23.63	42.90	−43.69	−11.94	800.36
1970	−56.30	33.53	7.98	−49.50	−35.63	−16.91	50.59	30.46	−3.90	−5.07	38.48	44.83	838.92
1971	29.58	10.33	25.54	37.38	−33.94	−16.67	−32.71	39.64	−10.88	−48.19	−7.66	58.86	890.20
1972	11.97	25.96	12.57	13.47	6.55	−31.69	−4.29	38.99	−10.46	2.25	62.69	1.81	1020.02
1973	−21.00	−43.95	−4.06	−29.58	−20.02	−9.70	34.69	−38.83	59.53	9.48	−134.33	28.61	850.86
1974	4.69	4.98	−13.85	−9.93	−34.58	0.24	−44.98	−78.85	−70.71	57.65	−46.86	−2.42	616.24
1975	87.45	35.36	29.10	53.19	10.95	46.70	−47.48	3.83	−41.46	42.16	24.63	−8.26	852.41
1976	122.87	−2.67	26.84	−2.60	−21.62	27.55	−18.14	−10.90	16.45	−25.26	−17.71	57.43	1004.65
1977	−50.28	−17.95	−17.29	7.77	−28.24	17.64	−26.23	−28.58	−14.38	−28.76	11.35	1.47	831.17
1978	−61.25	−27.80	15.24	79.96	3.29	−21.66	43.32	14.55	−11.00	−73.37	6.58	5.98	805.01
1979	34.21	−30.40	53.36	−7.28	−32.57	19.65	4.44	41.21	−9.05	−62.88	6.65	16.39	838.74
1980	37.11	−12.71	−77.39	31.31	33.79	17.07	67.40	−2.73	−0.17	−7.93	68.85	−29.35	963.99
1981	−16.72	27.31	29.29	−6.12	−6.00	−14.87	−24.54	−70.87	−31.49	2.57	36.43	−13.98	875.00
1982	−3.90	−46.71	−1.62	25.59	−28.82	−7.61	−3.33	92.71	−5.06	95.47	47.56	7.26	1046.54
1983	29.16	36.92	17.41	96.17	−26.22	21.98	−22.74	16.94	16.97	−7.93	50.82	−17.38	1258.64
1984	−38.06	−65.95	10.26	5.86	−65.90	27.55	−17.12	109.10	−17.67	0.67	−18.44	22.63	1211.57
1985	75.20	−2.76	−17.23	−8.72	57.35	20.05	11.99	−13.44	−5.38	45.68	97.82	74.54	1546.67
1986	24.32	138.00	109.55	−34.63	92.73	16.01	−117.41	123.03	−130.76	110.23	36.42	−18.28	1895.95
1987	262.09	65.95	80.70	−18.33	5.21	126.96	153.54	90.88	−66.67	−602.75	−159.98	105.28	1938.83
1988	19.39	113.40	−83.56	44.27	−1.21	110.59	−12.98	−97.08	81.26	35.74	−34.14	54.06	2168.57
1989	173.75	−83.93	35.23	125.18	61.35	−40.09	220.60	76.61	−44.45	−47.74	61.19	46.93	2753.20
1990	−162.66	36.71	79.96	−50.45	219.90	4.03	24.51	−290.84	−161.88	−10.15	117.32	74.01	2633.66
1991	102.73	145.79	31.68	−25.99	139.63	−120.75	118.07	18.78	−26.83	52.33	−174.42	274.15	3168.83
1992	54.56	44.28	−32.20	123.65	37.76	−78.36	75.26	−136.43	14.31	−45.38	78.88	−4.05	3301.11

continued

	Jan	Feb	Mar	Apr	May	Jun	Jul	Aug	Sep	Oct	Nov	Dec	Year's Close
1993	8.92	60.78	64.30	−7.56	99.88	−11.35	23.39	111.78	−96.13	125.47	3.36	70.14	3754.09
1994	224.27	−146.34	−196.06	45.73	76.68	−133.41	139.54	148.92	−70.23	64.93	−168.89	95.21	3834.44
1995	9.42	167.19	146.64	163.58	143.87	90.96	152.37	−97.91	178.52	−33.60	319.01	42.63	5117.12
1996	278.18	90.32	101.52	−18.06	74.10	11.45	−125.72	87.30	265.96	147.21	492.32	−73.43	6448.27
1997	364.82	64.65	−294.26	425.51	322.05	341.75	549.82	−600.19	322.84	−503.18	381.05	85.12	7908.25
1998	−1.75	639.22	254.09	263.56	−163.42	52.07	−68.73	−1344.22	303.55	749.48	524.45	64.88	9181.43
1999	177.40	−52.25	479.58	1002.88	−229.30	411.06	−315.65	174.13	−492.33	392.91	147.95	619.31	11497.12
2000	−556.59	−812.22	793.61	−188.01	−211.58	−74.44	74.09	693.12	−564.18	320.22	−556.65	372.36	10786.85
2001	100.51	−392.08	−616.50	856.19	176.97	−409.54	20.41	−573.06	−1102.19	227.58	776.42	169.94	10021.50
2002	−101.50	186.13	297.81	−457.72	−20.97	−681.99	−506.67	−73.09	−1071.57	805.10	499.06	−554.46	8341.63
2003	−287.82	−162.73	101.05	487.96	370.17	135.18	248.36	182.02	−140.76	526.06	−18.66	671.46	10453.92
2004	34.15	95.85	−226.22	−132.13	−37.12	247.03	−295.77	34.21	−93.65	−52.80	400.55	354.99	10783.01
2005	−293.07	276.29	−262.47	−311.25	274.97	−192.51	365.94	−159.31	87.10	−128.63	365.80	−88.37	10717.50
2006	147.36	128.55	115.91	257.82	−198.83	−18.09	35.46	195.47	297.92	401.66	141.20	241.22	12463.15
2007	158.54	−353.06	85.72	708.56	564.73	−219.02	−196.63	145.75	537.89	34.38	−558.29	−106.90	13264.82
2008	−614.46	−383.97	−3.50	557.24	−181.81	−1288.31	28.01	165.53	−692.89	−1525.65	−495.97	−52.65	8776.39
2009	−775.53	−937.93	545.99	559.20	332.21	−53.33	724.61	324.67	216.00	0.45	632.11	83.21	10428.05
2010	−360.72	257.93	531.37	151.98	−871.98	−362.61	691.92	−451.22	773.33	330.44	−112.47	571.49	11577.51
2011	314.42	334.41	93.39	490.81	−240.75	−155.45	−271.10	−529.71	−700.15	1041.63	90.67	171.88	12217.56
2012	415.35	319.16	259.97	1.59	−820.18	486.64	128.59	82.16	346.29	−340.67	−70.88	78.56	13104.14
2013	756.44	193.91	524.05	261.26	275.77	−205.97	589.94	−689.23	319.36	416.08	540.66	490.25	16576.66
2014	−877.81	622.86	135.95	123.18	136.33	109.43	−263.30	535.15	−55.55	347.62	437.72	−5.17	17823.07
2015	−658.12	967.75	−356.58	64.40	170.16	−391.17	70.35	−1161.83	−244.03	1379.54	56.38	−294.89	17425.03
2016	−958.73	50.20	1168.59	88.55	13.56	142.79	502.25	−31.36	−92.73	−165.73	981.16	639.02	19762.60
2017	101.49	948.15	−149.02	277.29	68.14	340.98	541.49	56.98	456.99	972.15	895.11	446.87	24719.22
2018	1430.17	−1120.19	−926.09	60.04	252.69								
TOTALS	−231.33	1345.09	3088.16	6360.30	603.98	−1863.93	3413.34	−2849.09	−1806.15	5126.56	6015.59	5013.19	
# Up	44	41	44	47	37	32	43	38	27	41	46	48	
# Down	25	28	25	22	32	36	25	30	41	27	22	20	

DOW JONES INDUSTRIALS MONTHLY CLOSING PRICES SINCE 1950

	Jan	Feb	Mar	Apr	May	Jun	Jul	Aug	Sep	Oct	Nov	Dec
1950	201.79	203.44	206.05	214.33	223.42	209.11	209.40	216.87	226.36	225.01	227.60	235.41
1951	248.83	252.05	247.94	259.13	249.65	242.64	257.86	270.25	271.16	262.35	261.27	269.23
1952	270.69	260.08	269.46	257.63	262.94	274.26	279.56	275.04	270.61	269.23	283.66	291.90
1953	289.77	284.27	279.87	274.75	272.28	268.26	275.38	261.22	264.04	275.81	281.37	280.90
1954	292.39	294.54	303.51	319.33	327.49	333.53	347.92	335.80	360.46	352.14	386.77	404.39
1955	408.83	411.87	409.70	425.65	424.86	451.38	465.85	468.18	466.62	454.87	483.26	488.40
1956	470.74	483.65	511.79	516.12	478.05	492.78	517.81	502.04	475.25	479.85	472.78	499.47
1957	479.16	464.62	474.81	494.36	504.93	503.29	508.52	484.35	456.30	441.04	449.87	435.69
1958	450.02	439.92	446.76	455.86	462.70	478.18	502.99	508.63	532.09	543.22	557.46	583.65
1959	593.96	603.50	601.71	623.75	643.79	643.60	674.88	664.41	631.68	646.60	659.18	679.36
1960	622.62	630.12	616.59	601.70	625.50	640.62	616.73	625.99	580.14	580.36	597.22	615.89
1961	648.20	662.08	676.63	678.71	696.72	683.96	705.37	719.94	701.21	703.92	721.60	731.14
1962	700.00	708.05	706.95	665.33	613.36	561.28	597.93	609.18	578.98	589.77	649.30	652.10
1963	682.85	662.94	682.52	717.70	726.96	706.88	695.43	729.32	732.79	755.23	750.52	762.95
1964	785.34	800.14	813.29	810.77	820.56	831.50	841.10	838.48	875.37	873.08	875.43	874.13
1965	902.86	903.48	889.05	922.31	918.04	868.03	881.74	893.10	930.58	960.82	946.71	969.26
1966	983.51	951.89	924.77	933.68	884.07	870.10	847.38	788.41	774.22	807.07	791.59	785.69
1967	849.89	839.37	865.98	897.05	852.56	860.26	904.24	901.29	926.66	879.74	875.81	905.11
1968	855.47	840.50	840.67	912.22	899.00	897.80	883.00	896.01	935.79	952.39	985.08	943.75
1969	946.05	905.21	935.48	950.18	937.56	873.19	815.47	836.72	813.09	855.99	812.30	800.36
1970	744.06	777.59	785.57	736.07	700.44	683.53	734.12	764.58	760.68	755.61	794.09	838.92
1971	868.50	878.83	904.37	941.75	907.81	891.14	858.43	898.07	887.19	839.00	831.34	890.20
1972	902.17	928.13	940.70	954.17	960.72	929.03	924.74	963.73	953.27	955.52	1018.21	1020.02
1973	999.02	955.07	951.01	921.43	901.41	891.71	926.40	887.57	947.10	956.58	822.25	850.86

continued

154

	Jan	Feb	Mar	Apr	May	Jun	Jul	Aug	Sep	Oct	Nov	Dec
1974	855.55	860.53	846.68	836.75	802.17	802.41	757.43	678.58	607.87	665.52	618.66	616.24
1975	703.69	739.05	768.15	821.34	832.29	878.99	831.51	835.34	793.88	836.04	860.67	852.41
1976	975.28	972.61	999.45	996.85	975.23	1002.78	984.64	973.74	990.19	964.93	947.22	1004.65
1977	954.37	936.42	919.13	926.90	898.66	916.30	890.07	861.49	847.11	818.35	829.70	831.17
1978	769.92	742.12	757.36	837.32	840.61	818.95	862.27	876.82	865.82	792.45	799.03	805.01
1979	839.22	808.82	862.18	854.90	822.33	841.98	846.42	887.63	878.58	815.70	822.35	838.74
1980	875.85	863.14	785.75	817.06	850.85	867.92	935.32	932.59	932.42	924.49	993.34	963.99
1981	947.27	974.58	1003.87	997.75	991.75	976.88	952.34	881.47	849.98	852.55	888.98	875.00
1982	871.10	824.39	822.77	848.36	819.54	811.93	808.60	901.31	896.25	991.72	1039.28	1046.54
1983	1075.70	1112.62	1130.03	1226.20	1199.98	1221.96	1199.22	1216.16	1233.13	1225.20	1276.02	1258.64
1984	1220.58	1154.63	1164.89	1170.75	1104.85	1132.40	1115.28	1224.38	1206.71	1207.38	1188.94	1211.57
1985	1286.77	1284.01	1266.78	1258.06	1315.41	1335.46	1347.45	1334.01	1328.63	1374.31	1472.13	1546.67
1986	1570.99	1709.06	1818.61	1783.98	1876.71	1892.72	1775.31	1898.34	1767.58	1877.81	1914.23	1895.95
1987	2158.04	2223.99	2304.69	2286.36	2291.57	2418.53	2572.07	2662.95	2596.28	1993.53	1833.55	1938.83
1988	1958.22	2071.62	1988.06	2032.33	2031.12	2141.71	2128.73	2031.65	2112.91	2148.65	2114.51	2168.57
1989	2342.32	2258.39	2293.62	2418.80	2480.15	2440.06	2660.66	2737.27	2692.82	2645.08	2706.27	2753.20
1990	2590.54	2627.25	2707.21	2656.76	2876.66	2880.69	2905.20	2614.36	2452.48	2442.33	2559.65	2633.66
1991	2736.39	2882.18	2913.86	2887.87	3027.50	2906.75	3024.82	3043.60	3016.77	3069.10	2894.68	3168.83
1992	3223.39	3267.67	3235.47	3359.12	3396.88	3318.52	3393.78	3257.35	3271.66	3226.28	3305.16	3301.11
1993	3310.03	3370.81	3435.11	3427.55	3527.43	3516.08	3539.47	3651.25	3555.12	3680.59	3683.95	3754.09
1994	3978.36	3832.02	3635.96	3681.69	3758.37	3624.96	3764.50	3913.42	3843.19	3908.12	3739.23	3834.44
1995	3843.86	4011.05	4157.69	4321.27	4465.14	4556.10	4708.47	4610.56	4789.08	4755.48	5074.49	5117.12
1996	5395.30	5485.62	5587.14	5569.08	5643.18	5654.63	5528.91	5616.21	5882.17	6029.38	6521.70	6448.27
1997	6813.09	6877.74	6583.48	7008.99	7331.04	7672.79	8222.61	7622.42	7945.26	7442.08	7823.13	7908.25
1998	7906.50	8545.72	8799.81	9063.37	8899.95	8952.02	8883.29	7539.07	7842.62	8592.10	9116.55	9181.43
1999	9358.83	9306.58	9786.16	10789.04	10559.74	10970.80	10655.15	10829.28	10336.95	10729.86	10877.81	11497.12
2000	10940.53	10128.31	10921.92	10733.91	10522.33	10447.89	10521.98	11215.10	10650.92	10971.14	10414.49	10786.85
2001	10887.36	10495.28	9878.78	10734.97	10911.94	10502.40	10522.81	9949.75	8847.56	9075.14	9851.56	10021.50
2002	9920.00	10106.13	10403.94	9946.22	9925.25	9243.26	8736.59	8663.50	7591.93	8397.03	8896.09	8341.63
2003	8053.81	7891.08	7992.13	8480.09	8850.26	8985.44	9233.80	9415.82	9275.06	9801.12	9782.46	10453.92
2004	10488.07	10583.92	10357.70	10225.57	10188.45	10435.48	10139.71	10173.92	10080.27	10027.47	10428.02	10783.01
2005	10489.94	10766.23	10503.76	10192.51	10467.48	10274.97	10640.91	10481.60	10568.70	10440.07	10805.87	10717.50
2006	10864.86	10993.41	11109.32	11367.14	11168.31	11150.22	11185.68	11381.15	11679.07	12080.73	12221.93	12463.15
2007	12621.69	12268.63	12354.35	13062.91	13627.64	13408.62	13211.99	13357.74	13895.63	13930.01	13371.72	13264.82
2008	12650.36	12266.39	12262.89	12820.13	12638.32	11350.01	11378.02	11543.55	10850.66	9325.01	8829.04	8776.39
2009	8000.86	7062.93	7608.92	8168.12	8500.33	8447.00	9171.61	9496.28	9712.28	9712.73	10344.84	10428.05
2010	10067.33	10325.26	10856.63	11008.61	10136.63	9774.02	10465.94	10014.72	10788.05	11118.49	11006.02	11577.51
2011	11891.93	12226.34	12319.73	12810.54	12569.79	12414.34	12143.24	11613.53	10913.38	11955.01	12045.68	12217.56
2012	12632.91	12952.07	13212.04	13213.63	12393.45	12880.09	13008.68	13090.84	13437.13	13096.46	13025.58	13104.14
2013	13860.58	14054.49	14578.54	14839.80	15115.57	14909.60	15499.54	14810.31	15129.67	15545.75	16086.41	16576.66
2014	15698.85	16321.71	16457.66	16580.84	16717.17	16826.60	16563.30	17098.45	17042.90	17390.52	17828.24	17823.07
2015	17164.95	18132.70	17776.12	17840.52	18010.68	17619.51	17689.86	16528.03	16284.00	17663.54	17719.92	17425.03
2016	16466.30	16516.50	17685.09	17773.64	17787.20	17929.99	18432.24	18400.88	18308.15	18142.42	19123.58	19762.60
2017	19864.09	20812.24	20663.22	20940.51	21008.65	21349.63	21891.12	21948.10	22405.09	23377.24	24272.35	24719.22
2018	26149.39	25029.20	24103.11	24163.15	24415.84							

	Jan	Feb	Mar	Apr	May	Jun	Jul	Aug	Sep	Oct	Nov	Dec	Year's Change
1950	1.7	1.0	0.4	4.5	3.9	−5.8	0.8	3.3	5.6	0.4	−0.1	4.6	21.8
1951	6.1	0.6	−1.8	4.8	−4.1	−2.6	6.9	3.9	−0.1	−1.4	−0.3	3.9	16.5
1952	1.6	−3.6	4.8	−4.3	2.3	4.6	1.8	−1.5	−2.0	−0.1	4.6	3.5	11.8
1953	−0.7	−1.8	−2.4	−2.6	−0.3	−1.6	2.5	−5.8	0.1	5.1	0.9	0.2	−6.6
1954	5.1	0.3	3.0	4.9	3.3	0.1	5.7	−3.4	8.3	−1.9	8.1	5.1	45.0
1955	1.8	0.4	−0.5	3.8	−0.1	8.2	6.1	−0.8	1.1	−3.0	7.5	−0.1	26.4
1956	−3.6	3.5	6.9	−0.2	−6.6	3.9	5.2	−3.8	−4.5	0.5	−1.1	3.5	2.6
1957	−4.2	−3.3	2.0	3.7	3.7	−0.1	1.1	−5.6	−6.2	−3.2	1.6	−4.1	−14.3
1958	4.3	−2.1	3.1	3.2	1.5	2.6	4.3	1.2	4.8	2.5	2.2	5.2	38.1

continued

	Jan	Feb	Mar	Apr	May	Jun	Jul	Aug	Sep	Oct	Nov	Dec	Year's Change
1959	0.4	−0.02	0.1	3.9	1.9	−0.4	3.5	−1.5	−4.6	1.1	1.3	2.8	8.5
1960	−7.1	0.9	−1.4	−1.8	2.7	2.0	−2.5	2.6	−6.0	−0.2	4.0	4.6	−3.0
1961	6.3	2.7	2.6	0.4	1.9	−2.9	3.3	2.0	−2.0	2.8	3.9	0.3	23.1
1962	−3.8	1.6	−0.6	−6.2	−8.6	−8.2	6.4	1.5	−4.8	0.4	10.2	1.3	−11.8
1963	4.9	−2.9	3.5	4.9	1.4	−2.0	−0.3	4.9	−1.1	3.2	−1.1	2.4	18.9
1964	2.7	1.0	1.5	0.6	1.1	1.6	1.8	−1.6	2.9	0.8	−0.5	0.4	13.0
1965	3.3	−0.1	−1.5	3.4	−0.8	−4.9	1.3	2.3	3.2	2.7	−0.9	0.9	9.1
1966	0.5	−1.8	−2.2	2.1	−5.4	−1.6	−1.3	−7.8	−0.7	4.8	0.3	−0.1	−13.1
1967	7.8	0.2	3.9	4.2	−5.2	1.8	4.5	−1.2	3.3	−2.9	0.1	2.6	20.1
1968	−4.4	−3.1	0.9	8.2	1.1	0.9	−1.8	1.1	3.9	0.7	4.8	−4.2	7.7
1969	−0.8	−4.7	3.4	2.1	−0.2	−5.6	−6.0	4.0	−2.5	4.4	−3.5	−1.9	−11.4
1970	−7.6	5.3	0.1	−9.0	−6.1	−5.0	7.3	4.4	3.3	−1.1	4.7	5.7	0.1
1971	4.0	0.9	3.7	3.6	−4.2	0.1	−4.1	3.6	−0.7	−4.2	−0.3	8.6	10.8
1972	1.8	2.5	0.6	0.4	1.7	−2.2	0.2	3.4	−0.5	0.9	4.6	1.2	15.6
1973	−1.7	−3.7	−0.1	−4.1	−1.9	−0.7	3.8	−3.7	4.0	−0.1	−11.4	1.7	−17.4
1974	−1.0	−0.4	−2.3	−3.9	−3.4	−1.5	−7.8	−9.0	−11.9	16.3	−5.3	−2.0	−29.7
1975	12.3	6.0	2.2	4.7	4.4	4.4	−6.8	−2.1	−3.5	6.2	2.5	−1.2	31.5
1976	11.8	−1.1	3.1	−1.1	−1.4	4.1	−0.8	−0.5	2.3	−2.2	−0.8	5.2	19.1
1977	−5.1	−2.2	−1.4	0.02	−2.4	4.5	−1.6	−2.1	−0.2	−4.3	2.7	0.3	−11.5
1978	−6.2	−2.5	2.5	8.5	0.4	−1.8	5.4	2.6	−0.7	−9.2	1.7	1.5	1.1
1979	4.0	−3.7	5.5	0.2	−2.6	3.9	0.9	5.3	N/C	−6.9	4.3	1.7	12.3
1980	5.8	−0.4	−10.2	4.1	4.7	2.7	6.5	0.6	2.5	1.6	10.2	−3.4	25.8
1981	−4.6	1.3	3.6	−2.3	−0.2	−1.0	−0.2	−6.2	−5.4	4.9	3.7	−3.0	−9.7
1982	−1.8	−6.1	−1.0	4.0	−3.9	−2.0	−2.3	11.6	0.8	11.0	3.6	1.5	14.8
1983	3.3	1.9	3.3	7.5	−1.2	3.5	−3.3	1.1	1.0	−1.5	1.7	−0.9	17.3
1984	−0.9	−3.9	1.3	0.5	−5.9	1.7	−1.6	10.6	−0.3	−0.01	−1.5	2.2	1.4
1985	7.4	0.9	−0.3	−0.5	5.4	1.2	−0.5	−1.2	−3.5	4.3	6.5	4.5	26.3
1986	0.2	7.1	5.3	−1.4	5.0	1.4	−5.9	7.1	−8.5	5.5	2.1	−2.8	14.6
1987	13.2	3.7	2.6	−1.1	0.6	4.8	4.8	3.5	−2.4	−21.8	−8.5	7.3	2.0
1988	4.0	4.2	−3.3	0.9	0.3	4.3	−0.5	−3.9	4.0	2.6	−1.9	1.5	12.4
1989	7.1	−2.9	2.1	5.0	3.5	−0.8	8.8	1.6	−0.7	−2.5	1.7	2.1	27.3
1990	−6.9	0.9	2.4	−2.7	9.2	−0.9	−0.5	−9.4	−5.1	−0.7	6.0	2.5	−6.6
1991	4.2	6.7	2.2	0.03	3.9	−4.8	4.5	2.0	−1.9	1.2	−4.4	11.2	26.3
1992	−2.0	1.0	−2.2	2.8	0.1	−1.7	3.9	−2.4	0.9	0.2	3.0	1.0	4.5
1993	0.7	1.0	1.9	−2.5	2.3	0.1	−0.5	3.4	−1.0	1.9	−1.3	1.0	7.1
1994	3.3	−3.0	−4.6	1.2	1.2	−2.7	3.1	3.8	−2.7	2.1	−4.0	1.2	−1.5
1995	2.4	3.6	2.7	2.8	3.6	2.1	3.2	−0.03	4.0	−0.5	4.1	1.7	34.1
1996	3.3	0.7	0.8	1.3	2.3	0.2	−4.6	1.9	5.4	2.6	7.3	−2.2	20.3
1997	6.1	0.6	−4.3	5.8	5.9	4.3	7.8	−5.7	5.3	−3.4	4.5	1.6	31.0
1998	1.0	7.0	5.0	0.9	−1.9	3.9	−1.2	−14.6	6.2	8.0	5.9	5.6	26.7
1999	4.1	−3.2	3.9	3.8	−2.5	5.4	−3.2	−0.6	−2.9	6.3	1.9	5.8	19.5
2000	−5.1	−2.0	9.7	−3.1	−2.2	2.4	−1.6	6.1	−5.3	−0.5	−8.0	0.4	−10.1
2001	3.5	−9.2	−6.4	7.7	0.5	−2.5	−1.1	−6.4	−8.2	1.8	7.5	0.8	−13.0
2002	−1.6	−2.1	3.7	−6.1	−0.9	−7.2	−7.9	0.5	−11.0	8.6	5.7	−6.0	−23.4
2003	−2.7	−1.7	1.0	8.0	5.1	1.1	1.6	1.8	−1.2	5.5	0.7	5.1	26.4
2004	1.7	1.2	−1.6	−1.7	1.2	1.8	−3.4	0.2	0.9	1.4	3.9	3.2	9.0
2005	−2.5	1.9	−1.9	−2.0	3.0	−0.01	3.6	−1.1	0.7	−1.8	3.5	−0.1	3.0
2006	2.5	0.05	1.1	1.2	−3.1	0.01	0.5	2.1	2.5	3.2	1.6	1.3	13.6
2007	1.4	−2.2	1.0	4.3	3.3	−1.8	−3.2	1.3	3.6	1.5	−4.4	−0.9	3.5
2008	−6.1	−3.5	−0.6	4.8	1.1	−8.6	−1.0	1.2	−9.1	−16.9	−7.5	0.8	−38.5
2009	−8.6	−11.0	8.5	9.4	5.3	0.02	7.4	3.4	3.6	−2.0	5.7	1.8	23.5
2010	−3.7	2.9	5.9	1.5	−8.2	−5.4	6.9	−4.7	8.8	3.7	−0.2	6.5	12.8
2011	2.3	3.2	−0.1	2.8	−1.4	−1.8	−2.1	−5.7	−7.2	10.8	−0.5	0.9	−0.003
2012	4.4	4.1	3.1	−0.7	−6.3	4.0	1.3	2.0	2.4	−2.0	0.3	0.7	13.4
2013	5.0	1.1	3.6	1.8	2.1	−1.5	4.9	−3.1	3.0	4.5	2.8	2.4	29.6
2014	−3.6	4.3	0.7	0.6	2.1	1.9	−1.5	3.8	−1.6	2.3	2.5	−0.4	11.4
2015	−3.1	5.5	−1.7	0.9	1.0	−2.1	2.0	−6.3	−2.6	8.3	0.1	−1.8	−0.7
2016	−5.1	−0.4	6.6	0.3	1.5	0.1	3.6	−0.1	−0.1	−1.9	3.4	1.8	9.5
2017	1.8	3.7	−0.04	0.9	1.2	0.5	1.9	0.1	1.9	2.2	2.8	1.0	19.4
2018	5.6	−3.9	−2.7	0.3	2.2								
TOTALS	70.2	2.9	80.7	100.0	17.9	−1.6	70.0	−6.0	−32.4	62.6	105.2	109.5	
AVG.	1.0	0.04	1.2	1.4	0.3	−0.02	1.0	−0.1	−0.5	0.9	1.5	1.6	
# Up	42	38	44	49	41	36	38	37	30	41	46	51	
# Down	27	31	25	20	28	32	30	31	37	27	22	17	

STANDARD & POOR'S 500 MONTHLY CLOSING PRICES SINCE 1950

	Jan	Feb	Mar	Apr	May	Jun	Jul	Aug	Sep	Oct	Nov	Dec
1950	17.05	17.22	17.29	18.07	18.78	17.69	17.84	18.42	19.45	19.53	19.51	20.41
1951	21.66	21.80	21.40	22.43	21.52	20.96	22.40	23.28	23.26	22.94	22.88	23.77
1952	24.14	23.26	24.37	23.32	23.86	24.96	25.40	25.03	24.54	24.52	25.66	26.57
1953	26.38	25.90	25.29	24.62	24.54	24.14	24.75	23.32	23.35	24.54	24.76	24.81
1954	26.08	26.15	26.94	28.26	29.19	29.21	30.88	29.83	32.31	31.68	34.24	35.98
1955	36.63	36.76	36.58	37.96	37.91	41.03	43.52	43.18	43.67	42.34	45.51	45.48
1956	43.82	45.34	48.48	48.38	45.20	46.97	49.39	47.51	45.35	45.58	45.08	46.67
1957	44.72	43.26	44.11	45.74	47.43	47.37	47.91	45.22	42.42	41.06	41.72	39.99
1958	41.70	40.84	42.10	43.44	44.09	45.24	47.19	47.75	50.06	51.33	52.48	55.21
1959	55.42	55.41	55.44	57.59	58.68	58.47	60.51	59.60	56.88	57.52	58.28	59.89
1960	55.61	56.12	55.34	54.37	55.83	56.92	55.51	56.96	53.52	53.39	55.54	58.11
1961	61.78	63.44	65.06	65.31	66.56	64.64	66.76	68.07	66.73	68.62	71.32	71.55
1962	68.84	69.96	69.55	65.24	59.63	54.75	58.23	59.12	56.27	56.52	62.26	63.10
1963	66.20	64.29	66.57	69.80	70.80	69.37	69.13	72.50	71.70	74.01	73.23	75.02
1964	77.04	77.80	78.98	79.46	80.37	81.69	83.18	81.83	84.18	84.86	84.42	84.75
1965	87.56	87.43	86.16	89.11	88.42	84.12	85.25	87.17	89.96	92.42	91.61	92.43
1966	92.88	91.22	89.23	91.06	86.13	84.74	83.60	77.10	76.56	80.20	80.45	80.33
1967	86.61	86.78	90.20	94.01	89.08	90.64	94.75	93.64	96.71	93.90	94.00	96.47
1968	92.24	89.36	90.20	97.59	98.68	99.58	97.74	98.86	102.67	103.41	108.37	103.86
1969	103.01	98.13	101.51	103.69	103.46	97.71	91.83	95.51	93.12	97.24	93.81	92.06
1970	85.02	89.50	89.63	81.52	76.55	72.72	78.05	81.52	84.21	83.25	87.20	92.15
1971	95.88	96.75	100.31	103.95	99.63	99.70	95.58	99.03	98.34	94.23	93.99	102.09
1972	103.94	106.57	107.20	107.67	109.53	107.14	107.39	111.09	110.55	111.58	116.67	118.05
1973	116.03	111.68	111.52	106.97	104.95	104.26	108.22	104.25	108.43	108.29	95.96	97.55
1974	96.57	96.22	93.98	90.31	87.28	86.00	79.31	72.15	63.54	73.90	69.97	68.56
1975	76.98	81.59	83.36	87.30	91.15	95.19	88.75	86.88	83.87	89.04	91.24	90.19
1976	100.86	99.71	102.77	101.64	100.18	104.28	103.44	102.91	105.24	102.90	102.10	107.46
1977	102.03	99.82	98.42	98.44	96.12	100.48	98.85	96.77	96.53	92.34	94.83	95.10
1978	89.25	87.04	89.21	96.83	97.24	95.53	100.68	103.29	102.54	93.15	94.70	96.11
1979	99.93	96.28	101.59	101.76	99.08	102.91	103.81	109.32	109.32	101.82	106.16	107.94
1980	114.16	113.66	102.09	106.29	111.24	114.24	121.67	122.38	125.46	127.47	140.52	135.76
1981	129.55	131.27	136.00	132.81	132.59	131.21	130.92	122.79	116.18	121.89	126.35	122.55
1982	120.40	113.11	111.96	116.44	111.88	109.61	107.09	119.51	120.42	133.71	138.54	140.64
1983	145.30	148.06	152.96	164.42	162.39	168.11	162.56	164.40	166.07	163.55	166.40	164.93
1984	163.41	157.06	159.18	160.05	150.55	153.18	150.66	166.68	166.10	166.09	163.58	167.24
1985	179.63	181.18	180.66	179.83	189.55	191.85	190.92	188.63	182.08	189.82	202.17	211.28
1986	211.78	226.92	238.90	235.52	247.35	250.84	236.12	252.93	231.32	243.98	249.22	242.17
1987	274.08	284.20	291.70	288.36	290.10	304.00	318.66	329.80	321.83	251.79	230.30	247.08
1988	257.07	267.82	258.89	261.33	262.16	273.50	272.02	261.52	271.91	278.97	273.70	277.72
1989	297.47	288.86	294.87	309.64	320.52	317.98	346.08	351.45	349.15	340.36	345.99	353.40
1990	329.08	331.89	339.94	330.80	361.23	358.02	356.15	322.56	306.05	304.00	322.22	330.22
1991	343.93	367.07	375.22	375.35	389.83	371.16	387.81	395.43	387.86	392.46	375.22	417.09
1992	408.79	412.70	403.69	414.95	415.35	408.14	424.21	414.03	417.80	418.68	431.35	435.71
1993	438.78	443.38	451.67	440.19	450.19	450.53	448.13	463.56	458.93	467.83	461.79	466.45
1994	481.61	467.14	445.77	450.91	456.50	444.27	458.26	475.49	462.69	472.35	453.69	459.27
1995	470.42	487.39	500.71	514.71	533.40	544.75	562.06	561.88	584.41	581.50	605.37	615.93
1996	636.02	640.43	645.50	654.17	669.12	670.63	639.95	651.99	687.31	705.27	757.02	740.74
1997	786.16	790.82	757.12	801.34	848.28	885.14	954.29	899.47	947.28	914.62	955.40	970.43
1998	980.28	1049.34	1101.75	1111.75	1090.82	1133.84	1120.67	957.28	1017.01	1098.67	1163.63	1229.23
1999	1279.64	1238.33	1286.37	1335.18	1301.84	1372.71	1328.72	1320.41	1282.71	1362.93	1388.91	1469.25
2000	1394.46	1366.42	1498.58	1452.43	1420.60	1454.60	1430.83	1517.68	1436.51	1429.40	1314.95	1320.28
2001	1366.01	1239.94	1160.33	1249.46	1255.82	1224.42	1211.23	1133.58	1040.94	1059.78	1139.45	1148.08
2002	1130.20	1106.73	1147.39	1076.92	1067.14	989.82	911.62	916.07	815.28	885.76	936.31	879.82
2003	855.70	841.15	849.18	916.92	963.59	974.50	990.31	1008.01	995.97	1050.71	1058.20	1111.92
2004	1131.13	1144.94	1126.21	1107.30	1120.68	1140.84	1101.72	1104.24	1114.58	1130.20	1173.82	1211.92
2005	1181.27	1203.60	1180.59	1156.85	1191.50	1191.33	1234.18	1220.33	1228.81	1207.01	1249.48	1248.29
2006	1280.08	1280.66	1294.83	1310.61	1270.09	1270.20	1276.66	1303.82	1335.85	1377.94	1400.63	1418.30
2007	1438.24	1406.82	1420.86	1482.37	1530.62	1503.35	1455.27	1473.99	1526.75	1549.38	1481.14	1468.36
2008	1378.55	1330.63	1322.70	1385.59	1400.38	1280.00	1267.38	1282.83	1166.36	968.75	896.24	903.25
2009	825.88	735.09	797.87	872.81	919.14	919.32	987.48	1020.62	1057.08	1036.19	1095.63	1115.10
2010	1073.87	1104.49	1169.43	1186.69	1089.41	1030.71	1101.60	1049.33	1141.20	1183.26	1180.55	1257.64
2011	1286.12	1327.22	1325.83	1363.61	1345.20	1320.64	1292.28	1218.89	1131.42	1253.30	1246.96	1257.60
2012	1312.41	1365.68	1408.47	1397.91	1310.33	1362.16	1379.32	1406.58	1440.67	1412.16	1416.18	1426.19

continued

157

STANDARD & POOR'S 500 MONTHLY CLOSING PRICES SINCE 1950 (continued)

	Jan	Feb	Mar	Apr	May	Jun	Jul	Aug	Sep	Oct	Nov	Dec
2013	1498.11	1514.68	1569.19	1597.57	1630.74	1606.28	1685.73	1632.97	1681.55	1756.54	1805.81	1848.36
2014	1782.59	1859.45	1872.34	1883.95	1923.57	1960.23	1930.67	2003.37	1972.29	2018.05	2067.56	2058.90
2015	1994.99	2104.50	2067.89	2085.51	2107.39	2063.11	2103.84	1972.18	1920.03	2079.36	2080.41	2043.94
2016	1940.24	1932.23	2059.74	2065.30	2096.96	2098.86	2173.60	2170.95	2168.27	2126.15	2198.81	2238.83
2017	2278.87	2363.64	2362.72	2384.20	2411.80	2423.41	2470.30	2471.65	2519.36	2575.26	2647.58	2673.61
2018	2823.81	2713.83	2640.87	2648.05	2705.27							

NASDAQ COMPOSITE MONTHLY PERCENT CHANGES SINCE 1971

	Jan	Feb	Mar	Apr	May	Jun	Jul	Aug	Sep	Oct	Nov	Dec	Year's Change
1971	10.2	2.6	4.6	6.0	–3.6	–0.4	–2.3	3.0	0.6	–3.6	–1.1	9.8	27.4
1972	4.2	5.5	2.2	2.5	0.9	–1.8	–1.8	1.7	–0.3	0.5	2.1	0.6	17.2
1973	–4.0	–6.2	–2.4	–8.2	–4.8	–1.6	7.6	–3.5	6.0	–0.9	–15.1	–1.4	–31.1
1974	3.0	–0.6	–2.2	–5.9	–7.7	–5.3	–7.9	–10.9	–10.7	17.2	–3.5	–5.0	–35.1
1975	16.6	4.6	3.6	3.8	5.8	4.7	–4.4	–5.0	–5.9	3.6	2.4	–1.5	29.8
1976	12.1	3.7	0.4	–0.6	–2.3	2.6	1.1	–1.7	1.7	–1.0	0.9	7.4	26.1
1977	–2.4	–1.0	–0.5	1.4	0.1	4.3	0.9	–0.5	0.7	–3.3	5.8	1.8	7.3
1978	–4.0	0.6	4.7	8.5	4.4	0.05	5.0	6.9	–1.6	–16.4	3.2	2.9	12.3
1979	6.6	–2.6	7.5	1.6	–1.8	5.1	2.3	6.4	–0.3	–9.6	6.4	4.8	28.1
1980	7.0	–2.3	–17.1	6.9	7.5	4.9	8.9	5.7	3.4	2.7	8.0	–2.8	33.9
1981	–2.2	0.1	6.1	3.1	3.1	–3.5	–1.9	–7.5	–8.0	8.4	3.1	–2.7	–3.2
1982	–3.8	–4.8	–2.1	5.2	–3.3	–4.1	–2.3	6.2	5.6	13.3	9.3	0.04	18.7
1983	6.9	5.0	3.9	8.2	5.3	3.2	–4.6	–3.8	1.4	–7.4	4.1	–2.5	19.9
1984	–3.7	–5.9	–0.7	–1.3	–5.9	2.9	–4.2	10.9	–1.8	–1.2	–1.8	2.0	–11.2
1985	12.7	2.0	–1.7	0.5	3.6	1.9	1.7	–1.2	–5.8	4.4	7.3	3.5	31.4
1986	3.3	7.1	4.2	2.3	4.4	1.3	–8.4	3.1	–8.4	2.9	–0.3	–2.8	7.5
1987	12.2	8.4	1.2	–2.8	–0.3	2.0	2.4	4.6	–2.3	–27.2	–5.6	8.3	–5.4
1988	4.3	6.5	2.1	1.2	–2.3	6.6	–1.9	–2.8	3.0	–1.4	–2.9	2.7	15.4
1989	5.2	–0.4	1.8	5.1	4.4	–2.4	4.3	3.4	0.8	–3.7	0.1	–0.3	19.3
1990	–8.6	2.4	2.3	–3.6	9.3	0.7	–5.2	–13.0	–9.6	–4.3	8.9	4.1	–17.8
1991	10.8	9.4	6.5	0.5	4.4	–6.0	5.5	4.7	0.2	3.1	–3.5	11.9	56.8
1992	5.8	2.1	–4.7	–4.2	1.1	–3.7	3.1	–3.0	3.6	3.8	7.9	3.7	15.5
1993	2.9	–3.7	2.9	–4.2	5.9	0.5	0.1	5.4	2.7	2.2	–3.2	3.0	14.7
1994	3.0	–1.0	–6.2	–1.3	0.2	–4.0	2.3	6.0	–0.2	1.7	–3.5	0.2	–3.2
1995	0.4	5.1	3.0	3.3	2.4	8.0	7.3	1.9	2.3	–0.7	2.2	–0.7	39.9
1996	0.7	3.8	0.1	8.1	4.4	–4.7	–8.8	5.6	7.5	–0.4	5.8	–0.1	22.7
1997	6.9	–5.1	–6.7	3.2	11.1	3.0	10.5	–0.4	6.2	–5.5	0.4	–1.9	21.6
1998	3.1	9.3	3.7	1.8	–4.8	6.5	–1.2	–19.9	13.0	4.6	10.1	12.5	39.6
1999	14.3	–8.7	7.6	3.3	–2.8	8.7	–1.8	3.8	0.2	8.0	12.5	22.0	85.6
2000	–3.2	19.2	–2.6	–15.6	–11.9	16.6	–5.0	11.7	–12.7	–8.3	–22.9	–4.9	–39.3
2001	12.2	–22.4	–14.5	15.0	–0.3	2.4	–6.2	–10.9	–17.0	12.8	14.2	1.0	–21.1
2002	–0.8	–10.5	6.6	–8.5	–4.3	–9.4	–9.2	–1.0	–10.9	13.5	11.2	–9.7	–31.5
2003	–1.1	1.3	0.3	9.2	9.0	1.7	6.9	4.3	–1.3	8.1	1.5	2.2	50.0
2004	3.1	–1.8	–1.8	–3.7	3.5	3.1	–7.8	–2.6	3.2	4.1	6.2	3.7	8.6
2005	–5.2	–0.5	–2.6	–3.9	7.6	–0.5	6.2	–1.5	–0.02	–1.5	5.3	–1.2	1.4
2006	4.6	–1.1	2.6	–0.7	–6.2	–0.3	–3.7	4.4	3.4	4.8	2.7	–0.7	9.5
2007	2.0	–1.9	0.2	4.3	3.1	–0.05	–2.2	2.0	4.0	5.8	–6.9	–0.3	9.8
2008	–9.9	–5.0	0.3	5.9	4.6	–9.1	1.4	1.8	–11.6	–17.7	–10.8	2.7	–40.5
2009	–6.4	–6.7	10.9	12.3	3.3	3.4	7.8	1.5	5.6	–3.6	4.9	5.8	43.9
2010	–5.4	4.2	7.1	2.6	–8.3	–6.5	6.9	–6.2	12.0	5.9	–0.4	6.2	16.9
2011	1.8	3.0	–0.04	3.3	–1.3	–2.2	–0.6	–6.4	–6.4	11.1	–2.4	–0.6	–1.8
2012	8.0	5.4	4.2	–1.5	–7.2	3.8	0.2	4.3	1.6	–4.5	1.1	0.3	15.9
2013	4.1	0.6	3.4	1.9	3.8	–1.5	6.6	–1.0	5.1	3.9	3.6	2.9	38.3
2014	–1.7	5.0	–2.5	–2.0	3.1	3.9	–0.9	4.8	–1.9	3.1	3.5	–1.2	13.4
2015	–2.1	7.1	–1.3	0.8	2.6	–1.6	2.8	–6.9	–3.3	9.4	1.1	–2.0	5.7
2016	–7.9	–1.2	6.8	–1.9	3.6	–2.1	6.6	1.0	1.9	–2.3	2.6	1.1	7.5
2017	4.3	3.8	1.5	2.3	2.5	–0.9	3.4	1.3	1.0	3.6	2.2	0.4	28.2
2018	7.4	–1.9	–2.9	0.04	5.3								
TOTALS	127.3	32.5	39.8	64.2	51.2	30.2	19.5	6.7	–23.3	38.0	76.7	85.2	
AVG.	2.7	0.7	0.8	1.3	1.1	0.6	0.4	0.1	–0.5	0.8	1.6	1.8	
# Up	31	26	30	31	30	25	25	26	26	26	32	28	
# Down	17	22	18	17	18	22	22	21	21	21	15	19	

Based on NASDAQ composite; prior to February 5, 1971, based on National Quotation Bureau indices.

NASDAQ COMPOSITE MONTHLY CLOSING PRICES SINCE 1971

	Jan	Feb	Mar	Apr	May	Jun	Jul	Aug	Sep	Oct	Nov	Dec
1971	98.77	101.34	105.97	112.30	108.25	107.80	105.27	108.42	109.03	105.10	103.97	114.12
1972	118.87	125.38	128.14	131.33	132.53	130.08	127.75	129.95	129.61	130.24	132.96	133.73
1973	128.40	120.41	117.46	107.85	102.64	100.98	108.64	104.87	111.20	110.17	93.51	92.19
1974	94.93	94.35	92.27	86.86	80.20	75.96	69.99	62.37	55.67	65.23	62.95	59.82
1975	69.78	73.00	75.66	78.54	83.10	87.02	83.19	79.01	74.33	76.99	78.80	77.62
1976	87.05	90.26	90.62	90.08	88.04	90.32	91.29	89.70	91.26	90.35	91.12	97.88
1977	95.54	94.57	94.13	95.48	95.59	99.73	100.65	100.10	100.85	97.52	103.15	105.05
1978	100.84	101.47	106.20	115.18	120.24	120.30	126.32	135.01	132.89	111.12	114.69	117.98
1979	125.82	122.56	131.76	133.82	131.42	138.13	141.33	150.44	149.98	135.53	144.26	151.14
1980	161.75	158.03	131.00	139.99	150.45	157.78	171.81	181.52	187.76	192.78	208.15	202.34
1981	197.81	198.01	210.18	216.74	223.47	215.75	211.63	195.75	180.03	195.24	201.37	195.84
1982	188.39	179.43	175.65	184.70	178.54	171.30	167.35	177.71	187.65	212.63	232.31	232.41
1983	248.35	260.67	270.80	293.06	308.73	318.70	303.96	292.42	296.65	274.55	285.67	278.60
1984	268.43	252.57	250.78	247.44	232.82	239.65	229.70	254.64	249.94	247.03	242.53	247.35
1985	278.70	284.17	279.20	280.56	290.80	296.20	301.29	297.71	280.33	292.54	313.95	324.93
1986	335.77	359.53	374.72	383.24	400.16	405.51	371.37	382.86	350.67	360.77	359.57	349.33
1987	392.06	424.97	430.05	417.81	416.54	424.67	434.93	454.97	444.29	323.30	305.16	330.47
1988	344.66	366.95	374.64	379.23	370.34	394.66	387.33	376.55	387.71	382.46	371.45	381.38
1989	401.30	399.71	406.73	427.55	446.17	435.29	453.84	469.33	472.92	455.63	456.09	454.82
1990	415.81	425.83	435.54	420.07	458.97	462.29	438.24	381.21	344.51	329.84	359.06	373.84
1991	414.20	453.05	482.30	484.72	506.11	475.92	502.04	525.68	526.88	542.98	523.90	586.34
1992	620.21	633.47	603.77	578.68	585.31	563.60	580.83	563.12	583.27	605.17	652.73	676.95
1993	696.34	670.77	690.13	661.42	700.53	703.95	704.70	742.84	762.78	779.26	754.39	776.80
1994	800.47	792.50	743.46	733.84	735.19	705.96	722.16	765.62	764.29	777.49	750.32	751.96
1995	755.20	793.73	817.21	843.98	864.58	933.45	1001.21	1020.11	1043.54	1036.06	1059.20	1052.13
1996	1059.79	1100.05	1101.40	1190.52	1243.43	1185.02	1080.59	1141.50	1226.92	1221.51	1292.61	1291.03
1997	1379.85	1309.00	1221.70	1260.76	1400.32	1442.07	1593.81	1587.32	1685.69	1593.61	1600.55	1570.35
1998	1619.36	1770.51	1835.68	1868.41	1778.87	1894.74	1872.39	1499.25	1693.84	1771.39	1949.54	2192.69
1999	2505.89	2288.03	2461.40	2542.85	2470.52	2686.12	2638.49	2739.35	2746.16	2966.43	3336.16	4069.31
2000	3940.35	4696.69	4572.83	3860.66	3400.91	3966.11	3766.99	4206.35	3672.82	3369.63	2597.93	2470.52
2001	2772.73	2151.83	1840.26	2116.24	2110.49	2160.54	2027.13	1805.43	1498.80	1690.20	1930.58	1950.40
2002	1934.03	1731.49	1845.35	1688.23	1615.73	1463.21	1328.26	1314.85	1172.06	1329.75	1478.78	1335.51
2003	1320.91	1337.52	1341.17	1464.31	1595.91	1622.80	1735.02	1810.45	1786.94	1932.21	1960.26	2003.37
2004	2066.15	2029.82	1994.22	1920.15	1986.74	2047.79	1887.36	1838.10	1896.84	1974.99	2096.81	2175.44
2005	2062.41	2051.72	1999.23	1921.65	2068.22	2056.96	2184.83	2152.09	2151.69	2120.30	2232.82	2205.32
2006	2305.82	2281.39	2339.79	2322.57	2178.88	2172.09	2091.47	2183.75	2258.43	2366.71	2431.77	2415.29
2007	2463.93	2416.15	2421.64	2525.09	2604.52	2603.23	2545.57	2596.36	2701.50	2859.12	2660.96	2652.28
2008	2389.86	2271.48	2279.10	2412.80	2522.66	2292.98	2325.55	2367.52	2091.88	1720.95	1535.57	1577.03
2009	1476.42	1377.84	1528.59	1717.30	1774.33	1835.04	1978.50	2009.06	2122.42	2045.11	2144.60	2269.15
2010	2147.35	2238.26	2397.96	2461.19	2257.04	2109.24	2254.70	2114.03	2368.62	2507.41	2498.23	2652.87
2011	2700.08	2782.27	2781.07	2873.54	2835.30	2773.52	2756.38	2579.46	2415.40	2684.41	2620.34	2605.15
2012	2813.84	2966.89	3091.57	3046.36	2827.34	2935.05	2939.52	3066.96	3116.23	2977.23	3010.24	3019.51
2013	3142.13	3160.19	3267.52	3328.79	3455.91	3403.25	3626.37	3589.87	3771.48	3919.71	4059.89	4176.59
2014	4103.88	4308.12	4198.99	4114.56	4242.62	4408.18	4369.77	4580.27	4493.39	4630.74	4791.63	4736.05
2015	4635.24	4963.53	4900.88	4941.42	5070.03	4986.87	5128.28	4776.51	4620.16	5053.75	5108.67	5007.41
2016	4613.95	4557.95	4869.85	4775.36	4948.05	4842.67	5162.13	5213.22	5312.00	5189.13	5323.68	5383.12
2017	5614.79	5825.44	5911.74	6047.61	6198.52	6140.42	6348.12	6428.66	6495.96	6727.67	6873.97	6903.39
2018	7411.48	7273.01	7063.44	7066.27	7442.12							

Based on NASDAQ composite; prior to February 5, 1971, based on National Quotation Bureau indices.

RUSSELL 1000 INDEX MONTHLY PERCENT CHANGES SINCE 1979

	Jan	Feb	Mar	Apr	May	Jun	Jul	Aug	Sep	Oct	Nov	Dec	Year's Change
1979	4.2	−3.5	6.0	0.3	−2.2	4.3	1.1	5.6	0.02	−7.1	5.1	2.1	16.1
1980	5.9	−0.5	−11.5	4.6	5.0	3.2	6.4	1.1	2.6	1.8	10.1	−3.9	25.6
1981	−4.6	1.0	3.8	−1.9	0.2	−1.2	−0.1	−6.2	−6.4	5.4	4.0	−3.3	−9.7
1982	−2.7	−5.9	−1.3	3.9	−3.6	−2.6	−2.3	11.3	1.2	11.3	4.0	1.3	13.7
1983	3.2	2.1	3.2	7.1	−0.2	3.7	−3.2	0.5	1.3	−2.4	2.0	−1.2	17.0
1984	−1.9	−4.4	1.1	0.3	−5.9	2.1	−1.8	10.8	−0.2	−0.1	−1.4	2.2	−0.1
1985	7.8	1.1	−0.4	−0.3	5.4	1.6	−0.8	−1.0	−3.9	4.5	6.5	4.1	26.7
1986	0.9	7.2	5.1	−1.3	5.0	1.4	−5.9	6.8	−8.5	5.1	1.4	−3.0	13.6
1987	12.7	4.0	1.9	−1.8	0.4	4.5	4.2	3.8	−2.4	−21.9	−8.0	7.2	0.02
1988	4.3	4.4	−2.9	0.7	0.2	4.8	−0.9	−3.3	3.9	2.0	−2.0	1.7	13.1
1989	6.8	−2.5	2.0	4.9	3.8	−0.8	8.2	1.7	−0.5	−2.8	1.5	1.8	25.9
1990	−7.4	1.2	2.2	−2.8	8.9	−0.7	−1.1	−9.6	−5.3	−0.8	6.4	2.7	−7.5
1991	4.5	6.9	2.5	−0.1	3.8	−4.7	4.6	2.2	−1.5	1.4	−4.1	11.2	28.8
1992	−1.4	0.9	−2.4	2.3	0.3	−1.9	4.1	−2.5	1.0	0.7	3.5	1.4	5.9
1993	0.7	0.6	2.2	−2.8	2.4	0.4	−0.4	3.5	−0.5	1.2	−1.7	1.6	7.3
1994	2.9	−2.9	−4.5	1.1	1.0	−2.9	3.1	3.9	−2.6	1.7	−3.9	1.2	−2.4
1995	2.4	3.8	2.3	2.5	3.5	2.4	3.7	0.5	3.9	−0.6	4.2	1.4	34.4
1996	3.1	1.1	0.7	1.4	2.1	−0.1	−4.9	2.5	5.5	2.1	7.1	−1.8	19.7
1997	5.8	0.2	−4.6	5.3	6.2	4.0	8.0	−4.9	5.4	−3.4	4.2	1.9	30.5
1998	0.6	7.0	4.9	0.9	−2.3	3.6	−1.3	−15.1	6.5	7.8	6.1	6.2	25.1
1999	3.5	−3.3	3.7	4.2	−2.3	5.1	−3.2	−1.0	−2.8	6.5	2.5	6.0	19.5
2000	−4.2	−0.4	8.9	−3.3	−2.7	2.5	−1.8	7.4	−4.8	−1.2	−9.3	1.1	−8.8
2001	3.2	−9.5	−6.7	8.0	0.5	−2.4	−1.4	−6.2	−8.6	2.0	7.5	0.9	−13.6
2002	−1.4	−2.1	4.0	−5.8	−1.0	−7.5	−7.5	0.3	−10.9	8.1	5.7	−5.8	−22.9
2003	−2.5	−1.7	0.9	7.9	5.5	1.2	1.8	1.9	−1.2	5.7	1.0	4.6	27.5
2004	1.8	1.2	−1.5	−1.9	1.3	1.7	−3.6	0.3	1.1	1.5	4.1	3.5	9.5
2005	−2.6	2.0	−1.7	−2.0	3.4	0.3	3.8	−1.1	0.8	−1.9	3.5	0.01	4.4
2006	2.7	0.01	1.3	1.1	−3.2	0.003	0.1	2.2	2.3	3.3	1.9	1.1	13.3
2007	1.8	−1.9	0.9	4.1	3.4	−2.0	−3.2	1.2	3.7	1.6	−4.5	−0.8	3.9
2008	−6.1	−3.3	−0.8	5.0	1.6	−8.5	−1.3	1.2	−9.7	−17.6	−7.9	1.3	−39.0
2009	−8.3	−10.7	8.5	10.0	5.3	0.1	7.5	3.4	3.9	−2.3	5.6	2.3	25.5
2010	−3.7	3.1	6.0	1.8	−8.1	−5.7	6.8	−4.7	9.0	3.8	0.1	6.5	13.9
2011	2.3	3.3	0.1	2.9	−1.3	−1.9	−2.3	−6.0	−7.6	11.1	−0.5	0.7	−0.5
2012	4.8	4.1	3.0	−0.7	−6.4	3.7	1.1	2.2	2.4	−1.8	0.5	0.8	13.9
2013	5.3	1.1	3.7	1.7	2.0	−1.5	5.2	−3.0	3.3	4.3	2.6	2.5	30.4
2014	−3.3	4.5	0.5	0.4	2.1	2.1	−1.7	3.9	−1.9	2.3	2.4	−0.4	11.1
2015	−2.8	5.5	−1.4	0.6	1.1	−2.0	1.8	−6.2	−2.9	8.0	0.1	−2.0	−1.1
2016	−5.5	−0.3	6.8	0.4	1.5	0.1	3.7	−0.1	−0.1	−2.1	3.7	1.7	9.7
2017	1.9	3.6	−0.1	0.9	1.0	0.5	1.9	0.1	2.0	2.2	2.8	1.0	19.3
2018	5.4	−3.9	−2.4	0.2	2.3								
TOTALS	40.1	13.1	44.0	59.8	40.0	6.9	28.4	7.4	−22.5	39.4	66.8	59.8	
AVG.	1.0	0.3	1.1	1.5	1.0	0.2	0.7	0.2	−0.6	1.0	1.7	1.5	
# Up	25	24	26	28	28	23	19	24	19	25	29	30	
# Down	15	16	14	12	12	16	20	15	20	14	10	9	

RUSSELL 1000 INDEX MONTHLY CLOSING PRICES SINCE 1979

	Jan	Feb	Mar	Apr	May	Jun	Jul	Aug	Sep	Oct	Nov	Dec
1979	53.76	51.88	54.97	55.15	53.92	56.25	56.86	60.04	60.05	55.78	58.65	59.87
1980	63.40	63.07	55.79	58.38	61.31	63.27	67.30	68.05	69.84	71.08	78.26	75.20
1981	71.75	72.49	75.21	73.77	73.90	73.01	72.92	68.42	64.06	67.54	70.23	67.93
1982	66.12	62.21	61.43	63.85	61.53	59.92	58.54	65.14	65.89	73.34	76.28	77.24
1983	79.75	81.45	84.06	90.04	89.89	93.18	90.18	90.65	91.85	89.69	91.50	90.38
1984	88.69	84.76	85.73	86.00	80.94	82.61	81.13	89.87	89.67	89.62	88.36	90.31
1985	97.31	98.38	98.03	97.72	103.02	104.65	103.78	102.76	98.75	103.16	109.91	114.39
1986	115.39	123.71	130.07	128.44	134.82	136.75	128.74	137.43	125.70	132.11	133.97	130.00
1987	146.48	152.29	155.20	152.39	152.94	159.84	166.57	172.95	168.83	131.89	121.28	130.02
1988	135.55	141.54	137.45	138.37	138.66	145.31	143.99	139.26	144.68	147.55	144.59	146.99
1989	156.93	152.98	155.99	163.63	169.85	168.49	182.27	185.33	184.40	179.17	181.85	185.11
1990	171.44	173.43	177.28	172.32	187.66	186.29	184.32	166.69	157.83	156.62	166.69	171.22
1991	179.00	191.34	196.15	195.94	203.32	193.78	202.67	207.18	204.02	206.96	198.46	220.61
1992	217.52	219.50	214.29	219.13	219.71	215.60	224.37	218.86	221.15	222.65	230.44	233.59
1993	235.25	236.67	241.80	235.13	240.80	241.78	240.78	249.20	247.95	250.97	246.70	250.71
1994	258.08	250.52	239.19	241.71	244.13	237.11	244.44	254.04	247.49	251.62	241.82	244.65
1995	250.52	260.08	266.11	272.81	282.48	289.29	299.98	301.40	313.28	311.37	324.36	328.89
1996	338.97	342.56	345.01	349.84	357.35	357.10	339.44	347.79	366.77	374.38	401.05	393.75
1997	416.77	417.46	398.19	419.15	445.06	462.95	499.89	475.33	500.78	483.86	504.25	513.79
1998	517.02	553.14	580.31	585.46	572.16	592.57	584.97	496.66	529.11	570.63	605.31	642.87
1999	665.64	643.67	667.49	695.25	679.10	713.61	690.51	683.27	663.83	707.19	724.66	767.97
2000	736.08	733.04	797.99	771.58	750.98	769.68	755.57	811.17	772.60	763.06	692.40	700.09
2001	722.55	654.25	610.36	658.90	662.39	646.64	637.43	597.67	546.46	557.29	599.32	604.94
2002	596.66	583.88	607.35	572.04	566.18	523.72	484.39	486.08	433.22	468.51	495.00	466.18
2003	454.30	446.37	450.35	486.09	512.92	518.94	528.53	538.40	532.15	562.51	568.32	594.56
2004	605.21	612.58	603.42	591.83	599.40	609.31	587.21	589.09	595.66	604.51	629.26	650.99
2005	633.99	646.93	635.78	623.32	644.28	645.92	670.26	663.13	668.53	656.09	679.35	679.42
2006	697.79	697.83	706.74	714.37	691.78	691.80	692.59	707.55	723.48	747.30	761.43	770.08
2007	784.11	768.92	775.97	807.82	835.14	818.17	792.11	801.22	830.59	844.20	806.44	799.82
2008	750.97	726.42	720.32	756.03	768.28	703.22	694.07	702.17	634.08	522.47	481.43	487.77
2009	447.32	399.61	433.67	476.84	501.95	502.27	539.88	558.21	579.97	566.50	598.41	612.01
2010	589.41	607.45	643.79	655.06	601.79	567.37	606.09	577.68	629.78	653.57	654.24	696.90
2011	712.97	736.24	737.07	758.45	748.75	734.48	717.77	674.79	623.45	692.41	688.77	693.36
2012	726.33	756.42	778.92	773.50	724.12	750.61	758.60	775.07	793.74	779.35	783.37	789.90
2013	831.74	840.97	872.11	886.89	904.44	890.67	937.16	909.28	939.50	979.68	1004.97	1030.36
2014	996.48	1041.36	1046.42	1050.20	1071.96	1094.59	1075.60	1117.71	1096.43	1121.98	1148.90	1144.37
2015	1111.85	1173.46	1156.95	1164.03	1176.67	1152.64	1173.55	1100.51	1068.46	1153.55	1154.66	1131.88
2016	1069.78	1066.58	1138.84	1143.76	1160.95	1161.57	1204.43	1203.05	1202.25	1177.22	1220.68	1241.66
2017	1265.35	1311.34	1310.06	1322.44	1336.18	1343.52	1368.57	1369.61	1396.90	1427.43	1467.42	1481.81
2018	1561.66	1501.23	1464.87	1468.28	1502.31							

RUSSELL 2000 INDEX MONTHLY PERCENT CHANGES SINCE 1979

	Jan	Feb	Mar	Apr	May	Jun	Jul	Aug	Sep	Oct	Nov	Dec	Year's Change
1979	9.0	–3.2	9.7	2.3	–1.8	5.3	2.9	7.8	–0.7	–11.3	8.1	6.6	38.0
1980	8.2	–2.1	–18.5	6.0	8.0	4.0	11.0	6.5	2.9	3.9	7.0	–3.7	33.8
1981	–0.6	0.3	7.7	2.5	3.0	–2.5	–2.6	–8.0	–8.6	8.2	2.8	–2.0	–1.5
1982	–3.7	–5.3	–1.5	5.1	–3.2	–4.0	–1.7	7.5	3.6	14.1	8.8	1.1	20.7
1983	7.5	6.0	2.5	7.2	7.0	4.4	–3.0	–4.0	1.6	–7.0	5.0	–2.1	26.3
1984	–1.8	–5.9	0.4	–0.7	–5.4	2.6	–5.0	11.5	–1.0	–2.0	–2.9	1.4	–9.6
1985	13.1	2.4	–2.2	–1.4	3.4	1.0	2.7	–1.2	–6.2	3.6	6.8	4.2	28.0
1986	1.5	7.0	4.7	1.4	3.3	–0.2	–9.5	3.0	–6.3	3.9	–0.5	–3.1	4.0
1987	11.5	8.2	2.4	–3.0	–0.5	2.3	2.8	2.9	–2.0	–30.8	–5.5	7.8	–10.8
1988	4.0	8.7	4.4	2.0	–2.5	7.0	–0.9	–2.8	2.3	–1.2	–3.6	3.8	22.4
1989	4.4	0.5	2.2	4.3	4.2	–2.4	4.2	2.1	0.01	–6.0	0.4	0.1	14.2
1990	–8.9	2.9	3.7	–3.4	6.8	0.1	–4.5	–13.6	–9.2	–6.2	7.3	3.7	–21.5
1991	9.1	11.0	6.9	–0.2	4.5	–6.0	3.1	3.7	0.6	2.7	–4.7	7.7	43.7
1992	8.0	2.9	–3.5	–3.7	1.2	–5.0	3.2	–3.1	2.2	3.1	7.5	3.4	16.4
1993	3.2	–2.5	3.1	–2.8	4.3	0.5	1.3	4.1	2.7	2.5	–3.4	3.3	17.0
1994	3.1	–0.4	–5.4	0.6	–1.3	–3.6	1.6	5.4	–0.5	–0.4	–4.2	2.5	–3.2
1995	–1.4	3.9	1.6	2.1	1.5	5.0	5.7	1.9	1.7	–4.6	4.2	2.4	26.2
1996	–0.2	3.0	1.8	5.3	3.9	–4.2	–8.8	5.7	3.7	–1.7	4.0	2.4	14.8
1997	1.9	–2.5	–4.9	0.1	11.0	4.1	4.6	2.2	7.2	–4.5	–0.8	1.7	20.5
1998	–1.6	7.4	4.1	0.5	–5.4	0.2	–8.2	–19.5	7.6	4.0	5.2	6.1	–3.4
1999	1.2	–8.2	1.4	8.8	1.4	4.3	–2.8	–3.8	–0.1	0.3	5.9	11.2	19.6
2000	–1.7	16.4	–6.7	–6.1	–5.9	8.6	–3.2	7.4	–3.1	–4.5	–10.4	8.4	–4.2
2001	5.1	–6.7	–5.0	7.7	2.3	3.3	–5.4	–3.3	–13.6	5.8	7.6	6.0	1.0
2002	–1.1	–2.8	7.9	0.8	–4.5	–5.1	–15.2	–0.4	–7.3	3.1	8.8	–5.7	–21.6
2003	–2.9	–3.1	1.1	9.4	10.6	1.7	6.2	4.5	–2.0	8.3	3.5	1.9	45.4
2004	4.3	0.8	0.8	–5.2	1.5	4.1	–6.8	–0.6	4.6	1.9	8.6	2.8	17.0
2005	–4.2	1.6	–3.0	–5.8	6.4	3.7	6.3	–1.9	0.2	–3.2	4.7	–0.6	3.3
2006	8.9	–0.3	4.7	–0.1	–5.7	0.5	–3.3	2.9	0.7	5.7	2.5	0.2	17.0
2007	1.6	–0.9	0.9	1.7	4.0	–1.6	–6.9	2.2	1.6	2.8	–7.3	–0.2	–2.7
2008	–6.9	–3.8	0.3	4.1	4.5	–7.8	3.6	3.5	–8.1	–20.9	–12.0	5.6	–34.8
2009	–11.2	–12.3	8.7	15.3	2.9	1.3	9.5	2.8	5.6	–6.9	3.0	7.9	25.2
2010	–3.7	4.4	8.0	5.6	–7.7	–7.9	6.8	–7.5	12.3	4.0	3.4	7.8	25.3
2011	–0.3	5.4	2.4	2.6	–2.0	–2.5	–3.7	–8.8	–11.4	15.0	–0.5	0.5	–5.5
2012	7.0	2.3	2.4	–1.6	–6.7	4.8	–1.4	3.2	3.1	–2.2	0.4	3.3	14.6
2013	6.2	1.0	4.4	–0.4	3.9	–0.7	6.9	–3.3	6.2	2.5	3.9	1.8	37.0
2014	–2.8	4.6	–0.8	–3.9	0.7	5.2	–6.1	4.8	–6.2	6.5	–0.02	2.7	3.5
2015	–3.3	5.8	1.6	–2.6	2.2	0.6	–1.2	–6.4	–5.1	5.6	3.1	–5.2	–5.7
2016	–8.8	–0.1	7.8	1.5	2.1	–0.2	5.9	1.6	0.9	–4.8	11.0	2.6	19.5
2017	0.3	1.8	–0.1	1.0	–2.2	3.3	0.7	–1.4	6.1	0.8	2.8	–0.6	13.1
2018	2.6	–4.0	1.1	0.8	5.9								
TOTALS	56.6	44.2	57.1	57.8	55.7	24.2	–11.2	7.6	–14.0	–9.9	80.5	97.7	
AVG.	1.4	1.1	1.4	1.4	1.4	0.6	–0.3	0.2	–0.4	–0.3	2.1	2.5	
# Up	22	23	29	25	26	24	19	22	22	22	26	30	
# Down	18	17	11	15	14	15	20	17	17	17	13	9	

THE ULTIMATE GUIDE TO MARKET-BEATING RETURNS, FROM *STOCK TRADER'S ALMANAC* EDITOR-IN-CHIEF **JEFFREY HIRSCH**

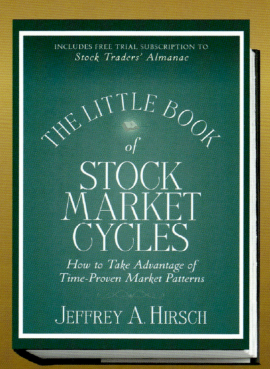

To profit from the stock market, you must be able to predict its patterns. *The Little Book of Stock Market Cycles* brings together everything you need to know about recurring trends in one insightful and accessible volume, backed by the wisdom of the pre-eminent authority on market cycles and seasonal patterns.

The perfect companion to the *Stock Trader's Almanac*, this little book is big on practical advice and proven strategies that you can put to use right away to consistently outperform the market.

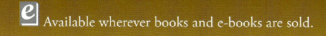
Available wherever books and e-books are sold.

WILEY

	Jan	Feb	Mar	Apr	May	Jun	Jul	Aug	Sep	Oct	Nov	Dec
1979	44.18	42.78	46.94	48.00	47.13	49.62	51.08	55.05	54.68	48.51	52.43	55.91
1980	60.50	59.22	48.27	51.18	55.26	57.47	63.81	67.97	69.94	72.64	77.70	74.80
1981	74.33	74.52	80.25	82.25	84.72	82.56	80.41	73.94	67.55	73.06	75.14	73.67
1982	70.96	67.21	66.21	69.59	67.39	64.67	63.59	68.38	70.84	80.86	87.96	88.90
1983	95.53	101.23	103.77	111.20	118.94	124.17	120.43	115.60	117.43	109.17	114.66	112.27
1984	110.21	103.72	104.10	103.34	97.75	100.30	95.25	106.21	105.17	103.07	100.11	101.49
1985	114.77	117.54	114.92	113.35	117.26	118.38	121.56	120.10	112.65	116.73	124.62	129.87
1986	131.78	141.00	147.63	149.66	154.61	154.23	139.65	143.83	134.73	139.95	139.26	135.00
1987	150.48	162.84	166.79	161.82	161.02	164.75	169.42	174.25	170.81	118.26	111.70	120.42
1988	125.24	136.10	142.15	145.01	141.37	151.30	149.89	145.74	149.08	147.25	142.01	147.37
1989	153.84	154.56	157.89	164.68	171.53	167.42	174.50	178.20	178.21	167.47	168.17	168.30
1990	153.27	157.72	163.63	158.09	168.91	169.04	161.51	139.52	126.70	118.83	127.50	132.16
1991	144.17	160.00	171.01	170.61	178.34	167.61	172.76	179.11	180.16	185.00	176.37	189.94
1992	205.16	211.15	203.69	196.25	198.52	188.64	194.74	188.79	192.92	198.90	213.81	221.01
1993	228.10	222.41	229.21	222.68	232.19	233.35	236.46	246.19	252.95	259.18	250.41	258.59
1994	266.52	265.53	251.06	252.55	249.28	240.29	244.06	257.32	256.12	255.02	244.25	250.36
1995	246.85	256.57	260.77	266.17	270.25	283.63	299.72	305.31	310.38	296.25	308.58	315.97
1996	315.38	324.93	330.77	348.28	361.85	346.61	316.00	333.88	346.39	340.57	354.11	362.61
1997	369.45	360.05	342.56	343.00	380.76	396.37	414.48	423.43	453.82	433.26	429.92	437.02
1998	430.05	461.83	480.68	482.89	456.62	457.39	419.75	337.95	363.59	378.16	397.75	421.96
1999	427.22	392.26	397.63	432.81	438.68	457.68	444.77	427.83	427.30	428.64	454.08	504.75
2000	496.23	577.71	539.09	506.25	476.18	517.23	500.64	537.89	521.37	497.68	445.94	483.53
2001	508.34	474.37	450.53	485.32	496.50	512.64	484.78	468.56	404.87	428.17	460.78	488.50
2002	483.10	469.36	506.46	510.67	487.47	462.64	392.42	390.96	362.27	373.50	406.35	383.09
2003	372.17	360.52	364.54	398.68	441.00	448.37	476.02	497.42	487.68	528.22	546.51	556.91
2004	580.76	585.56	590.31	559.80	568.28	591.52	551.29	547.93	572.94	583.79	633.77	651.57
2005	624.02	634.06	615.07	579.38	616.71	639.66	679.75	666.51	667.80	646.61	677.29	673.22
2006	733.20	730.64	765.14	764.54	721.01	724.67	700.56	720.53	725.59	766.84	786.12	787.66
2007	800.34	793.30	800.71	814.57	847.19	833.69	776.13	792.86	805.45	828.02	767.77	766.03
2008	713.30	686.18	687.97	716.18	748.28	689.66	714.52	739.50	679.58	537.52	473.14	499.45
2009	443.53	389.02	422.75	487.56	501.58	508.28	556.71	572.07	604.28	562.77	579.73	625.39
2010	602.04	628.56	678.64	716.60	661.61	609.49	650.89	602.06	676.14	703.35	727.01	783.65
2011	781.25	823.45	843.55	865.29	848.30	827.43	797.03	726.81	644.16	741.06	737.42	740.92
2012	792.82	810.94	830.30	816.88	761.82	798.49	786.94	812.09	837.45	818.73	821.92	849.35
2013	902.09	911.11	951.54	947.46	984.14	977.48	1045.26	1010.90	1073.79	1100.15	1142.89	1163.64
2014	1130.88	1183.03	1173.04	1126.86	1134.50	1192.96	1120.07	1174.35	1101.68	1173.51	1173.23	1204.70
2015	1165.39	1233.37	1252.77	1220.13	1246.53	1253.95	1238.68	1159.45	1100.69	1161.86	1198.11	1135.89
2016	1035.38	1033.90	1114.03	1130.84	1154.79	1151.92	1219.94	1239.91	1251.65	1191.39	1322.34	1357.13
2017	1361.82	1386.68	1385.92	1400.43	1370.21	1415.36	1425.14	1405.28	1490.86	1502.77	1544.14	1535.51
2018	1574.98	1512.45	1529.43	1541.88	1633.61							

10 BEST DAYS BY PERCENT AND POINT

	BY PERCENT CHANGE				BY POINT CHANGE		
DAY	CLOSE	PNT CHANGE	% CHANGE	DAY	CLOSE	PNT CHANGE	% CHANGE
DJIA 1901 to 1949							
3/15/33	62.10	8.26	15.3	10/30/29	258.47	28.40	12.3
10/6/31	99.34	12.86	14.9	11/14/29	217.28	18.59	9.4
10/30/29	258.47	28.40	12.3	10/5/29	341.36	16.19	5.0
9/21/32	75.16	7.67	11.4	10/31/29	273.51	15.04	5.8
8/3/32	58.22	5.06	9.5	10/6/31	99.34	12.86	14.9
2/11/32	78.60	6.80	9.5	11/15/29	228.73	11.45	5.3
11/14/29	217.28	18.59	9.4	6/19/30	228.97	10.13	4.6
12/18/31	80.69	6.90	9.4	9/5/39	148.12	10.03	7.3
2/13/32	85.82	7.22	9.2	11/22/28	290.34	9.81	3.5
5/6/32	59.01	4.91	9.1	10/1/30	214.14	9.24	4.5
DJIA 1950 to MAY 2018							
10/13/08	9387.61	936.42	11.1	10/13/08	9387.61	936.42	11.1
10/28/08	9065.12	889.35	10.9	10/28/08	9065.12	889.35	10.9
10/21/87	2027.85	186.84	10.2	3/26/18	24202.60	669.40	2.8
3/23/09	7775.86	497.48	6.8	8/26/15	16285.51	619.07	4.0
11/13/08	8835.25	552.59	6.7	2/6/18	24912.77	567.02	2.3
11/21/08	8046.42	494.13	6.5	11/13/08	8835.25	552.59	6.7
7/24/02	8191.29	488.95	6.4	3/16/00	10630.60	499.19	4.9
10/20/87	1841.01	102.27	5.9	3/23/09	7775.86	497.48	6.8
3/10/09	6926.49	379.44	5.8	11/21/08	8046.42	494.13	6.5
7/29/02	8711.88	447.49	5.4	11/30/11	12045.68	490.05	4.2
S&P 500 1930 to MAY 2018							
3/15/33	6.81	0.97	16.6	10/13/08	1003.35	104.13	11.6
10/6/31	9.91	1.09	12.4	10/28/08	940.51	91.59	10.8
9/21/32	8.52	0.90	11.8	8/26/15	1940.51	72.90	3.9
10/13/08	1003.35	104.13	11.6	3/26/18	2658.55	70.29	2.7
10/28/08	940.51	91.59	10.8	3/16/00	1458.47	66.32	4.8
2/16/35	10.00	0.94	10.4	1/3/01	1347.56	64.29	5.0
8/17/35	11.70	1.08	10.2	9/30/08	1166.36	59.97	5.4
3/16/35	9.05	0.82	10.0	11/13/08	911.29	58.99	6.9
9/12/38	12.06	1.06	9.6	3/23/09	822.92	54.38	7.1
9/5/39	12.64	1.11	9.6	3/18/08	1330.74	54.14	4.2
NASDAQ 1971 to MAY 2018							
1/3/01	2616.69	324.83	14.2	1/3/01	2616.69	324.83	14.2
10/13/08	1844.25	194.74	11.8	12/5/00	2889.80	274.05	10.5
12/5/00	2889.80	274.05	10.5	4/18/00	3793.57	254.41	7.2
10/28/08	1649.47	143.57	9.5	5/30/00	3459.48	254.37	7.9
4/5/01	1785.00	146.20	8.9	10/19/00	3418.60	247.04	7.8
4/18/01	2079.44	156.22	8.1	10/13/00	3316.77	242.09	7.9
5/30/00	3459.48	254.37	7.9	6/2/00	3813.38	230.88	6.4
10/13/00	3316.77	242.09	7.9	4/25/00	3711.23	228.75	6.6
10/19/00	3418.60	247.04	7.8	3/26/18	7220.54	227.87	3.3
5/8/02	1696.29	122.47	7.8	4/17/00	3539.16	217.87	6.6
RUSSELL 1000 1979 to MAY 2018							
10/13/08	542.98	56.75	11.7	10/13/08	542.98	56.75	11.7
10/28/08	503.74	47.68	10.5	10/28/08	503.74	47.68	10.5
10/21/87	135.85	11.15	8.9	8/26/15	1081.77	39.00	3.7
3/23/09	446.90	29.36	7.0	3/26/18	1474.81	38.09	2.7
11/13/08	489.83	31.99	7.0	3/16/00	777.86	36.60	4.9
11/24/08	456.14	28.26	6.6	1/3/01	712.63	35.74	5.3
3/10/09	391.01	23.46	6.4	11/13/08	489.83	31.99	7.0
11/21/08	427.88	24.97	6.2	9/30/08	634.08	31.74	5.3
7/24/02	448.05	23.87	5.6	8/9/11	647.85	30.57	5.0
7/29/02	477.61	24.69	5.5	12/5/00	728.44	30.36	4.4
RUSSELL 2000 1979 to MAY 2018							
10/13/08	570.89	48.41	9.3	10/13/08	570.89	48.41	9.3
11/13/08	491.23	38.43	8.5	9/18/08	723.68	47.30	7.0
3/23/09	433.72	33.61	8.4	8/9/11	696.16	45.20	6.9
10/21/87	130.65	9.26	7.6	11/30/11	737.42	41.32	5.9
10/28/08	482.55	34.15	7.6	10/4/11	648.64	39.15	6.4
11/24/08	436.80	30.26	7.4	11/13/08	491.23	38.43	8.5
3/10/09	367.75	24.49	7.1	10/27/11	765.43	38.28	5.3
9/18/08	723.68	47.30	7.0	11/9/16	1232.16	37.02	3.1
8/9/11	696.16	45.20	6.9	5/10/10	689.61	36.61	5.6
10/16/08	536.57	34.46	6.9	8/11/11	695.89	35.68	5.4

10 <u>WORST</u> DAYS BY PERCENT AND POINT

	BY PERCENT CHANGE				BY POINT CHANGE		
DAY	CLOSE	PNT CHANGE	% CHANGE	DAY	CLOSE	PNT CHANGE	% CHANGE
DJIA 1901 to 1949							
10/28/29	260.64	−38.33	−12.8	10/28/29	260.64	−38.33	−12.8
10/29/29	230.07	−30.57	−11.7	10/29/29	230.07	−30.57	−11.7
11/6/29	232.13	−25.55	−9.9	11/6/29	232.13	−25.55	−9.9
8/12/32	63.11	−5.79	−8.4	10/23/29	305.85	−20.66	−6.3
3/14/07	55.84	−5.05	−8.3	11/11/29	220.39	−16.14	−6.8
7/21/33	88.71	−7.55	−7.8	11/4/29	257.68	−15.83	−5.8
10/18/37	125.73	−10.57	−7.8	12/12/29	243.14	−15.30	−5.9
2/1/17	88.52	−6.91	−7.2	10/3/29	329.95	−14.55	−4.2
10/5/32	66.07	−5.09	−7.2	6/16/30	230.05	−14.20	−5.8
9/24/31	107.79	−8.20	−7.1	8/9/29	337.99	−14.11	−4.0
DJIA 1950 to MAY 2018							
10/19/87	1738.74	−508.00	−22.6	2/5/18	24345.75	−1175.21	−4.6
10/26/87	1793.93	−156.83	−8.0	2/8/18	23860.46	−1032.89	−4.2
10/15/08	8577.91	−733.08	−7.9	9/29/08	10365.45	−777.68	−7.0
12/1/08	8149.09	−679.95	−7.7	10/15/08	8577.91	−733.08	−7.9
10/9/08	8579.19	−678.91	−7.3	3/22/18	23957.89	−724.42	−2.9
10/27/97	7161.15	−554.26	−7.2	9/17/01	8920.70	−684.81	−7.1
9/17/01	8920.70	−684.81	−7.1	12/1/08	8149.09	−679.95	−7.7
9/29/08	10365.45	−777.68	−7.0	10/9/08	8579.19	−678.91	−7.3
10/13/89	2569.26	−190.58	−6.9	2/2/18	25520.96	−665.75	−2.5
1/8/88	1911.31	−140.58	−6.9	8/8/11	10809.85	−634.76	−5.6
S&P 500 1930 to MAY 2018							
10/19/87	224.84	−57.86	−20.5	2/5/18	2648.94	−113.19	−4.1
3/18/35	8.14	−0.91	−10.1	9/29/08	1106.39	−106.62	−8.8
4/16/35	8.22	−0.91	−10.0	2/8/18	2581.00	−100.66	−3.8
9/3/46	15.00	−1.65	−9.9	10/15/08	907.84	−90.17	−9.0
10/18/37	10.76	−1.10	−9.3	4/14/00	1356.56	−83.95	−5.8
10/15/08	907.84	−90.17	−9.0	12/1/08	816.21	−80.03	−8.9
12/1/08	816.21	−80.03	−8.9	8/8/11	1119.46	−79.92	−6.7
7/20/33	10.57	−1.03	−8.9	8/24/15	1893.21	−77.68	−3.9
9/29/08	1106.39	−106.62	−8.8	6/24/16	2037.41	−75.91	−3.6
7/21/33	9.65	−0.92	−8.7	10/9/08	909.92	−75.02	−7.6
NASDAQ 1971 to MAY 2018							
10/19/87	360.21	−46.12	−11.4	4/14/00	3321.29	−355.49	−9.7
4/14/00	3321.29	−355.49	−9.7	4/3/00	4223.68	−349.15	−7.6
9/29/08	1983.73	−199.61	−9.1	4/12/00	3769.63	−286.27	−7.1
10/26/87	298.90	−29.55	−9.0	2/8/18	6777.16	−274.82	−3.9
10/20/87	327.79	−32.42	−9.0	2/5/18	6967.53	−273.42	−3.8
12/1/08	1398.07	−137.50	−9.0	4/10/00	4188.20	−258.25	−5.8
8/31/98	1499.25	−140.43	−8.6	1/4/00	3901.69	−229.46	−5.6
10/15/08	1628.33	−150.68	−8.5	3/27/18	7008.81	−211.73	−2.9
4/3/00	4223.68	−349.15	−7.6	6/24/16	4707.98	−202.06	−4.1
1/2/01	2291.86	−178.66	−7.2	3/14/00	4706.63	−200.61	−4.1
RUSSELL 1000 1979 to MAY 2018							
10/19/87	121.04	−28.40	−19.0	2/5/18	1466.98	−61.29	−4.0
10/15/08	489.71	−49.11	−9.1	9/29/08	602.34	−57.35	−8.7
12/1/08	437.75	−43.68	−9.1	2/8/18	1429.23	−55.18	−3.7
9/29/08	602.34	−57.35	−8.7	10/15/08	489.71	−49.11	−9.1
10/26/87	119.45	−10.74	−8.3	4/14/00	715.20	−45.74	−6.0
10/9/08	492.13	−40.05	−7.5	8/8/11	617.28	−45.56	−6.9
8/8/11	617.28	−45.56	−6.9	12/1/08	437.75	−43.68	−9.1
11/20/08	402.91	−29.62	−6.9	8/24/15	1056.36	−43.45	−4.0
8/31/98	496.66	−35.77	−6.7	6/24/16	1128.04	−42.53	−3.6
10/27/97	465.44	−32.96	−6.6	10/9/08	492.13	−40.05	−7.5
RUSSELL 2000 1979 to MAY 2018							
10/19/87	133.60	−19.14	−12.5	8/8/11	650.96	−63.67	−8.9
12/1/08	417.07	−56.07	−11.9	2/5/18	1491.09	−56.18	−3.6
10/15/08	502.11	−52.54	−9.5	12/1/08	417.07	−56.07	−11.9
10/26/87	110.33	−11.26	−9.3	10/15/08	502.11	−52.54	−9.5
10/20/87	121.39	−12.21	−9.1	10/9/08	499.20	−47.37	−8.7
8/8/11	650.96	−63.67	−8.9	9/29/08	657.72	−47.07	−6.7
10/9/08	499.20	−47.37	−8.7	8/4/11	726.80	−45.98	−6.0
11/19/08	412.38	−35.13	−7.9	8/24/15	1111.69	−45.10	−3.9
4/14/00	453.72	−35.50	−7.3	6/24/16	1127.54	−44.68	−3.8
11/14/08	456.52	−34.71	−7.1	2/8/18	1463.79	−44.18	−2.9

10 BEST WEEKS BY PERCENT AND POINT

	BY PERCENT CHANGE				BY POINT CHANGE		
WEEK ENDS	CLOSE	PNT CHANGE	% CHANGE	WEEK ENDS	CLOSE	PNT CHANGE	% CHANGE
DJIA 1901 to 1949							
8/6/32	66.56	12.30	22.7	12/7/29	263.46	24.51	10.3
6/25/38	131.94	18.71	16.5	6/25/38	131.94	18.71	16.5
2/13/32	85.82	11.37	15.3	6/27/31	156.93	17.97	12.9
4/22/33	72.24	9.36	14.9	11/22/29	245.74	17.01	7.4
10/10/31	105.61	12.84	13.8	8/17/29	360.70	15.86	4.6
7/30/32	54.26	6.42	13.4	12/22/28	285.94	15.22	5.6
6/27/31	156.93	17.97	12.9	8/24/29	375.44	14.74	4.1
9/24/32	74.83	8.39	12.6	2/21/29	310.06	14.21	4.8
8/27/32	75.61	8.43	12.6	5/10/30	272.01	13.70	5.3
3/18/33	60.56	6.72	12.5	11/15/30	186.68	13.54	7.8
DJIA 1950 to MAY 2018							
10/11/74	658.17	73.61	12.6	2/16/18	25219.38	1028.48	4.3
10/31/08	9325.01	946.06	11.3	11/11/16	18847.66	959.38	5.4
8/20/82	869.29	81.24	10.3	10/31/08	9325.01	946.06	11.3
11/28/08	8829.04	782.62	9.7	3/9/18	25335.74	797.68	3.3
3/13/09	7223.98	597.04	9.0	12/2/11	12019.42	787.64	7.0
10/8/82	986.85	79.11	8.7	11/28/08	8829.04	782.62	9.7
3/21/03	8521.97	662.26	8.4	6/8/18	25316.53	681.32	2.8
8/3/84	1202.08	87.46	7.9	12/1/17	24231.59	673.60	2.9
9/28/01	8847.56	611.75	7.4	3/17/00	10595.23	666.41	6.7
7/17/09	8743.94	597.42	7.3	3/21/03	8521.97	662.26	8.4
S&P 500 1930 to MAY 2018							
8/6/32	7.22	1.12	18.4	2/16/18	2732.22	112.67	4.3
6/25/38	11.39	1.72	17.8	6/2/00	1477.26	99.24	7.2
7/30/32	6.10	0.89	17.1	11/28/08	896.24	96.21	12.0
4/22/33	7.75	1.09	16.4	3/9/18	2786.57	95.32	3.5
10/11/74	71.14	8.80	14.1	10/31/08	968.75	91.98	10.5
2/13/32	8.80	1.08	14.0	12/2/11	1244.28	85.61	7.4
9/24/32	8.52	1.02	13.6	11/11/16	2164.45	79.27	3.8
10/10/31	10.64	1.27	13.6	4/20/00	1434.54	77.98	5.8
8/27/32	8.57	1.01	13.4	10/24/14	1964.58	77.82	4.1
3/18/33	6.61	0.77	13.2	7/2/99	1391.22	75.91	5.8
NASDAQ 1971 to MAY 2018							
6/2/00	3813.38	608.27	19.0	6/2/00	3813.38	608.27	19.0
4/12/01	1961.43	241.07	14.0	2/16/18	7239.47	364.98	5.3
11/28/08	1535.57	151.22	10.9	2/4/00	4244.14	357.07	9.2
10/31/08	1720.95	168.92	10.9	3/3/00	4914.79	324.29	7.1
3/13/09	1431.50	137.65	10.6	4/20/00	3643.88	322.59	9.7
4/20/01	2163.41	201.98	10.3	3/9/18	7560.81	302.94	4.2
12/8/00	2917.43	272.14	10.3	12/8/00	2917.43	272.14	10.3
4/20/00	3643.88	322.59	9.7	4/12/01	1961.43	241.07	14.0
10/11/74	60.42	5.26	9.5	1/5/18	7136.56	233.17	3.4
2/4/00	4244.14	357.07	9.2	10/24/14	4483.72	225.28	5.3
RUSSELL 1000 1979 to MAY 2018							
11/28/08	481.43	53.55	12.5	2/16/18	1512.36	62.68	4.3
10/31/08	522.47	50.94	10.8	6/2/00	785.02	57.93	8.0
3/13/09	411.10	39.88	10.7	11/28/08	481.43	53.55	12.5
8/20/82	61.51	4.83	8.5	3/9/18	1543.49	52.77	3.5
6/2/00	785.02	57.93	8.0	10/31/08	522.47	50.94	10.8
9/28/01	546.46	38.48	7.6	12/2/11	687.44	47.63	7.4
10/16/98	546.09	38.45	7.6	11/11/16	1199.16	44.50	3.9
8/3/84	87.43	6.13	7.5	10/24/14	1092.59	43.55	4.2
12/2/11	687.44	47.63	7.4	4/20/00	757.32	42.12	5.9
3/21/03	474.58	32.69	7.4	3/3/00	756.41	41.55	5.8
RUSSELL 2000 1979 to MAY 2018							
11/28/08	473.14	66.60	16.4	11/11/16	1282.38	118.94	10.2
10/31/08	537.52	66.40	14.1	12/9/16	1388.07	73.82	5.6
6/2/00	513.03	55.66	12.2	12/2/11	735.02	68.86	10.3
3/13/09	393.09	42.04	12.0	11/28/08	473.14	66.60	16.4
12/2/11	735.02	68.86	10.3	10/31/08	537.52	66.40	14.1
11/11/16	1282.38	118.94	10.2	2/16/18	1543.55	65.71	4.5
10/14/11	712.46	56.25	8.6	3/9/18	1597.14	63.97	4.2
7/17/09	519.22	38.24	8.0	10/14/11	712.46	56.25	8.6
10/16/98	342.87	24.47	7.7	6/2/00	513.03	55.66	12.2
12/18/87	116.94	8.31	7.7	10/31/14	1173.51	54.69	4.9

10 WORST WEEKS BY PERCENT AND POINT

	BY PERCENT CHANGE				BY POINT CHANGE		
WEEK ENDS	CLOSE	PNT CHANGE	% CHANGE	WEEK ENDS	CLOSE	PNT CHANGE	% CHANGE
			DJIA 1901 to 1949				
7/22/33	88.42	−17.68	−16.7	11/8/29	236.53	−36.98	−13.5
5/18/40	122.43	−22.42	−15.5	12/8/28	257.33	−33.47	−11.5
10/8/32	61.17	−10.92	−15.2	6/21/30	215.30	−28.95	−11.9
10/3/31	92.77	−14.59	−13.6	10/19/29	323.87	−28.82	−8.2
11/8/29	236.53	−36.98	−13.5	5/3/30	258.31	−27.15	−9.5
9/17/32	66.44	−10.10	−13.2	10/31/29	273.51	−25.46	−8.5
10/21/33	83.64	−11.95	−12.5	10/26/29	298.97	−24.90	−7.7
12/12/31	78.93	−11.21	−12.4	5/18/40	122.43	−22.42	−15.5
5/8/15	62.77	−8.74	−12.2	2/8/29	301.53	−18.23	−5.7
6/21/30	215.30	−28.95	−11.9	10/11/30	193.05	−18.05	−8.6
			DJIA 1950 to MAY 2018				
10/10/08	8451.19	−1874.19	−18.2	10/10/08	8451.19	−1874.19	−18.2
9/21/01	8235.81	−1369.70	−14.3	3/23/18	23533.20	−1413.31	−5.7
10/23/87	1950.76	−295.98	−13.2	9/21/01	8235.81	−1369.70	−14.3
10/16/87	2246.74	−235.47	−9.5	2/9/18	24190.90	−1330.06	−5.2
10/13/89	2569.26	−216.26	−7.8	2/2/18	25520.96	−1095.75	−4.1
3/16/01	9823.41	−821.21	−7.7	1/8/16	16346.45	−1078.58	−6.2
7/19/02	8019.26	−665.27	−7.7	8/21/15	16459.75	−1017.65	−5.8
12/4/87	1766.74	−143.74	−7.5	3/16/01	9823.41	−821.21	−7.7
9/13/74	627.19	−50.69	−7.5	10/3/08	10325.38	−817.75	−7.3
9/12/86	1758.72	−141.03	−7.4	4/14/00	10305.77	−805.71	−7.3
			S&P 500 1930 to MAY 2018				
7/22/33	9.71	−2.20	−18.5	10/10/08	899.22	−200.01	−18.2
10/10/08	899.22	−200.01	−18.2	3/23/18	2588.26	−163.75	−6.0
5/18/40	9.75	−2.05	−17.4	4/14/00	1356.56	−159.79	−10.5
10/8/32	6.77	−1.38	−16.9	2/9/18	2619.55	−142.58	−5.2
9/17/32	7.50	−1.28	−14.6	9/21/01	965.80	−126.74	−11.6
10/21/33	8.57	−1.31	−13.3	1/8/16	1922.03	−121.91	−6.0
10/3/31	9.37	−1.36	−12.7	8/21/15	1970.89	−120.65	−5.8
10/23/87	248.22	−34.48	−12.2	10/3/08	1099.23	−113.78	−9.4
12/12/31	8.20	−1.13	−12.1	2/2/18	2762.13	−110.74	−3.9
3/26/38	9.20	−1.21	−11.6	8/5/11	1199.38	−92.90	−7.2
			NASDAQ 1971 to MAY 2018				
4/14/00	3321.29	−1125.16	−25.3	4/14/00	3321.29	−1125.16	−25.3
10/23/87	328.45	−77.88	−19.2	3/23/18	6992.67	−489.32	−6.5
9/21/01	1423.19	−272.19	−16.1	7/28/00	3663.00	−431.45	−10.5
10/10/08	1649.51	−297.88	−15.3	11/10/00	3028.99	−422.59	−12.2
11/10/00	3028.99	−422.59	−12.2	3/31/00	4572.83	−390.20	−7.9
10/3/08	1947.39	−235.95	−10.8	2/9/18	6874.49	−366.46	−5.1
7/28/00	3663.00	−431.45	−10.5	1/8/16	4643.63	−363.78	−7.3
10/24/08	1552.03	−159.26	−9.3	1/28/00	3887.07	−348.33	−8.2
12/15/00	2653.27	−264.16	−9.1	8/21/15	4706.04	−342.20	−6.8
12/1/00	2645.29	−259.09	−8.9	10/6/00	3361.01	−311.81	−8.5
			RUSSELL 1000 1979 to MAY 2018				
10/10/08	486.23	−108.31	−18.2	10/10/08	486.23	−108.31	−18.2
10/23/87	130.19	−19.25	−12.9	4/14/00	715.20	−90.39	−11.2
9/21/01	507.98	−67.59	−11.7	3/23/18	1436.72	−88.62	−5.8
4/14/00	715.20	−90.39	−11.2	2/9/18	1449.68	−78.59	−5.1
10/3/08	594.54	−65.15	−9.9	1/8/16	1063.55	−68.33	−6.0
10/16/87	149.44	−14.42	−8.8	9/21/01	507.98	−67.59	−11.7
11/21/08	427.88	−41.15	−8.8	8/21/15	1099.81	−66.86	−5.7
9/12/86	124.95	−10.87	−8.0	10/3/08	594.54	−65.15	−9.9
8/5/11	662.84	−54.93	−7.7	2/2/18	1528.27	−60.71	−3.8
7/19/02	450.64	−36.13	−7.4	8/5/11	662.84	−54.93	−7.7
			RUSSELL 2000 1979 to MAY 2018				
10/23/87	121.59	−31.15	−20.4	10/10/08	522.48	−96.92	−15.7
4/14/00	453.72	−89.27	−16.4	1/8/16	1046.20	−89.69	−7.9
10/10/08	522.48	−96.92	−15.7	4/14/00	453.72	−89.27	−16.4
9/21/01	378.89	−61.84	−14.0	10/3/08	619.40	−85.39	−12.1
10/3/08	619.40	−85.39	−12.1	8/5/11	714.63	−82.40	−10.3
11/21/08	406.54	−49.98	−11.0	3/23/18	1510.08	−75.97	−4.8
10/24/08	471.12	−55.31	−10.5	2/9/18	1477.84	−69.43	−4.5
8/5/11	714.63	−82.40	−10.3	5/7/10	653.00	−63.60	−8.9
3/6/09	351.05	−37.97	−9.8	9/23/11	652.43	−61.88	−8.7
11/14/08	456.52	−49.27	−9.7	9/21/01	378.89	−61.84	−14.0

10 **BEST** MONTHS BY PERCENT AND POINT

	BY PERCENT CHANGE				BY POINT CHANGE		
MONTH	CLOSE	PNT CHANGE	% CHANGE	MONTH	CLOSE	PNT CHANGE	% CHANGE
DJIA 1901 to 1949							
APR-1933	77.66	22.26	40.2	NOV-1928	293.38	41.22	16.3
AUG-1932	73.16	18.90	34.8	JUN-1929	333.79	36.38	12.2
JUL-1932	54.26	11.42	26.7	AUG-1929	380.33	32.63	9.4
JUN-1938	133.88	26.14	24.3	JUN-1938	133.88	26.14	24.3
APR-1915	71.78	10.95	18.0	AUG-1928	240.41	24.41	11.3
JUN-1931	150.18	21.72	16.9	APR-1933	77.66	22.26	40.2
NOV-1928	293.38	41.22	16.3	FEB-1931	189.66	22.11	13.2
NOV-1904	52.76	6.59	14.3	JUN-1931	150.18	21.72	16.9
MAY-1919	105.50	12.62	13.6	AUG-1932	73.16	18.90	34.8
SEP-1939	152.54	18.13	13.5	JAN-1930	267.14	18.66	7.5
DJIA 1950 to MAY 2018							
JAN-1976	975.28	122.87	14.4	JAN-2018	26149.39	1430.17	5.8
JAN-1975	703.69	87.45	14.2	OCT-2015	17663.54	1379.54	8.5
JAN-1987	2158.04	262.09	13.8	MAR-2016	17685.09	1168.59	7.1
AUG-1982	901.31	92.71	11.5	OCT-2011	11955.01	1041.63	9.5
OCT-1982	991.72	95.47	10.7	APR-1999	10789.04	1002.88	10.2
OCT-2002	8397.03	805.10	10.6	NOV-2016	19123.58	981.16	5.4
APR-1978	837.32	79.96	10.6	OCT-2017	23377.24	972.15	4.3
APR-1999	10789.04	1002.88	10.2	FEB-2015	18132.70	967.75	5.6
NOV-1962	649.30	59.53	10.1	FEB-2017	20812.24	948.15	4.8
NOV-1954	386.77	34.63	9.8	NOV-2017	24272.35	895.11	3.8
S&P 500 1930 to MAY 2018							
APR-1933	8.32	2.47	42.2	OCT-2015	2079.36	159.33	8.3
JUL-1932	6.10	1.67	37.7	JAN-2018	2823.81	150.20	5.6
AUG-1932	8.39	2.29	37.5	MAR-2000	1498.58	132.16	9.7
JUN-1938	11.56	2.29	24.7	MAR-2016	2059.74	127.51	6.6
SEP-1939	13.02	1.84	16.5	OCT-2011	1253.30	121.88	10.8
OCT-1974	73.90	10.36	16.3	FEB-2015	2104.50	109.51	5.5
MAY-1933	9.64	1.32	15.9	SEP-2010	1141.20	91.87	8.8
APR-1938	9.70	1.20	14.1	APR-2001	1249.46	89.13	7.7
JUN-1931	14.83	1.81	13.9	AUG-2000	1517.68	86.85	6.1
JAN-1987	274.08	31.91	13.2	FEB-2017	2363.64	84.77	3.7
NASDAQ 1971 to MAY 2018							
DEC-1999	4069.31	733.15	22.0	FEB-2000	4696.69	756.34	19.2
FEB-2000	4696.69	756.34	19.2	DEC-1999	4069.31	733.15	22.0
OCT-1974	65.23	9.56	17.2	JUN-2000	3966.11	565.20	16.6
JAN-1975	69.78	9.96	16.6	JAN-2018	7411.48	508.09	7.4
JUN-2000	3966.11	565.20	16.6	AUG-2000	4206.35	439.36	11.7
APR-2001	2116.24	275.98	15.0	OCT-2015	5053.75	433.59	9.4
JAN-1999	2505.89	313.20	14.3	MAY-2018	7442.12	375.85	5.3
NOV-2001	1930.58	240.38	14.2	NOV-1999	3336.16	369.73	12.5
OCT-2002	1329.75	157.69	13.5	FEB-2015	4963.53	328.29	7.1
OCT-1982	212.63	24.98	13.3	JUL-2016	5162.13	319.46	6.6
RUSSELL 1000 1979 to MAY 2018							
JAN-1987	146.48	16.48	12.7	OCT-2015	1153.55	85.09	8.0
OCT-1982	73.34	7.45	11.3	JAN-2018	1561.66	79.85	5.4
AUG-1982	65.14	6.60	11.3	MAR-2016	1138.84	72.26	6.8
DEC-1991	220.61	22.15	11.2	OCT-2011	692.41	68.96	11.1
OCT-2011	692.41	68.96	11.1	MAR-2000	797.99	64.95	8.9
AUG-1984	89.87	8.74	10.8	FEB-2015	1173.46	61.61	5.5
NOV-1980	78.26	7.18	10.1	AUG-2000	811.17	55.60	7.4
APR-2009	476.84	43.17	10.0	SEP-2010	629.78	52.10	9.0
SEP-2010	629.78	52.10	9.0	APR-2001	658.90	48.54	8.0
MAY-1990	187.66	15.34	8.0	JUL-2013	937.16	46.49	5.2
RUSSELL 2000 1979 to MAY 2018							
FEB-2000	577.71	81.48	16.4	NOV-2016	1322.34	130.95	11.0
APR-2009	487.56	64.81	15.3	OCT-2011	741.06	96.90	15.0
OCT-2011	741.06	96.90	15.0	MAY-2018	1633.61	91.73	5.9
OCT-1982	80.86	10.02	14.1	SEP-2017	1490.86	85.58	6.1
JAN-1985	114.77	13.28	13.1	FEB-2000	577.71	81.48	16.4
SEP-2010	676.14	74.08	12.3	MAR-2016	1114.03	80.13	7.8
AUG-1984	106.21	10.96	11.5	SEP-2010	676.14	74.08	12.3
JAN-1987	150.48	15.48	11.5	OCT-2014	1173.51	71.83	6.5
DEC-1999	504.75	50.67	11.2	JUL-2016	1219.94	68.02	5.9
JUL-1980	63.81	6.34	11.0	FEB-2015	1233.37	67.98	5.8

10 <u>WORST</u> MONTHS BY PERCENT AND POINT

	BY PERCENT CHANGE				BY POINT CHANGE		
MONTH	CLOSE	PNT CHANGE	% CHANGE	MONTH	CLOSE	PNT CHANGE	% CHANGE
DJIA 1901 to 1949							
SEP-1931	96.61	−42.80	−30.7	OCT-1929	273.51	−69.94	−20.4
MAR-1938	98.95	−30.69	−23.7	JUN-1930	226.34	−48.73	−17.7
APR-1932	56.11	−17.17	−23.4	SEP-1931	96.61	−42.80	−30.7
MAY-1940	116.22	−32.21	−21.7	SEP-1929	343.45	−36.88	−9.7
OCT-1929	273.51	−69.94	−20.4	SEP-1930	204.90	−35.52	−14.8
MAY-1932	44.74	−11.37	−20.3	NOV-1929	238.95	−34.56	−12.6
JUN-1930	226.34	−48.73	−17.7	MAY-1940	116.22	−32.21	−21.7
DEC-1931	77.90	−15.97	−17.0	MAR-1938	98.95	−30.69	−23.7
FEB-1933	51.39	−9.51	−15.6	SEP-1937	154.57	−22.84	−12.9
MAY-1931	128.46	−22.73	−15.0	MAY-1931	128.46	−22.73	−15.0
DJIA 1950 to MAY 2018							
OCT-1987	1993.53	−602.75	−23.2	OCT-2008	9325.01	−1525.65	−14.1
AUG-1998	7539.07	−1344.22	−15.1	AUG-1998	7539.07	−1344.22	−15.1
OCT-2008	9325.01	−1525.65	−14.1	JUN-2008	11350.01	−1288.31	−10.2
NOV-1973	822.25	−134.33	−14.0	AUG-2015	16528.03	−1161.83	−6.6
SEP-2002	7591.93	−1071.57	−12.4	FEB-2018	25029.20	−1120.19	−4.3
FEB-2009	7062.93	−937.93	−11.7	SEP-2001	8847.56	−1102.19	−11.1
SEP-2001	8847.56	−1102.19	−11.1	SEP-2002	7591.93	−1071.57	−12.4
SEP-1974	607.87	−70.71	−10.4	JAN-2016	16466.30	−958.73	−5.5
AUG-1974	678.58	−78.85	−10.4	FEB-2009	7062.93	−937.93	−11.7
JUN-2008	11350.01	−1288.31	−10.2	MAR-2018	24103.11	−926.09	−3.7
S&P 500 1930 to MAY 2018							
SEP-1931	9.71	−4.15	−29.9	OCT-2008	968.75	−197.61	−16.9
MAR-1938	8.50	−2.84	−25.0	AUG-1998	957.28	−163.39	−14.6
MAY-1940	9.27	−2.92	−24.0	AUG-2015	1972.18	−131.66	−6.3
MAY-1932	4.47	−1.36	−23.3	FEB-2001	1239.94	−126.07	−9.2
OCT-1987	251.79	−70.04	−21.8	JUN-2008	1280.00	−120.38	−8.6
APR-1932	5.83	−1.48	−20.2	SEP-2008	1166.36	−116.47	−9.1
FEB-1933	5.66	−1.28	−18.4	NOV-2000	1314.95	−114.45	−8.0
OCT-2008	968.75	−197.61	−16.9	JAN-2016	1940.24	−103.70	−5.1
JUN-1930	20.46	−4.03	−16.5	JAN-2016	1940.24	−103.70	−5.1
AUG-1998	957.28	−163.39	−14.6	SEP-2002	815.28	−100.79	−11.0
NASDAQ 1971 to MAY 2018							
OCT-1987	323.30	−120.99	−27.2	NOV-2000	2597.93	−771.70	−22.9
NOV-2000	2597.93	−771.70	−22.9	APR-2000	3860.66	−712.17	−15.6
FEB-2001	2151.83	−620.90	−22.4	FEB-2001	2151.83	−620.90	−22.4
AUG-1998	1499.25	−373.14	−19.9	SEP-2000	3672.82	−533.53	−12.7
OCT-2008	1720.95	−370.93	−17.7	MAY-2000	3400.91	−459.75	−11.9
MAR-1980	131.00	−27.03	−17.1	JAN-2016	4613.95	−393.46	−7.9
SEP-2001	1498.80	−306.63	−17.0	AUG-1998	1499.25	−373.14	−19.9
OCT-1978	111.12	−21.77	−16.4	OCT-2008	1720.95	−370.93	−17.7
APR-2000	3860.66	−712.17	−15.6	AUG-2015	4776.51	−351.77	−6.9
NOV-1973	93.51	−16.66	−15.1	MAR-2001	1840.26	−311.57	−14.5
RUSSELL 1000 1979 to MAY 2018							
OCT-1987	131.89	−36.94	−21.9	OCT-2008	522.47	−111.61	−17.6
OCT-2008	522.47	−111.61	−17.6	AUG-1998	496.66	−88.31	−15.1
AUG-1998	496.66	−88.31	−15.1	AUG-2015	1100.51	−73.04	−6.2
MAR-1980	55.79	−7.28	−11.5	NOV-2000	692.40	−70.66	−9.3
SEP-2002	433.22	−52.86	−10.9	FEB-2001	654.25	−68.30	−9.5
FEB-2009	399.61	−47.71	−10.7	SEP-2008	634.08	−68.09	−9.7
SEP-2008	634.08	−68.09	−9.7	JUN-2008	703.22	−65.06	−8.5
AUG-1990	166.69	−17.63	−9.6	JAN-2016	1069.78	−62.10	−5.5
FEB-2001	654.25	−68.30	−9.5	FEB-2018	1501.23	−60.43	−3.9
NOV-2000	692.40	−70.66	−9.3	MAY-2010	601.79	−53.27	−8.1
RUSSELL 2000 1979 to MAY 2018							
OCT-1987	118.26	−52.55	−30.8	OCT-2008	537.52	−142.06	−20.9
OCT-2008	537.52	−142.06	−20.9	JAN-2016	1035.38	−100.51	−8.8
AUG-1998	337.95	−81.80	−19.5	SEP-2011	644.16	−82.65	−11.4
MAR-1980	48.27	−10.95	−18.5	AUG-1998	337.95	−81.80	−19.5
JUL-2002	392.42	−70.22	−15.2	AUG-2015	1159.45	−79.23	−6.4
AUG-1990	139.52	−21.99	−13.6	JUL-2014	1120.07	−72.89	−6.1
SEP-2001	404.87	−63.69	−13.6	SEP-2014	1101.68	−72.67	−6.2
FEB-2009	389.02	−54.51	−12.3	JUL-2002	392.42	−70.22	−15.2
NOV-2008	473.14	−64.38	−12.0	AUG-2011	726.81	−70.22	−8.8
SEP-2011	644.16	−82.65	−11.4	NOV-2008	473.14	−64.38	−12.0

10 BEST QUARTERS BY PERCENT AND POINT

	BY PERCENT CHANGE				BY POINT CHANGE		
QUARTER	CLOSE	PNT CHANGE	% CHANGE	QUARTER	CLOSE	PNT CHANGE	% CHANGE
DJIA 1901 to 1949							
JUN-1933	98.14	42.74	77.1	DEC-1928	300.00	60.57	25.3
SEP-1932	71.56	28.72	67.0	JUN-1933	98.14	42.74	77.1
JUN-1938	133.88	34.93	35.3	MAR-1930	286.10	37.62	15.1
SEP-1915	90.58	20.52	29.3	JUN-1938	133.88	34.93	35.3
DEC-1928	300.00	60.57	25.3	SEP-1927	197.59	31.36	18.9
DEC-1904	50.99	8.80	20.9	SEP-1928	239.43	28.88	13.7
JUN-1919	106.98	18.13	20.4	SEP-1932	71.56	28.72	67.0
SEP-1927	197.59	31.36	18.9	JUN-1929	333.79	24.94	8.1
DEC-1905	70.47	10.47	17.4	SEP-1939	152.54	21.91	16.8
JUN-1935	118.21	17.40	17.3	SEP-1915	90.58	20.52	29.3
DJIA 1950 to MAY 2018							
MAR-1975	768.15	151.91	24.7	DEC-2017	24719.22	2314.13	10.3
MAR-1987	2304.69	408.74	21.6	MAR-2013	14578.54	1474.40	11.3
MAR-1986	1818.61	271.94	17.6	DEC-2016	19762.60	1454.45	7.9
MAR-1976	999.45	147.04	17.2	DEC-2013	16576.66	1446.99	9.6
DEC-1998	9181.43	1338.81	17.1	DEC-1998	9181.43	1338.81	17.1
DEC-1982	1046.54	150.29	16.8	DEC-2011	12217.56	1304.18	12.0
JUN-1997	7672.79	1089.31	16.5	SEP-2009	9712.28	1265.28	15.0
DEC-1985	1546.67	218.04	16.4	JUN-1999	10970.80	1184.64	12.1
SEP-2009	9712.28	1265.28	15.0	DEC-2003	10453.92	1178.86	12.7
JUN-1975	878.99	110.84	14.4	DEC-2001	10021.50	1173.94	13.3
S&P 500 1930 to MAY 2018							
JUN-1933	10.91	5.06	86.5	DEC-1998	1229.23	212.22	20.9
SEP-1932	8.08	3.65	82.4	DEC-1999	1469.25	186.54	14.5
JUN-1938	11.56	3.06	36.0	DEC-2013	1848.36	166.81	9.9
MAR-1975	83.36	14.80	21.6	DEC-2017	2673.61	154.25	6.1
DEC-1998	1229.23	212.22	20.9	MAR-2012	1408.47	150.87	12.0
JUN-1935	10.23	1.76	20.8	MAR-2013	1569.19	143.00	10.0
MAR-1987	291.70	49.53	20.5	SEP-2009	1057.08	137.76	15.0
SEP-1939	13.02	2.16	19.9	MAR-1998	1101.75	131.32	13.5
MAR-1943	11.58	1.81	18.5	JUN-1997	885.14	128.02	16.9
MAR-1930	25.14	3.69	17.2	DEC-2011	1257.60	126.18	11.2
NASDAQ 1971 to MAY 2018							
DEC-1999	4069.31	1323.15	48.2	DEC-1999	4069.31	1323.15	48.2
DEC-2001	1950.40	451.60	30.1	MAR-2017	5911.74	528.62	9.8
DEC-1998	2192.69	498.85	29.5	MAR-2000	4572.83	503.52	12.4
MAR-1991	482.30	108.46	29.0	DEC-1998	2192.69	498.85	29.5
MAR-1975	75.66	15.84	26.5	MAR-2012	3091.57	486.42	18.7
DEC-1982	232.41	44.76	23.9	SEP-2016	5312.00	469.33	9.7
MAR-1987	430.05	80.72	23.1	DEC-2001	1950.40	451.60	30.1
JUN-2003	1622.80	281.63	21.0	DEC-2017	6903.39	407.43	6.3
JUN-1980	157.78	26.78	20.4	DEC-2013	4176.59	405.11	10.7
JUN-2009	1835.04	306.45	20.0	DEC-2015	5007.41	387.25	8.4
RUSSELL 1000 1979 to MAY 2018							
DEC-1998	642.87	113.76	21.5	DEC-1998	642.87	113.76	21.5
MAR-1987	155.20	25.20	19.4	DEC-1999	767.97	104.14	15.7
DEC-1982	77.24	11.35	17.2	DEC-2013	1030.36	90.86	9.7
JUN-1997	462.95	64.76	16.3	MAR-2012	778.92	85.56	12.3
DEC-1985	114.39	15.64	15.8	DEC-2017	1481.81	84.91	6.1
JUN-2009	502.27	68.60	15.8	MAR-2013	872.11	82.21	10.4
DEC-1999	767.97	104.14	15.7	SEP-2009	579.97	77.70	15.5
SEP-2009	579.97	77.70	15.5	DEC-2011	693.36	69.91	11.2
JUN-2003	518.94	68.59	15.2	JUN-2009	502.27	68.60	15.8
MAR-1991	196.15	24.93	14.6	JUN-2003	518.94	68.59	15.2
RUSSELL 2000 1979 to MAY 2018							
MAR-1991	171.01	38.85	29.4	DEC-2010	783.65	107.51	15.9
DEC-1982	88.90	18.06	25.5	DEC-2016	1357.13	105.48	8.4
MAR-1987	166.79	31.79	23.5	DEC-2014	1204.70	103.02	9.4
JUN-2003	448.37	83.83	23.0	MAR-2013	951.54	102.19	12.0
SEP-1980	69.94	12.47	21.7	SEP-2016	1251.65	99.73	8.7
DEC-2001	488.50	83.63	20.7	DEC-2011	740.92	96.76	15.0
JUN-1983	124.17	20.40	19.7	SEP-2013	1073.79	96.31	9.9
JUN-1980	57.47	9.20	19.1	SEP-2009	604.28	96.00	18.9
DEC-1999	504.75	77.45	18.1	MAR-2006	765.14	91.92	13.7
SEP-2009	604.28	96.00	18.9	DEC-2013	1163.64	89.85	8.4

170

10 <u>WORST</u> QUARTERS BY PERCENT AND POINT

	BY PERCENT CHANGE				BY POINT CHANGE		
QUARTER	CLOSE	PNT CHANGE	% CHANGE	QUARTER	CLOSE	PNT CHANGE	% CHANGE
DJIA 1901 to 1949							
JUN-1932	42.84	–30.44	–41.5	DEC-1929	248.48	–94.97	–27.7
SEP-1931	96.61	–53.57	–35.7	JUN-1930	226.34	–59.76	–20.9
DEC-1929	248.48	–94.97	–27.7	SEP-1931	96.61	–53.57	–35.7
SEP-1903	33.55	–9.73	–22.5	DEC-1930	164.58	–40.32	–19.7
DEC-1937	120.85	–33.72	–21.8	DEC-1937	120.85	–33.72	–21.8
JUN-1930	226.34	–59.76	–20.9	SEP-1946	172.42	–33.20	–16.1
DEC-1930	164.58	–40.32	–19.7	JUN-1932	42.84	–30.44	–41.5
DEC-1931	77.90	–18.71	–19.4	JUN-1940	121.87	–26.08	–17.6
MAR-1938	98.95	–21.90	–18.1	MAR-1939	131.84	–22.92	–14.8
JUN-1940	121.87	–26.08	–17.6	JUN-1931	150.18	–22.18	–12.9
DJIA 1950 to MAY 2018							
DEC-1987	1938.83	–657.45	–25.3	DEC-2008	8776.39	–2074.27	–19.1
SEP-1974	607.87	–194.54	–24.2	SEP-2001	8847.56	–1654.84	–15.8
JUN-1962	561.28	–145.67	–20.6	SEP-2002	7591.93	–1651.33	–17.9
DEC-2008	8776.39	–2074.27	–19.1	SEP-2011	10913.38	–1500.96	–12.1
SEP-2002	7591.93	–1651.33	–17.9	SEP-2015	16284.00	–1335.51	–7.6
SEP-2001	8847.56	–1654.84	–15.8	MAR-2009	7608.92	–1167.47	–13.3
SEP-1990	2452.48	–428.21	–14.9	JUN-2002	9243.26	–1160.68	–11.2
MAR-2009	7608.92	–1167.47	–13.3	SEP-1998	7842.62	–1109.40	–12.4
SEP-1981	849.98	–126.90	–13.0	JUN-2010	9774.02	–1082.61	–10.0
JUN-1970	683.53	–102.04	–13.0	MAR-2008	12262.89	–1001.93	–7.6
S&P 500 1930 to MAY 2018							
JUN-1932	4.43	–2.88	–39.4	DEC-2008	903.25	–263.11	–22.6
SEP-1931	9.71	–5.12	–34.5	SEP-2011	1131.42	–189.22	–14.3
SEP-1974	63.54	–22.46	–26.1	SEP-2001	1040.94	–183.48	–15.0
DEC-1937	10.55	–3.21	–23.3	SEP-2002	815.28	–174.54	–17.6
DEC-1987	247.08	–74.75	–23.2	MAR-2001	1160.33	–159.95	–12.1
DEC-2008	903.25	–263.11	–22.6	JUN-2002	989.82	–157.57	–13.7
JUN-1962	54.75	–14.80	–21.3	MAR-2008	1322.70	–145.66	–9.9
MAR-1938	8.50	–2.05	–19.4	SEP-2015	1920.03	–143.08	–6.9
JUN-1970	72.72	–16.91	–18.9	JUN-2010	1030.71	–138.72	–11.9
SEP-1946	14.96	–3.47	–18.8	SEP-1998	1017.01	–116.83	–10.3
NASDAQ 1971 to MAY 2018							
DEC-2000	2470.52	–1202.30	–32.7	DEC-2000	2470.52	–1202.30	–32.7
SEP-2001	1498.80	–661.74	–30.6	SEP-2001	1498.80	–661.74	–30.6
SEP-1974	55.67	–20.29	–26.7	MAR-2001	1840.26	–630.26	–25.5
DEC-1987	330.47	–113.82	–25.6	JUN-2000	3966.11	–606.72	–13.3
MAR-2001	1840.26	–630.26	–25.5	DEC-2008	1577.03	–514.85	–24.6
SEP-1990	344.51	–117.78	–25.5	JUN-2002	1463.21	–382.14	–20.7
DEC-2008	1577.03	–514.85	–24.6	MAR-2008	2279.10	–373.18	–14.1
JUN-2002	1463.21	–382.14	–20.7	SEP-2015	4620.16	–366.71	–7.4
SEP-2002	1172.06	–291.15	–19.9	SEP-2011	2415.40	–358.12	–12.9
JUN-1974	75.96	–16.31	–17.7	SEP-2000	3672.82	–293.29	–7.4
RUSSELL 1000 1979 to MAY 2018							
DEC-2008	487.77	–146.31	–23.1	DEC-2008	487.77	–146.31	–23.1
DEC-1987	130.02	–38.81	–23.0	SEP-2011	623.45	–111.03	–15.1
SEP-2002	433.22	–90.50	–17.3	SEP-2001	546.46	–100.18	–15.5
SEP-2001	546.46	–100.18	–15.5	SEP-2002	433.22	–90.50	–17.3
SEP-1990	157.83	–28.46	–15.3	MAR-2001	610.36	–89.73	–12.8
SEP-2011	623.45	–111.03	–15.1	SEP-2015	1068.46	–84.18	–7.3
JUN-2002	523.72	–83.63	–13.8	JUN-2002	523.72	–83.63	–13.8
MAR-2001	610.36	–89.73	–12.8	MAR-2008	720.32	–79.50	–9.9
SEP-1981	64.06	–8.95	–12.3	JUN-2010	567.37	–76.42	–11.9
JUN-2010	567.37	–76.42	–11.9	DEC-2000	700.09	–72.51	–9.4
RUSSELL 2000 1979 to MAY 2018							
DEC-1987	120.42	–50.39	–29.5	SEP-2011	644.16	–183.27	–22.1
DEC-2008	499.45	–180.13	–26.5	DEC-2008	499.45	–180.13	–26.5
SEP-1990	126.70	–42.34	–25.0	SEP-2015	1100.69	–153.26	–12.2
SEP-2011	644.16	–183.27	–22.1	SEP-2001	404.87	–107.77	–21.0
SEP-2002	362.27	–100.37	–21.7	SEP-2002	362.27	–100.37	–21.7
SEP-2001	404.87	–107.77	–21.0	SEP-1998	363.59	–93.80	–20.5
SEP-1998	363.59	–93.80	–20.5	SEP-2014	1101.68	–91.28	–7.7
SEP-1981	67.55	–15.01	–18.2	MAR-2008	687.97	–78.06	–10.2
MAR-2009	422.75	–76.70	–15.4	MAR-2009	422.75	–76.70	–15.4
MAR-1980	48.27	–7.64	–13.7	JUN-2010	609.49	–69.15	–10.2

10 **BEST** YEARS BY PERCENT AND POINT

	BY PERCENT CHANGE				BY POINT CHANGE		
YEAR	CLOSE	PNT CHANGE	% CHANGE	YEAR	CLOSE	PNT CHANGE	% CHANGE
DJIA 1901 to 1949							
1915	99.15	44.57	81.7	1928	300.00	97.60	48.2
1933	99.90	39.97	66.7	1927	202.40	45.20	28.8
1928	300.00	97.60	48.2	1915	99.15	44.57	81.7
1908	63.11	20.07	46.6	1945	192.91	40.59	26.6
1904	50.99	15.01	41.7	1935	144.13	40.09	38.5
1935	144.13	40.09	38.5	1933	99.90	39.97	66.7
1905	70.47	19.48	38.2	1925	156.66	36.15	30.0
1919	107.23	25.03	30.5	1936	179.90	35.77	24.8
1925	156.66	36.15	30.0	1938	154.76	33.91	28.1
1927	202.40	45.20	28.8	1919	107.23	25.03	30.5
DJIA 1950 to MAY 2018							
1954	404.39	123.49	44.0	2017	24719.22	4956.62	25.1
1975	852.41	236.17	38.3	2013	16576.66	3472.52	26.5
1958	583.65	147.96	34.0	2016	19762.60	2337.57	13.4
1995	5117.12	1282.68	33.5	1999	11497.12	2315.69	25.2
1985	1546.67	335.10	27.7	2003	10453.92	2112.29	25.3
1989	2753.20	584.63	27.0	2006	12463.15	1745.65	16.3
2013	16576.66	3472.52	26.5	2009	10428.05	1651.66	18.8
1996	6448.27	1331.15	26.0	1997	7908.25	1459.98	22.6
2003	10453.92	2112.29	25.3	1996	6448.27	1331.15	26.0
1999	11497.12	2315.69	25.2	1995	5117.12	1282.68	33.5
S&P 500 1930 to MAY 2018							
1933	10.10	3.21	46.6	2017	2673.61	434.78	19.4
1954	35.98	11.17	45.0	2013	1848.36	422.17	29.6
1935	13.43	3.93	41.4	1998	1229.23	258.80	26.7
1958	55.21	15.22	38.1	1999	1469.25	240.02	19.5
1995	615.93	156.66	34.1	2003	1111.92	232.10	26.4
1975	90.19	21.63	31.5	1997	970.43	229.69	31.0
1997	970.43	229.69	31.0	2009	1115.10	211.85	23.5
1945	17.36	4.08	30.7	2014	2058.90	210.54	11.4
2013	1848.36	422.17	29.6	2016	2238.83	194.89	9.5
1936	17.18	3.75	27.9	2006	1418.30	170.01	13.6
NASDAQ 1971 to MAY 2018							
1999	4069.31	1876.62	85.6	1999	4069.31	1876.62	85.6
1991	586.34	212.50	56.8	2017	6903.39	1520.27	28.2
2003	2003.37	667.86	50.0	2013	4176.59	1157.08	38.3
2009	2269.15	692.12	43.9	2009	2269.15	692.12	43.9
1995	1052.13	300.17	39.9	2003	2003.37	667.86	50.0
1998	2192.69	622.34	39.6	1998	2192.69	622.34	39.6
2013	4176.59	1157.08	38.3	2014	4736.05	559.46	13.4
1980	202.34	51.20	33.9	2012	3019.51	414.36	15.9
1985	324.93	77.58	31.4	2010	2652.87	383.72	16.9
1975	77.62	17.80	29.8	2016	5383.12	375.71	7.5
RUSSELL 1000 1979 to MAY 2018							
1995	328.89	84.24	34.4	2013	1030.36	240.46	30.4
1997	513.79	120.04	30.5	2017	1481.81	240.15	19.3
2013	1030.36	240.46	30.4	1998	642.87	129.08	25.1
1991	220.61	49.39	28.8	2003	594.56	128.38	27.5
2003	594.56	128.38	27.5	1999	767.97	125.10	19.5
1985	114.39	24.08	26.7	2009	612.01	124.24	25.5
1989	185.11	38.12	25.9	1997	513.79	120.04	30.5
1980	75.20	15.33	25.6	2014	1144.37	114.01	11.1
2009	612.01	124.24	25.5	2016	1241.66	109.78	9.7
1998	642.87	129.08	25.1	2012	789.90	96.54	13.9
RUSSELL 2000 1979 to MAY 2018							
2003	556.91	173.82	45.4	2013	1163.64	314.29	37.0
1991	189.94	57.78	43.7	2016	1357.13	221.24	19.5
1979	55.91	15.39	38.0	2017	1535.51	178.38	13.1
2013	1163.64	314.29	37.0	2003	556.91	173.82	45.4
1980	74.80	18.89	33.8	2010	783.65	158.26	25.3
1985	129.87	28.38	28.0	2009	625.39	125.94	25.2
1983	112.27	23.37	26.3	2006	787.66	114.44	17.0
1995	315.97	65.61	26.2	2012	849.35	108.43	14.6
2010	783.65	158.26	25.3	2004	651.57	94.66	17.0
2009	625.39	125.94	25.2	1999	504.75	82.79	19.6

172

10 <u>WORST</u> YEARS BY PERCENT AND POINT

	BY PERCENT CHANGE				BY POINT CHANGE		
YEAR	CLOSE	PNT CHANGE	% CHANGE	YEAR	CLOSE	PNT CHANGE	% CHANGE
DJIA 1901 to 1949							
1931	77.90	−86.68	−52.7	1931	77.90	−86.68	−52.7
1907	43.04	−26.08	−37.7	1930	164.58	−83.90	−33.8
1930	164.58	−83.90	−33.8	1937	120.85	−59.05	−32.8
1920	71.95	−35.28	−32.9	1929	248.48	−51.52	−17.2
1937	120.85	−59.05	−32.8	1920	71.95	−35.28	−32.9
1903	35.98	−11.12	−23.6	1907	43.04	−26.08	−37.7
1932	59.93	−17.97	−23.1	1917	74.38	−20.62	−21.7
1917	74.38	−20.62	−21.7	1941	110.96	−20.17	−15.4
1910	59.60	−12.96	−17.9	1940	131.13	−19.11	−12.7
1929	248.48	−51.52	−17.2	1932	59.93	−17.97	−23.1
DJIA 1950 to MAY 2018							
2008	8776.39	−4488.43	−33.8	2008	8776.39	−4488.43	−33.8
1974	616.24	−234.62	−27.6	2002	8341.63	−1679.87	−16.8
1966	785.69	−183.57	−18.9	2001	10021.50	−765.35	−7.1
1977	831.17	−173.48	−17.3	2000	10786.85	−710.27	−6.2
2002	8341.63	−1679.87	−16.8	2015	17425.03	−398.04	−2.2
1973	850.86	−169.16	−16.6	1974	616.24	−234.62	−27.6
1969	800.36	−143.39	−15.2	1966	785.69	−183.57	−18.9
1957	435.69	−63.78	−12.8	1977	831.17	−173.48	−17.3
1962	652.10	−79.04	−10.8	1973	850.86	−169.16	−16.6
1960	615.89	−63.47	−9.3	1969	800.36	−143.39	−15.2
S&P 500 1930 to MAY 2018							
1931	8.12	−7.22	−47.1	2008	903.25	−565.11	−38.5
1937	10.55	−6.63	−38.6	2002	879.82	−268.26	−23.4
2008	903.25	−565.11	−38.5	2001	1148.08	−172.20	−13.0
1974	68.56	−28.99	−29.7	2000	1320.28	−148.97	−10.1
1930	15.34	−6.11	−28.5	1974	68.56	−28.99	−29.7
2002	879.82	−268.26	−23.4	1990	330.22	−23.18	−6.6
1941	8.69	−1.89	−17.9	1973	97.55	−20.50	−17.4
1973	97.55	−20.50	−17.4	2015	2043.94	−14.96	−0.7
1940	10.58	−1.91	−15.3	1981	122.55	−13.21	−9.7
1932	6.89	−1.23	−15.1	1977	95.10	−12.36	−11.5
NASDAQ 1971 to MAY 2018							
2008	1577.03	−1075.25	−40.5	2000	2470.52	−1598.79	−39.3
2000	2470.52	−1598.79	−39.3	2008	1577.03	−1075.25	−40.5
1974	59.82	−32.37	−35.1	2002	1335.51	−614.89	−31.5
2002	1335.51	−614.89	−31.5	2001	1950.40	−520.12	−21.1
1973	92.19	−41.54	−31.1	1990	373.84	−80.98	−17.8
2001	1950.40	−520.12	−21.1	2011	2605.15	−47.72	−1.8
1990	373.84	−80.98	−17.8	1973	92.19	−41.54	−31.1
1984	247.35	−31.25	−11.2	1974	59.82	−32.37	−35.1
1987	330.47	−18.86	−5.4	1984	247.35	−31.25	−11.2
1981	195.84	−6.50	−3.2	1994	751.96	−24.84	−3.2
RUSSELL 1000 1979 to MAY 2018							
2008	487.77	−312.05	−39.0	2008	487.77	−312.05	−39.0
2002	466.18	−138.76	−22.9	2002	466.18	−138.76	−22.9
2001	604.94	−95.15	−13.6	2001	604.94	−95.15	−13.6
1981	67.93	−7.27	−9.7	2000	700.09	−67.88	−8.8
2000	700.09	−67.88	−8.8	1990	171.22	−13.89	−7.5
1990	171.22	−13.89	−7.5	2015	1131.88	−12.49	−1.1
1994	244.65	−6.06	−2.4	1981	67.93	−7.27	−9.7
2015	1131.88	−12.49	−1.1	1994	244.65	−6.06	−2.4
2011	693.36	−3.54	−0.5	2011	693.36	−3.54	−0.5
1984	90.31	−0.07	−0.1	1984	90.31	−0.07	−0.10
RUSSELL 2000 1979 to MAY 2018							
2008	499.45	−266.58	−34.8	2008	499.45	−266.58	−34.8
2002	383.09	−105.41	−21.6	2002	383.09	−105.41	−21.6
1990	132.16	−36.14	−21.5	2015	1135.89	−68.81	−5.7
1987	120.42	−14.58	−10.8	2011	740.92	−42.73	−5.5
1984	101.49	−10.78	−9.6	1990	132.16	−36.14	−21.5
2015	1135.89	−68.81	−5.7	2007	766.03	−21.63	−2.7
2011	740.92	−42.73	−5.5	2000	483.53	−21.22	−4.2
2000	483.53	−21.22	−4.2	1998	421.96	−15.06	−3.4
1998	421.96	−15.06	−3.4	1987	120.42	−14.58	−10.8
1994	250.36	−8.23	−3.2	1984	101.49	−10.78	−9.6

173

STRATEGY PLANNING AND RECORD SECTION

CONTENTS

175 Portfolio at Start of 2019

176 Additional Purchases

178 Short-Term Transactions

180 Long-Term Transactions

182 Interest/Dividends Received During 2018/Brokerage Account Data 2019

183 Weekly Portfolio Price Record 2019

185 Weekly Indicator Data 2019

187 Monthly Indicator Data 2019

188 Portfolio at End of 2019

189 If You Don't Profit from Your Investment Mistakes, Someone Else Will/ Performance Record of Recommendations

190 Individual Retirement Account (IRA): Most Awesome Mass Investment Incentive Ever Devised

191 G. M. Loeb's "Battle Plan" for Investment Survival

192 G. M. Loeb's Investment Survival Checklist

These forms are available at our website, www.stocktradersalmanac.com.

PORTFOLIO AT START OF 2019

DATE ACQUIRED	NO. OF SHARES	SECURITY	PRICE	TOTAL COST	PAPER PROFITS	PAPER LOSSES

ADDITIONAL PURCHASES

DATE ACQUIRED	NO. OF SHARES	SECURITY	PRICE	TOTAL COST	REASON FOR PURCHASE PRIME OBJECTIVE, ETC.

ADDITIONAL PURCHASES

DATE ACQUIRED	NO. OF SHARES	SECURITY	PRICE	TOTAL COST	REASON FOR PURCHASE PRIME OBJECTIVE, ETC.

SHORT-TERM TRANSACTIONS

Pages 178–181 can accompany next year's income tax return (Schedule D). Enter transactions as completed to avoid last-minute pressures.

NO. OF SHARES	SECURITY	DATE ACQUIRED	DATE SOLD	SALE PRICE	COST	LOSS	GAIN

TOTALS:
Carry over to next page

SHORT-TERM TRANSACTIONS *(continued)*

NO. OF SHARES	SECURITY	DATE ACQUIRED	DATE SOLD	SALE PRICE	COST	LOSS	GAIN

TOTALS:

LONG-TERM TRANSACTIONS

Pages 178–181 can accompany next year's income tax return (Schedule D). Enter transactions as completed to avoid last-minute pressures.

NO. OF SHARES	SECURITY	DATE ACQUIRED	DATE SOLD	SALE PRICE	COST	LOSS	GAIN

TOTALS:
Carry over to next page

180

NO. OF SHARES	SECURITY	DATE ACQUIRED	DATE SOLD	SALE PRICE	COST	LOSS	GAIN

TOTALS:

INTEREST/DIVIDENDS RECEIVED DURING 2019

SHARES	STOCK/BOND	FIRST QUARTER		SECOND QUARTER		THIRD QUARTER		FOURTH QUARTER	
		$		$		$		$	

BROKERAGE ACCOUNT DATA 2019

	MARGIN INTEREST	TRANSFER TAXES	CAPITAL ADDED	CAPITAL WITHDRAWN
JAN				
FEB				
MAR				
APR				
MAY				
JUN				
JUL				
AUG				
SEP				
OCT				
NOV				
DEC				

WEEKLY PORTFOLIO PRICE RECORD 2019 (FIRST HALF)

Place purchase price above stock name and weekly closes below.

STOCKS Week Ending	1	2	3	4	5	6	7	8	9	10
JANUARY 4										
11										
18										
25										
FEBRUARY 1										
8										
15										
22										
MARCH 1										
8										
15										
22										
29										
APRIL 5										
12										
19										
26										
MAY 3										
10										
17										
24										
31										
JUNE 7										
14										
21										
28										

WEEKLY PORTFOLIO PRICE RECORD 2019 (SECOND HALF)

Place purchase price above stock name and weekly closes below.

STOCKS Week Ending	1	2	3	4	5	6	7	8	9	10
JULY 5										
12										
19										
26										
AUGUST 2										
9										
16										
23										
30										
SEPTEMBER 6										
13										
20										
27										
OCTOBER 4										
11										
18										
25										
NOVEMBER 1										
8										
15										
22										
29										
DECEMBER 6										
13										
20										
27										

WEEKLY INDICATOR DATA 2019 (FIRST HALF)

	Week Ending	Dow Jones Industrial Average	Net Change for Week	Net Change on Friday	Net Change Next Monday	S&P or NASDAQ	NYSE Advances	NYSE Declines	New Highs	New Lows	CBOE Put/Call Ratio	90-Day Treas. Rate	Moody's AAA Rate
JANUARY	4												
	11												
	18												
	25												
FEBRUARY	1												
	8												
	15												
	22												
MARCH	1												
	8												
	15												
	22												
	29												
APRIL	5												
	12												
	19												
	26												
MAY	3												
	10												
	17												
	24												
	31												
JUNE	7												
	14												
	21												
	28												

WEEKLY INDICATOR DATA 2019 (SECOND HALF)

	Week Ending	Dow Jones Industrial Average	Net Change for Week	Net Change on Friday	Net Change Next Monday	S&P or NASDAQ	NYSE Advances	NYSE Declines	New Highs	New Lows	CBOE Put/Call Ratio	90-Day Treas. Rate	Moody's AAA Rate
JULY	5												
	12												
	19												
	26												
AUGUST	2												
	9												
	16												
	23												
	30												
SEPTEMBER	6												
	13												
	20												
	27												
OCTOBER	4												
	11												
	18												
	25												
NOVEMBER	1												
	8												
	15												
	22												
	29												
DECEMBER	6												
	13												
	20												
	27												

186

MONTHLY INDICATOR DATA 2019

	DJIA% Last 3 + 1st 2 Days	DJIA% 9th to 11th Trading Days	DJIA% Change Rest of Month	DJIA% Change Whole Month	% Change Your Stocks	Gross Domestic Product	Prime Rate	Trade Deficit $ Billion	CPI % Change	% Unem- ployment Rate
JAN										
FEB										
MAR										
APR										
MAY										
JUN										
JUL										
AUG										
SEP										
OCT										
NOV										
DEC										

INSTRUCTIONS:

Weekly Indicator Data (pages 185–186). Keeping data on several indicators may give you a better feel of the market. In addition to the closing DJIA and its net change for the week, post the net change for Friday's Dow and also the following Monday's. A series of "down Fridays" followed by "down Mondays" often precedes a downswing (see page 74). Tracking either the S&P or NASDAQ composite, and advances and declines, will help prevent the Dow from misleading you. New highs and lows and put/call ratios (www.cboe. com) are also useful indicators. All these weekly figures appear in weekend papers or *Barron's*. Data for the 90-day Treasury Rate and Moody's AAA Bond Rate are quite important for tracking short- and long-term interest rates. These figures are available from:

> Weekly U.S. Financial Data
> Federal Reserve Bank of St. Louis
> P.O. Box 442
> St. Louis, MO 63166
> **http://research.stlouisfed.org**

Monthly Indicator Data. The purpose of the first three columns is to enable you to track the market's bullish bias near the end, beginning and middle of the month, which has been shifting lately (see pages 82, 145 and 146). Market direction, performance of your stocks, gross domestic product, prime rate, trade deficit, Consumer Price Index, and unemployment rate are worthwhile indicators to follow. Or, readers may wish to gauge other data.

PORTFOLIO AT END OF 2019

DATE ACQUIRED	NO. OF SHARES	SECURITY	PRICE	TOTAL COST	PAPER PROFITS	PAPER LOSSES

IF YOU DON'T PROFIT FROM YOUR INVESTMENT MISTAKES, SOMEONE ELSE WILL

No matter how much we may deny it, almost every successful person on Wall Street pays a great deal of attention to trading suggestions—especially when they come from "the right sources."

One of the hardest things to learn is to distinguish between good tips and bad ones. Usually, the best tips have a logical reason behind them, which accompanies the tip. Poor tips usually have no reason to support them.

The important thing to remember is that the market discounts. It does not review, it does not reflect. The Street's real interest in "tips," inside information, buying and selling suggestions and everything else of this kind emanates from a desire to find out just what the market has on hand to discount. The process of finding out involves separating the wheat from the chaff—and there is plenty of chaff.

HOW TO MAKE USE OF STOCK "TIPS"

- The source should be **reliable**. (By listing all "tips" and suggestions on a Performance Record of Recommendations, such as the form below, and then periodically evaluating the outcomes, you will soon know the "batting average" of your sources.)

- The story should make sense. Would the merger violate antitrust laws? Are there too many computers on the market already? How many years will it take to become profitable?

- The stock should not have had a recent sharp run-up. Otherwise, the story may already be discounted, and confirmation or denial in the press would most likely be accompanied by a sell-off in the stock.

PERFORMANCE RECORD OF RECOMMENDATIONS

STOCK RECOMMENDED	BY WHOM	DATE	PRICE	REASON FOR RECOMMENDATION	SUBSEQUENT ACTION OF STOCK

INDIVIDUAL RETIREMENT ACCOUNT (IRA): MOST AWESOME MASS INVESTMENT INCENTIVE EVER DEVISED

MAX IRA INVESTMENTS OF $5,500* A YEAR COMPOUNDED AT VARIOUS INTEREST RATES OF RETURN FOR DIFFERENT PERIODS

Annual Rate	5 Yrs	10 Yrs	15 Yrs	20 Yrs	25 Yrs	30 Yrs	35 Yrs	40 Yrs	45 Yrs	50 Yrs
1%	$28,336	$58,118	$89,418	$122,316	$156,891	$193,230	$231,423	$271,564	$313,752	$358,093
2%	29,195	61,428	97,016	136,308	179,690	227,587	280,469	338,855	403,318	474,490
3%	30,076	64,943	105,363	152,221	206,542	269,515	342,518	427,148	525,258	638,994
4%	30,981	68,675	114,535	170,331	238,215	320,806	421,291	543,546	692,288	873,256
5%	31,911	72,637	124,616	190,956	275,624	383,684	521,600	697,619	922,268	1,208,985
6%	32,864	76,844	135,699	214,460	319,860	460,909	649,665	902,262	1,240,295	1,692,658
7%	33,843	81,310	147,884	241,258	372,221	555,902	813,524	1,174,853	1,681,635	2,392,423
8%	34,848	86,050	161,284	271,826	434,249	672,902	1,023,562	1,538,796	2,295,843	3,408,195
9%	35,878	91,082	176,019	306,705	507,782	817,164	1,293,186	2,025,605	3,152,523	4,886,426
10%	36,936	96,421	192,224	346,514	595,000	995,189	1,639,697	2,677,685	4,349,374	7,041,647
11%	38,021	102,088	210,045	391,958	698,493	1,215,022	2,085,404	3,552,048	6,023,428	10,187,848
12%	39,134	108,100	229,643	443,843	821,337	1,486,609	2,659,047	4,725,283	8,366,697	14,784,112
13%	40,275	114,479	251,195	503,085	967,176	1,822,233	3,397,621	6,300,172	11,647,933	21,500,837
14%	41,445	121,245	274,892	570,726	1,140,330	2,237,054	4,348,701	8,414,497	16,242,841	31,315,649
15%	42,646	128,421	300,946	647,956	1,345,916	2,749,763	5,573,401	11,252,746	22,675,938	45,652,055
16%	43,876	136,031	329,588	736,123	1,589,985	3,383,389	7,150,149	15,061,631	31,678,448	66,579,439
17%	45,138	144,100	361,069	836,762	1,879,695	4,166,271	9,179,470	20,170,648	44,268,235	97,100,943
18%	46,431	152,653	395,665	951,616	2,223,497	5,133,252	11,790,069	27,019,253	61,859,935	141,566,978
19%	47,756	161,720	433,676	1,082,661	2,631,368	6,327,131	15,146,529	36,192,731	86,416,412	206,267,876
20%	49,115	171,327	475,432	1,232,141	3,115,075	7,800,418	19,459,052	48,469,462	120,656,646	300,281,459

* At press time—2019 Contribution Limit will be indexed to inflation.

G. M. LOEB'S "BATTLE PLAN" FOR INVESTMENT SURVIVAL

LIFE IS CHANGE: Nothing can ever be the same a minute from now as it was a minute ago. Everything you own is changing in price and value. You can find that last price of an active security on the stock ticker, but you cannot find the next price anywhere. The value of your money is changing. Even the value of your home is changing, though no one walks in front of it with a sandwich board consistently posting the changes.

RECOGNIZE CHANGE: Your basic objective should be to profit from change. The art of investing is being able to recognize change and to adjust investment goals accordingly.

WRITE THINGS DOWN: You will score more investment success and avoid more investment failures if you write things down. Very few investors have the drive and inclination to do this.

KEEP A CHECKLIST: If you aim to improve your investment results, get into the habit of keeping a checklist on every issue you consider buying. Before making a commitment, it will pay you to write down the answers to at least some of the basic questions—How much am I investing in this company? How much do I think I can make? How much do I have to risk? How long do I expect to take to reach my goal?

HAVE A SINGLE RULING REASON: Above all, writing things down is the best way to find "the ruling reason." When all is said and done, there is invariably a single reason that stands out above all others, why a particular security transaction can be expected to show a profit. All too often, many relatively unimportant statistics are allowed to obscure this single important point.

Any one of a dozen factors may be the point of a particular purchase or sale. It could be a technical reason—an increase in earnings or dividend not yet discounted in the market price—a change of management—a promising new product—an expected improvement in the market's valuation of earnings—or many others. But, in any given case, one of these factors will almost certainly be more important than all the rest put together.

CLOSING OUT A COMMITMENT: If you have a loss, the solution is automatic, provided you decide what to do at the time you buy. Otherwise, the question divides itself into two parts. Are we in a bull or bear market? Few of us really know until it is too late. For the sake of the record, if you think it is a bear market, just put that consideration first and sell as much as your conviction suggests and your nature allows.

If you think it is a bull market, or at least a market where some stocks move up, some mark time and only a few decline, do not sell unless:

✓ You see a bear market ahead.
✓ You see trouble for a particular company in which you own shares.
✓ Time and circumstances have turned up a new and seemingly far better buy than the issue you like least in your list.
✓ Your shares stop going up and start going down.

A subsidiary question is, which stock to sell first? Two further observations may help:

✓ Do not sell solely because you think a stock is "overvalued."
✓ If you want to sell some of your stocks and not all, in most cases it is better to go against your emotional inclinations and sell first the issues with losses, small profits or none at all, the weakest, the most disappointing and so on.

Mr. Loeb is the author of *The Battle for Investment Survival*, John Wiley & Sons.

G. M. LOEB'S INVESTMENT SURVIVAL CHECKLIST

OBJECTIVES AND RISKS

DISCARD

Security		Price	Shares	Date

"Ruling reason" for commitment	Amount of commitment $_____
	% of my investment capital _____%

Price objective	Est. time to achieve it	I will risk _____ points	Which would be $_____

TECHNICAL POSITION

Price action of stock:

❑ Hitting new highs   ❑ In a trading range

❑ Pausing in an uptrend   ❑ Moving up from low ground

❑ Acting stronger than market   ❑ _____

Dow Jones Industrial Average

Trend of market

SELECTED YARDSTICKS

	Price Range		Earnings Per Share Actual or Projected	Price/Earnings Ratio Actual or Projected
	High	Low		
Current year Previous year				

Merger possibilities	Years for earnings to double in past
Comment on future	Years for market price to double in past

PERIODIC RECHECKS

Date	Stock Price	DJIA	Comment	Action taken, if any

COMPLETED TRANSACTIONS

Date closed	Period of time held	Profit or loss

Reason for profit or loss